GENRE IN THE CLASSROOM
Multiple Perspectives

Edited by

Ann M. Johns
San Diego State University

LAWRENCE ERLBAUM ASSOCIATES, PUBLISHERS
2002 Mahwah, New Jersey London

Lawrence Erlbaum Associates, Inc., Publishers
10 Industrial Avenue
Mahwah, NJ 07430

Cover design by Kathryn Houghtaling Lacey

Library of Congress Cataloging-in-Publication Data

Genre in the classroom : multiple perspectives / Ann M. Johns, ed.
p. cm.
Includes bibliographical references and index.
ISBN 0-8058-3073-1 (cloth : alk. paper)
ISBN 0-8058-3074-X (pbk. : alk. paper)
1. English language—Study and teaching—Foreign speakers.
2. Academic writing—Study and teaching. 3. Literary form—Study and teaching. 4. Literature—Study and teaching. I. Johns, Ann M.
PE1128.A2 G436 2001
428'.007—dc21 00-067769
CIP

Books published by Lawrence Erlbaum Associates are printed on acid-free paper, and their bindings are chosen for strength and durability.

Printed in the United States of America
10 9 8 7 6 5 4 3 2 1

Contents

PART VII CONCLUSION AND RESPONSES

Preface

Ann M. Johns

This collection began to take shape in 1996 while I was participating in a three-day colloquium organized by John Swales on "Genre and Thick Description" at the International Association of Applied Linguistics Conference in Finland. We heard rich, "thickly described" theory and research papers, but the discussions of pedagogy were relegated to last–and quite thin. Participants had the same kinds of experiences (i.e., hearing excellent theoretical and research papers, but few pedagogical ones) at the Second International Genre Conference in Vancouver, organized in 1998 by Richard Coe. There, I concluded with others that we practitioners needed a volume that focused on pedagogy in which the various important theoretical camps were represented.

When Naomi Silverman, of Lawrence Erlbaum Associates, encouraged me in this venture, I began to solicit chapters and compile the manuscripts. As I continued to work, I became increasingly appreciative of Naomi's guidance and of the prompt responses made by assistant editor, Lori Hawver. I am also grateful for the very careful work of Laurie Mendenblik, the indexer. Central to the success of most volumes are the reviewers. The contributors and I are particularly grateful to reviewer John Hedgecock, who understood the volume's purposes and whose comments were very useful to us all as we revised our chapters.

The contributors of the volume's chapters are a very capable group, as their work will attest. I am most grateful to them for submitting and revising their texts to make them appropriate and for being patient with me as I took care of the business of putting a book together. As readers will notice, the conclusion is rather unusual: William Grabe's contribution, followed by commentaries by major figures from each of the theoretical camps represented. Of course, I am very pleased with Bill's chapter and with the expert responses, which should dissuade any readers from believing that there is one "true way" to approach genre theory or practice.

I would also like to thank some local people in San Diego, particularly Harry Polkinhorn of San Diego State University Press, who made excellent suggestions and helped with the editing, and Jim McMenamin, who worked long hours to edit and make the manuscripts camera-ready.

GENRE IN THE CLASSROOM
Multiple Perspectives

Introduction: Genre in the Classroom

Ann M. Johns
San Diego State University

In the past 15 years or so, a major paradigm shift has been taking place in literacy studies at the theoretical, and, in some locales, pedagogical levels. During the 1970s and most of the 1980s, experts focused primarily upon psycholinguistic/cognitive literacy theories and "The Process Approach" (see Feez, this volume; Johns, 1990, 1997; Silva, 1990), which resulted in learner-centered classrooms. However, in the late 1980s, the 1990s, and beyond, much of the theoretical interest has shifted to a contextual approach, to analyses of the situations in which writing takes place. In these theories, the writer is viewed as a social being , and texts are viewed as *genre* exemplars: purposeful, situated, and "repeated" (Miller, 1984) social responses.

The term *genre* is not new, of course. For more than a century, genres have been defined as written texts that are "(a) primarily literary, (b) entirely defined by textual regularities in form and content, (c) fixed and immutable, and (d) classifiable into neat and mutually exclusive categories and subcategories" (Freedman & Medway, 1994b, p. 1). The current reconceptualizations of genre challenge each of these traditional features. Experts argue that although all types of texts, literary and otherwise, might initially be identified by knowledgeable readers and writers through their conventions, as "typical forms of utterances" (Bakhtin, 1984, p. 63), those who understand and utilize specific genres have other cognitive and socially constructed tools that facilitate both text recognition and production. These include notions about context, content, readers' and writers' roles, community values, and so on (see, especially, Berkenkotter & Huckin, 1995; Halliday & Hasan, 1989; Purves, 1991). Thus, genre has become a term that refers to complex oral or written responses by speakers or writers to the demands of a social context. Yet, as Hyon (1996) and others have noted, there are considerable differences among theorists and practitioners about how genres should be described and what this term means for the classroom.

The manner in which genre is discussed within the various theoretical camps reveals the intellectual tensions that are inherent in conceptualization and application of this term. The first, and perhaps central, tension arises from divergent theoretical foci: whether a theory is solidly grounded in language and text structure or whether it stems primarily from social theories of context and community. Flowerdew (this volume) refers to those views that foreground language and the texts themselves as *linguistic*, "applying theories of functional grammar and discourse and concentrating on the lexico-grammatical and rhetorical realization of communicative purposes." Proponents of the Sydney School, and, to some extent, English for Specific Purposes, tend to fall into this category. Those who foreground rhetorical situation are considered by Flowerdew to be *contextually grounded*[1] "[originating with] the purposes and functions of genres and the attitudes, beliefs, values and behaviors of members of the discourse communities within which genres are situated." This juxtaposition between linguistic and contextual foregrounding is a major organizational principle in this volume.

There are other tensions among the theories and practices discussed here, perhaps less obvious to the reader, but nonetheless important for an understanding of the complexity of the issues involved. One relates to stability, or the lack thereof: whether genres can be captured, taught, and acquired in the classroom; or whether, in fact, they are so slippery and evolving–and thus thoroughly contextualized–that building a curriculum around them is a virtual impossibility. Another tension involves the relationships among genres, power, and authority. Do we, as theorists and practitioners, promote an "accommodationist," pragmatic approach in which genres are considered positive artifacts of a target culture that students must acquire to succeed, or do we take a more critical approach, encouraging our students to resist a culture's hegemonic texts (see, for example, Benesch, 1993; Hyon, 1996)?

In addition to these theoretical and ideological questions, there are specific, and contestable, curricular questions. What level of genre specificity and description is appropriate for the classroom? Should we be teaching "macro-genres," such as narrative and exposition, as Grabe (this volume) suggests, or "sub-genres," such as the literature review discussed in Swales and Lindemann in this volume? Should we select what some in the Sydney School refer to as "elemental" genres, general texts from a culture such as "procedure," "report," and "recount" (Feez, this volume), or should the genres we choose be more specific to our individual classrooms and students' professional goals, as Hyon (this volume) and other ESP practitioners argue? What *are* genres, anyway, and how do we teachers differentiate them from the more traditional "text types" (Paltridge, this volume)?

As will be seen, these tensions and questions have been addressed in quite different ways by the authors and schools represented here.

---

[1]Actually, Flowerdew uses the term *non-linguistic*; however, it seems quite inappropriate to discuss the very interesting theories of the New Rhetoric in terms of the "other!"

THE SYDNEY SCHOOL

Australia is the place in which practitioners have been most successful in applying genre theory and research to pedagogy, particularly in the publicly supported primary and secondary schools and in adult migrant education. Arguing that learner-centered classrooms and The Process Approach generally "promote a situation in which only the brightest, middle-class monolingual students will benefit" (Martin, 1985b), a number of theorists and researchers, including Martin (1993a), Christie (1991b), Feez, and Macken-Horarik (both in this volume), have worked with teachers to create a genre-based pedagogy consistent with Systemic Functional Linguistics, originated by Michael Halliday (1978). In the classroom, and in the world,

> a text is understood as functioning in a context, where context is said to operate at two levels: at the level of *register*, where *field* (social activity), *tenor* (the interpersonal relationships among people using language) and *mode* (the part played by language in building communication) all have consequences for the choices made in the linguistic system; and at the level of *genre*, where *social purpose* in using language also has consequences for linguistic choices made. For any given instance of language use, a genre is selected (be that a report, a narrative, a trade encounter, and so on) and particular choices are made with respect to field, tenor, and mode, all of which are realized in language choices. (Christie, 1991a, p. 142)

From Halliday's theory, and the research that arises from it, have come conclusions about how grammatical and macrostructural resources are exploited for particular generic purposes. For example, genre researchers have explored the ways in which phenomena are identified and sorted into taxonomies in science,[2] and then discussed by members of the scientific community in selected registers and community-sanctioned genres (Halliday & Martin, 1993). Feez (this volume) notes that research has extended into many contexts, and "researchers (in Australia) have . . . developed increasingly sophisticated understandings about the nature of texts . . . in terms of how genre interacts with register in a variety of contexts of situation and how these interactions predict particular language choices at the level of both discourse and lexicogrammar" (p. 54). Using these insights, practitioners have developed pedagogical frameworks in which genres and registers are related to the goals, values, and "staged" processes of a culture.

One widely accepted instructional approach found in Sydney-School curricula is the teaching/learning cycle (Reproduced in Hyon, 1996, p. 705), in which teachers first model texts from a genre and discuss text features, then assist students to explore the genre's social purposes (see also Macken-Horarik, this volume). As students become comfortable with particular text types, they are given an increasing amount of independence and encouraged to negotiate text structure and content.

---

[2]For a detailed, and fascinating, discussion of the professional taxonomizing process and its resultant texts, see Swales' "textography" of the University of Michigan herbarium (1998, pp. 79–142).

Genre theory and pedagogy have had a profound impact upon Australian literacy education for a number of reasons, not the least of which are the university/school partnerships and the support of major government agencies through the Literacy and Education Research Network (LERN). The first two chapters of this volume are written by practitioners who discuss these relationships and the pedagogies that result. After a thorough introduction to theory and pedagogical practice (Chapter 1), Macken-Horarik describes the development of lessons in a secondary-school science classroom associated with the Disadvantaged Schools Program in Sydney. In Chapter 2, Feez provides a history of the Adult Migrant Education Project and then outlines a genre-based curriculum built on specific student objectives. After completing these two chapters, and consulting Martin's response to the Grabe chapter (this volume), readers should have a rich understanding of the theory, history, and pedagogical practices–and the issues of contention–in the Sydney School.

RELATED APPROACHES

Each of the two chapters in the Related Approaches section draws from Systemic Functional Linguistics (SFL) but extends the discussion to other concerns and other student populations. In Chapter 3, Paltridge addresses one of the murkiest issues raised by the Sydney School and others: the relationships between the terms *genre* and *text-type*,[3] terms that are sometimes used interchangeably in the literature.[4] In Current-Traditional Rhetoric (CTR), popular in North American composition studies in the 1950s and 1960s, text type, or *rhetorical mode*, was the guiding curricular principle. At that time, writing was considered to be merely "a matter of arrangement, of fitting sentences and paragraphs into prescribed patterns . . . such as illustration, exemplification, comparison, contrast, partition, classification, diphenan, causal analysis, and so on" (Silva, 1990, pp. 13–14). Maintaining that *genre* refers to named, socially constructed discourse, and *text type* to organizational patterns within more complex discourses, Paltridge argues that the two concepts interact in interesting, and important, ways in authentic texts. He demonstrates how he integrates genre and text type analyses into an English for Academic Purposes (EAP) program in an Australian university.

As in the case of the first three chapters, Flowerdew's "linguistic approach" (Chapter 4) makes extensive use of Halliday's theories, particularly of *field, tenor,* and *mode*. He discusses assisting students to understand the ways in which language supports genres' social purposes. Flowerdew applies Davies' (1994, 1995; Johns & Davies, 1983) theories of *topic types* to scientific texts in the classroom. Then he demonstrates, in considerable detail, a pedagogy adapted to the needs of English for Academic Purposes students within a Middle Eastern context.

---

[3]See also the juxtaposition of "genre" and "register" studies in Bhatia (1997b) and this volume.

[4]See also Pang's discussion of genre and text type in this volume.

ENGLISH FOR SPECIFIC PURPOSES (ESP)

As noted earlier, contributions to this volume were initially selected to represent the three genre schools described by Hyon (1996): the Sydney School, ESP, and the New Rhetoric. However, since some ESP scholars, particularly in North America, draw from New Rhetoric and SFL, separating ESP from other theoretical strands is becoming increasingly difficult. To confuse matters even more, ESP terms such as English for Academic Purposes (EAP) are employed by teachers who subscribe to several theoretical camps, though their curricula may differ considerably.

The principal reason it is difficult to identify English for Specific Purposes (ESP) with a particular linguistic or pedagogical tradition is that the movement is inherently pragmatic, and pedagogies are situated, generally based on local needs assessment and situational and discourse analyses (Johns & Dudley-Evans, 1991; Dudley-Evans & St John, 1998). In some ESP contexts, particularly in international, English as a Foreign Language (EFL) environments, the teaching and testing emphases continue to be almost exclusively on grammar or vocabulary; in others, on a single skill, such as reading, and in others, on a specific genre, such as the research paper. ESP pedagogies range from those that draw from SFL or structural linguistics to those that draw from the New Rhetoric or from literacy approaches that were more common in the 1950s and 1960s. This is because ESP practitioners "distrust theories that do not quite work out in the litmus-paper realities of [their own] classroom[s]" (Swales, 1988, p. xvii).

Despite the taxonomic problems in ESP, Swales and Lindemann appear under this rubric (Chapter 5) because the first author is recognized as the most important and productive current proponent of this school. Swales' text-based theory of moves (1981, 1990), central to ESP genre analysis, is familiar to anyone who reads the ESP literature. However, his work may also be related conceptually to the Sydney School, for "moves" seem to be closely allied to the "stages" described in the first two chapters of this volume.

Chapter 5 presents a study of advanced EAP students' judgments about the organization, metadiscourse, claims, generalizations, and summaries in a literature review. Though text-based, it is much more rhetorical in focus than earlier ESP work. Because of this, it seems to fit nicely into the blurred, transition points in ESP between analyzing features of texts and relating those features to the values and rhetorical purposes of discourse communities.[5]

Hyon's contribution (Chapter 6) has been chosen for the ESP section because it takes a single-skill approach to an EAP classroom study, asking whether the direct teaching of genres assists students to *read* academic texts. After determining through a needs assessment that four genres–a hard-news story, a feature article, a textbook, and a research article–are most relevant to her students' reading needs, Hyon devoted her course to training in the formal and functional features of these written texts, an approach that she considers basic to ESP course design (Hyon,

[5]See Swales (1990) for an oft-cited discussion of discourse communities.

1996). She concludes that her students' reading does improve when genre awareness is heightened.

BRIDGING TEXT AND CONTEXT

This section includes chapters that, for several reasons, straddle the linguistic/contextual dichotomy mentioned by Flowerdew (this volume), either because purely linguistic applications are inappropriate for the contexts discussed or because the authors make a concerted and focused attempt to balance language and context.

Pang's chapter (Chapter 7) represents a direct attempt to bridge the gap between text and context, between the linguistic and the situational foci of genre studies. Using a movie review, he hypothesizes for one group of his Hong Kong students that "by learning to study the lexico-grammatical features of texts of a certain genre, learners should be more capable [of writing] in that genre." For a second, comparable group, he hypothesizes that "given the context, learners trained in contextual analysis should be able to generate appropriate text, using appropriate language from the [lexico-grammatical] system." His research shows that each groups of students made progress in certain areas and concludes that both linguistic and contextual approaches should be applied in order for students to have a full understanding of the language and contexts of genres.

The chapter by Samraj (Chapter 8) is also transitional. Although she comes from ESP and Systemic Functional backgrounds, Samraj draws heavily from the New Rhetoric and its presentations of context as both rhetorical situation (purpose, audience, and occasion) and context of situation (Coe, 1994b). She discusses two courses in a graduate program, Wildlife Behavior and Resource Policy, in which the institutional context, various disciplines, the classroom, and the workplace influence the nature of the texts produced and faculty evaluation of student work. If she had not conducted textual analyses as part of her study, and if she had not advocated for some direct teaching of genres, her chapter would have been fully as appropriate for the next section: The New Rhetoric.

THE NEW RHETORIC

It is common for New Rhetoric theorists and researchers to argue that genres are too complex and varied to be taken from their original rhetorical situations and taught in the classroom (Freedman, 1994). Genre knowledge is viewed by many in this theoretical camp as "living in the social unconscious of discourse community; for individual writers, [this knowledge] is at least partially subliminal . . . many (perhaps most) experts use their genres without explicit understanding" (Coe, 1994b, p. 158). New Rhetoricians also claim that most authentic reading and writing are dialogic (Hunt, 1994a) in that all relevant texts and other influences are integral to an ongoing discussion among participants. In addition, genres are seen as dynamic and evolving, "passing theories of communicative interaction," which take concrete form in specific texts (Berkenkotter & Huckin, 1995; Kent, 1993, p. 167). Thus, for several reasons, the classroom appears to be an inauthentic place for dialogue, development of passing theories, and acquisition of professional, and some academic, genres.

Those in New Rhetoric (NR) can be distinguished from the genre theorists and practitioners discussed earlier in other ways, as well. They generally fall at the *contextual* end of Flowerdew's dichotomy, preferring to start (and sometimes end) with a discussion of the rhetorical situation rather than with a more specific analysis of lexico-grammatical elements within the text.[6] They argue that context is complex, consisting of much more than the traditional rhetorical situation (audience, purposes, occasion) described in many native-English-speaker composition textbooks. Among other things, context relates to who and what texts are in power. The "critical" theorists address the socially constructed power relationships between hegemonic texts (and text writers) and the students or novices who are learning about (and oppressed by) them. Coe (1994b, p. 161) lists a number of questions about a genre that might be posed:

1. What sorts of communication does this genre encourage? What sorts does it constrain against?
2. Does it empower some people while silencing others?
3. Are its effects dysfunctional beyond their immediate context?
4. What are the political and ethical implications of the rhetorical situation assumed by a particular genre?
5. What does the genre dignify (for example, about a discourse community)?

The consequences of ignoring the "critical" area of genre analysis are major, according to NR theorists. Herndl (1993) argues that the uncritical genre theories and pedagogies "lend [themselves] to a mode of reporting that reproduces the dominant discourse of [their] research site[s] and spend relatively little energy analyzing the modes and possibilities for dissent, resistance, and revision" (p. 349).

The emphasis on genres as textual tools, exploited for social, and sometimes hegemonic, purposes within communities by knowledgeable experts, has resulted in a considerable amount of research into situated texts outside of the classroom. Publications focus on the historical evolution of genres (Bazerman, 1997), the social processes involved in constructing important genres for a specific, powerful audience (Myers, 1985), the study of genres in a workplace (Van Nostrand, 1994), and contrastive studies of the attribution and uses of power within genres (Scollon, 1997).

[6]This could be explained by the fact that most New Rhetoricians come from native-English speakers' rhetorical traditions, molded, in part, by postmodernism and literary theory. Several native-speaker compositionists have told me that they have had little experience with linguistics or grammatical analysis.

By contrast, those from the more linguistic traditions have been educated in applied linguistics and ESL/EFL teaching, so they view language as central to a discussion of genres.

Thus, the New Rhetoric has led to considerable theorizing and research about contexts and ideologies. As a result, many proponents are skeptical about genre pedagogies, about the ways in which schooling might assist students in acquiring, critiquing, and using genres for their own purposes.

Fortunately for teachers, some New Rhetoric practitioners do attempt to teach genres within classrooms, keeping in mind the cautions and comments of their colleagues. Three such practitioners are represented here. Adam and Artemeva (Chapter 9), after a careful review of the research and the cautions found in the New Rhetoric literature, describe their attempt to provide authenticity in genre processing for their English for Academic Purposes classroom through the use of dialogic and collaborative writing in electronic newsgroups. Using this venue, ESL students were able to discuss and create texts about a familiar subject, language learning. Empowered by a topic about which they were experts, the students "learned how to participate in a discussion, to listen to others' opinions, and to consider their ideas in light of new information."

Coe (Chapter 10) argues that we must understand genre as "the motivated, functional relationship between text type and rhetorical situation." After presenting a list of principles for understanding this view, he suggests that if we are to attempt a genre pedagogy in the classroom, we must "call into question several assumptions about writing that underlie traditional English composition instruction," particularly the belief that there are broadly applicable principles of good writing for every rhetorical situation. He then discusses a series of classroom writing assignments that lead to a complex genre, the political brief, a situated text that addresses multiple audiences.

PEDAGOGICAL QUANDARIES

The three chapters in this section draw from various theories and focus on the messy and challenging issues that face teachers as they attempt to create and apply genre pedagogies.

In Chapter 11, Guleff discusses the relationships between reading and writing processes and specific text products, a topic also raised by Coe (1994a and this volume). Initially intimidated by a complex, situated academic genre, the ethnographic paper in a sociology class, the author's novice students were led through a series of minitasks that enabled them to write a paper in which participant observation, organization and analysis of field notes, and examination of model texts were central intertextual elements. After this teaching experience, Guleff concludes that "The [reductionist] Writing Process," as constituted in many composition classes, is inadequate for the demands of the complex genres required in academic classrooms and in the professions.

Dudley-Evans (Chapter 12) discusses a problem that cannot be solved through approaches familiar to his ESP tradition: the teaching of a mixed pedagogical genre ("the essay assignment") to international graduate students. This quote expresses part of his dilemma: "[texts from this genre] do not have a number of delineated sections . . . and even when there is one, a number of approaches to structuring that section may exist." Stymied by the variety of texts that resulted from "the essay assignment" in different disciplines at his British university, Dudley-Evans developed a number of units on general principles of academic writing, and then ensured that his students worked closely with their departments on textual elements that are discourse community-specific, such as the use of citation and textual organization. Like many practitioners, he attempted to balance "general EAP" with the necessity for "positioning," that is, "asking students about what they are writing in terms of how well it is positioning them as members of their chosen discourse communities" (Swales & Feak, 1994, p. 3).

Johns (Chapter 13), working with novice undergraduates in the United States, found that students brought to her classes limited, and limiting, theories of pedagogical genres, based on their previous secondary-school literacy experiences. She and her coinstructor, an historian, attempted to destabilize their students' theories about one slippery pedagogical genre, "the research paper," by introducing them to distinct ways to gather data and construct texts. She and her colleague assigned a variety of units, or mini-tasks, leading up to the final text product in order to ensure that the students would not be overwhelmed. Because there are almost as many types of assigned undergraduate research papers as there are faculty (see, for example, Prior, 1991; Larson, 1982), Johns encouraged students to be open-minded and flexible in their academic classrooms rather than resorting to rigid and autonomous theories of texts which allow for little flexibility and negotiation.

CONCLUSION

This volume does not include a traditional conclusion, that is, a summing up of the information and arguments presented by the contributors. Instead, its conclusion begins with a chapter by a leading applied linguist and reading theorist (Grabe) that challenges many of the arguments in the text. This chapter is followed by responses from major theorists and practitioners from each of the three schools represented here.

In the focus chapter, Grabe uses reading research to directly address the issues of genre boundaries and breadth. Drawing from studies in educational literacy, cultural psychology, cognitive development, applied linguistics, and corpus analysis (especially Biber, 1988, 1995a & b), Grabe argues that there are two families of macro-genres, the narrative and the expository, "drawing on distinct and identifiable combinations of formal resources, occurring in identifiable social contexts, and using distinct organizing devices as aspects of discourse construction." He claims that accepting these two top-level organizing principles will assist us to understand how readers and writers structure their worlds. He also argues that this understanding can also assist teachers in reconsidering their textual practices and prevent scholars from dabbling in "unanchored theorizing."

In order to highlight these and other issues, three noted theorists/practitioners were invited to respond to the Grabe chapter. The first response, by James Martin of the Sydney School,[7] raises a number of issues that all theorists and pedagogues must consider: the topical, linguistic, and contextual features of genre families, genre boundaries and histories, and the ways in which we can most successfully organize and taxonomize genres for pedagogical purposes. His argumentation, and his visual representations of genre staging, are both persuasive and challenging–and they tell us a great deal about topics considered within the Sydney School.

Vijay Bhatia, a prominent exponent of the English for Specific Purposes group, deals with some of the same central topics, particularly the categorizing of genres. Taking a considerably different approach from Martin, Bhatia argues that there are certain versatile "generic values [especially writer purposes] that are realized in terms of a set of typical lexico-grammatical features." These values, then, influence "genre colonies," grounded in broad rhetorical contexts, which, in turn, lead to more specific, nameable, individual genres. He argues that the distinct differences between the ESP School and the Sydney School lie where the curriculum begins, either with textual purposes (Sydney School) or with individual, community-identified genres (ESP). Again, the visual and verbal argumentation is informative and thought-provoking.

Carol Berkenkotter, using a mixed-genre style in her text, praises Grabe for his extensive literature review of reading research but raises objections, commonly heard among New Rhetoricians, about confining discussions of genre to text type. If this is done, Berkenkotter argues, teachers risk the possibility of returning to "the obsolete pedagogy of teaching the traditional modes of discourse." This argument is helpful because, in this way, she questions the basic assumptions of textually grounded ("linguistic") theories and pedagogies.

The purpose of this volume is to bring together various understandings of genre and discussions of the ways in which this complex concept has been realized, or critiqued, as teachers attempt to apply it to academic classrooms. There has been no attempt at coherence among the chapters; instead, the intention was to show the multiplicity of discussions and applications of the concept.

Despite the central differences among theorists and practitioners, there are, I believe, at least eight principles on which they could agree, and these are important for our own understanding of the new directions in theory and practice. These principles are:

1. Texts are socially constructed. The influence of community and culture, however these are defined, is considerable, in both text processing and production.
2. Texts are purposeful, and their functions are at least partially determined by the context and community long before the writer (or reader) begins to process them.

[7]Martin notes that this term, "The Sydney School," is "in need of fuzzy borders if family differences be told"!

3. Some genres, like some language registers, are valued more than others within a community. This is a reality that can be accepted, or critiqued, by teachers, researchers, theorists, and students.
4. Textual conventions are often subject to community constraints, and the writer needs to consider working within these boundaries. Form, as well as other text features, is strongly influenced by the conventions of a genre and the particular situation in which the text is being produced.
5. The grammar of expository texts, including the metadiscourse, is functional; that is, it serves community and writer purposes within a genre and context.
6. What is present, and absent, in texts, such as content and argumentation, is often regulated by a community or the particular context in which the text is operating.
7. Genres are ideologically driven; even, or especially, in educational institutions, there are no texts that are free from the values and purposes of those involved in producing and processing them.
8. Finally, the language of texts, whether it be vocabulary, grammar, metadiscourse, or other features, should never be taught separately from rhetorical considerations. Language is purposefully chosen and used by expert writers (see Johns, in press).

Thus, there is some agreement on points that bring literacy studies to a different place than was the case in the past. I hope that this volume will enrich the readers' understanding of how genre principles are theorized and practiced, leading to a more contextualized approach to the teaching of literacies.

Part I

The Sydney School

1

"Something to Shoot For": A Systemic Functional Approach to Teaching Genre in Secondary School Science

Mary Macken-Horarik
University of Canberra, Australia

It has become something of a truism in conversations among "Sydney School" linguists that students at risk of school failure fare better within a visible curriculum. In this view, such students need explicit induction into the genres of power if they are to participate in mainstream textual and social processes within and beyond the school. But what does "explicit induction" mean in pedagogic terms, and what kinds of metalinguistic resources are going to serve learners well in this process? Many claims and counter-claims have been made about the role of genre in both textual and social processes (see, for example, Callaghan & Rothery, 1988; Cope & Kalantzis, 1993; Lee, 1997; Luke, 1996; Martin, 1993a; Reid, 1987). This chapter is one contribution to the ongoing dialogue between theorists of the Sydney School and beyond.[1] It focuses on the role of a systemic functional metalanguage in the process of initiating students into subject-specific literacies rather than with social processes more broadly.[2] More particularly, it explores the role of genre and register in one teacher's mediation of the demands and possibilities of scientific literacy.

The classroom work on which this chapter is based was itself part of a larger project associated with the Disadvantaged Schools Program (hereafter, DSP)

---

[1] The term "Sydney School" is a convenient fiction that enables me to situate my work within educational applications of systemic functional linguistics as reported in North American and British publications. In fact, much of the work by the "Sydney School" has been undertaken in sites far from even the major Australian cities like Brisbane, Adelaide, Perth, Melbourne, and Darwin.

[2] Of course, we cannot really separate learning processes and outcomes from social processes. But the focus of our attention in this chapter is on the immediate pay-off for learning of an investment in tools such as genre within a systemic functional orientation to teaching literacy.

situated in Erskineville, Sydney. There have been two important school literacy projects coordinated by the DSP. The first was the *Language and Social Power Project*, which focused on the application of genre-based approaches to teaching literacy in primary and secondary schools (see Callaghan, Knapp, & Noble, 1993; Callaghan & Rothery, 1988, for fuller accounts of this project). The second was the *Write it Right Project,* which extended the work of the earlier project to incorporate register-sensitive accounts of secondary school literacy in its interface with work-place literacies (see Christie & Martin, 1997, for a full review of this research). The current chapter is based on case-study material, which emerged primarily during the first project.

Most of the junior secondary-school teachers involved in DSP in-services wanted access to resources and assistance that would help them to integrate literacy and learning in different subjects with perceivable pay-offs for both subject-area learning *and* literacy. It was against this background that Margaret Watts and I began to work cooperatively on classroom-based research in 1990. Margaret was one of the DSP science teachers who had become interested in the notion of genre when she saw how positively it impacted on students struggling with the literacy demands of science. In her early applications of the model, Margaret introduced her students to the full range of scientific genres such as procedures, recounts, explanations, reports, and expositions. Her students analyzed the generic structure of these written genres and spent time producing texts similar to her prototypes. All had some degree of success with each genre. But, as Margaret later realized, some genres (like explanations), which are crucial to the construction of scientific knowledge, are more difficult to teach than others (like procedures).

This chapter takes up the point at which Margaret began work on explanation with a Year 10 class in a new school, drawing on her earlier experiences and pushing the model in the direction of greater usefulness to secondary-school teachers. The contextual framework reviewed here is based solidly on her classroom work (as well as that of others in DSP schools). It shows how the systemic functional metalanguage (related to the tools of genre and register) can be used in planning for, reflecting on, and assessing student literacy across the curriculum.

Margaret claimed that the metalanguage drawn from systemic functional linguistics (hereafter SFL) gave her "something to shoot for" when teaching scientific literacy. Her words form the title of this chapter because I believe they capture the attraction that this metalanguage and its associated pedagogy have for many teachers. To anticipate my argument a little, the metalanguage gives teachers "something to shoot for" because it enables them to characterize goals for learning in semiotic terms—to turn them into meanings. Using the context–text framework presented in the next section (see especially Table 1.2), Margaret formulated learning goals in terms of the demands of particular genres and register values. In addition to this, she shared aspects of the metalanguage (especially genre) with her students as well as using it herself (especially register) to reflect on her students' difficulties and achievements. She found that the texts her students produced yielded valuable evidence about what they had learned and the kinds of assistance they still needed—especially those from non-English-speaking backgrounds. As will be seen, she was able to turn this framework to rhetorical ends.

The chapter is divided into two halves. In the first half, I outline those aspects of SFL that secondary teachers have drawn on in their teaching, setting out the contextual framework and dealing with the pedagogy adopted by Margaret and other DSP teachers. In the second half of the chapter, I show how Margaret applied this model in a unit of work on reproduction technologies with her class of 15- and 16-year-olds (in New South Wales, Year 10 is the final year of junior secondary high school). My reflections attempt to mediate the significance of her work for development of the contextual framework (initially reported on in Macken & Rothery, 1991).

A CONTEXTUAL FRAMEWORK FOR TEACHING LITERACY ACROSS THE CURRICULUM

A viable contextual framework for teaching literacy across the curriculum has to face two ways: toward the specificities of learning in particular subject areas, and toward the commonalities of higher order academic learning more generally. This is important because in the later years of secondary schooling, students learn through language, and the texts they encounter are increasingly abstract, technical, and metaphorical. Furthermore, the framework must enable teachers to move in mutually predictable ways between the learning contexts they set up for students and the kinds of texts they encounter there.

The following contextual framework assumes that there is a principled and mutually determining relationship between language use and its social environment. It was Michael Halliday who first proposed a systematic connection between social context and text meanings. In the late 1970s, he observed that the internal organization of language itself corresponded to the external organization of social context:

> The context of situation, the context in which the text unfolds, is encapsulated in the text, not in a kind of piecemeal fashion, not at the other extreme in any mechanical way, but through a systematic relationship between the social environment on the one hand, and the functional organization of language on the other. If we treat both text and context as semiotic phenomena, as modes of meaning, so to speak, we can get from one to the other in a revealing way. (Halliday & Hasan, 1985, pp. 11–12)

Halliday represents the immediate social environment in terms of *context of situation*. This tripartite construct comprises three crucial variables: *field*, referring to the nature of the social action taking place; *tenor*, referring to the roles taken up by interactants in the interaction; and *mode*, referring primarily to the channel of communication—whether spoken or written or some combination of the two

(Halliday, 1985, p. 12). Taken together, these three contextual variables determine the *register* of a text (the patterns of meanings associated with the context). Thus, contextual variation produces register variation. The twin notions of context of situation and register are useful because they show how context "gets into" text and how context itself is "recovered from" a text.

In later educational applications of SFL, linguists such as Jim Martin, Joan Rothery, and others added another layer to context of situation. They built on the notion of *genre* as it is used in literary or film criticism to include all "staged, goal-oriented, social processes" (Martin, 1984). They argued that scientific reports, procedures, service encounters, and government submissions are just as much genres as the more familiar examples of narrative fiction or film. In this extension of the functional language model, the notion of *genre* is "tuned into" the social purpose of a text and captures its distinctive global (or schematic) structure. The notion of *register*, on the other hand, relates to the context of situation in which a text is produced (and heard or read) and accounts for the text's distinctive patterns of meaning (see Table 1.3 for a composite view).

The first educational implementations of the model in the early to mid-1980s raised teachers' consciousness about the category of genre and introduced them to a wider range of text types than was currently available (Martin, 1984). In the educational climate of this time, it is arguable that teachers would have tolerated only a very simple metalanguage. The growth model of literacy and associated regimes such as process writing exercised a hegemony in the literacy curriculum in those days, and teachers were cautioned to "bite their tongues" rather than tell students anything about what or how to write (Rothery, 1989; Christie in Christie, 1990; Gilbert, 1990, for extended discussion of these issues). Early curriculum materials foregrounded only simple structural differences between genres and provided teachers with essential information about the structural elements (schematic stages) of key written genres, their social purposes, and social location. The material reproduced in Table 1.1 was developed by Joan Rothery and me for teacher in-services in DSP schools during the late 1980s. It is representative of the kind of genre metalanguage teachers worked with at that time in the classroom for a range of genres across the primary and secondary curriculum.

SOME KEY WRITTEN GENRES ACROSS THE SECONDARY CURRICULUM

We represent the *schematic structure* of a text as a predictable sequence of stages (the more common term is *generic structure*). Each established genre can be identified as a sequence of obligatory and optional elements or stages. For example, the *Recount* genre typically consists of an obligatory *Orientation*, which provides information about the situation of the participants, followed by a *Record of Events*, which tells about what happened to these participants. At the end of the Recount there is an optional *Reorientation* stage, which brings the listener/reader back into the present. We represent this schematic structure as a sequence of elements, using the ^ formalism to indicate "is followed by" and the round brackets to indicate optionality in the structure. The whole sequence of elements is enclosed in curly brackets. We can represent the schematic structure of the Recount as follows: {Orientation ^ Record of Events ^ (Reorientation)}. As you can see, these same formalisms are adopted in the following table. Table 1.1 sets out the social purpose, social location, schematic structure, and descriptions of text stages for eight prototypical genres in our culture.

Table 1.1

A Look at Eight Key Genres for Teaching Writing across the Curriculum

	Social Purpose	*Social Location*	*Schematic Structure*	*Description of Stages*
Recount	Retells events for the purpose of informing or entertaining. Events usually arranged in a temporal sequence.	Recounts are found in personal letters or oral & written histories, police records, insurance claims and excursion "write-ups."	{Orientation ^ Record of Events ^ (Re-orientation)}	**Orientation:** provides information about the situation; **Record of events:** presents events in temporal sequence; **Re-orientation:** optional stage bringing the events into the present.
Information Report	Describes "the ways things are" in our natural, built, & social environment by firstly classifying things & then describing their special characteristics.	Information reports package information and are found in encyclopedias, brochures, and government documents. They are useful for locating information on a topic.	{General Statement (or Classification) Description of Aspects.^ Description of Activities}	**General Statement:** provides information about the subject matter; **Description of Aspects:** lists and elaborates the parts or qualities of the subject matter; **Description of Activities:** could be behaviors, functions, or uses.
Explanation	Accounts for how or why things are as they are. An explanation sets out the logical steps in a process.	Explanations are written by experts for textbooks, for nature programs, environmental leaflets, health-care booklets, and so on.	{General Statement ^ Implication Sequence ^ (State)}	**General Statement:** provides information about the phenomena to be explained; **Implication Sequence:** sets out steps in a process or the factors influencing a phenomenon in a logical sequence.

Exposition	Argues for a particular point of view on an issue. An exposition gives reasons to support a thesis and elaborates these using evidence.	Expositions are written in school essays for subjects like History or English. They also occur in editorials, commentaries, and political debates.	{Thesis [Position ^ Preview] ^ Arguments^n [Elaboration ^ Assertion] ^ Reiteration}	**Thesis:** proposes a viewpoint on a topic or issue; **Position ^ Preview:** a position is stated & the arguments listed. **Arguments^n**: the arguments are asserted & elaborated in turn. **Reiteration**: returns to the thesis & concludes.
	Social Purpose	**Social Location**	**Schematic Structure**	**Description of Stages**
Discussion	Discusses an issue in the light of some kind of "frame" or position. Provides more than one point of view on an issue.	Discussions are found in essays, editorials, & public forums, which canvass a range of views on issues. They also occur in panel discussions & research summaries.	{Issue ^ Arguments for & against ^ Conclusion}	**Issue:** gives information about the issue and how it is to be framed; **Arguments for & against:** canvasses points of view on the issue. (similarities & differences or advantages & disadvantages) **Conclusion:** recommends a final position on the issue.
Procedure	Instructs in how to do something through a sequence of steps.	Procedures can be found in science experiments and in instructional manuals such as gardening and cookbooks and technical instruction sheets.	{Goal ^ Steps 1-n ^ (Results)}	**Goal:** gives information about the purpose of the activity (might be in the title or in the opening paragraphs); **Steps 1-n:** presents the activities needed to achieve the goal. They need to be put in right order. **Results:** optional stage describing the final state or "look" of activity.
Narrative	Entertains & instructs via reflection on experience. Deals with problematic events which individuals have to resolve for better or worse.	Narratives are found across all aspects of cultural life, in novels, short stories, movies, sit coms, and radio dramas. They are important in subjects such as English.	{Orientation ^ (Complication. Evaluation) ^ Resolution}	**Orientation:** provides relevant information about the characters' situation; **Complication:** introduces one or more problems for characters to solve; **Evaluation:** highlights the significance of the events for characters; **Resolution:** sorts out the problems for better or worse.

News Story	Presents recent events regarded as "news-worthy" or of public importance.	News stories are found in newspapers, television, & radio broadcasts.	{Lead ^ Key Events ^ Quotes}	**Lead:** provides newsworthy information about the events (the "hook"); **Key Events:** Provides background information about events or story; **Quotes:** provides commentary from relevant sources about significance of the events.

How do these schematic structures map onto texts? The curriculum materials produced at the time contained model texts annotated for their schematic stages and distinctive language features (see, for example, Callaghan & Rothery, 1988, and Macken et al., 1989a). Teachers used texts like the following one when modeling the structure of a particular genre for their students. This text was written by one of the case-study students and its grammatical idiosyncrasies have been preserved as in the original.

Model Explanation

GENERAL STATEMENT	Follows is an explanation of why an offspring from a couple in the IVF program receiving either sperm, ovum or both would not bear a baby that looks like the birth mother.
IMPLICATION SEQUENCE	When an ovum is produced in the woman's ovary, it is given 23 of the mother's 46 chromosomes. These chromosomes make up the nucleus of the cells in the ovum. Lying along each chromosome are 1000 or more genes. Contained in these genes is DNA or the genetic information that determines such characteristics as eye color, nose shape, height and many other characteristics. This process also occurs in the father's sperm. He too passes on his genetics to the unborn zygote. Thus when fertilization occurs,the baby's characteristics are decided, the dominant genes develop while the recessive genes lay dormant, to be passed on in the next generation.
STATE	This therefore explains the fact that it doesn't matter who the embryo implants and grows in. What really matters is who produced the ova and sperm in the beginning.

Rodney, Year 10

Teachers in both primary and secondary schools emphasize the generative power of metalanguage. As the model text indicates, each stage of the genre has a functional label, one that foregrounds the rhetorical function of each part in relation to the whole generic structure. This kind of metalanguage enables teachers to be explicit with learners about the semantic demands of any writing task. In fact, one pervasive claim made by teachers is that this model of genre facilitates a global orientation to texts in their students. They learn to construe texts in structural terms—to see them as rhetorical wholes composed of functional elements.

Of course, it is important that our representations of genre allow for both predictability and innovation. Although some genres are socially acceptable and others unthinkable in particular social contexts, new genres emerge in times of cultural, technological, and political change. With the onset of the AIDS virus in Western cultures, for example, advertisements promoting safe sex became acceptable. Prior to this, the narrative was an unlikely genre to use in condom advertisements situated in public places such as bus and train stations. The massive and unprecedented threat to public health led to new combinations of genre (narrative) and register (written mode in public advertisements, about safe sex and addressed to passing members of the public).

Building on the twin notions of genre and register, we now have a framework that affords multiple foci on learning contexts—one that enables us to highlight areas of stability and of transformation in register/genre combinations. Table 1.2 presents the four-part model of context, which has been applied by DSP teachers in the literacy projects related to the functional-language model.

Note: the questions "why," "what," "who," and "how" in this table were developed as simple glosses for each contextual category. "Why" points to the purposefulness of genres, "what" to the "aboutness" of a text's subject matter, "who" to those involved in the act of communication, and "how" to the means by which the communication is achieved.

Table 1.2
Critical Aspects of Context

GENRE (WHY?)	Genres are staged, goal-oriented language processes; we use different genres to get things done in language; the goals or purposes of the users affect the type of text they construct. Each stage of the text contributes to achieving the overall social purpose of the participants.
FIELD (WHAT?)	This is the social activity of the participants (what is going on). Subject matter is one aspect of field. In written language, the field is the subject matter. This is because the reader is dependent on language alone to re-construct the field.
TENOR (WHO?)	This refers to the relationship assumed between participants in the communication event (who is taking part). What are the status, familiarity, and degree of feeling assumed in the interaction? In written language, the relationship assumed is often one of differential status (apprentice to expert), with marked social distance between writer and reader (that is, an impersonal tenor).
MODE (HOW?)	This refers to the role played by language (how language is being used). The simplest distinction is that between spoken and written language. Mode can be represented as a continuum—moving from texts which are most "spoken" to those which are most "written." The mode is also influenced by semiotic distance of two kinds: (a) the distance of the speaker or

> writer from the events about which language is used (from language in action to language as reflection); and (b) the distance of the participants themselves in the interactions (from communication with maximum feed back to that with delayed or no feedback).

Like other social contexts in the community, the context of formal school learning can thus be described and modeled in terms of four main variables: (a) the social purpose(s) of the participants influencing choice and inflection of genre; (b) the social activities of the participants in a particular field; (c) the role relationships assumed by interactants influencing the tenor; and (d) the channel and/or medium of communication chosen affecting its mode. These four variables—categorized as *genre, field, tenor*, and *mode*—can be used to contextualize the interpretive and the productive demands of any situation.

How does contextualization work in practice? In any formal act of interpretation, readers faced with an unfamiliar text will typically attempt to recognize its overall design and purpose (to place it generically). They will also attempt to unpack the particular treatment it gives to its subject matter (assign it to one field or another). In negotiating the text, they will respond to the reading position(s) that the text opens up (comply with or resist its tenor), and they will manage all these tasks through language itself (negotiate the written or spoken demands of the text's mode). The extent to which learners can negotiate these dimensions of the task will determine the extent to which they engage with it successfully.

The same dimensions can be applied to the production of a text. Faced with a particular writing task, students need to select a genre relevant to their purpose(s), marshal their knowledge of a given field, adopt the appropriate tenor for the task in hand, and operationalize these decisions through control of spoken or written language. Of course, contextualization is a dynamic and on-line process. Decisions about the interpretive or productive demands of a given context or text are multilevel and simultaneous. However, this analytical framework serves as a heuristic, which enables us to "factor out" the contextual constraints operating in any situation and to use them as tools for reflecting on language use.

Many DSP teachers have drawn productively on this framework when articulating their goals for learning in any given unit of work. They will probe and reflect on the learning context they have set up in the classroom using one or more of the categories of genre, field, tenor, and mode. In addition to this, they may ask themselves at some time during a unit of work whether students are coming to terms with the demands of the genre under focus, whether their learners are making the correct inferences about the field from the learning activities they have been through, and so on. Finally, teachers will assess the products of students' learning (for example, their written and sometimes their spoken texts) from the point of view of their control of the structure of the genre, their knowledge of the field of study, their adoption of the appropriate tenor(s), and their command of the language of the spoken or written mode. The model thus serves as a tool for planning for, reflecting on, and assessing students' learning through consideration of the texts they encounter and produce.

PEDAGOGY

Many DSP teachers involved in literacy education seek guidance on pedagogy. Strategies such as modeling and joint construction were promoted in the "teaching–learning cycle" used at this time (see Macken, Martin, Kress, Kalantzis, Rothery, & Cope, 1989a; Feez, this volume). The teaching–learning cycle incorporates the insights of linguists like Halliday (1975) and Painter (1986) into child language development and those of educators such as Brian Gray, whose research into literacy learning among Aboriginal children has been formative in genre-based pedagogy in Australia (Gray, 1986; 1987). The approach is based on the assumption that language is learned "through guidance and interaction" in the context of shared experience (Painter, 1986). In what is popularly termed an *explicit pedagogy*, the teacher inducts learners into the linguistic demands of genres which are important to participation in school learning and in the wider community.

What kinds of strategies are salient in this pedagogy? Those that scaffold learners' work on unfamiliar genres. The cycle introduced in many teacher in-services and curriculum materials involves three stages:

1. *Modeling*: The teacher builds up the context relevant to the field of inquiry and provides learners with models of the genre in focus in this context, helping learners explore the social purpose of the text, its prototypical elements of structure, and its distinctive language features.
2. *Joint Negotiation of Text*: The teacher prepares learners for joint production of a new text in the focus genre. Teachers and students compose a new text together, drawing on shared knowledge of both the learning context itself and the structure and features of the genre.
3. *Independent Construction of Text*: The learners work on their own texts using processes such as drafting, conferencing, editing, and publishing (Macken et al., 1989a & 1989b). Many teachers have used the strategies suggested in the cycle, but their pedagogies have not been lockstep or rigidly applied. In fact, early research on educational applications of genre in different New South Wales schools revealed difference rather than sameness in the teacher inflections of the model (see Macken et al., 1989b, for extensive discussion of initial case-study schools).

Thus, although there is no "right way" to sequence teaching–learning activities, it is important that teachers provide maximum assistance to students in their early work on a text, gradually shifting responsibility onto the learners as they achieve greater control of the new genre. In this way, teacher input to any text negotiation is at a maximum in early phases of scaffolding and reduces to a minimum as students gain control of and learn to exploit the linguistic possibilities of a given genre.

Furthermore, as Margaret and other teachers involved in the DSP Project discovered, modeling and joint negotiation are labor-intensive strategies. But they are valuable because they afford learners a "loan of consciousness" that assists them in the production of a particular genre in a given register. Without this kind of support, many students are thrown back onto their own resources too early and thus fail to produce texts that are both contextually adequate and educationally valued. This applies especially to students from non-English-speaking backgrounds who are often most disadvantaged in classrooms marked by invisible pedagogies (see Callaghan & Rothery, 1988, and Macken et al., 1989a, for extended treatment of pedagogical issues). The teaching–learning cycle acknowledges the crucial mediating role teachers play in the literacy education of their students.

A SYSTEMIC FUNCTIONAL APPROACH: MARGARET'S EXPERIENCE

This section focuses on Margaret's application of this model (metalanguage and pedagogy) to a 10-week unit on human reproduction and its technologies with a special focus on the explanation genre. Margaret and I met weekly over the course of the unit, during which time I visited her classroom, collected teaching resources, scrutinized students' writing, and adapted the contextual framework in the light of all these factors. The case-study material is presented from the point of view of the planning, teaching, reflection, and assessment strategies Margaret undertook during this unit.

PLANNING

Initially, Margaret planned to cover elementary principles of human reproduction and inheritance, and then move on to the use of technologies like in vitro fertilization and genetic engineering. But she did not want to stop there. She also wanted her students to contextualize these base-level understandings in alternative (contradictory) ways as they considered some of the real-life ethical and social issues raised by the application of such technologies. Hence, although field has never been a neutral construct for Margaret, she did want her students to debate the issues with "a good science base." She knew that the students would not be able to discuss the ethical problems surrounding genetic engineering without a thorough grasp of its procedures, and they could not understand even these if they hadn't first built up adequate understandings of how babies are conceived and develop. Similarly, in order to explain to a woman in an IVF program why the child she is carrying may not look like her, they would have to draw on their earlier work on human reproduction and IVF and integrate this with new understandings about inheritance.

The students' work on the explanation genre was designed to guide them into understandings about the field. Her choice of this genre was apposite because explanation is central to the construction of scientific knowledge. Of course, Margaret knew that she would need to spend some initial time on genre analysis itself. But she wanted this metalinguistic work to yield benefits for students' later scientific work. To this end, Margaret planned to increase the ideational complexity of each explanation her students wrote so that the cognitive load increased over time and so that their writing served to induct them into the field itself. In short, in this unit, literacy and learning were to be intimately related.

The case-study population was uneven in that it included 15- and 16-year-old students from both non-English-speaking and Anglo-Celtic backgrounds. Because this unit was to focus on scientific writing, students were told (and appeared to accept) that they would be challenged at a fairly high level and that their work would be monitored by both Margaret and me. As is obvious from their writing, the students approached each learning task with seriousness of purpose and with enthusiasm.

Margaret's initial program notes indicated that at the end of this unit, students should be able to:

- Use the explanation genre effectively.
- Explain the processes of sexual reproduction in humans, in vitro fertilization, genetic engineering, and inheritance (both dominant and recessive).
- List and describe the technologies for intervening in or altering the outcomes of human reproduction.
- Discuss the ethical and medical issues arising out of new reproduction technologies.
- Read and discuss various issues treated in a number of articles (newspapers, scientific journals, textbooks), and different media (print and television, for example, "A Current Affair").

Her goals can also be characterized in contextual terms, using the notions of genre and register. The specialized literacy demands of the context can be represented as follows:

Purpose: Explaining natural and technological phenomena (focus on explanation genre);
Field: Biological and technological processes surrounding human reproduction (focus on specialized field knowledge);
Tenor: Students as apprentices, learning to take up the role of authorities in this field (focus on expert tenor); and
Mode: Written language (focus on producing epistemic texts).

The twin notions of genre and register thus work as semiotic frames for planning the learning context. In Margaret's classroom they serve as complementary ways of characterizing the literacy demands of the science curriculum.

TEACHING: BUILDING UP THE FIELD

What steps, then, did Margaret take to move students from their current understandings of the field to those privileged within the discipline?

Students' common-sense knowledge about human reproduction was mediated by individual and communal experiences in their everyday lives and certainly would not have been uniform. In fact, many of the students had already done some introductory work on elementary principles of human reproduction in Year 8, so Margaret began by reviewing what they had already learned and establishing a common knowledge base for the lessons to follow.

A complete account of the work done in this initial period is beyond the scope of this chapter. However, I offer here a brief description of the kind of activities students undertook in building up knowledge of the field of human reproduction and its technologies.

In initial classroom work, Margaret minimized the semantic load of each learning activity on students and supported them through strategies like oral rehearsal of activity sequences related to menstruation, intercourse, and gestation, using the visual support of diagrams and flow charts. Students were not expected to work alone at this stage and tended to complete all exercises in groups. In this phase of their work on this topic, language was only a part of what was going on, and learners could rely on extralinguistic cues to help them decode and encode the meanings of each text. They tended to shunt between verbal and visual representations of the activity sequences relevant to reproduction. In one exercise, for example, students were asked to draw up a table that summarized the events from 0 hours to 12 days after conception (that is, fertilization). Science Text 1 is an example of this type of activity. Here, Laurent outlines the stages in egg development using a timeline:

Science Text 1: Egg Development

TIME (days)	**EVENTS**
1.5 days	Zygote splits into 2 cells
2 days	Zygote splits into 4 cells
3 days	Ball of 16–32 cells is formed
4 days	Hollow ball of 64–128 cells
4–5 days	Embryo still free in uterus
6–7 days	Embryo attaching to wall
11–12 days	Embryo embedded

Activities like this were important prerequisites to understanding the in vitro fertilization procedure (IVF). Students used excerpts from textbooks, news articles, and videos as they built up specialized knowledge of the field. In one activity, for example, the class watched a video about the biological and technological processes behind IVF and then wrote a short account of the process based on the notes they made during this program.

TEACHING: WORKING ON THE EXPLANATION GENRE

At this point, Margaret stopped work on "science" and began classroom work on the explanation genre itself. In previous weeks, she had pretested the students on their ability to write an explanation about how the sex of a child is determined. This initial piece of writing gave Margaret and me valuable feedback about students' starting points in relation to both the field and to the focus genre. We were able to "tune in" to the difficulties experienced by poorer writers, particularly those like Hoa who had only been in the country for two years.

Following this, and because they hadn't received any explicit introduction to the structure and nature of written genres in science, Margaret presented the class with some prototypical examples of explanations, reports, procedures, expositions, and discussions. Students matched each text with its "social purpose" and discussed some of the differences between these genres. In a later class, they focused on contrasts between two key genres—explanations and information reports. One student observed that explanations seemed to be more about "things in action" and reports about "things in place." Margaret drew attention to the different social and scientific purposes of the genres, pointing out that explanations focus on processes and information reports on taxonomies. Students discussed the differences between the structure and language of these two genres, identifying language features such as causal connectors and dynamic verbs in explanations and what they called *static verbs* in information reports. Their animated classroom discussions occurred over several days.

Following this analytical work on genre, Margaret structured the students' first explanation. Using an overhead projector, she analyzed the task—Explain the in vitro fertilization process—for the class, breaking it down into its component stages. She presented verbs like "fertilize," "block," "transfer," and "ovulate" on the board, because they are critical to reconstruction of this process. Margaret modeled the structure of the explanation both orally and visually, using the following "board notes":

Science Text 2: Board Notes for the First Explanation

Task: Explain the in vitro fertilization process

1. Define IVF
2. Outline situation: people who need IVF
   (for example, fertilize, block, transfer, travel)

3. Explain procedure
   (for example, ovulate, masturbate, remove, transfer, place, mix)

.... Embryo implantation

.... Return of embryo
(for example, insert implant, remove, wait, menstruate)

These notes are interesting because they facilitate features of both genre and register awareness. The stages of the required text are outlined on the left-hand side of the notes, and the technical terms relevant to the field are presented down the right-hand side.

Following the modeling session, which involved a great deal of classroom talk and troubleshooting, students worked in small groups jointly constructing their own explanations. The final drafts of the first writing task are revealing because they show how students built on both knowledge of the field (its activity sequences and technical terminology) and the structure of the genre (schematic stages) to write their first text. Science Text 3 is one of these texts:

Science Text 3: Explanation of How IVF Works

IVF involves fertilization of the egg outside the woman's body.

Participants are infertile couples, where either the woman has a damaged fallopian tube or the man has a low sperm count, wishing to have a child.

When the man produces the sperm, it is mixed with the egg that has been removed from the woman's ovary. Fertilization occurs on the petri dish. Two or three days later, the embryo is placed into the uterus by way of a long thin tube. At about this time the egg would be arriving from the fallopian tube in normal circumstances. Four or five days after the insertion of the egg, it should start to attach itself to the wall of the womb. If this occurs successfully, the embryo embeds and continues to develop.

Beth

Beth's text is a coherent explanation of the IVF process: the reader can easily reconstruct the procedure on the basis of what she has written. The writer has drawn on her earlier work on the technical names for sexual organs (for example, "ovary," "uterus," "fallopian tube," "embryo") and shows understanding of their functions in each phase of development from conception onwards. Furthermore, she has integrated her knowledge of this biological process (fertilization) with that of a clinical intervention in this process (IVF) through the explanation itself. Her control of the genre facilitates her command of the field: she is integrating her learning of science *through* her learning of writing.

At this stage of their work on the genre, students' texts were heavily "reproductive" in a number of ways. Margaret did not expect her students to produce original material in an unfamiliar genre without assistance. Rather, she played a guiding role in her induction of students into the structure of the explanation genre and its deployment in this field.

The class produced three written explanations during this period, each of which built on an earlier knowledge base:

Task 1: Explain the process of in vitro fertilization
Task 2: Write a letter to a couple who have embarked on the IVF program. Explain to the woman why it is that the child she is carrying may not look like her.
Task 3: Explain how the material of inheritance may be changed.

Students could not possibly write a good explanation without a thorough grasp of the field. Furthermore, each new explanation presents learners with a new ideational challenge. They move from the more concrete and temporally sequenced processes of Task 1 to the more abstract and logically sequenced processes of Task 3. In other words, each task is cognitively more demanding. But the complexity of these writing tasks has an interpersonal as well as an ideational dimension. Explaining the process of inheritance and drawing out its implications for IVF parents, for example, demands not only a technical understanding of both IVF and inheritance but also an ability to reformulate this in terms understandable to a lay audience. In Task 2, students are challenged to "talk from within the discipline out," as they learn to take alternative perspectives on the IVF process—those of the scientist with his or her specialized knowledge of inheritance and those of the layperson with a commonsense understanding of how children come to be like their parents.

From the point of view of development of the written *mode*, learners were reading and writing texts that were increasingly distant from immediate experience. Although in early days they had been able to draw heavily on diagrams, flow charts, and observations of illustrated or filmic treatments of the topic in their writing, their later texts had to carry far more of the communicative burden. The students had to create texts that could stand alone—that were "constitutive" of their own situation (see Table 1.4). This was an important move from the point of view of their growing control of scientific discourse. The specialized knowledge of science is represented primarily through written language and is typically less congruent with observable activity sequences and with the "here and now" of "you and me."

In short, as Tables 1.3 and 1.4 indicate, students experienced an increasing challenge on all dimensions of register as time went on, and Margaret had to support their efforts in such a way that they were only given as much as they could handle at any one time.

TEACHING: CRITICAL LITERACY

What about the critical literacy dimension to this classroom work? How did Margaret help her students use this knowledge base to dialogue with other discourses and to view knowledge construction as open to question?

Well, it is important to note the kinds of reading students engaged in during this unit. Classroom textual practices were rich and varied. Students were exposed to textbook materials, newspaper articles on issues such as IVF, gene-splicing, genetic engineering, and written texts of various kinds to accompany video materials. In addition to this, the class notice board was covered with newspaper and magazine articles on these topics—collected by both teacher and students. On several occasions, the early part of the lesson was spent on the latest notice-board acquisitions and the issues they raised. Students also watched and wrote up a number of videos on sex determination, on IVF, and on the issue of surrogacy and motherhood. Each time they discussed these issues, the students were problematizing specialized knowledge. In fact, the critical literacy orientation of this class occurred at the interface between the scientific and the social, and focused on the impact on people's lives of new scientific and technological developments.

Margaret did not defer discussion of critical social issues until the end of the unit. But there was always a rhythm to her interventions here. She only asked students to consider an issue when they knew enough about the "science" behind it to participate effectively. For example, the class did talk about how the Donor Gamete Program challenges our traditionally accepted concepts of motherhood. They were asked: "Who owns the child in this program—the donor of the gamete or the woman whose uterus grows the baby?" Students' ability to participate effectively in these discussions was dependent on their understanding of the biological and technological processes underpinning this program as well as their understanding of its social impact. Of course, not every student engaged in each discussion with the same degree of interest. There were some for whom the issues had a burning personal significance. One student, for example, who was an adopted child and had recently made contact with her birth mother, had discovered that she was carrier for an inherited disease. As she began to apply her understandings of inheritance to the study of sex-linked diseases, questions like the following took on a frightening personal relevance:

> Thalassemia is an inherited blood disease common among people of Mediterranean origin. It is caused by a single recessive gene. People with Thalassemia Minor are heterozygous. People with Thalassemia Major are homozygous recessive. What advice would you give a couple who are heterozygous and want to have children?

In responding to this question, students first had to apply their knowledge of Mendelian inheritance to work out that the couple had a 50% chance of having children with Thalassemia Minor. The science provided them with an empirical foundation on which to base the advice they would give the couple. But in applying their knowledge of inheritance to human situations, they were forced to confront the values underpinning the different views of people with a stake in the issue.

As well as using science to help them think through the issues, students also problematized science from the point of view of the social. For example, they talked and wrote about the advantages and disadvantages of genetic engineering, taking up such questions as the dangers to future generations of errors in genetic experiments or the possibility of new forms of germ warfare falling into the wrong hands.

One of the final tasks the class completed involved critical reading of three news reports about new genetic technology for checking birth defects in human embryos. Science Text 4 presents the text of one of these reports:

Science Text 4
Doctors find cure for cystic fibrosis
From Margaret Harris in London

> **Doctors in London and Berlin have developed a test which can eliminate cystic fibrosis.**
>
> The test—which relies on genetic analysis of a single cell removed from an eight-celled embryo conceived using in vitro fertilization techniques—will be used to allow women known to be carrying genetic diseases to have normal children.
>
> Careful removal of one cell at this early stage should not damage the embryo. If, when the cell has been analyzed, the embryo is proven to be free of the cystic fibrosis gene, the embryo can be implanted in its mother's womb and develop into a normal healthy baby.
>
> Writing up their work in the *British Medical Journal*, the London team from Hammersmith Hospital said they were ready to use these techniques to eliminate a wide range of genetic diseases. Easiest to identify are the sex-linked diseases carried on the "X" chromosome because only males are seriously affected.
>
> Embryos of mothers known to carry the hemophilia gene can have their cells examined to determine whether or not they are males. Only female embryos will be implanted in mothers known to be carrying the hemophilia gene.
>
> Although the research team at Hammersmith Hospital says their techniques will eliminate serious genetic diseases like cystic fibrosis, campaigners opposed to genetic research, genetic manipulation and abortion say their work should be stopped.

Margaret asked the class to apply their scientific knowledge to a reading of texts like these. One of her questions was: "Are these cures? If not, what is the news report describing?" Science Text 5 is one student's response to this question. Note how he draws on both his scientific knowledge of reproduction and his capacity for critique of media hype to answer this question.

Science Text 5: Response to a News Article on Cystic Fibrosis

> The so called cures that doctors have come up with for cystic fibrosis are nothing more than prevention of the inherited disease being developed in an embryo.
>
> Rodney

In answering questions such as this one, students were learning to be more critical of media representations of the so-called "cures" found by science but from an informed base. Rodney's ability to modify the noun "cures" with "so called" indicates an ability to distance himself from the verbal representations of others (even those of experts). An important step on the way to becoming critically literate is to see others' texts as constructs that can be resisted and challenged.

Margaret's pedagogy shifted as students moved into greater critical work on reproduction technologies. As she judged that they were ready to take up more reflexive perspectives on the field, Margaret stepped out of her instructional role and gave students greater control over the content and pacing of their learning.

Strategies like modeling and joint negotiation diminished as her students became more independent in their reading, talking, and writing.

In the final writing task of the unit, students were asked to explain how the material of inheritance can be changed (Writing Task 3, mentioned earlier). Many produced texts that displayed a sophisticated understanding of the field of genetic engineering and embodied a more reflective stance on its ethical implications for contemporary society. The final three paragraphs of Beth's text are reproduced as Science Text 6.

Science Text 6: Changing the Material of Inheritance

> Today, with all our wonderful technology, it is now possible for scientists themselves to change genes. It is called genetic engineering, involving joining together genes in new and, they hope, helpful ways. One example is the combining of a bacteria and an insulin gene. This has been successful in producing insulin for diabetics, but could prove fatal if a lethal type of this bacteria is accidentally formed.
>
> Genetic engineering has already been tried on animals and one achievement is having changed fruit flies' eye color. It is now the humans' turn. Doctors can change the genes in human eggs when they are in test tubes, and try to get rid of genes causing inherited disorders. Here again, they could make mistakes, creating deformed children.
>
> If this is further developed, scientists could create the sort of egg they want in a laboratory. They could specifically make people, clones, to do certain things. Inheritance would mean nothing then, because the child wouldn't really have any parents. Already it is causing big moral problems and they can only get worse.
>
> Beth

Like all those produced later in the unit, this text "talks about" reproduction technologies in new ways. The writer, Beth, has acquired a confident grasp of the biology behind genetic mutations but is now able to contextualize this knowledge socially. Although she acknowledges the hopes of scientists, she also distances herself from them. She writes about both the positive outcomes of the genetic engineering (producing insulin for treatment of diabetics) and its problematic aspects (the lethal possibilities of creation of artificial bacteria). In fact, her writing indicates a new level of meta-awareness, one that is able to reconstruct *and* relativize scientific processes. Beth's final explanation builds on, but goes beyond, the foundational understandings of the field and into the domain of the reflexive.

Reflecting on Learning

What about the potential of the contextual framework for reflecting on the demands of different contexts and for mapping literacy development in science?

Well, if we take the field and mode variables, it is possible to indicate the kind of progress learners made in this unit and to generalize about their progress in science more generally. From the point of view of the *field*, Margaret's students were moving from common-sense knowledge into specialized knowledge of reproduction technologies and shunting between specialized and reflexive perspectives. From the point of view of *mode*, they were moving from language in action (typical of diagram labeling and tabular representations of processes) into the language of reflection (typical of scientific explanations and hypotheses).

We can represent the challenge of *field* in the following simple table:

Table 1.3
Moving into Field

Building up knowledge of the field	*1* *common-sense knowledge*	*2* *specialized knowledge*	*3* *reflexive knowledge*
	based on personal and commun-al experience	based on educational knowledge	based on contradictory experiences and discourses

As her implementation of this framework makes clear, Margaret was not interested in replacing their common-sense interpretations of phenomena but in adding to these the knowledge that biology makes possible. Technicality is part of this. Learning to use the scientific terminology relevant to human reproduction and its technologies (the technical tokens plus the scientific value they are given) allowed her students to take up alternative perspectives on this field. Technicality enables learners to interpret a context in more than one way: they are no longer stranded in common-sense knowledge of a topic but can incorporate specialized knowledge into their discourses about the topic. Developing critical perspectives on this technicality takes learners one step further, enabling them to shunt between specialized and reflexive domains of knowledge.

We can adopt a similar mechanism to reflect on the challenge of the written *mode*. Table 1.4 moves away from an overly simplistic distinction between spoken and written language into a mode distinction based on the notion of "semiotic distance" (see Martin, 1984, 1993a, for extended discussion of this). As Margaret's unit attests, early work in a new field tends to be embedded in visual and other nonverbal contexts, and the language used is "ancillary" to experience, as in Science Text 1, which tabulates events in relation to a timeline. Later work in the field tends to move students into language that is "constitutive" of experience, as in Science Text 3, which communicates by means of language alone. Then there are texts that recontextualize, critique, or subvert experience, as in Science Texts 5 and 6. These texts introduce different voices and viewpoints into a text and in effect recontextualize it. Movement from the production of "language in action" texts to "language as reflection" texts can be presented as movement along the mode continuum.

Table 1.4
Moving into Mode

Building up knowledge of the field	*1 ancillary texts*	*2 constitutive texts*	*3 recontextualizing texts*
	"language in action"		"language as reflection"

Although language is not her subject specialty, Margaret always works directly on the language features of the texts she wants her students to produce. In her own words: "I explicitly model the language demands of the genre. I show them and tell them how to do it: step one, two, three, and so on. I show the connectors, the processes. I am *really* down at language level" (Margaret Watts, personal communication).

In fact, in the course of our consultations, Margaret often raised questions with me about how to assist the less confident students with written language. These conversations took us beyond macro considerations of text structure and into micro considerations of syntax and lexis.

How did we develop connections between the global structure of the genre and the local structures such as wording of sentences? For the most part, we drew on SFL, which relates the linguistic features of texts to the demands of the contexts in which they are produced. Table 1.5 displays some of the text features Margaret brought to students' attention as she worked with them on their explanations.

Table 1.5
Moving from Context to Text in Assessing Students' Writing

Context	*Text Features*
Genre: Explanation	• How one factor influences another over time • Logical & temporal sequencing
Field: Giving information about how IVF works	• Action verbs carrying meaning about processes (material processes) • Things in general (generic participants and universal present tense) • technical terms (technical nominal groups)
Tenor: Addressed to an unfamiliar expert/audience	• unmodulated statements rather than questions • Focus on factual data rather than personal observations; non-attitudinal (generic participants as subject rather than observer or addressee)
Mode: Written to be read; semiotically distant	• Text is appropriate to context • Text hangs together

• First position in the clause is angled to the overall purpose of genre (focusing on processes)

Assessing Texts

Finally, we used the texts students wrote as evidence of what they had achieved in relation to the demands of the learning context. We could apply contextually apposite criteria to our assessments of these and use them as cues in our conferences with the writers.

Some of the field- and mode-related questions we posed in relation to students' texts include the following:

• *Building Up Field Knowledge: Becoming Specialized*
(a) Does the student recreate the activity sequences relevant to this field?
(b) Are these activity sequences logically related (for example, show appropriate relations of addition, time, cause, condition, manner, purpose, consequence, and so on)?
(c) Does the student build a clear picture of when, where, how, and why activity sequences occur?
(d) Does the student understand and use technical terms properly?

• *Controlling Mode: Becoming Subject-Literate*
(a) (Macro) Is the text coherent? Does each part contribute to the overall unity of the text and help realize the writer's purpose (for example, to explain clearly how a process occurs)?
(b) (Text-wide) Is the text cohesive, that is, does it hang together (for example, could the reader reconstruct the activity sequence from the text alone)?
(c) (Micro) Does the text show control of the sentence (for example, are clauses combined appropriately to link processes)?

I want to dwell briefly on the application of these contextually sensitive criteria to assessment of the writing of one non-English-speaking student. Hoa was one of those in this class who had great difficulty with the written demands of this unit of work. We can consider Science Texts 7 and 8 from the point of view of genre, field (Hoa's control of subject matter), and mode (his control of written language).

Science Text 7 is Hoa's first explanation.

Science Text 7: Hoa's First Explanation (about the IVF Process)

IVF stands for In-Vitro Fertilization. It mainly affected by women or male reproductive organs do not function properly as it required.

The method IVF is by removing eggs from the ovaries into a test tubes, and the fertilization is done through by men masturbation.

> Once the action took place the ova has be sperm and fertilize and then it transfer back into the woman ovaries, there the egg can be develops into an human child.
>
> This kind of operation cost $1000 or $1500.
>
> Hoa

With respect to the criteria outlined in Margaret's board notes, this text is a poor example of the explanation *genre*. There is no definition, its description of the situation of the typical IVF participants is unclear, and, although the explanation sequence *is* recoverable from the text, it would not be explicable to a reader other than the teacher.

This text also reveals that Hoa is struggling with the *field*. Although relevant to the subject of IVF, it is difficult for the reader to reconstruct the activity sequences of the IVF process. In fact, some of the sequences in the text are simply inaccurate. For example, fertilization does not occur as a result of masturbation, and the egg does not immediately develop into a human child. Hoa has confused some terms (eggs and sperm), and it is clear that the technical terminology is a problem for him, especially when it comes to using the appropriate terms to "fill out" the activity sequences.

From the point of view of *mode*, the text is certainly not fully coherent or cohesive, though knowledge of the structure of the genre has given it a minimal coherence. As scrutiny of Science Text 3 shows, this text is patterned in a similar way to the other explanations of the class. Once we move to microconsiderations such as syntax, however, coherence breaks down. The clauses in this text are not combined so as to interrelate the processes logically. Hoa mixes up processes and participants ("men masturbation"; "ova has be sperm"), and he leaves out some processes altogether ("The method IVF is ? "by removing"), or he uses inappropriate verbs in the explanation sequence ("It mainly affected by women or male reproductive organs"). Hoa, like many Asian students, finds the English tense system difficult to control. In explanations of phenomena, the favored tense is the universal present tense ("Once the action takes place" instead of "Once the action took place").

Science Text 8 is Hoa's final explanation, taken from the class test given at the end of the unit. In this task, students were presented with a diagram of a woman's reproductive organs and asked to explain why diseased or damaged fallopian tubes would stop a woman "falling" pregnant. Hoa wrote this text under examination conditions. The enforced independence of its creation provides us with vital information about his long-term development in control of the explanation genre, the field of human reproduction, and the written mode.

Science Text 8: Hoa's Final Explanation

> The disease of damage fallopian tube will stop a woman fallen pregnant because once the tube is damaged or blocks, the eggs can no longer travel from the fallopian tube to the uterus. If the fallopian tube is damage the sperm would not be able to travel along the tube into the ovary to fertilize the eggs.
>
> Hoa

Hoa's examination text is a better example of the explanation genre, and it reveals increasing command of *field* knowledge. Technical terms are now clearly understood and fill out the relevant activity sequences properly. Circumstantial meanings, realized through prepositional phrases, enable the reader to build a clear picture of the events explained (e.g., "disease of the fallopian tubes"; "*from the fallopian tubes to the uterus*"; "sperm would not be able to travel along the tube into the ovary"). With respect to *mode*, this text, though quite short, is basically coherent and cohesive. Readers can reconstruct the relevant activity sequences from the text alone, and, apart from some minor flaws to do with verb choice ("fallen" instead of "falling") and consistency of tense ("damaged or blocks" instead of "damaged or blocked"), clauses are combined appropriately and integrated well into the sentence.

In summary, then, while these functional criteria relate to literacy in particular, they also tell us a lot about processes of learning in general. We can use them to reflect on Hoa's overall development as a student of biology as well as his confidence with writing.

CONCLUSION

In concluding this chapter, I want to make three points: first, about the contextual framework itself; second, about pedagogy; and finally about the place of explicitness within the development of a generalized rhetorical competence.

First, the contextual framework in focus here is a semiotic construct that foregrounds the meanings (registers) and text types (genres) at stake in a given learning situation. The contextual dimensions enable the teacher to set the linguistic probabilities of this context. Once she or he has made decisions about the nature of the content to be explored and the activities by which it will be investigated (its field), the roles students will play in this classroom work (its tenor), and the semiotic dimension of this task (its media and modes), there are certain register possibilities already "in the air," so to speak. Becoming conscious of the contextual pressures of a given learning environment, the teacher is better able to situate and motivate the kinds of reading and writing he or she asks students to do. As Margaret herself expressed this idea, "Making the context–text connection is important. I know where I'm going and the possible problems the kids are going to have. I also know what types of writing they will need to concentrate on in a unit of work, so I can organize the learning situation so as to orient them in a particular direction" (Margaret Watts, personal communication).

Educational learning privileges specialized registers and genres but encompasses those of everyday and reflexive domains because it has an interface with the worlds that learners inhabit before they come to school and after they leave it. This implies that the same situation can evoke a different register for different participants. The meaning potential of any classroom setting could be amplified in (at least) three ways: everyday, specialized, or reflexive. Any contextual framework that is adequate to both the diversity of students' starting points and the potential of learning itself needs to allow for different interpretations of the demands and possibilities of any situation. This is important if teachers are to assist students whose interpretation of the classroom context diverges significantly from their own. They need a contextual model that enables them both to sense when the students are assigning an unproductive register to a task and to imagine what effect this is having on their ability to participate in classroom learning.

Second, although ultimately learning is the responsibility of the learner, it is also true that the teacher has a crucial role in organizing learning challenges for students. Teaching is intervention, but the kind of intervention required will vary according to the stage students are at in their learning and to the purposes of the teacher. The business of teaching involves making choices from moment to moment about what is going on and where students need to go next. No pedagogy can take away responsibility from the teacher for making these moment-by-moment choices about where he or she is going and why. For students who come from backgrounds in which reading is not a priority, the teacher has a crucial role to play in initiating them into the demands of written genres. Modeling and joint negotiation should be seen as part of a repertoire of teaching strategies, not a pedagogic sequence set in concrete.

Margaret expressed similar sentiments on her use of the teaching–learning cycle in her science classroom: "The cycle makes good sense. It's a useful model for teaching literacy as a starting point. I no longer use it in a strict sequence any more. But I make decisions about what kinds of assistance my kids need and use aspects of the cycle according to where they're at and where we're going" (Margaret Watts, personal communication). The contextual framework offers teachers a way of analyzing the learning context and deciding which teaching strategies are central at each stage to best realize the overall goals for learning. Thus, teachers do need to orchestrate the learning situation but with the aim of increasing students' capacity for independence in the long run.

Third, making language explicit does not mean separating it from a more generalized rhetorical competence. Whether it is driving a car, playing the trombone, or writing a letter to the local council, learning to do something for the first time means being (often uncomfortably) conscious of the process. It is only when we have been doing something for a long time that we "automatize" it—lodge it deep in the guts, so to speak—so that we no longer have to think about it every time we do it. Teaching students about language and how to use it often requires a high degree of consciousness and explicitness in early stages. It is one aspect of the teacher's contribution to students' long-term rhetorical competence.

SFL is well suited to this kind of rhetorical competence. Because it is a contextually sensitive and functional grammar, it enables us to move in a mutually predictive way between context and text. In classrooms such as Margaret's, it was used very effectively as a metalinguistic resource for reflecting on students' language use and for assisting their production of complex texts essential to participation in scientific learning. Coupled with the drive to ameliorate the fates of learners without ready access to the discourses and genres of the elite, the work of the Sydney School has taken on the energy and zeal of an educational campaign. This case study represents one vivid expression of this combination of linguistic explicitness and educational interventionism.

2

Heritage and Innovation in Second Language Education

Susan Feez

National Centre for English Language Teaching & Research (NCELTR)

Macquarie University, Australia

This chapter is an account of the intersection of two stories. The first is the story of Australia's immigration program, an icon of Australia's postwar social history that in recent times has been the focus of considerable scrutiny and change. The second is the story of a home-grown language pedagogy, known as the *genre approach*, which itself has sometimes been accorded an iconic status, a status that those who work within the pedagogy have neither sought nor found especially helpful because it so often obscures the energetic dialogue between linguists and language educators that continues to drive the evolution of the approach. The stories of these two icons have intersected in the Adult Migrant English Program,[1] usually referred to as the AMEP, an English-language program offered by the Commonwealth government to all migrants on their arrival in Australia. This intersection has evolved into a national English as a Second Language (ESL) curriculum framework that endeavors to integrate a 50-year-old English language teaching heritage with the language teaching innovations developed by the genre theorists.

The fact that, in the 21st century, icons are neither immutable nor immobile is not surprising. What may be surprising in these self-serving times is that the two icons, whose stories intersect in classrooms where adult migrants are taught English, have both emerged from a desire to provide opportunities for success to those who lacked them. Perhaps it is no coincidence that such an intersection should occur in Australia with its strong tradition of a "fair go" for everyone. The question of whether and how Australians can maintain that tradition in this century is the backdrop against which the genre debate within the field of language and literacy is played out.

---

[1]In Australia the term "migrant" is used to refer to immigrants who become permanent residents.

Many of us working to develop genre-based language pedagogy in Australia have been quite surprised to lift our heads from the day-to-day challenges of curriculum and syllabus design, materials development, and classroom implementation to find that the diverse work we have been involved in for several years across many educational sectors and all states of the Commonwealth is now collectively known as the work of the "Sydney School" (Hyon, 1996). It is quite flattering in one sense to be seen as a force in the field deserving of our own label, especially for those of us who live in Sydney, but there is also a danger that the label becomes as reductive of what we do pedagogically as it is of where we live geographically.

The account that follows is offered as one example of how genre pedagogy, as it has evolved in Australia, has been applied, in this case, to the development of a language curriculum for the Adult Migrant English Program during a period of social, industrial, and educational change. Rising unemployment and reduced funding for migrant English programs emerging from these changes have put pressure on migrants to develop their English-language and literacy skills as quickly and effectively as possible in order to be successful in employment, in the community, and in further education.

Genre theory, as it has developed in Australia, has made it possible to identify what people need to be able to do with language in order to be successful in education, in the community, and in employment. The capacity of this pedagogy to support literacy development is enhanced because it is located within the model of language generated by systemic functional linguistics, a richly descriptive linguistics developed over several decades in Europe and Australia by the British linguist Halliday (1994) and his students and colleagues. This model of language describes in systematic detail how the language system is organized so people can use it as a resource to construct texts that vary in response to the demands of different social contexts. Rothery, a pioneer of genre pedagogy in Australia, summarized the value of such a model of language to literacy pedagogy in the following way:

> A strong and rich model of language description enables us to model the curriculum in terms of its literacy requirements, to map possible paths of development in literacy and learning and to develop criteria for assessment and evaluation. In short, it offers the opportunity to develop a language-based approach to learning. (Rothery, 1996, p. 87)

The application of Halliday's model of language within the genre approach represents the third time his work has influenced curriculum innovation in the AMEP in Australia. For an understanding of how the two earlier waves of Halliday's influence helped shape curriculum in the AMEP, it is necessary to go back to the program's beginnings.

THE ADULT MIGRANT ENGLISH PROGRAM

The Australian Adult Migrant English Program (AMEP) is more than 50 years old. It began on the ships that brought migrants to Australia from post-World War II

Europe. It continued in the migrant hostels, the initial accommodation offered to people, many of them refugees, arriving from all corners of the globe as war, injustice, poverty, lack of opportunity, and even Northern Hemisphere winters made life in a country on the other side of the planet seem more appealing than staying at home. The AMEP continues to be delivered in education centers scattered across Australia's major metropolitan areas and larger industrial towns as well as through distance education even further afield.

Since World War II, people from all continents and hundreds of language groups have settled in Australia. The settlement of some of these people has been spectacularly successful, others are still working on it, but the vast majority in between have made a comfortable and rewarding life for themselves and their families. Most have made the local variety of English their own and are contributing to its evolution. Many people believe that the AMEP has been an important element in the successful integration of so many people of such diverse backgrounds into Australian society, which is both multicultural and cohesive.

The evolution of English-language teaching expertise in the AMEP has been a process of interpreting developments in applied linguistics and customizing them to meet the demands of the learning contexts into which non-English-speaking migrants have been arriving in Australia. It is useful to chronicle briefly these developments in order to locate the genre approach within the evolving body of knowledge and practice available to language teachers.

The body of knowledge and practice available to teachers determines the judgments they make as they plan courses of language study. Nunan (1988, p.10) pointed out that "these judgements are not value free, but reflect our beliefs about the nature of language and learning." In other words, teacher judgments are an outcome of conscious and unconscious theories about language and language learning. Theories about language will determine the approach used to break down the object of study—language—into manageable chunks and to decide which of these chunks are selected as the content of a language course. Theories about language learning will determine the approach used to incorporate and sequence these chunks of content into a series of classroom activities.

Up to the 1990s, the approaches to curriculum and syllabus design in the AMEP were roughly organized under two general headings: structural approaches, in which individual sentences and their constituents were the focus of study, and learner-centred, needs-based, communicative approaches, which were more concerned with longer stretches of naturally-occurring language. Halliday's work played a part in the genesis of both these approaches.

STRUCTURAL APPROACHES IN THE AMEP

At the beginning of the 20th century, language teaching in the West traditionally consisted of students working through lists of isolated grammatical structures and lexical items, then using these to translate literary texts. This grammar–translation method was based on the teaching of Latin to classical scholars (Richards & Rodgers, 1986, pp. 1–13). Unfortunately, the teaching of rhetoric—that is, the teaching of how to use whole stretches of language to achieve a communicative purpose—was no longer taught as it had been in Europe during classical and medieval times (Christie, 1990). As the 20th century unfolded and populations became more mobile, people wanted to interact with speakers of other languages for more than just elite literary and intellectual purposes. In response to this demand, British applied linguists developed situational language teaching, and the work of the American structuralists led to the development of the Audiolingual Method (For an account of these developments, see Howatt, 1984, and Richards & Rodgers, 1986.).

Although many early AMEP teachers relied on grammar–translation methods and Australian syllabus writers of the time were influenced by the American structuralists, it was British situational language teaching, described by Richards and Rodgers (1986, p. 35) as "a type of British 'structuralism,'" that had the strongest influence on the AMEP curriculum from its beginnings to the end of the 1970s. In this approach, structures were "linked to situations in which they could be used" (Richards & Rodgers, 1986, p. 35), reflecting the work of British linguists, in particular Firth and Halliday, who were linking structure and context, or more specifically, exploring how structure and meaning were related to context and situation.

> The emphasis now is on the description of language activity as part of the whole complex of events which, together with the participants and relevant objects, make up actual situations (Halliday, McIntosh, & Strevens, 1964, p. 38, quoted in Richards & Rodgers, 1986, p. 35).

Richards and Rodgers (1986, p. 35) summarized situational language teaching in the following way: ". . . in contrast to American structuralist views on language, language was viewed as purposeful activity related to goals and situations in the real world."

In common with the American Audiolingual Method, however, situational approaches valued correct language habits and accurate forms. In the classroom, this translated into behaviorist teaching techniques involving response, repetition, and memorization in the form of imitation drills and substitution exercises.

The "Australian Situational Method" (Bottomley, 1994) was a response to the immediate need of non-English-speaking migrants to be able to use "real-world" English as quickly as possible on arrival. This method was formalized into a centralized syllabus based on a series of graded textbooks called *Situational English for Newcomers to Australia* (Australian Government Publishing Service, 1975), which were supported by radio programs. Using these books, learners in the AMEP worked systematically through the teaching units, each usually based on a dialogue placed within an everyday setting such as *In the restaurant* or *Buying a train ticket*. The dialogues introduced lexical items and grammatical structures that were practiced by the learners in follow-up activities. When we read those dialogues today, they seem quaint, even comical, and certainly not authentic. Nevertheless, they shifted the focus of language teaching to the situations in which learners needed to use language, and they did make it possible for learners to acquire quickly the formulaic elements of simple spoken exchanges in certain settings, especially during the initial period of building "survival" English.

Structural approaches, as exemplified by the Australian situational syllabus, were very innovative for their time. Many of the categories used by language teachers today to organize their material originated with these syllabi. It was at this time that teachers began to be concerned with the different macroskills of language—listening, speaking, reading, and writing—and to use themes and topics as course design tools. In addition, they began to use classroom-management strategies involving elicitation techniques and pair and group work. Presentation and practice techniques were devised that incorporated realia, concrete and visual materials, gesture, and mime. Teachers also began to specify teaching objectives in terms of what the learner should be able to do with English at the end of the course.

Despite the attempt to link structures to situations in the Australian situational syllabus, it retained many of the limitations of structural syllabi in general. Language forms were learned in isolation and in a fixed progression irrespective of the learner's needs and goals. Language learning was atomistic, product-oriented, teacher-centered, and concerned, above all, with accuracy. As Yalden (1987a, p. 26) pointed out:

> In teaching approaches based on [the structural syllabus], form and meaning are assumed to be in a one-to-one relation, and meaning is to be learned together with particular grammatical forms. Meaning (other than purely lexical meaning) is thought to be self-evident, and is not taught as such. Yet in the grammatical syllabus, even when we have described the grammatical and lexical meaning of a sentence, we still have not accounted for the way in which it is used in an utterance, and still less in an exchange of utterances between two or more speakers.

Even where situational versions of structural approaches made links between language learning and real-world language use, as in the Australian syllabus, this was not enough:

> The absence of the functional component from the situational syllabus is one of the major limiting factors [. . .] in terms of preparing learning for real life situations. [. . .] we can easily "situationalise" a grammatical syllabus, but that in so doing, we will not have resolved the problem [. . .] of teaching words and sentences as isolates. (Yalden, 1987a, pp. 38–39)

It was only a matter of time before structural approaches to language teaching would be challenged by approaches that their proponents claimed were more "natural" ways of learning a language, especially once Chomsky had rejected the ideas of both the structuralists and behaviorists, claiming that language use was "not imitated behavior but . . . created anew from underlying knowledge of abstract rules" (Richards & Rodgers, 1986, p. 59). The AMEP was to be influenced profoundly by the quest for a "natural" approach to language learning.

LEARNER-CENTERED, NEEDS-BASED COMMUNICATIVE APPROACHES IN THE AMEP

By the 1980s, in line with the development of more "natural" approaches to language teaching, the AMEP had discarded its centralized structural syllabus and moved to an individualized syllabus in which teachers were responsible for syllabus design. Brindley and Hood (1990, pp. 223–224) noted that "this radical change in the teacher's role was not without its problems as teachers tried to grapple with the complexities of designing individualized programs with little institutional support." In practice, AMEP teachers responded in an eclectic way to these curriculum developments. They tended to select and sequence syllabus elements according to their perception of what "worked" in the classroom. The repertoire of syllabus elements and methodologies teachers drew on at that time can be roughly grouped according to whether they were informed by studies into second-language acquisition or by theories of language and language learning concerned with communication and social activity.

Proponents of theories of second-language acquisition, following Chomsky, saw language learners as being involved in a process of actively testing their own interpretations of the new language, with the result that nonstandard approximations of the target language by learners, or *interlanguage*, began to be seen by AMEP teachers not as a deficiency, but as an important stage in language development and as a source of valuable information about a learner's progress (Corder, 1981; Selinker, 1991). AMEP teachers strove to provide learners with the quality "roughly-tuned" language input that Krashen (1988) proposed was critical to successful second-language acquisition, that is, language input comprehensible to learners but just beyond what they are able to produce themselves. AMEP teachers at that time, in tandem with many of their colleagues overseas, felt that if language learners had enough of this kind of input in a stress-free environment, then they would acquire the target language unconsciously, effortlessly, and fluently.

To achieve a stress-free learning environment, AMEP teachers looked to the progressive pedagogies that had emerged after the social upheavals of the 1960s in Western democracies that had challenged, among other things, the authoritarian role of teachers in traditional pedagogies. Progressive pedagogies encourage teachers to develop more equal and respectful relationships with their students and to facilitate humane, interesting, and interactive educational settings. They led to the development of methodologies that highlight the needs, interests, feelings, and motivations of learners and that encourage learners to make their own decisions, to take risks, and to discover knowledge as they need it. In particular, AMEP teachers were influenced by the development of learning principles appropriate to adults, incorporating, for example, techniques for self-directed and contract learning (Knowles, 1990). Many AMEP teachers were also influenced by Third-World educators such as Freire (1972), whose pedagogies included the goals of social and political freedom, as well as personal freedom.

The influence of progressive pedagogies led to the following beliefs about teaching, having wide currency within the AMEP by the end of the 1980s:

- Too much intervention stifles the individual's motivation, self-expression, and personal development and takes responsibility away from the learner, disrupting, even destroying, the learning process.
- Because learners, especially adult learners, should "own" and take responsibility for both the process and the product of their learning, teachers should negotiate the curriculum with the learners based on their needs.
- Fluency is more important than accuracy.

Meanwhile, in Australian primary[2] and secondary schools, "whole language" and "process writing" had taken hold as the expression of progressive approaches to language education.

At the same time as AMEP teachers were working from second-language acquisition and progressive perspectives, they were also becoming increasingly aware of developments in language teaching stemming from the work of linguists who were concerned with meaning, function, and social context, in particular Hymes in the United States and Halliday in the United Kingdom.

Hymes (1972a) coined the term *communicative competence* to challenge Chomsky's competence and performance opposition and to account for the two kinds of knowledge successful language users apply, that is, linguistic knowledge and knowledge about what language is appropriate in particular social contexts. This term spawned an array of approaches to language teaching known collectively as *communicative language teaching*. (See the following for accounts of these approaches: Brumfit, 1986; Melrose, 1991, pp. 1–16; Richards & Rodgers, 1986; Yalden, 1987b). By the end of the 1980s, communicative language teaching had become the basis of AMEP curriculum.

Meanwhile Halliday, working within the European linguistic tradition, had developed a systematic way of describing language in terms of the meanings people make with it and what people do with it, that is, in terms of the functions of meaningful language use within social contexts (Halliday, 1975, 1976, 1978). As Yalden (1987a, p. 50) noted, "Linguistics in Europe has never excluded from consideration the relationship between language and the context of its use."

Hymes and Halliday influenced the AMEP indirectly through the English-language teaching syllabus documents prepared by the Council of Europe in the early 1970s (van Ek & Alexander, 1980). Their influence resulted in these documents being based not on isolated individual grammatical structures and

---

[2]In Australia "primary"-school education refers to the first seven years of compulsory education.

lexical items, but on units of meaning expressed in stretches of language longer than a single clause or sentence. The units of meaning used in the syllabus were those identified by Wilkins (1976), who attempted to "demonstrate the systems of meanings that lay behind the communicative uses of language" (Richards & Rodgers, 1986, p. 65), and thus to identify all the types of meaning language learners need to express through the target language. Wilkins described two types of meaning, *notions* and *functions*. Notion refers to the language used to express a general area of meaning such as *time*, *quantity*, and *emotion*. Functions are units of meaning identified on the basis of their communicative purpose, for example, *greeting*, *persuading,* and *suggesting*. An influential inventory of functions and notions was presented to teachers in the AMEP in the early 1980s.

Teachers in the Australian AMEP have probably been influenced so strongly by applications of the evolving ideas of the sociolinguists because, as Yalden (1987a, p. 81) pointed out, "Most second-language learners are highly concerned with language as social behaviour, and that is why Halliday's and Hymes' work provides so many valuable insights in applied linguistic theory." Migrants arriving in Australia are overwhelmingly involved with adapting to new modes of social behavior, new social roles, and the language used to express these.

Following a major review of the AMEP, completed at the beginning of the 1980s, needs-based and learner-centered approaches became the official AMEP syllabus model. Teachers were also asked to determine language proficiency with reference to proficiency scales, the most well-known being the Australian Second Language Proficiency Ratings (ASLPR; Ingram & Wiley, 1984), which incorporated extended stretches of language, or discourse, grammar, phonology, and graphology, in a systematic description of what learners could do with language at different levels.

Hagan (1994, p. 30) described the approach to curriculum taken in the 1980s by the Adult Migrant English Service (AMES), which delivers the AMEP in New South Wales, in the following way:

> The needs-based learner-centred approach to curriculum design was embraced enthusiastically by NSW AMES during the 1980s. It was to some extent a rejection of the prescribed structurally-based syllabus models popular during the 1960s and 1970s. According to the needs-based approach teachers were responsible for assessing learner needs and designing appropriate courses to meet those needs. There was also a great emphasis placed on the use of authentic classroom materials, a wide variety of methodologies and an individualised approach to course design.

For each new class they taught, teachers were expected to analyze the needs of learners (Brindley, 1984), to negotiate language-learning objectives with the learners, and to use functional–notional inventories to select and sequence syllabus elements. In addition, teachers began to recognize the skills and strategies learners needed to develop if they were to become effective listeners, speakers, readers, and writers. Teachers were encouraged to implement learner-centered methodologies in which self-directed learning and fluency were valued over teacher-centered methods demanding memorization or accuracy.

As the 1980s progressed, AMEP teachers became increasingly aware of criticism being leveled at inventories of notions and functions, for example, by Candlin (as cited in Melrose, 1991, pp. 19–20) and Widdowson (1979), because, although they were lists of units of meaning rather than lists of words and structures, they remained inventories of isolated components and as such could not really be of value in developing communicative competence.

> . . . communicative competence is not a compilation of items in memory, but a set of strategies or creative procedures for realising the value of linguistic elements in contexts of use, an ability to make sense as a participant in discourse, whether spoken or written. . . . (Widdowson, 1979, p. 248, as quoted in Yalden, 1987a, p. 77)

Increasingly, teachers tried to provide learners with opportunities to use extended chunks of language, or discourse, to achieve communicative purposes in a context rather than simply providing opportunities for memorizing isolated vocabulary and grammatical structures.

In practice, however, the task of integrating all of these components and ideas into a coherent and principled course proved to be overwhelming for many teachers. To make the task manageable, teachers tried to devise situations in which the students could practice using different words and structures in "natural" contexts of use. Many such manifestations of communicative language teaching, especially those influenced most strongly by progressive pedagogies, failed to recognize that Hymes' notion of communicative competence encompassed both linguistic knowledge and communicative practice, often with the result that fluency was emphasized at the expense of accuracy.

A second extensive review of the AMEP (Campbell, 1986) and accompanying studies (including Nunan, 1987, and Brindley, 1985) revealed that learners in the AMEP had little continuity or sense of progression or achievement, a consequence of the practical difficulties teachers were facing. To overcome these difficulties, teachers requested "nonmandatory curriculum guidelines to assist them in planning courses to meet the needs of commonly recurring learner groups" (Nunan, 1987, p. 59). In addition, communicative approaches did not seem to be able to address the phenomenon of "stabilized" learners, those learners who, once they had achieved an interlanguage that allowed them to survive in Australia, did not progress to more standard forms of English. In many AMEP classrooms, the opportunity for learners to interact with standard English was limited, because teachers were trying not to intervene in learning. Teacher interaction with learners involved practices that many teachers saw as interventionist, so classroom interaction tended to be between learners more than between teacher and learners.

In sharp contrast to the belief of many teachers that language is acquired naturally through exposure or input, it had become evident to others that there was a need for planned intervention by teachers in the language learning of AMEP students, intervention that incorporated "an interactive model of grammar and discourse, one that demonstrates the necessity and importance of both levels of language to the language learning process and to the attainment of communicative competence" (Celce-Murcia, 1990, p. 146).

Those recognizing the need for a more interventionist approach were encouraged by developments in the wider field of English-language teaching. Widdowson (1990, p. 164), for example, challenged natural approaches in the following way:

> To try to replicate the conditions of natural communicative use of language in classrooms is mistaken for two basic reasons. First, to do so is to deny the whole purpose of pedagogy, which is to contrive economical and more effective means for language learning than is provided by natural exposure and experience. Second, natural language use typically deflects attention from language itself and presupposes a knowledge of the language system as a basic resource which learners have, by definition, not yet acquired.

The first response to the pressures for change was the development and implementation of a series of curriculum resource documents, the National Curriculum Project Frameworks (Burton & Nunan, 1988). This was followed by the development of a learner pathways framework (Colman, 1988a, 1988b). Hagan (1994, p. 32) stated that a "major advantage of the learner pathways framework was that it allowed learner needs and goals to be described in a common language." In the context of the early 1990s, however, this was not enough.

This period brought rising unemployment and the overhaul of vocational training. AMEP learners needed English levels that prepared them for work or further training, and they needed credentials to add to their job-seeking portfolios (Hagan, 1994, p. 32). A national ESL credential was needed to ensure that people from non-English-speaking backgrounds would be able to access and exploit the new training environment. To be accredited within the new system, the ESL curriculum framework leading to the national ESL credential had to be written in terms of explicit outcomes, or competencies.

Alongside the pressures for change, there were also pressures within the AMEP to retain the best of the accumulated heritage of the situational and the needs-based communicative years. For example, the AMEP review had shown that ESL learners wanted and needed to be taught language structures explicitly and systematically. At the same time, AMEP teachers were concerned that a narrow training focus was not appropriate to educating migrants who needed "to develop the capacity to deal with the new, the innovative and the unexpected" (Bottomley, 1994, p. 22). To accommodate all these demands, the national ESL curriculum needed to provide explicit learning outcomes within a common training pathway, be flexible enough to meet individual learner need within diverse teaching contexts, and reflect language use in real life, that is, communication in context in the form of discourse, not in the form of isolated elements.

The problem facing the writers of the national ESL curriculum was to identify a discourse-oriented unit of language that could both accommodate notions of communication and fluency and provide a framework for the explicit teaching of grammatical, lexical, phonological, and graphological knowledge and skills. The discourse unit would need to focus on meaning in context as well as on accuracy. In addition, the curriculum writers needed to model a workable pedagogy for explicit intervention in the process of language learning.

It may have been an accident of geography that the writers of the new curriculum were based in Sydney at the Adult Migrant English Service, which delivered AMEP programs in New South Wales. To address their problem, these writers looked to the work of Halliday, now also based in Sydney, and his colleagues and students working within the field of systemic functional linguistics, in particular, those who, since the early 1980s, had been developing what had become called the *genre approach* to writing in schools. Genre theory provided the writers of the new AMEP curriculum with both a discourse-oriented unit of language around which to write generalized curriculum outcomes and an interactive pedagogy for intervening in language development. In this way, for the third time, Halliday's influence was to be felt in the AMEP.

THE GENESIS OF GENRE PEDAGOGY IN AUSTRALIA

Cope and Kalantzis (1993, p. 231) summarized the genesis of genre pedagogy in Australia in the following way:

> It was Michael Halliday, founding Professor of Linguistics at the University of Sydney from late 1975, who was to provide the catalyst for the development of genre theory. [. . .] Halliday's idea was to bring together linguists and educators to forge educational linguistics into a transdisciplinary, rather than simply an interdisciplinary, field. . . . Linguists must begin working with teachers and teachers in turn would begin to see linguistics as a practical, rather than an esoteric tool which they could use in their everyday work. In other words experts would start to examine the same problems from different points of view.

Using Halliday's theory, which systematically links context with language use, systemic functional linguists investigate the way language varies from context to context. They are also interested, within that variation, in the relatively stable underlying patterns or "shapes" that organize texts so they are culturally and socially functional. The exploration and description of these patterns and their relationship to language variation has been the focus of genre theory and the resource which genre pedagogy exploits.

Kress (1991, p. 10) listed the following assumptions shared by the genre theorists:

> 1. that forms of text (genres) are the result of processes of social production;
> 2. that, given the relative stability of social structures, forms of text produced in and by specific social institutions, that is, the resultant genres, will attain a certain degree of stability and of persistence over time;
> 3. that consequently, texts in their generic form are not produced *ab initio* each time by

an individual (or individuals) expressing an inner meaning, but are, rather, the effects of the action of individual social agents acting *both* within the bounds of their social history *and* the constraints of particular contexts, and with a knowledge of existing generic types;
4. that, given the social provenance of genres, different genres "have," convey, and give access to different degrees and kinds of social power;
5. that genres have specifiable linguistic characteristics which are neither fully determined nor largely under the control of individual speakers or writers;
6. that knowledge of the characteristics of texts and of their social place and power can and should form a part of any curriculum, whether in one subject area, or "across the curriculum."

Genre pedagogy in Australia began when, mindful of Hasan's work on generalized text structure (Halliday & Hasan, 1985; Hasan, 1978), Martin and Rothery investigated and categorized many hundreds of samples of primary-school student writing as a first step in developing "a language-based approach to teaching and learning" (Rothery, 1996, p. 92). The different types of texts, or genres, they identified and described were distinguished by distinctive patterns of lexical, grammatical, and cohesive choices which "construct the function of the stages of the genres" (Rothery, 1996, p. 93). The generic organizational structure of a text supports the text's purpose, whether that purpose has to do with learning an aspect of the school curriculum or participating in the wider culture beyond school. Significantly, Martin and Rothery found that not all genres were valued equally in school learning and that access to the highly valued genres was not distributed equally to all students in classrooms where there was no intervention in writing development. (For an account of this work, see Martin, 1993a, and Rothery, 1996.)

Since Martin and Rothery's original work, research in Australia across a variety of contexts—for example, secondary school subject areas, academic disciplines, and workplaces—has revealed an increasing repertoire of genres. Researchers have also developed increasingly sophisticated understandings about the nature of texts belonging to these genres in terms of how genre interacts with different varieties of language across different contexts of use and of how these interactions predict particular patterns of language that can be described in terms of the user's choice of lexis, grammatical structures, and cohesive devices. For example, researchers have considered:

• the nature of texts belonging to factual genres (Martin, 1985b) and texts belonging to story genres (Martin, 1996a; Plum, 1988; Rothery, 1990);
• how the genres of a particular academic discipline or institution constitute the knowledge, social practices, and values of that discipline or institution, how different genres are valued in the different contexts in which they are used, and how genres cluster or are sequenced in these contexts (Christie & Martin, 1997; Halliday & Martin, 1993; Iedema, 1994a; Rose, McInnes, & Korner, 1992);
• how genres change over time, the potential of different genres to expand their

meaning potential across different dimensions in different contexts, and the commonalities shared by different genres (Hood, 1996; Iedema, Feez, & White, 1994; Martin & Matthiessen, 1991);

- the characteristics of dynamic open-ended genres, such as casual conversation (Eggins & Slade, 1997) and news stories (Iedema, 1994b; White, 1997) in contrast to those genres that progress in a more stable and predictable way towards closure;
- discourse units that are more than a clause but less than a text (Cloran, 1994; Macken-Horarik, 1996); and
- how genre patterns are combined and customized in longer and more complex texts in order to achieve specialized and sophisticated purposes (Drury, 1992; Martin, 1994).

This body of research continues to develop, much of it in response to the issues raised by teachers working across all educational sectors and, more recently, to issues raised by professionals and others trying to gain more insight into critical communication processes in a variety of workplaces and community contexts. As researchers and practitioners in Australia augment the range and scope of genre descriptions, they also debate contrasting interpretations of genre and the different models of genre pedagogy these generate. The result is a rich bank of knowledge and understanding that language educators can use and interpret in their work as new challenges and solutions emerge both in the classroom and at the level of curriculum and syllabus development.

Genre pedagogy is a response to the realization that knowledge about the stable patterns and possibilities of variation within texts across a range of social institutions is a form of cultural capital. The work of Martin and Rothery showed that not all students in our educational institutions have equal access to this cultural capital and that those with reduced access are less likely to achieve successful educational outcomes.

In collaboration with teachers, Rothery developed a pedagogy that would integrate learning about language into the teaching of writing and into literacy teaching across the curriculum. In this pedagogy, teachers were encouraged to adopt "an authoritative negotiating role" (Cope, Kalantzis, Kress, & Martin, 1993, pp. 233–234). Halliday's model of language, specifically his functional grammar, lies at the heart of genre pedagogy.

Halliday's model provides teachers with a grammar that focuses on meaning rather than form and focuses on whole texts and their organisation as well as on sentences. This means that when teachers are helping their students create texts for different purposes and audiences, they can point explicitly to what has to be done. Students no longer have to guess what is expected when they write.

This model is therefore especially helpful for working class, migrant and Aboriginal students who suffer most when they are expected to do things but are not shown how. For teachers, the model provides clear guidance for setting up social situations in the classroom that enable students to learn how to write and use other modes of language appropriate for different social purposes (Callaghan & Rothery, 1988, pp. 19–20).

The genre pedagogy was initially presented to teachers in the form of a cycle of teaching and learning designed to build literacy in primary schools (For a diagram and detailed description of the teaching–learning cycle, see Rothery, 1996, pp. 101–104). As Rothery (1996, p. 102) noted: "We have always represented it as a circle to indicate there are different points of entry for students according to their development in learning and literacy."

The cycle of teaching and learning models a literacy teaching methodology that reflects Halliday's (1992, p. 19) view of learning as "a semiotic process: as learning to mean and to expand one's meaning potential." Halliday's view is supported by his own and Painter's research into first-language development (Halliday, 1975; Painter, 1985, 1996). Halliday views educational learning as an organized process in which the construction of meaning can take place systematically:

> Education, I take it, means enabling people to learn; not just to learn in the natural, commonsense ways in which we learn in our daily lives, but to learn in an organised, progressive and systematic manner according to some generally accepted principles about what people ought to know. (Halliday, 1981, p.1)

The genre-based cycle of teaching and learning exemplifies a "visible pedagogy" (Bernstein, 1990, p. 73) in which what is to be learned and assessed is made clear to students and in which teacher–learner interaction is valued, as well as interaction between learners. The design of the teaching–learning cycle draws on the work of the Russian psychologist Vygotsky (1978) and its interpretation by Bruner (1986).

Vygotsky's work suggests that pedagogies that are only concerned with existing independent functioning will not give the learner the chance to progress. By contrast, pedagogies that support learners as they move toward their potential level of performance make genuine learning and progress possible. Second-language teachers can hear an echo of Krashen's notion of "roughly-tuned" input in Vygotsky's idea of "potential performance." Vygotsky's insights, however, suggest that learners are not going to reach their potential performance through input alone, but rather through an interactive process. Pedagogies based on Vygotsky's work model learning as a collaboration between teacher and learner with the teacher taking on an authoritative role similar to that of an expert supporting an apprentice. Vygotsky pointed out that this collaboration always involves language in the form of a dialogue between teacher and learner. Bruner (1986, p. 74) used the term *scaffolding* to describe the teacher's role in the collaboration.

Vygotsky's notion of collaborative learning provides a theoretical basis for genre pedagogy, making it possible to plan language learning as a process of social construction with two key characteristics, scaffolding and joint construction. Scaffolding occurs when the teacher contributes what learners are not yet able to do alone or do not yet know. Teachers adjust, and strategically diminish, their contribution, supporting learners as they progress towards their potential level of independent performance. Joint construction occurs when the teacher and the learner share the responsibility for functioning until the learner has the knowledge and skills to perform independently and with sole responsibility.

Gray (1987, pp. 35–38) listed four points that teachers need to consider as they implement genre pedagogy:

1. Joint construction involves negotiation between the teacher and learner, not domination by the teacher. Both the teacher and learner need to have a shared understanding of the context and of the meanings being negotiated. Problems are shared, and the teacher only asks direct questions when learners show they have a chance of success. Throughout this process learners are thinking and making choices to contribute to the joint construction.
2. Teachers have to create contexts in which the use of the target language is legitimate and meaningful. Teachers also have to decide what kinds of texts to use.
3. Jointly constructed and negotiated meanings are best supported or scaffolded within predictable and familiar routines, or cycles, of interaction and activity over extended periods of time.
4. Teachers use scaffolding to monitor the level of difficulty as control is gradually handed over to the learner.

Gray also exemplified how even the most common classroom activities can be used to further the language development of learners. According to Gray (1983, pp. 39–49), what is important is that language occurs as "part of a goal-oriented activity and becomes part of a socially constructed text."

As learners gradually gain increasing control of the genres they need to use English effectively in the social contexts they are participating in, they can begin to engage with English-speaking culture in productive ways. For those whose background has not prepared them for the culture of the classroom, the genre pedagogy allows them gradually to take over this culture and to make it their own. For many AMEP students, this move is a critical step, especially when the culture of a formal learning environment is as challenging as the culture of the new language.

Over the last decade or more, the original teaching–learning cycle developed by Rothery to teach writing in primary schools has been adapted to teach literacy across the curriculum in secondary schools (Christie & Martin, 1997; Rothery, 1996), to teach tertiary literacy (Webb & Drury, 1995), and to teach ESL and adult literacy (Cornish, 1992, p. 17; Hammond, 1989, 1990; Hammond, Burns, Joyce, Brosnan, & Gerot, 1992; Hood, 1996b; Joyce, 1992, p. 44). A parallel model for scaffolding the teaching of spoken language in ESL has been developed by Burns, Joyce, & Gollin (1996, p. 88).

Common to all variations on genre pedagogy is the emphasis on developing a critical literacy in students. (See Rothery, 1996, p. 116–120). Through making the literacy practices and literacy demands of different types of texts in English-speaking cultures more visible, genre pedagogy also makes more visible the values and worldviews embodied in those texts. These values and worldviews are, therefore, openly available for discussion, negotiation, criticism, and challenge (Christie, 1991d, p. 11; Christie, 1995). Most variations of genre pedagogy,

> Curriculum is concerned with the planning, implementation, evaluation, management and administration of education programs.
>
> Syllabus can be defined as a plan of what is to be taught in a language program. A syllabus may contain all or any of the following: topics, text types, objectives, grammar, phonology, skills and tasks. It also gives an indication of the order in which these elements should be taught. (Nunan, 1988, as quoted in NSW AMES, 1995, p. 25)

THE CURRICULUM LEVEL

It is at the general level of curriculum that the certificate framework is written. The outcomes of the framework are organized into a pathway of four levels of language learning: beginner, postbeginner, intermediate, and advanced. The learners are able to work through the pathway at a pace related to their educational background. As they move through the pathway, they work in increasingly specialized contexts, from a general learning context at beginner and postbeginner levels to more specialized contexts related to employment, further study, or community access.

Genre theory was used to write discourse-oriented learning outcomes in terms of very general text categories, for example, *description*, *recount*, *instructions*, or *information text*. These categories were then anchored in terms of macroskill—listening, speaking, reading, or writing—in order to describe what a learner should be able to do with language at the end of a course of study at that level, for example:

- *Can demonstrate understanding of a spoken information text*
- *Can tell a recount*
- *Can read written instructions*
- *Can write a description*

The outcomes are grouped into language-learning domains: listening and speaking, reading, and writing. This organization makes it possible to break the curriculum into smaller modules for students who need intensive work in oracy or literacy where one of these areas lags behind the other. The structure of the complete learning pathway available to students through the CSWE framework is illustrated in Figure 2.1.

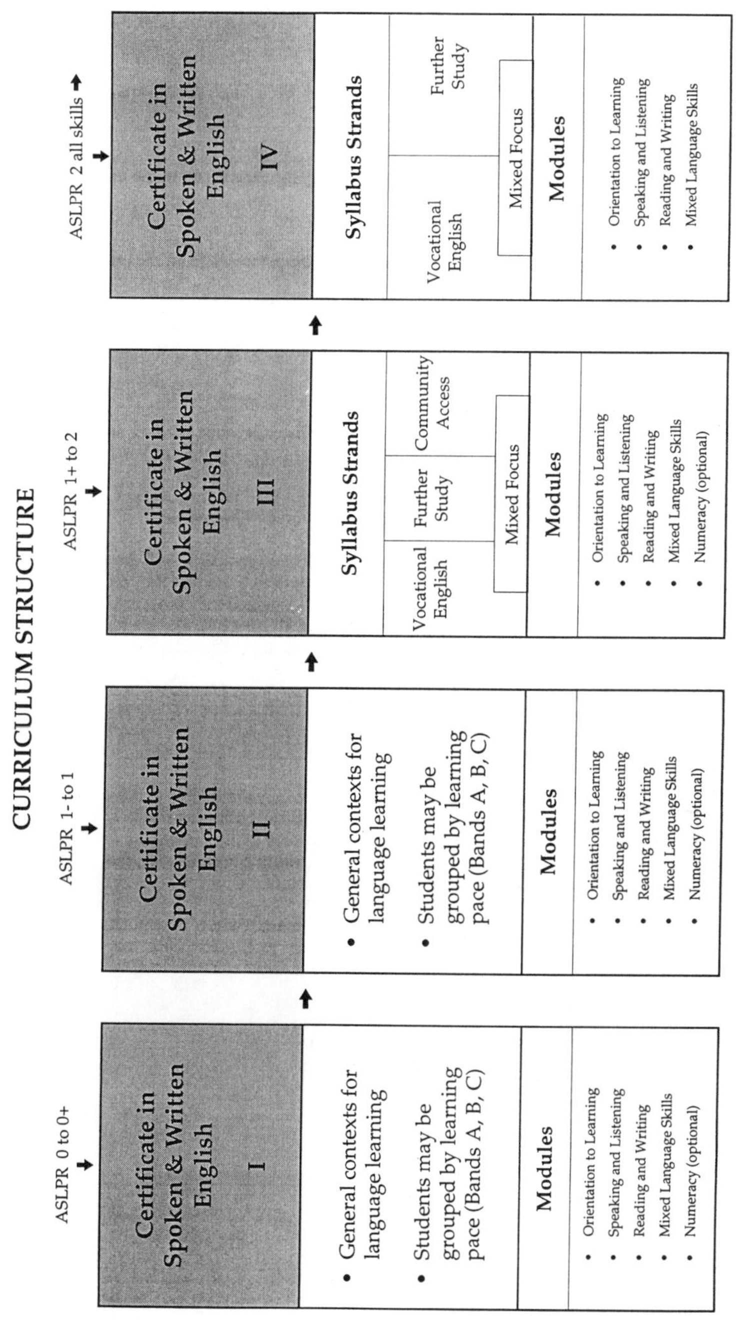

© NSW AMES

Fig. 2.1. Certificates in Spoken and Written English

The way curriculum outcomes are organized into domains within a level is illustrated by the following list (Fig. 2.2) of outcomes for *Certificate in Spoken and Written English I*, the beginners' level.

---

1. Can undertake the roles and responsibilities of a learner in a formal learning environment
2. Can use a range of learning strategies and resources

---

3. Can demonstrate understanding of a spoken information text
4. Can provide personally relevant information using spoken language
5. Can request information/goods using spoken language
6. Can tell a short recount

---

7. Can read social sight signs
8. Can read simple written instructions
9. Can read a short information text
10. Can read a short narrative/recount

---

11. Can complete a simple formatted text
12. Can write a short description
13. Can write a short recount

Fig. 2.2. Certificate I in Spoken and Written English

ELEMENTS	PERFORMANCE CRITERIA
Discourse Structure i. can use appropriate staging ii.. can use conjunctions **Grammar and Vocabulary** iii. can use vocabulary appropriate to topic iv. can construct simple clauses v. can construct simple noun groups vi. can use verbs 'to be' and/or 'to have' in the present tense vii. can use personal pronouns viii. can express location using prepositional phrases	• uses appropriate staging eg statement of topic, description of place, person or thing • joins simple clauses with conjunctions eg 'and', 'but', 'because' • uses vocabulary appropriate to topic • constructs simple clauses • constucts simple noun groups and uses adjectives eg 'A small flat', 'My flat is small' • uses 'to be' and/or 'to have' in the present tense • uses personal pronouns as required • uses prepositional phrases to indicate location as required
RANGE STATEMENTS	**EVIDENCE GUIDE**
• at least 5 clauses with correct tense forms • uses at least 1 conjunction • familiar and relevant topic • recourse to dictionary • may include a few grammatical, punctuation and spelling errors but errors should not interfere with meaning or dominate text • may redraft	**Sample Tasks** • learners describe a place or thing from personal experience • learners describe a picture of a place or thing • learners describe a person in a photograph

Fig. 2.3. Can Write a Short Description (CSWE1, Competency 12)

Genre theory was used not only to identify the generalized, text-based outcomes of the framework but also to identify the key language features of the text type to be studied as learners worked to achieve an outcome. These features are written as elements of the outcome. Performance criteria for assessment are based on the elements. Thus, the performance criteria for each outcome draw on what genre theory has told us about the predictable language features of that type of text. Elements, and their related performance criteria, are organized, using Halliday's stratified language model, into features relating to the whole text, lexical and grammatical features, and phonological or graphological features (For an overview of the stratified, systemic functional language model, see Eggins, 1994, pp. 1–24). The number and complexity of the performance criteria for each outcome depend on the learner's level. The range within which students will be assessed against those criteria, and an evidence guide, are also indicated for each outcome. Figure 2.3 is an example of a writing outcome for Certificate 1, the beginner level.

The explicit outcomes of the CSWE mean that learners studying within the framework know what is expected of them at any point in the learner pathway. They are also able to map their own progress. In addition, teachers working within the AMEP, and in other contexts where the CSWE is used, share a common framework for course design and for assessment. Although the general curriculum framework is common, the design of individual courses and their assessment are carried out at the level of syllabus. Because the general curriculum framework is differentiated from the more specific level of syllabus design in this way, teachers are able to address the diverse needs of learners in different classes while reporting against a common framework with common performance criteria.

THE SYLLABUS LEVEL

It is at the syllabus level that teachers customize the general outcomes of the CSWE to address the specific language-learning needs of their students. They are able to do this by drawing on Halliday's register theory, through which the immediate context of language use can be systematically linked to the meanings, words, and structures of texts.

For each curriculum outcome, teachers identify the immediate contexts in which learners will be using texts belonging to the general text category of that outcome. Text examples from these contexts can then be selected for inclusion in the course. In order to select appropriate contexts of use, teachers prepare course objectives on the basis of an analysis of learner need.

To design a systematic plan of course content customized to the learners in their class, teachers work through the following steps:

1. Analyze learner need and set specific syllabus objectives, including language-learning objectives related to the immediate contexts where learners need to use English, and link these objectives to the curriculum outcomes;

2. Identify and select what needs to be learned; the syllabus elements, including texts, topics, cohesive devices, grammatical structures, vocabulary, related skills, and strategies;
3. Sequence the syllabus elements into an effective progression of teaching and learning; and
4. Monitor learner progress during the course and assess learner achievement at the end of the course against the curriculum outcomes.

The language outcomes in the CSWE framework are already written in terms of whether they are spoken or written, that is, in terms of *mode*. In Halliday's three-dimensional model of situational register, mode is the role language plays in the situation. Mode determines whether the language is spoken or written, as well as the channel through which communication takes place. For the particular contexts of use relevant to their students, teachers may need to refine further the mode description of some outcomes as they select the texts for a course. For example, they may need to teach a particular spoken text in the context of speaking on the telephone as well as speaking face-to-face. They will then need to reveal to learners how the language changes structurally, grammatically, lexically, and phonologically to ensure effective communication in both situations. In addition to mode, again drawing on Halliday's model of register, teachers identify the social activities and topics that relate to the chosen situation of use (the *field*), as well as the relationships of those involved in the situation (the *tenor*). (See Eggins, 1994, pp. 49–80, for a more detailed introduction to Halliday's model of register.)

The competency presented in Figure 2.3, *Can write a short description* (CSWE I, Competency 12), will be used to illustrate how a general outcome can be customized at the level of syllabus.

This outcome is a general statement of a beginner's ability to produce a purposeful, whole, written text belonging to the genre of *description*. There is a variety of possible texts that the learners might produce at the end of a cycle of teaching and learning to meet the requirements of this competency. The target text might be from any number of specific situations of use, or registers, depending on learner need and course objectives. Here are some examples of situated texts appropriate for general English classes at beginner level:

- a description of a place of beauty or interest visited on an excursion (field) for a class book (mode) being prepared for visitors to the teaching center on open day (tenor);
- a description of a mystery object (field) written on cards (mode) to be used with classmates in a guessing game (tenor);
- a description of things or people of interest or value, for example, types of fish or flowers, the uniform of a favorite sporting team, a painting, sculpture or piece of music, a person's country of origin, home, child or grandchild

(field) to be combined with illustrations in a book (mode) for children (tenor); and
- a description of a new home (field) written on a postcard or in a letter (mode) to a friend (tenor).

An example drawing on situations of use in which learners need to access a service within the community might be a description of something lost or damaged or in need of repair, for example, a damaged or stolen car, lost jewellery, house repairs (field), written on a form (mode) as if for the police, insurance company, or landlord (tenor).

An example based on a workplace situation could be a description of a faulty machine (field) on a shift hand-over report (mode) for the foreman (tenor).

The elements and performance criteria of the outcome are listed in two categories of language features discourse structure, which relates to the recognizable parts of the genre pattern and the way clauses are linked to construct a cohesive, unified text—and grammar and vocabulary.

Each of these elements is addressed within the specific context of situation in which the learners are attempting to write a description. If, for example, learners were drafting a description of a damaged car in order to complete an insurance claim form, they would need to be familiar with the general social context in which insurance claims are made in Australia. They would also need to know something of the subject matter, damaged cars, and the social activity, insurance (field). As they explore the field, they build a vocabulary for talking about it at a level accessible to beginner learners. In addition, the students would need to learn about filling in forms (the mode), for example, recognizing abbreviations, writing in specified spaces, and using block letters. The learners will also need to know the appropriate tenor for completing claim forms. For example, unlike a personal letter to a friend, insurance claims are more effective if they are formal and appear to be objective. This means that a personal evaluation such as *My car is a mess*, which might elicit sympathy from a friend, is unlikely to further the cause of an insurance claim. The teacher would also need to devise activities for teaching the features identified in the elements of the outcome, that is, grammatical structures such as simple noun groups and simple, present-tense, declarative clauses as well as personal pronouns and simple conjunctions to unify the clauses within the stages of a description text.

The expression level of language is accounted for in the graphology statement that appears below the competency description. This statement gives a general view of the graphological features that can be expected in the writing of beginner learners. Teachers need to incorporate presentation and practice of these features into course design. For the insurance claim form example used earlier, legible lettering and accurate spelling are critical to the effectiveness of the text.

The process of syllabus design also involves linking the different types of texts being taught in the course into related units of work. For example, a unit of work on writing descriptions at CSWE Level 1 can be linked to related units of work teaching learners to use texts which belong to the recount genre. Both spoken and written recounts are included in the outcomes of CSWE I. Related spoken recounts might include learners telling the police and telling friends what happened when the car was damaged. Related written recounts might include writing to friends or onto an insurance claim form what happened when the car was damaged. In all these cases the field remains constant, allowing learners to recycle what they have learned about the social activity and subject matter, including, for example, vocabulary.

An important aspect of syllabus design within the CSWE framework is the integration of assessment into the course. *Assessment* is concerned with learner achievement and is often contrasted with *evaluation*, which is concerned with the quality and effectiveness of a course or program. Assessment within the CSWE framework enables and supports learners' language development; that is, learners are given a reasonable opportunity to demonstrate what they have learned during their course of study against the explicit criteria of the curriculum. This approach to assessment is described by Macken and Slade (1993, pp. 205–206, 207) in the following way:

> . . . an effective language assessment program must be linguistically principled, explicit, criterion-referenced, and must inform different types of assessment, including diagnostic, formative and summative assessment. . . . Shared criteria based on a sound knowledge of language and its varieties will enable teachers to reflect on the strengths and to diagnose weaknesses in the texts produced by their students.

Instead of grading and ranking learners against vague notions of general language proficiency, this form of assessment makes it possible to record what each learner can do in his or her own right at the end of a course of study. Within the CSWE curriculum framework, this can be done at two levels. The CSWE outcomes provide common general statements and related performance criteria against which all AMEP teachers can assess learner achievement within a common framework. Course objectives provide a more specific, syllabus-level focus for assessment of individual learner progress. Teachers can use the data collected at both levels to evaluate their course design.

The syllabus-design model that the CSWE curriculum framework supports has been called a text-based model (Feez & Joyce, 1998a). Text-based syllabus design can be compared with what Ur (1996, p. 178) described as a "mixed or multi-strand" syllabus for English-language teaching. This is a syllabus model that combines different syllabus elements—such as topics, texts, structures, lexis, skills, and strategies—"in order to be maximally comprehensive" (Ur, 1996, p. 178). A text-based syllabus is a mixed syllabus in which the organizing principle is the study of whole texts in context. Genre pedagogy, and its interactive cycle of teaching and learning, provides teachers with a framework for selecting, organizing, and sequencing the comprehensive mix of text-based syllabus elements in a principled way.

The process of sequencing *what* is to be taught within the CSWE curriculum framework involves deciding *how* to teach it. When teachers make decisions on how they will teach a syllabus, they draw on a methodology. Methodology accounts for the process of language learning. It is at the level of methodology that the unpredictable can happen, that the best-laid plans will need to revised, that the immediate day-to-day demands of language teaching and learning have to be accommodated. In the context of the CSWE, methodology brings the customized syllabus to the learners.

The text-based methodology used to support students learning English as a second language within the CSWE framework is represented graphically in the following circle diagram (Fig. 2.4). This methodology is built around different phases of classroom interaction adapted from Rothery's original teaching and learning cycle (Rothery, 1996).

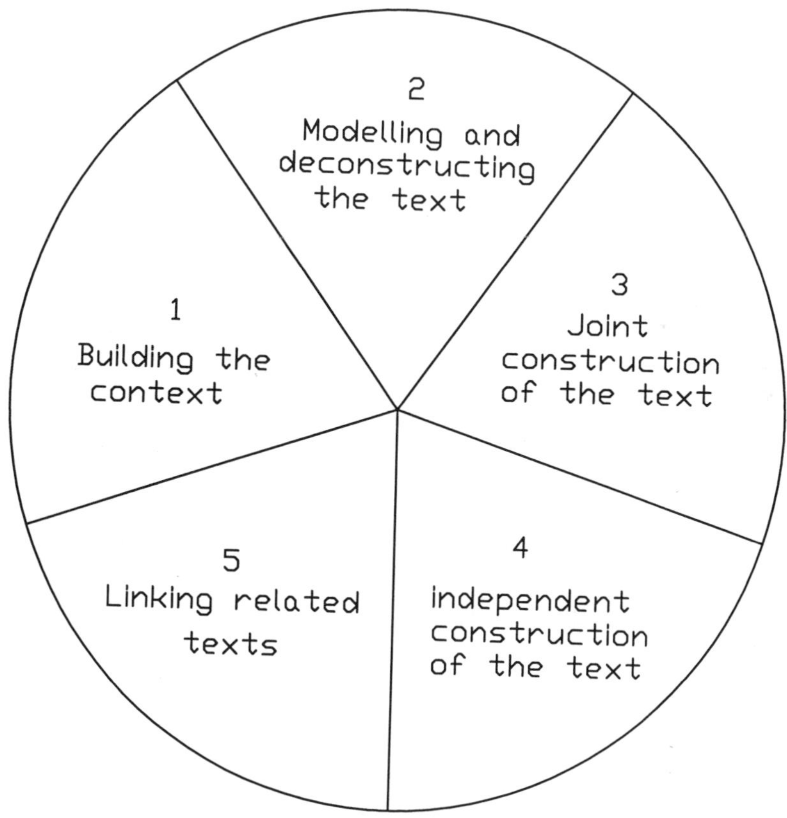

Fig. 2.4. A Teaching Learning Cycle (From Feez & Joyce, 1998a)

As the diagram shows, one whole phase of interaction is devoted to context-building, an important foundation step for second-language learners. In this step, the teacher designs opportunities for learners to experience and explore the cultural and situational aspects of the social context of the target text through activities such as brainstorming; listening and talking to others; reading relevant material; viewing realia, pictures, or video; and taking part in role-plays, cross-cultural comparisons, guided research, or field trips. For example, to build the context for filling out an insurance claim, students might view a television advertisement for a car-insurance company and build up vocabulary lists. They might research information about insurance written in their first language to identify key words and concepts they need to understand in English. They might interview, in English or in their first language, people who have played different roles in the context of car insurance in Australia. They might complete a table comparing the nature of car insurance in their country of origin and in Australia. During the context-building phase, learners' attention is first drawn to the different types of texts that they may be called on to use in the context of car insurance in Australia. Classroom interaction in the subsequent phases of the teaching–learning cycle are based on the shared experience of the context built up by teachers and learners during this phase.

The next phase of classroom interaction is devoted to modeling and deconstructing the text. During this phase, the teacher strongly directs the interaction, introducing learners to model texts belonging to the target genre in the context they have been exploring. Learners' attention is drawn to the structure and language features of the models. This is the stage in which second-language learners learn the grammar of the target language, but in the context of purposeful language use. For example, activities relevant to writing descriptions would provide practice in structuring simple declarative clauses using present-tense forms of the verbs *to be* and *to have* and using noun groups that include descriptive adjectives. The activities might include opportunities to learn, and even memorize, the forms of these features.

The strong scaffolding of the first two phases of classroom interaction is weakened in the joint-construction phase. The teacher begins to relinquish responsibility to the learners as the learners' expanding knowledge allows them to take over. During this stage, groups of learners contribute to the construction of a text belonging to the target-text type. They are guided by the teacher through all stages of the preparation and drafting process, explicitly discussing and negotiating the meanings they are making as they go.

During the final phase, the independent-construction phase, the scaffolding is taken away and learners research the context and construct their own texts independently, consulting with other learners and the teacher only as needed. Achievement assessment can be carried out at this stage of the cycle or immediately following its successful completion. At the end of the cycle, links are made to related text types, so learners have the opportunity to recycle what they have learned in other contexts of use, comparing and contrasting different texts and their uses and effectiveness.

In practice, the teaching–learning cycle is modified to suit the needs of different learners. Learners can enter at any point of the cycle, returning to a stage for review as needed or skipping stages if they are not ready or if they do not need them. In most adult ESL classes, the context-building phase is essential. Some beginning learners with minimal formal learning in their first language, however, may not go beyond the joint-construction phase for some more challenging text types. In contrast, many tertiary-educated adult learners with sophisticated study skills find the joint-construction phase unnecessary. These learners go directly to the independent-construction stage once the text type has been modeled.

A characteristic of the teaching–learning cycle that makes it so valuable to AMEP teachers is that it allows them to draw on a variety of classroom teaching methods. Teaching methods are configurations of tasks, activities, classroom-management styles, and assessment procedures. As teachers in the AMEP decide which method to use at each phase of the cycle, they draw on a second-language teaching repertoire that has been built up over 50 years. Teachers are inevitably eclectic as they select teaching methods. The ultimate test is that it "works." The genre approach makes it possible for teachers to select, modify, and locate a variety of methods in a principled and strategic way. In other words, they select from the language-teaching repertoire methods that make it possible to build the type of classroom interaction required by the different phases of the cycle.

For example, context-building lends itself to discovery-learning techniques, themes, and focus questions, task-based approaches, learner-centred and communicative activities, guided research, group projects, vocabulary-building, skills development, field work, and diagnostic assessment. The teacher acts as an initiator, resource, and guide for the learners as they explore the territory of the target text. The modeling and deconstructing stage is the one in which direct teaching about language takes place. Learners are given opportunities to investigate and manipulate text structure and to study grammar, vocabulary, and the systematic links between form and meaning, text and context. Practice can be generated through communicative, even authentic, activities. There may also be a place for activities that recall structural approaches, if learners need to memorize irregular forms or practice pronunciation, for example. At this stage, the teacher intervenes explicitly and authoritatively in the learning process.

As the joint-construction and independent-construction stages unfold, the teacher gradually steps back further into the role of facilitator, for example, facilitating a context to generate authentic use of a target-text type. Once learners are working independently with a text type, drafting and conferencing techniques or adaptations of these can be very useful for writing and for reflecting on written text. Communicative activities can also be adapted to generate purposeful independent speaking and listening, and theme-based project work can be used to generate all macroskills in an integrated way.

In summary, one of the most useful aspects of genre-based pedagogy in ESL is that it allows teachers to unhook effective teaching methods from approaches that have been left behind in the evolution of language-teaching theory and practice. These methods can then be relocated strategically into the phases of the teaching–learning cycle according to the type of interaction required.

Overall, the AMEP has benefited greatly from basing its new curriculum on genre pedagogy. Second language learners now have the opportunity to progress in relation to prototypical cultural and linguistic patterns while being able to customize their own texts to meet the demands of their immediate situations. In this way these learners have a chance, not offered before in the AMEP, of consciously building cultural and linguistic capital that they can exploit in the new society they are entering. A teaching methodology that reveals explicitly and systematically how context shapes text also provides learners with the opportunity to reflect on, and to make cross-cultural comparisons and critiques of, the orientations and values inherent in what they are learning.

A study into changes in teaching practice within the AMEP in response to the implementation of the CSWE curriculum frameworks revealed the following:

> Most commonly expressed by teachers were changes related to a greater sense of the pathways along which students would progress beyond their own immediate teaching context, and therefore a need to sharpen up their planning processes, to plan in more collaborative ways, and to be more focused in their teaching. For some this meant less freedom to react to immediate concerns and contexts. For most, however, it meant a clearer sense of direction for learners and the ability to give more explicit feedback on progress. (Hood, 1995, p. 32)

MANAGING CHANGE

Curriculum innovation in a time of considerable, and often unsettling, social change is fraught with difficulty. This has been true of the implementation of the CSWE curriculum framework in the AMEP as it has of parallel curriculum innovations in Australia derived from genre pedagogy, a notable example being the recent implementation of a text-based English syllabus for kindergarten to Year 6 students in New South Wales primary schools.

Those who initiated curriculum change in the AMEP were aware that they were embarking on a challenging project (See Brindley & Hood, 1990). They looked at the work of scholars investigating curriculum change, for example, Fullan (1982, 1991), to map out the phases of the change cycle—initiation, implementation, and continuation—and to guide these phases at both institutional and classroom level. They attempted to build the "coherent picture" Fullan proposed so that "people who are involved in or affected by educational change can make sense of what they and others are doing" (Fullan, 1982, p. 4).

Curriculum renewal in response to consultation with students, teachers, and program managers has been built into the process of curriculum change. In addition, classroom materials and resources modeling a text-based approach to syllabus design have been published (for example, Brown & Cornish, 1997; Clemens &

Crawford, 1994; Cornish, 1992; Delaruelle, 1998; Feez & Joyce, 1998a; Joyce, 1992; NSW AMES Writing Team, 1997). Professional development has included extensive training in educational linguistics, course design, and assessment. Teachers have been supported if they wish to pursue relevant further study. Since the implementation of the new curriculum framework, there has also been an ongoing cycle of national, classroom-based, collaborative-action research. The action-research model provides teachers with a useful technique for reflecting on and renovating classroom practice (see Burns & Hood, 1995, 1997, 1998; Burns & Joyce, 1999).

Genre pedagogy, like language pedagogy generally, is evolving and changing. The way teachers in the AMEP are working with the pedagogy is also changing as different teachers interpret it in different ways. When teachers first applied genre pedagogy, many superimposed the paradigms of the grammar-translation and structural approaches onto descriptions of text structure and language features. This resulted in teachers teaching text structure as fixed rule rather than in terms of functional variation within malleable prototypes. It also resulted in some teachers feeling they had to abandon the learner-centered methods developed as part of needs-based, communicative approaches and return to teacher-centered classrooms. As teachers gain knowledge, skill, confidence, and a sense of ownership of the curriculum, they are becoming increasingly adventurous and innovative in the way they adapt and integrate the best of our language-teaching heritage into text-based approaches. Teachers are also able to articulate the areas of genre theory they would like to see renovated or developed in relation to ESL.

It is classroom-based experimentation and reflection of this kind that is driving some of the most interesting theoretical developments in genre today. For example, an area of research of particular interest to ESL teachers is the mapping of language development in terms of configurations of language features across whole texts. Martin's work on text typology, topology, and agnation promises a theoretical basis for this research (Hood, 1996; Martin & Matthiessen, 1991).

At present, changing political and economic agendas are contributing to enormous structural change in the AMEP in Australia. The development of the *Certificates in Spoken and Written English* curriculum framework occurred in the context of a stable, collegiate educational environment oriented to public service. The AMEP is now delivered in a more fragmented and commercially oriented environment, as required by the ethos of competition currently driving public policy in Australia. It is not yet clear whether the new environment has the capacity to nurture the AMEP heritage so that it continues to provide an evidence-based foundation for principled curriculum evolution and innovation into the future. Whatever the future holds for migrant education, and for language education more generally throughout Australia, it seems certain, however, that language teachers who have used genre pedagogy to renew their teaching practice will continue to teach explicitly about text in context, linking grammar and lexis systematically to text, in order to assist learners to do with spoken and written English what they would not be able to do on their own.

Part II

Related Approaches

3
Genre, Text Type, and the English for Academic Purposes (EAP) Classroom

Brian Paltridge
Auckland University of Technology

Genre and its application in second-language classrooms is discussed in many of the journals in the area of second-language teaching and learning and in the more recent books on discourse analysis for language teachers (Burns, Joyce, & Gollin, 1996; McCarthy & Carter, 1994; Nunan, 1993; Paltridge, 1999). Genre is also discussed in many of the more recent books aimed at the professional development of second-language teachers (Dudley-Evans & St John, 1998; Feez & Joyce, 1998a; Grabe & Kaplan, 1996; Johns, 1997; Tribble, 1996; Jordan, 1997; Thornbury, 1997). Less attention, however, has been given to the relationship between genre and text type in much of this work. It may seem on a first reading of the genre analysis literature that the terms *genre* and *text type* refer to the same aspect of genre knowledge; in fact, very often these two terms are used interchangeably. There is not, however, universal agreement that genre and text type refer to the same aspect of a text. Biber (1988), for example, described a large-scale, corpus-based study of 23 genres, just under one million words and 67 different linguistic features, from which he drew a distinction between genre and text type that has important implications for the EAP classroom.

Biber (1989, p. 6) observed that texts within particular genres "can differ greatly in their linguistic characteristics; for example, newspaper articles can range from extremely narrative and colloquial in linguistic form to extremely informational and elaborated in form." On the other hand, he found that different genres can be quite similar linguistically. For example, newspaper articles and articles in popular magazines are often nearly identical in form.

On the basis of these observations, Biber drew a distinction between genre and text type that is extremely helpful for EAP classrooms. For him, the term genre characterized texts on the basis of external criteria, such as a text that is written or spoken by a particular person, for a particular audience, in a particular context, for a particular purpose, and viewed by the discourse community as being an example of the particular genre. Examples of genres, taken from this perspective, include university calendars, documented essays, research reports, lectures, and tutorials. Text types, on the other hand, represent rhetorical modes such as "problem–solution," "exposition," or "argument" type texts that are similar in terms of internal discourse patterns, irrespective of genre. *Genre* and *text type* thus represent different yet complementary perspectives on texts, both of which are useful and important for second-language classrooms.

The letter to the editor shown in Figure 3.1 provides an example of a particular text type—an argument—occurring within the context of the genre "letter to the editor." It is important to note that when someone is actually writing a letter to an editor, he or she needs to know much more than the final published text shows; he or she also needs to have an understanding of the conventions and expectations associated with letters to the editor, even though it is only the body of the letter that finally appears in print. Figure 3.1 shows this text as it might originally have been written, analyzed in terms of its generic structure (for the particular genre) and its text structure (as an instance of the text type "argument").

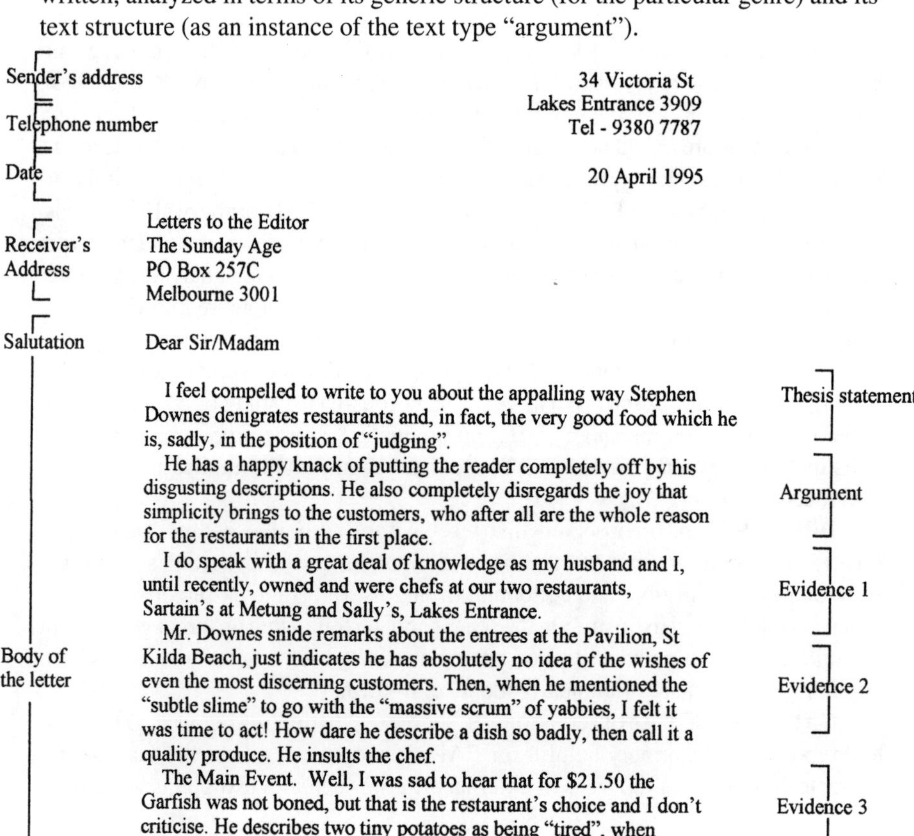

34 Victoria St
Lakes Entrance 3909
Tel - 9380 7787

20 April 1995

Letters to the Editor
The Sunday Age
PO Box 257C
Melbourne 3001

Dear Sir/Madam

I feel compelled to write to you about the appalling way Stephen Downes denigrates restaurants and, in fact, the very good food which he is, sadly, in the position of "judging".

He has a happy knack of putting the reader completely off by his disgusting descriptions. He also completely disregards the joy that simplicity brings to the customers, who after all are the whole reason for the restaurants in the first place.

I do speak with a great deal of knowledge as my husband and I, until recently, owned and were chefs at our two restaurants, Sartain's at Metung and Sally's, Lakes Entrance.

Mr. Downes snide remarks about the entrees at the Pavilion, St Kilda Beach, just indicates he has absolutely no idea of the wishes of even the most discerning customers. Then, when he mentioned the "subtle slime" to go with the "massive scrum" of yabbies, I felt it was time to act! How dare he describe a dish so badly, then call it a quality produce. He insults the chef.

The Main Event. Well, I was sad to hear that for $21.50 the Garfish was not boned, but that is the restaurant's choice and I don't criticise. He describes two tiny potatoes as being "tired", when obviously it is the receiver who is "spoilt" and "tired" of judging so much food

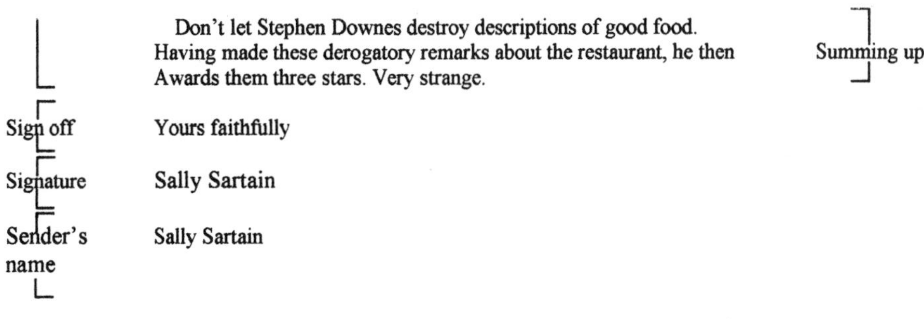
Don't let Stephen Downes destroy descriptions of good food.
Having made these derogatory remarks about the restaurant, he then
Awards them three stars. Very strange.

Yours faithfully

Sally Sartain

Sally Sartain

FIG 3.1: A letter to the editor/argument text (S. Sartain, 1995, April 30. Letter to the Editor. *The Sunday Age*, p. 16.)

The text shown in Figure 3.2 is an example of a problem–solution type text, also occurring within the context of the genre "letter to the editor." Clearly, not all letters to the editor are "argument" or "problem–solution" type texts, nor are all letters to the editor so clear in terms of text type categories as is the case with these two examples. However, in their original form, they would, for the most part, follow the conventions and expectations associated with letters to the editor (and formal letters in general); in terms of text type, they have many different possibilities.

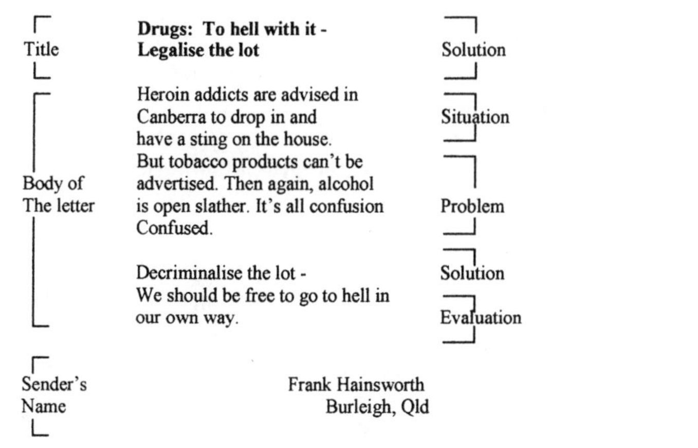
Drugs: To hell with it -
Legalise the lot

Heroin addicts are advised in
Canberra to drop in and
have a sting on the house.
But tobacco products can't be
advertised. Then again, alcohol
is open slather. It's all confusion
Confused.

Decriminalise the lot -
We should be free to go to hell in
our own way.

Frank Hainsworth
Burleigh, Qld

FIG. 3.2: A letter to the editor/problem–solution text. F. Hainsworth, 1995, July 9. Letter to the Editor. *The Sunday Age*, p. 12.

Figure 3.3 shows a problem–solution text within the context of an academic genre, the abstract section of a research report, analyzed in terms of its generic structure as an instance of a "research report abstract," and in terms of its text structure, as an instance of a "problem–solution" text.

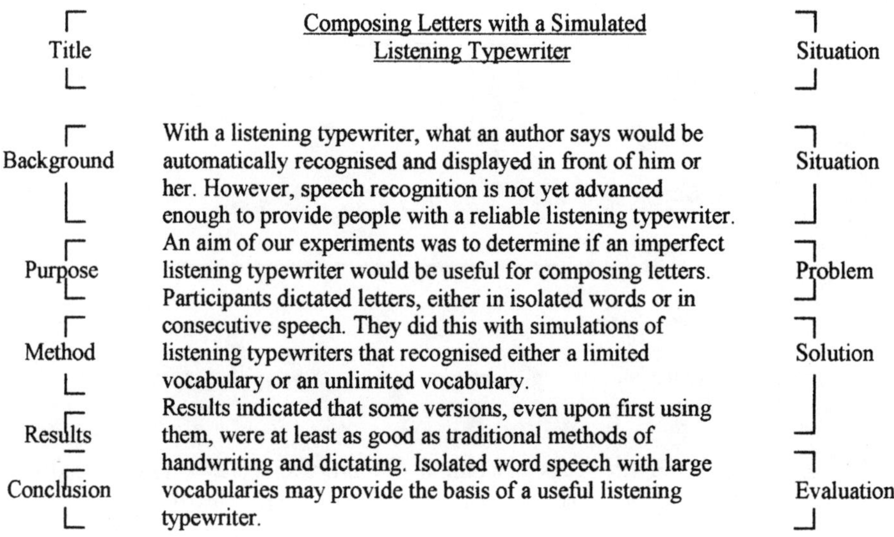
Composing Letters with a Simulated Listening Typewriter

With a listening typewriter, what an author says would be automatically recognised and displayed in front of him or her. However, speech recognition is not yet advanced enough to provide people with a reliable listening typewriter. An aim of our experiments was to determine if an imperfect listening typewriter would be useful for composing letters. Participants dictated letters, either in isolated words or in consecutive speech. They did this with simulations of listening typewriters that recognised either a limited vocabulary or an unlimited vocabulary. Results indicated that some versions, even upon first using them, were at least as good as traditional methods of handwriting and dictating. Isolated word speech with large vocabularies may provide the basis of a useful listening typewriter.

FIG. 3.3: Abstract of an experimental research report/problem-solution text (based on Weissberg & Buker, 1990, p. 185)

Other examples of text types being associated with more than one genre can be found in the work of Hoey (1983), where problem–solution texts are described within the context of advertisements, scientific reports, short stories, and novels; general–particular texts are described within the context of poems, novels, and scientific texts; and matching–contrast texts are described within the context of poems and letters to the editor. Crombie's (1985) work on discourse structures also provided examples of problem–solution texts within the context of scientific reports and advertisements, and topic–restriction–illustration texts within the context of advertisements and news reports.

Jordan (1997), drawing on work such as that carried out by Lackstrom, Selinker, & Trimble (1985), called this focus on text types a *rhetorical–functional* perspective on textual patterning. The rhetorical functions he listed include "descriptions," "narratives," "instructions," "explanations," "definitions," "exemplifications," "classifications," "compare and contrast," "cause and effect," and "discussion and argumentation/problem–solution" type texts. Tribble (1996) presented a similar perspective, listing commonly taught text types such as "expositions," "examples," "processes," "definitions," "cause and effect," "compare and contrast," "division and classification," "descriptions," "narration," and "argumentation and persuasion."

Genre and text type, thus, deal with aspects of language in different ways. This distinction is somewhat similar to the distinction that systemic genre analysts are now making between what they term *elemental genres* (see Feez, this volume) and *macro-genres*; that is, between smaller text types such as "narratives," "anecdotes," "recounts," "arguments," "reports," "explanations," "expositions," "descriptions," "instructions," "procedures," and "discussions" that together make up larger, more complex texts, or *macro-genres*, such as news stories and laboratory and research reports (Martin, 1994, 1995, 1997a; O'Carroll, Drury, & Jones, 1998; Veel, 1998).

A similar distinction is also made in the area of translation studies where genres are described as conventionalized forms of texts that reflect the communicative goals of particular social situations (such as novels, poems, editorials, jokes, advertisements, recipes, and news broadcasts), and text types as more basic kinds of rhetorical expression (such as argumentative, expository, instructional, informative, persuasive, and descriptive type texts; see Colina, 1997; Hatim & Mason, 1990).

For Bazerman (1998), this latter view primarily describes patterns of semantic organization such as narration, description, report, and accompanying linguistic and staged textual features "that may come to dominate passages of text longer than a sentence" (p. 24). As he pointed out, this conception differs from his own view of genre, which is more in line with, for example, Swales' (1990) and Biber's (1988) definitions of the term (see, e.g., Bazerman, 1994). Bloor (1998) described text types such as narration, description, and argumentation as "language styles" that might be used in the construction of many different genres. As she pointed out, the genre "story" might well include narrative and description-type texts, as might a medical research report genre contain anecdotes written as narratives to provide examples of particular cases.

Other discussions of the notion of text type can be found in the work of Werlich (1976) who, in his book *A Text Grammar of English*, provided detailed descriptions of five basic text types: description, narration, exposition, argumentation, and instruction. Text type research is also discussed by Pilegaard and Frandsen (1996) in the *Handbook of Pragmatics*. They argued that genre and text type studies are often confused with one another. In their view, there is a general line of demarcation between these two particular orientations: those that examine what they termed *text genres* (such as novels, legal texts, or business letters), and those that examine *text types* (such as narrative, expository, or argumentative type texts). They saw the distinction between these two perspectives as being based on text internal criteria (for text types) and text external features and differences relating to the extralinguistic context (for text genres). They pointed out, however, that this distinction between internal and external criteria is difficult to uphold with both genres and text types often being classified in terms of both text-internal and text-external parameters.

There is, unfortunately, no strong consensus on the best way to describe these kinds of discourse patternings—or indeed how to categorize them. For example, Silva (1990), describing the work of Current-Traditional Rhetoric teaching of academic writing in North America in the 1950s and 1960s, referred to *rhetorical modes*. The focus here is on the organization of content at the discourse and paragraph levels in the context of, for example, narration, description, exposition, and argumentation type texts. Other work, such as Johns (1986), Johns and Davies

(1983), and Johns and Paz (1997), draws more on schema theoretical principles and the notion of content slots or "constituent structures" in teaching students to write problem–solution texts, arguing for the importance of focusing on content, function, and form in academic writing instruction. Others, such as Kiniry and Rose (1993), described "critical reading and writing strategies" such as defining, summarizing, classifying, and comparing, which writers use across genres in different academic disciplines.

Work in this area is further complicated by the problem, as Horowitz (1986a) pointed out, that key words such as "describe" can mean different things in different settings. For example, an essay prompt starting with "Describe the causes of . . ." is as much (if not more) asking for a cause and effect type text rather than what might narrowly be called a description. Other assignment questions that contain the word "describe" might ask a student to describe the relationship between concepts or events, whereas others may require a listing or physical description of something (Horowitz, 1986a). Equally, there are various types of "summary." Ratterey (1985), for example, listed five different kinds. Furthermore, as Johns (1997) and others (e.g., Larson, 1982) pointed out, there is no single stable form that might be termed an "academic essay" or a "research paper" that applies in all academic classrooms (or indeed the one single meaning of essay prompts such as "describe"). In these sorts of cases, students can benefit greatly from asking teaching staff questions such as: What does a research paper mean to you? How would you organize a research paper? Do you have examples of papers written for your classes? (Johns 1997, p. 24), or, In this assignment question, what do you mean by "describe?" Students can then use this information as the basis for making decisions about how they will read for and write their academic assignments (see Johns, 1997; also Johns, this volume, for discussions of how this can be usefully done).

GENRE, TEXT TYPE, AND WRITING IN ACADEMIC SETTINGS

A number of studies have examined the written genre requirements of students studying in English-medium universities. Rose (1983), for example, examined essay prompts, take-home examinations, and assignment topics given to undergraduate students in 17 academic departments at the University of California, Los Angeles. He found that most writing assignments required exposition and argument type texts. Furthermore, he observed that the academic audiences for this writing seemed to vary in what they considered to be acceptable or appropriate in their particular area of study.

At Western Illinois University, Horowitz (1986b) found that, among the 54 writing tasks he examined, students were required to write research essays (15), assignments that required the connection of theory and data (10), summaries of/reactions to readings (9), reports on a specified experience (9), case studies (5), research projects (5), and annotated bibliographies (1). For undergraduate students, in particular, these writing tasks were often quite controlled in that students were given detailed instructions for the organization of the content of their assignment, or a thesis statement was provided that students were required to address in their piece of written work.

At Georgia State University, Canseco and Byrd (1989) found that, across 84 graduate business courses, the most common writing requirement was the formal examination, followed by written versions of problems presented in a textbook or by the instructor, then projects, case studies, and reports. Students were also required, although to a lesser extent, to produce surveys, business plans, audits, critiques, evaluations, diaries, project proposals, and political polls. Some of these pieces of written work involved a small-group or teamwork approach to data collection and reporting. In contrast with Horowitz's study, Canseco and Byrd found only a small number of assignment tasks that specified the content of the students' pieces of writing.

In an examination of the reading and writing requirements of students in an undergraduate history course at Georgia State University, Carson, Chase, Gibson, & Hargrove (1992) found that the main writing requirements came in the form of taking notes from set texts and lectures, book reviews, and examinations. These examinations most typically asked students to write compare-and-contrast, analysis, and cause-and-effect type texts. In particular, students needed to be able to recognize the content and writing requirements of examination questions when they were stated explicitly, and to predict what was expected when the question was less explicit.

Braine (1995), at the University of South Alabama, looked at the writing requirements of undergraduate students in 17 courses in the natural sciences and engineering and found that, of the 80 assignments he examined, students were required to write mostly five genres. These were summary/reactions, experimental reports (laboratory), experimental reports (design), case studies, and research papers. More than 75 % of the writing tasks assigned, however, required them to write an experimental report.

A study carried out by Hale, Taylor, Bridgeman, Carson, Kroll, & Kantor (1996) for the redevelopment of the TOEFL test is particularly relevant to this discussion. In their investigation, like Rose (1983) and Carson et al. (1992), the authors looked at both the genres and text types students need to command in English medium academic settings. They examined the written genre and text type requirements of 162 undergraduate and graduate courses in eight North American universities. The researchers found the most common written genres were documented essays, summaries, plans/proposals, and book reviews. They also found that students were sometimes required to write short papers of less than half a page in response to a given question or other stimulus. This was especially the case in the physical/mathematical sciences and engineering. By contrast, they found that students in the social sciences and humanities were more often required to write longer research essays. These essays most frequently asked students to write exposition and argument type texts and, in particular, cause-and-effect, problem–solution, classification/enumeration, compare/contrast, and analysis type texts.

Other studies (e.g., Behrens, 1980; Bernhardt, 1985; Bridgeman & Carlson, 1983; Casanave & Hubbard, 1992; Ostler, 1980; Trimmer, 1985) also investigated written genre requirements in North American universities. Although providing useful information, these studies are not discussed here because they used survey methods, or student reporting (alone), to gather their data, rather than an examination of actual tasks set by instructors. They also did not examine genre and text type requirements, the principal focus of this chapter.

AN AUSTRALIAN STUDY

The research carried out by Hale et al. (1996) provided the basis for a study done by Moore and Morton (1998) into the written genre and text type requirements of undergraduate and postgraduate students in two Australian universities, Monash University and the University of Melbourne. Moore and Morton focused, in particular, on disciplines where there were high enrollments of international students. They collected 155 writing tasks from undergraduate and postgraduate courses at both universities and sorted the tasks into genre and text type categories. They then followed up their analysis by interviewing academic staff as a way of supplementing their observations and analysis. The genres they found students were required to write are summarized in Table 3.1.

Table 3.1

Written Genre Requirements in Two Australian Universities

	GENRE TOTAL (% of writing tasks)	*UNDERGRADUATE (% of writing tasks)*	*POSTGRADUATE (% of writing tasks)*
Essay	58.1	58.4	56.7
Case study	9.7	7.2	20
Exercise	7.7	9.6	
Research report other than experimental	6.4	6.4	6.7
Review	4.5	4.8	3.3
Experimental research report	3.9	4.8	-
Literature review	1.3	.8	3.3
Research proposal	1.3	-	6.7
Summary	1.3	1.6	-
Short answer	1.3	1.6	-
Other *	4.5	4.8	3.3

Annotated reference, letter, project brief, resume, home page, computer program, educational program proposal.

(Moore & Morton, 1998, p. 17)

As can be seen from this table, the most common written genre was the academic essay. This was followed by case-study reports, exercises that required the application of some discipline–specific tool or model to a particular situation, research reports, reviews, literature reviews, research proposals, summaries, and short answers that required the reproduction of previously provided items of knowledge (such as from lectures or textbooks). It should not be taken from this table that these genre categories are, however, completely discrete and separate from each other. The categories assigned to the assignments tasks are the ones either confirmed or suggested by the academic staff who set the questions. Clearly, however, a research proposal or an experimental research report might well entail a literature review. Equally, a review or an essay may contain summary elements as well. Students thus need to be aware that many academic writing tasks require this sort of genremixing and embedding (see, e.g., Bhatia, 1997a; Martin, 1995). In terms of text type, about a quarter of the tasks required evaluation type texts. For example:

> Evaluation
> To what extent can people be regarded as the most important resource of an organization? (Management).
> (Moore & Morton, 1998, p. 21)

Following this, Moore and Morton found the most common text types were descriptions, summaries, compare and contrast, and explanation. For example:

> Descriptions
> Describe what is meant by international, domestic, and mass tourism (Tourism)
>
> Summaries
> What are the main points Christine Haliwell is making about the status of women in her chapter: Women in Asia: Anthropology and the study of women"? (Anthropology)
>
> Compare and contrast
> Where do the arguments of Oakey and Gati differ? (History)
>
> Explanation
> Adolescent mental health is a growth industry. Discuss factors that have contributed to this growth. (Medicine) (Moore & Morton, 1998, p. 22)

Other text types included recommendations, hortations (tasks that require students to make some judgment about the desirability of particular course of action or state of affairs), predictions, and instructions. For example:

Recommendation
What strategies can be used to make Internet contributors self-regulating?
(Computing)

Hortation
Because no person is an island, society should regulate private behavior. Discuss.
(Politics)

Prediction
What major changes in the Australian business environment are likely to impact on managers over the next decade?
(Management)

Instruction
Outline to any potential users precisely how the program is to be used.
(Computing–in an assignment requiring the writing of a computer program)
(Moore & Morton, 1998, pp. 22–23)

The text types observed in Moore and Morton's study are summarized in Table 3.2. Some of these (such as "evaluations," "descriptions," "compare and contrast," and "explanations") have been well described in terms of typical discourse patternings, whereas others (such as "recommendations," "hortations," and "predictions") have been much less so. These latter cases might, however, be seen as subsets of "argument" type texts, which are well described in the EAP literature, but nevertheless have different overriding purposes other than just "to argue a case," something that students need to keep in mind when writing their texts.

Analyses such as these show that although EAP students are required to be familiar with a number of different written genres, they also need a high-level understanding of the range of text types that might be appropriate to draw on for writing these genres.

Table 3.2

Written Text Type Requirements in Two Australian Universities (Moore & Morton, 1998)

TEXT TYPE	*TOTAL (% of writing tasks)*	*UNDERGRADUATE (% of writing tasks)*	*POSTGRADUATE (% of writing tasks)*
Evaluation	26.5	26.8	25.3
Description	18.1	17.2	1.5
Summary	14	14.9	10.2
Compare and contrast	13.7	15.6	16.3
Explanation	10.9	10.8	11.3
Recommendation	8.9	7	16.4
Hortation	3.8	4.5	1.2
Prediction	2.8	2.2	5.4
Instruction	1.3	1	2.4

AN EXAMPLE FROM THE CLASSROOM

Clearly, then, EAP programs need to focus on both genre and text type in their course of instruction. There are many examples of courses and published teaching materials that focus on each of these notions separately. There are, however, fewer examples where the notions of genre and text type are integrated into the single academic English program. This is an important omission, given the need for students to have an understanding of both genre and text type and how they interact with one another in EAP settings. To quote from a recent article on genre-based teaching:

> For any genre, a range of text types may be appropriate, but the range is far from infinite, and an error in setting the multiple dimensions along which a text type may vary can result in the creation of an inappropriate text type. (Caudrey, 1998)

His comment presents second-language writers with an especially complex task when taking genre requirements and expectations into account.

Paltridge (1995) described a first-year, tertiary-level course that aims to include a focus on the notions of genre and text type within the broader context of academic language and skills development. The course is both language- and content-based, in the subject area of English as an International Language. The program focuses on the development of a number of key academic genres as well as providing an opportunity for personal language and learning-skills development. Furthermore, the program integrates process- and product-oriented approaches to language-program design with content-based approaches to the teaching of academic writing. It draws on Raimes' (1991) notion of a balanced process approach to language-program development, which pays attention to form, content, and reader expectations along with a focus on the individual writer.

The specific aims of the program are to develop students' abilities to read and extract information from a range of genres relevant to the gathering of information for academic purposes, to write a range of genres and text types that meet the demands and expectations of an English-medium academic-learning environment, and to recognize required genres and text types in assessment and evaluation procedures and create appropriate responses to these questions.

The content in which learning tasks are embedded includes topics such as English as an international language, native and nonnative varieties of English, attitudes toward English, intercultural communication, communication strategies, and the influence of English on other languages. This thematic approach is supported by research into the effect of subject-matter knowledge and its impact on writing performance, such as that carried out by Tedick, who found that the extent to which ESL writers are familiar with subject matter has "dramatic influences on their writing performance" (1990, p. 138). It is also supported by studies such as that carried out by Adamson, who concluded that "academic skills are best taught in connection with authentic content material" (1990, p. 67).

The course reflects an integrated approach to language use in that students develop their ability to transfer from one mode of language use to another in a way that reflects the language behavior and expectations of an English-language academic learning environment. For example, students read and discuss texts on related topics for the creation of pieces of written work and in preparation for an examination on the particular topic.

Writing tasks in the program aim to cover some of the key written genres required in an English-medium academic learning environment. These include documented essays, summaries of and reactions to readings, annotated bibliographies, reports, case studies, and research projects. Text types focused on in these pieces of writing include argument, problem–solution, description, discussion, cause and effect, and compare and contrast.

Examples of topic areas, assignment tasks, and text types focused on in the program are shown in Table 3.3. All students enrolled in the course are required to write a documented essay—on either "English as an International Language" or "What English for Second-Language learners?" They then choose from one of the other assignments shown in Table 3.3 for their second piece of in-course work. That is, they have a choice of a summary of readings, a report on a survey of student attitudes, an annotated bibliography, a case study that looks at the communication strategies of an individual learner, or a broader, more general research project. Each of these genres provides the context for focusing on a number of different text types—in this case, description, compare and contrast, problem-solution, argument, discussion, compare and contrast, and cause and effect.

Table 3.3

A Genre-Based EAP Program: Assignment Tasks, Genres, and Text Types (Paltridge, 1995)

Topic area	*Assignment tasks*	*Genre and text type*
English as an International Language	Why is English an International Language? What problems arise when English is used as an International Language, and what can be done to help solve them?	Documented essay (description/ compare and contrast/problem solution)
What English for second-language learners?	Yukawa (1989) argues that it is not necessary for second language learners to match native English speaking linguistic and sociolinguistic abilities. What do you think should be the linguistic and sociolinguistic goals of second-language learners of English. Why?	Documented essay (argument)
World Englishes	What are World Englishes? Look at the references given by Kachru (1989) and and summarize several key readings on	Summary of readings (description)

	the subject. Be sure to include examples of World Englishes as well as examples of how English is used in the world and the people who use it.	
Attitudes toward English	Prepare and carry out a study of your fellow students' attitudes towards English. Focus, in particular, on their reasons for studying English, and their opinions regarding different varieties of English.	Report (discussion)
Intercultural communication	Identify a collection of key books or articles on the subject of intercultural communication, and write an annotated bibliography of these readings.	Annotated bibliography (description)
Communication strategies	Observe a fellow student in this course over a period of several weeks and identify the communication strategies s/he uses when speaking English. Discuss your observations with the student, then compare the results of your study with those of Tarone and Yule (1987).	Case study (compare and contrast)
The effect of English on other languages	Look at a particular topic in a newspaper, journal, or magazine project in a language other than English over a regular period. What borrowings from English can you find? Use these examples to discuss how and why languages change.	Research (cause and effect)

Students are also required to do a final examination that summarizes the content of the course and focuses on the range of text types considered in the program. In this examination, students write long- and short-answer questions as well as draw on skills developed in the course in analyzing and responding to examination questions. In preparation for this examination, particular attention is given to the analysis of examination prompts and identification of appropriate text types. For example, students analyze examination questions in order to identify what might be the most appropriate text type for the particular question.

AN ESSAY WRITING ACTIVITY

Possible essay topics students can choose to write about in this course are: What is English as an International Language? What problems arise when English is used as an International Language, and what can be done to help solve them? In the initial stages of preparation for the essay, students consider the social and cultural context of the genre they are preparing to write. This includes discussion of:

- the setting of the genre (e.g., a first-year course, at a university, etc.);
- the purpose of the genre (e.g., to display knowledge and understanding in a particular area, to demonstrate particular skills, to convince the reader, etc.);
- the content of the genre (including what claims are acceptable in particular areas of study, and what claims are not);
- the writer of the genre, his or her role and purpose in writing the text;
- the intended audience for the particular genre, their role and purpose in reading the text, how they will react to what they read, and the criteria they will use for assessing the text;
- the relationship between readers and writers of the genre and how this impacts on what is said and how it is said;
- general discourse community expectations and conventions for the genre, as well as particular expectations, conventions, and requirements of the particular area of study;
- text type requirements for the instance of the particular genre and how this is signaled (or not) to the writer;
- the background knowledge, values, and understandings it is assumed writers of the particular genre will share with their readers, including what is important to the intended audience and what is not;
- the relationship the genre has with other genres (such as lectures, set texts, journal articles, research reports, etc.).

As a way of exploring these issues, students examine the texts they are reading in preparation for their assignments in terms of these aspects. They discuss, in particular, how different contextual features (such as author, audience, setting, and subject matter) lead to the particular style, positioning, presentation, and use of language in the texts. Students also discuss how a text on the same topic and in a similar context might be presented in their own language and culture, and consider ways in which these texts might be similar to or different from each other. Students also discuss how the text they have examined might change if one of the contextual features of the text were changed such as a different author, audience, setting, purpose, or subject matter. An example of a worksheet used for this kind of exercise is shown in Figure 3.4.

Figure 3.4

A Context/Genre Analysis Worksheet (adapted from Paltridge, 2000)

What is the text about?

What is the purpose of the text?

What is the setting of the text?
(e.g., in a text book, a newspaper, etc.)

What is the tone of the text?
(e.g., formal, informal, etc)

Who is the author of the text?
What is his/her educational background?
academic status?
social status?
What is his/her purpose in writing the text?

Who is the intended audience of the text?

What is the relationship between the author
and intended audience of the text?

What rules or expectations limit
how the text might be written?

What shared cultural knowledge is assumed
by the text?

What shared values and understandings
are implied in the text?

What text type/s seem to be mostly
represented in the text?

What other texts does this text assume
you have a knowledge of?

How is the language of the text influenced by each of these factors?

Clearly, some of the reading prompts shown in Fig. 3.4 are more difficult for students less familiar with particular genres than others. This is especially the case with those prompts that are related to rules and expectations and shared cultural knowledge. Here, the teacher can help students by providing examples from the text being examined and discussing reasons for particular language and discourse features, then asking students to find similar examples themselves. For example, once the way academic writers often "hedge" is pointed out to students, and the reasons for this, they can then continue to find other examples of this particular linguistic strategy in their texts. Equally, students might identify examples of argument type texts throughout the reading passage they are examining and be asked to consider why the writer might have chosen this particular strategy.

The instruction, with the guidance and support of the teacher, commences "beyond the text" by exploring the contexts in which the texts that the students are learning to write are located, as well as reasons for the linguistic choices they might make.

Students are given further suggestions for the content of their essay by referring them to a chart presented by Strevens (1987, p. 63), which summarizes the notion of English as an International Language, contrasting it with English as Foreign Language, English as a Second Language, and English as an Intranational Language. The material encourages students to incorporate description and compare-and-contrast text type components (by comparing English as an International Language with English as a Foreign Language, etc.) into their essays. Students learn that an assignment question may often require them to draw on, and integrate, a number of different text types, rather than just the single one, into their piece of academic writing.

Students are also given a problem–solution "expectation network" (Johns, 1986) to use as a checklist for their reading and note-taking for their essay (Fig. 3.5). Students make notes under each of the "content slots" presented in the chart as a way of ensuring they attend to each of these constituent components of problem–solution texts in as much detail as possible. They then use the Strevens chart and the notes they have taken using the problem–solution network to write an outline for their essay, taking notes under headings that reflect the content and discourse organization they choose to follow. Students then draw up what McCarthy and Carter (1994, pp. 58–62) termed a *text frame* for their essay, that is, a diagram representation of the structural organization of their text, which they then use to write their individual assignments.

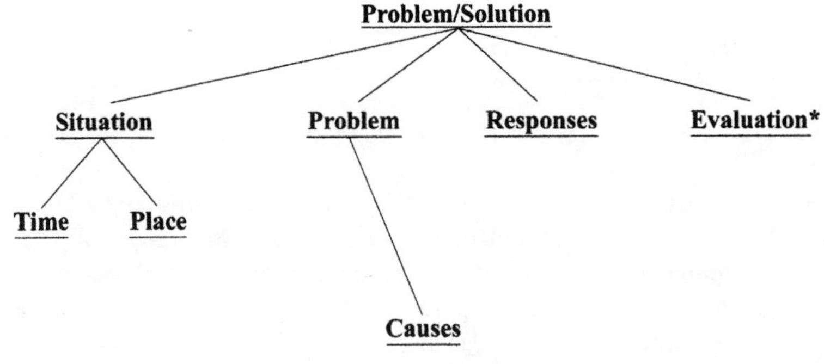

***Nonobligatory.**

Figure 3.5. A Model Expectation Network for Problem–Solution Texts (Johns, 1986, p. 77)

Students are reminded, however, that the kind of essay they write for a particular course is not necessarily (or indeed at all) universal across different academic disciplines and needs to be adapted or completely changed for other assignment questions in other areas of study (see Dudley-Evans, this volume). As Kusel (1992) pointed out, we cannot assume that rhetorical patterning is uniform from subject to subject within the same institution, or in the same subject area in different institutions, nor can we let our students assume this might be the case.

Dudley-Evans (1995) made a similar observation in his distinction between "general" and "particular" expectations of different academic disciplines. By "general expectations" he meant general transferable patterns of textual organization that might be transferred from one area of study to another, such as the overall organization of a piece of academic writing. By "particular expectations" he meant the ways in which these general patterns need to be adapted to meet the expectations and requirements of a particular field of study. As he argued, "An approach to the teaching of academic writing that implies that there are common patterns of organization that always apply in all disciplines [can be] dangerously misleading" (Dudley-Evans, 1993, p. 147). Thus, even though we can hypothesize about the general expectations in terms of how an academic assignment might be written, we also need to be sure to consider the particular expectations of the academic audience our students are writing for (see Johns, 1995, 1997, for ways of helping students write texts that meet the institutional and audience expectations of their particular field of study).

CONCLUSION

Clearly, more than knowledge of rhetorical structures is needed for students to succeed in academic settings. Genre knowledge also includes an understanding of the social and cultural contexts in which genres are located, as well as how these factors impact upon the language choices made within them. Furthermore, as Berkenkotter and Huckin (1995) argued, genre knowledge also includes a sense of what it is appropriate to write about in such contexts. This is especially important for ESL classrooms in that many descriptions of genres might focus on the language and structure of a text, but pay much less attention to the issue of appropriate content (Connor, 1996). Berkenkotter and Huckin also argued that a genre's conventions reveal much about the norms and values of a particular discourse community. This is especially the case in academic settings where these norms and values often tend to be "hidden" rather than overtly stated (Ongstad, 1999).

This "situated" view of genre is highly relevant for second language and novice classrooms in that it takes us beyond the language and form of a genre to a consideration of the ways in which a genre "is embedded in the communicative activities of the members of a discipline" (Berkenkotter & Huckin, 1995, p. 2). It also gives us insights into the ways students both acquire and use genre knowledge as they participate in the knowledge-producing activities of their field or profession.

Focusing on genre and text type in EAP classrooms, then, provides a context in which students can gain access to academic discourses that will, hopefully, enable them to participate more successfully in academic settings. Pennycook (1996), in a discussion of genre and the second-language classroom, argued that we need to develop our students' abilities and awareness to reflect on language and its uses in the acquisition of the genres they need to control. We can do this, in part, by assisting our students in unpacking texts in a way that helps them understand the context of production and interpretation of their particular texts, as well as how they might position themselves, and what they want to say, in order to achieve their particular goals (Cadman, 1997). This is often difficult for ESL students who come from a context where the conventions and expectations of academic writing may be quite different from the situation they now find themselves in (Ballard & Clanchy, 1984; Cleheran & Moodie, 1997). A focus on genre and text type in EAP classrooms provides one way in which these aspects of genre knowledge can be considered in a way that is helpful and useful to our learners.

4

Genre in the Classroom: A Linguistic Approach

John Flowerdew
City University of Hong Kong

In her widely quoted state-of-the-art article, Hyon (1996) distinguished three "worlds" of genre scholarship—English for Specific Purposes, New Rhetoric, and Australian—categorized according to the different theoretical and pedagogical orientations of their proponents. Although Hyon had valid reasons for grouping work in genre analysis into these three worlds, for my purpose in this chapter two groupings are more useful than three. The fundamental difference for me is between *linguistic* and *nonlinguistic* approaches. ESP and the Australian school take a linguistic approach, applying theories of functional grammar and discourse and concentrating on the lexico-grammatical and rhetorical realization of the communicative purposes embodied in a genre, whereas the New Rhetoric group is less interested in lexico-grammar and rhetorical structure and more focused on situational context—the purposes and functions of genres and the attitudes, beliefs, values, and behaviors of the members of the discourse communities within which genres are situated. The methodology used by the linguistic approach of the ESP and Australian groups is basically that of functional grammar, but with more concern for social context than is usual in that tradition and an additional interest in organizational patterns at the discourse level. New Rhetoric methodology, by contrast, tends to be more ethnographic than linguistic.

In making this distinction between the two approaches, I am not saying that the linguistic approach does not consider context and never uses ethnographic techniques, nor that the New Rhetoric is never concerned with linguistic realization. My point is that the outcome of the analysis is likely to be lexico-grammatical/rhetorical with the former and situational with the latter. Putting it another way, the linguistic approach looks to the situational context to interpret the linguistic and discourse structures, whereas the New Rhetoric may look to the text to interpret the situational context. The two approaches can be represented in a simple diagram (Fig. 4.1) as follows:

Fig. 4.1

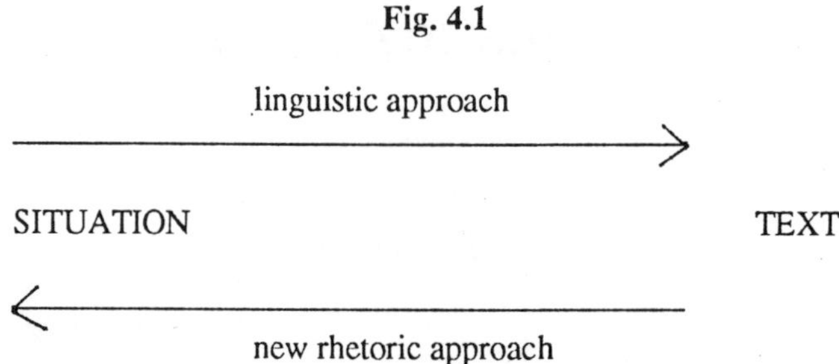

As far as pedagogical application of the two approaches is concerned, as Hyon (1996, p. 701) noted, the focus of the Australian and ESP approach is "on teaching students the formal, staged qualities of genres so that they can recognize these features in the texts that they read and use them in the texts that they write." In contrast, for the New Rhetoric, pedagogical application has been concerned with making students and professionals aware of the situational characteristics and social functions of the genres in which they engage. As Bazerman (1988, cited in Hyon, 1996, p. 699) has put it, the goal of writing instruction should not be just to give students, "the formal trappings of the genres they need to work in," but to make them aware that "The more [they] understand the fundamental assumptions and aims of [their] community, the better able [they]will be . . . to evaluate whether the rhetorical habits [they] and [their] colleagues bring to the task are appropriate and effective." It is not my purpose to argue for the advantages of either one of these two fundamental approaches, although I focus on the linguistic approach in this chapter.

From the perspective of an applied linguist, which is what I see myself as, the approach recommended will depend on the purpose of the analysis. In my own work, I have adopted both approaches. While I was working in the Middle East, I had the task of designing ESP curricula and materials for beginning university science students. The target audience for these curricula and materials had only minimal proficiency in general English, and the need was to develop their ability to cope with fairly elementary lectures and reading materials in science and engineering. One piece of research I conducted to feed into curriculum design in this context was to analyze the form and function of definitions, which I identified as an important feature of the lecture genre as my students encountered it. Genre analysis here took the form of the development of a taxonomy of the different functional and formal features of this important speech act as they occurred in a corpus of lectures of the types my target audience would be exposed to (Flowerdew, 1992).

In contrast to this earlier work, my more recent research in Hong Kong, with my colleagues Lindsay Miller and David Li, although again concerning itself with the *academic lecture* genre, has been focused less on the actual language and more on the situational context (Flowerdew, Li, & Miller, 1992, 1995, 1996a, 1996b; Flowerdew et al., 1998). Interviews with lecturers and students and observation of lectures have highlighted the somewhat different perspectives these two groups have of the lecture experience. The "thick" descriptions that my colleagues and I have been able to make of these perceptions, without actually describing the language of the lectures, have, like the more linguistically focused work in the Middle East, nevertheless been designed to facilitate student understanding. The explanation of the lecture experience embodied in these thick descriptions can be presented in an appropriate form to both students and lecturers, thereby helping students to understand their role better, on the one hand, and lecturers to adapt their lecturing to come closer to student expectations, on the other.

PURPOSE

Having presented my genre credentials, so to speak, I now turn to the context of the research I want to describe in this chapter. As already stated, my approach here is linguistic. I want to demonstrate the extent to which genre theory in the linguistic tradition is able to produce meaningful descriptions that can be applied, and suitably adapted, to helping nonnative speakers of English express themselves in the technical genres they encounter in the course of their studies. Although by no means wishing to downplay the value of the more situationally oriented applications of genre theory to the classroom, I think it is important that this linguistic approach, which has yielded valuable results in various contexts internationally, is represented in this collection of articles devoted to genre in the classroom.

Writing in 1973 in his influential *Introducing Applied Linguistics*, Pit Corder (1973, p. 93) stated:

> So long as linguistic theory is concerned only with the internal structure of sentences, as it has predominantly been over the centuries, the sort of descriptions the teacher needs in order to systematically develop communicative competence in his pupils will be lacking. Linguistic theories simply do not exist at the present time which give more than an anecdotal account of the relations between sentences in discourse or dialogue or the way in which utterances vary systematically in relation to differences in the situational context. Until such theories of communicative competence are much better developed the teacher will have to work on a principle of hit and miss exposure, hoping that the learner will discover on his own the discourse rules, or "speaking rules" of the language as we have called them.

It is my contention that linguistic theory—in functional systemic linguistics and in genre analysis—has developed in the 25 years since Corder's statement to a point where the lack of sequential and functional descriptions to which Corder referred has, at least to some extent, been made up for. My first purpose in this chapter is to demonstrate the way in which the sort of descriptions that can now be made, due to the advances achieved in grammar and discourse since Corder, can be carried out and applied. Following this, my second purpose is to show how such text analysis can then, in turn, be applied to the development of pedagogical materials designed to lead to the communicative competence to which Corder referred.

CONTEXT

The context for the work is the Middle Eastern university setting I described previously and the students with limited ability in general English, who needed to begin their study of science or engineering through the medium of English. I will concentrate here on the writing skill.

An immediate problem facing the curriculum designer in considering how to develop students' ability in appropriate writing skills in this context was the question of what genre or genres to focus on. Needs analysis indicated that content lecturers required very little writing at all in the first two years of the three-year degree course that their students followed. In their third year, however, students were expected to write lengthy, final-year projects. The reason for the minimal requirement in the first two years was that content professors had quickly come to the conclusion that tasks that required any sort of extended writing were beyond the proficiency level of the students. As a result, the professors developed tasks (multiple-choice, single word answer, and so on) that required hardly any writing at all. For reasons concerned with international standards and validation, the content staff nevertheless still required the project in the final third year.

From the point of view of the English specialist, this situation exacerbated the problem of developing competency in writing. On the one hand, students were not getting any practice in writing during the first two years of their content courses because their teachers judged them incapable. On the other hand, motivating students to want to spend time on developing their writing ability was difficult, given that they could perceive no immediate need for this skill. At the same time, the problems with the third-year projects were not being addressed, given that students were not doing anything to prepare themselves for a demanding writing task in their final year of study.

As a result of this situation, the English staff initiated collaboration with content teachers to develop writing tasks for the first year that would be appropriate in terms of content, would be within the proficiency level of the students, and that the language staff could help the students prepare for. Two genres were identified with members of the biology department where a writing requirement could be incorporated at a very basic level: *examination/quiz responses* and *laboratory report descriptions*. Both of these genres, analysis and literature review confirmed, required a relatively narrow set of text types, such as "physical structure and function," "physical process," "classification," and "definition." These text types, it was further confirmed, were also typical of the biology textbook, thus providing a useful resource for comparison and contrast with the genres that were to be the focus of the writing course. Collaboration with the content staff was important here, because it meant that the writing that the language staff were preparing students to be able to do had a real purpose. The notion of communicative purpose is essential to a definition of genre (Bhatia, 1993; Martin, 1992; Swales, 1990). Without the real purpose for writing provided by the content staff, the language staff would have been teaching students to write text types, but not to perform genres.[1]

ANALYSIS

In the following section, I will demonstrate how genre analysis was able to provide a description of the text type of physical structure that provided the basis for language teaching materials. This, in turn, prepared the students to perform the genres of examination/quiz response and laboratory report required by the content staff.

Schematic Structure

Following Bhatia (1993), Hasan (1977, 1979, 1984), Martin (1992), Swales (1990), Ventola (1987) and others, a first stage in the rhetorical/lexico-grammatical analysis of a genre is to break it down into its component stages, or moves, to provide a template of its schematic structure.[2]

My analysis here draws on work by Florence Davies (Davies, 1994, 1995; Davies & Greene, 1984; Johns & Davies, 1983),[3] who proposes a typology of elementary scientific texts according to topic, each topic type exhibiting a particular macro- or schematic structure of information slots. These information, or content, slots correspond to the moves in genre analysis, as conducted by Swales, Bhatia, and others, although these moves are conceptual, rather than the speech-act (or illocutionary) categories of the other researchers just mentioned.[4] Johns and Davies

[1]See Davies (1995) and Paltridge (1996, and this volume) on the distinction between text type and genre.

[2]Although I refer to identification of schematic structure as the first stage in genre analysis, this is an idealization for the purpose of exposition. In actual fact, various interrelated levels of analysis go on at the same time: identification of communicative purpose(s), schematic structure, grammatical features, lexical features, etc.

[3]Earlier work along similar lines was conducted by discourse analysts at the University of Washington: Larry Selinker, Louis Trimble, Robert Vroman, Thomas Huckin, and Mary Todd Trimble. This work is summarized in Trimble (1985).

[4]This question of moves corresponding to illocutionary or conceptual categories is an aspect of genre analysis that has not received much attention, although it highlights an important issue relating to the relation between form and meaning. In the persuasive genres analyzed by Swales and Bhatia, it seems appropriate to foreground persuasive aspects of textual meaning and hence illocutionary or speech-act

do not specify their ordering of information slots.

Topic types include physical structure, process, characteristics, mechanism, theory, principle, force, instruction, and so on. For "physical structure" texts—which can describe phenomena as diverse as a suspension bridge, a flowering plant, a skeleton, or a blast furnace—the schematic structure is as follows (note that the ordering is not specified in Johns & Davies):

- the parts of the structure
- the location of the parts
- the properties or attributes of the parts
- the function of the parts

This structure can be demonstrated by the following prototypical (made up) text, as in Text 1:

Text 1

(1) The skin has two layers. (2) The epidermis is the outer layer. (3) The dermis is the inner layer. (4) The epidermis consists of stratified epithelial tissues. (5) The dermis consists of fibrous connective tissues. (6) The epidermis protects the body. (7) The dermis contains blood vessels and stores fat.

In this text, sentence 1 refers to the parts of the structure, sentences 2 and 3 to the location of the parts, sentences 4 and 5 to the properties of the parts, and sentences 6 and 7 to the function of the parts.

Insofar as this text follows exactly the order of the schematic structure, it can be seen as a prototypical, unmarked text (Swales, 1990; Ventola, 1987). Most authentic texts will not reflect this prototype so exactly, however. The (authentic) text in Text 2, although exhibiting all elements of the formula, shows how: (a) the elements may be ordered differently, (for example, in sentence 1 the slot "parts"["a tooth"] is followed by the slot "attribute" ["has three regions"]); (b) some elements may be repeated throughout the text (for example, new "parts" are introduced, such as "bony socket," "dentine," "enamel," and so on); and (c) elements can be embedded one within another (for example, in sentence 1, "location" is embedded within "parts").

---

categories. Where more descriptive language is concerned, however, conceptual categories are more appropriately foregrounded. Whichever type of meaning is emphasized in establishing the move structure, however, there is the problem of ignoring the other type of meaning. This problem has been discussed at some length in speech-act theory in language teaching (see Flowerdew, 1990). At the clause level, this is less of a problem, because Halliday's ideational and interpersonal functions can deal with conceptual and illocutionary meaning respectively. Halliday's textual function also deals with another type of meaning; how the meaning of one part of the discourse relates to the others. Davies (1994) referred to these three types of meaning in written language as "informing," "interacting," and "organizing". Of related interest, Berkenkotter and Huckin (1995) also allowed for both illocutionary and conceptual meaning as important aspects of genre knowledge: ". . . a sense of what content is appropriate to a particular purpose in a particular situation at a particular point in time," as they put it (p. 13).

Text 2

(1) A tooth has three regions: the crown is the part projecting above the gum, the neck is embedded in the soft gum and the root is out of sight anchoring the tooth in its bony socket. (2) Inside the tooth is a fairly hard material which contains some living tissues. (3) This is the dentine. (4) The dentine cannot withstand wear, so in the crown and neck it is covered with a layer of hard, non-living enamel. (5) The dentine in the root is covered with a substance called cement, which helps to fix the tooth in its socket. (6) Inside the dentine, in the center of the tooth is a hollow pulp cavity containing nerves, a small artery and a small vein.
(Ewington & Moore (1971), cited in Johns & Davies, 1983, p. 5).

In addition, more complex texts may embed elements of different text types. Thus, for example, a physical structure text may include elements of a process text, as in the text in Text 3, where the FUNCTION of one of the parts is developed into an account of the PROCESS involved (the relevant section is underlined).

Text 3

Two main layers compose the skin: an outer and thinner layer, the epidermis, and an inner and thicker layer, the dermis.

The cells of stratified epithelial tissue which make up the epidermis are closely packed together and are arranged in several layers. Only the cells of the innermost layer of the epidermis reproduce themselves. <u>As they increase in number, they move up towards the surface and dislodge the dead horny cells of the outer layer. These flake off by the thousands onto our clothes, into our bath water, and onto things we handle</u>.

Connective tissue composes the dermis. Instead of cells being crowded close together like the epithelial cells of the epidermis, they are scattered far apart, with many fibers in between. Some of the fibers are tough and strong (collagenous or white fibers), and others are stretchable and elastic (elastic fibers). Some of the cells of the dermis store fat. A rich network of capillaries lies in the dermis and also immediately beneath it. The epidermis contains no blood vessels, however.

Anthony (1983).

Although the prototype as exemplified in Text 1 does not correspond to an authentic text, it is nevertheless useful for pedagogical purposes in providing a simplified model that can be presented to lower proficiency students. A text corresponding to this structure would be accepted by the content staff (language and content staff agreed on what were acceptable text structures). In fact, it might be said that such a text, if produced by a student, would be considered appropriate.

Lexico-Grammatical Analysis

Grammatical Analysis. Assuming the made-up text in Text 1 was used in pedagogical material, having specified the topic (genre) type and the moves, linguistic description could then identify the key functional/grammatical categories. The grammatical analysis employs categories found, for example, in Quirk, Greenbaum, Leech, & Svartvik (1985); Halliday (1994); Martin (1992); and Leech and Svartvik (1994).

In this text, as in physical structure texts in general, the major grammatical features are as follows:

stative relations: *The skin has two layers.*
The epidermis is the outer layer.
process relations: *The epidermis protects the body.*
The dermis stores fat.
location: - *inner, outer*
non-specific and specific reference:
An epidermis, a dermis
The outer layer, the epidermis

A similar range of grammatical features is found in Texts 2 and 3.

Lexical Analysis. Moving now to the next level of analysis, lexis, we see that the following items occur in the text in Text 1:

nominals: *skin, epidermis, dermis, layer, tissue, fat, body*
adjectives: *stratified, epithelial, fibrous, connective, inner, outer*
verbs: *protect, store*

Some of these items can be considered as technical (for example, *epidermis, dermis, epithelial*), specific to the study of the skin. Others, however, are of more general use, or subtechnical, in descriptions of physical structure (*inner, outer, protect, store*). For pedagogic application, the more general items, which are likely to occur in other physical structure texts, will be the focus.

Analysis of a More Complex Authentic Text

The previous analysis was on the made-up text (Text 1) for the purpose of illustration. If that text was used for beginning learners, material derived from the more complex authentic texts (Text 2, Text 3) might be introduced later. Based on these texts, the schematic structure would specify obligatory vs. nonobligatory moves, and variable ordering of the elements, with embedding and repetition. Learners could be shown how these phenomena operate by examining a range of authentic texts such as these. It is very important to stress the aspects of schematic variation, so that students are not given the impression that texts will always follow the prototypical pattern.

Given that the lexico-grammatical items for the earlier unit had been covered, work based on models such as those exemplified in Text 2 and Text 3 might operate at a more sophisticated level. At this point, it is useful to apply Halliday's tripartite division of the context of situation into *field, tenor,* and *mode.* Field corresponds to the subject matter and activity type of the text; tenor refers to the relation between the participants in the text; and mode is the rhetorical channel and function of the discourse—what part the text is playing (Halliday, 1994, p. 390; Martin, 1992, p. 404). Field, tenor, and mode are associated with the three macro-functions of ideational, interpersonal, and textual meaning respectively. The syllabus might focus at this stage on particular linguistic features associated with the three contextual parameters and their associated functions of this type of text as follows:

FIELD (subject matter and activity type of the text)
description of physical entities:
stative verbs to describe parts, location, and attributes:
- *has, is*

material process verbs to describe function:
- *anchoring, fix*

postmodification to express location or function:
- *the dentine in the root*
- *the part projecting above the gum*
- *a hollow pulp cavity containing nerves*

technical vocabulary to refer to parts of the structure:
- *crown, gum, neck, soft gum, root, bony socket, tissue, dentine, enamel, cement, pulp cavity, nerves, artery, vein*

subtechnical vocabulary to refer to location, attributes, and function:
- *regions, project, embedded, anchoring, withstand, nonliving, substance, fix, hollow*

TENOR (the relation between the participants in the text)
impersonal style expressive of "objectivity" of scientific and academic writing:
agentless passive:
- *the neck is embedded in . . .*
- *it* (the dentine) *is covered with . . .*
- *the dentine in the root is covered with . . .*

existential verbs:
- *is, has*

"universal" present tense suggesting that states, actions, or events are eternal or happen at all times:
- *is, has, contains, helps*

MODE (the rhetorical channel and function of the discourse: what part the text is playing)
written, elementary scientific textbook
lexical repetition:
- *the dentine . . . the dentine . . . the dentine . . . the dentine*

definite article referring to unique entity:
- *the crown, the neck, the soft gum, the dentine*

marked theme (Halliday, 1994) to emphasize location or attribute:
- *inside the tooth is ...*
- *a fairly hard material . . . This is the dentine.*
- *inside the dentine, in the center of the tooth, is a hollow pulp cavity*

apposition for listing parts:
- *A tooth has three regions: the crown . . . the neck . . . and the root.*

A further unit, taking the third cited text as its model, would probably not be presented until process texts had been dealt with. The learner would thus be combining two sets of knowledge about the two text types. As with schematic structure, it is important not to leave students with the impression that the form/function relations illustrated in this analysis are always the same; on the contrary, a range of texts should be used as examples to develop a sense of functional variation.

PEDAGOGICAL APPLICATION

Considering now the possible pedagogical application of the generic description just illustrated, I want to emphasize that, although this is a linguistic description, classroom application is not necessarily prescriptive. The Middle Eastern context in which this was actually used could be described as prescriptive to a certain degree, insofar as needs analysis conducted with students, content staff, and administrators had identified a "traditional" approach to language learning and a desire for a focus on formal grammar. I agree with Holliday (1994) that it is very important for expatriate educators to adapt their methods to the local culture (Flowerdew & Miller, 1995, 1996a) and accordingly make no apologies for what might look a rather prescriptive approach.

In addition, given that they are immersed in a whole range of genres on a daily basis, L1 students are able to identify the specific features of an unfamiliar genre by comparing and contrasting it with the wide range of genres with which they are already familiar. For foreign language learners, however, the situation is rather different. The language-learning materials may be the only contact these students have with the target language. There is, therefore, no way that they can be familiar with the subtle variations in language form that apply to various genres. Foreign-language learners are thus not in a position to negotiate their way into engaging in a new genre as L1 students are. Some overt focus on form seems to me essential, therefore, in a foreign-language context.

With this need for focus on form in the Middle Eastern context in mind, pedagogical materials were developed that systematically introduced and practiced the linguistic features identified in the analysis. However, accepting that there was a need for a focus on form, the material was nevertheless presented in such a way as to minimize prescription. Use of the metalanguage employed in the prior description was avoided, except for previously known terms such as noun, verb, adjective, and tense. The linguistic material was also introduced in a variety of ways and was carefully graded over the course of the program. The following is a list of activities that were incorporated into the materials:

1. Presentation of complete text or range of texts with similar schematic structure, as models for writing (modeling).
2. Identification of text structure of model texts by means of information transfer activities, such as completing tables, or by color-coding different information slots.
3. Exercises in metacommunicating—glossing model texts in terms of their structural moves and examining the linguistic realizations of the various moves.
4. Reassembling jumbled model texts into the correct sequence in order to create awareness of schematic structure.
5. Examining relations of form and meaning for individual moves.
6. Cloze exercises focusing on key signaling items of moves of model texts.
7. Intensive lexico-grammatical language work. Discrete items, as per the generic description, are singled out for intensive presentation and practice, for example, formation and use of passive, postmodification, subtechnical lexis.
8. Completion of model texts with moves or sentences deleted.
9. Exercises in paraphrasing. Students provide alternative possible encodings for the moves.
10. Eliciting information to be included in the writing task, based on the schematic structure.
11. Creating tables or charts based on the schematic structure.
12. Creating the text from the schematic structure table or chart.
13. Group/pair work assessing the effectiveness of the finished text.
14. Comparing text types across different genres.

A top-down as well as a bottom-up approach was used in presenting the material, where top-down corresponded to a problem-solving and hypothesis-testing attempt at communication before any input was provided by the teacher, whereas bottom-up corresponded to the more traditional presentation, practice, production-sequence methodology.

An important feature of the approach being described was language and content staff teaching in collaboration. As mentioned earlier, tasks were built into the content course that required the production by students of the structure and function text type that was the focus of the language work. This writing was assessed for both content and language. Students thus immediately saw the relevance of the language class work they were doing. In addition, and importantly, students were introduced into the social dimension of generic awareness, by discovering what was and what was not acceptable to their content teachers. Discussion of these factors was incorporated into the language classes, and students developed an awareness of the extent to which linguistic appropriateness and accuracy were important if they were to satisfy the demands of their content teachers.

It is emphasized that the structure text types were not the only ones students were exposed to. Additional text types were introduced as the writing progressed, and comparison and contrast of the different text types was incorporated into the course. At the same time, students were attending lectures and taking a course in listening. This allowed for comparison and contrast of the different text types across the different genres, important for developing a sense of generic variation. (See my paper [Flowerdew, 1993] on the interrelation between different genres and appropriate methodology.)

CONCLUSION

This chapter has presented a model of what I call a linguistic approach to genre pedagogy in an L2 context. The linguistic and generic description that the model bases itself on may lend itself to a prescriptive approach, and for cultural reasons what could be considered to be prescriptive was applied in the context within which the materials were developed, albeit with the understanding that students need to be sensitized to generic variation and that overprescription and stereotyping were to be avoided. The rationale for this moderately prescriptive approach is twofold. First, local cultural views should be respected. Second, in L2 contexts, students need systematic exposure to and practice in target genres in order to develop a sensitivity to a range of generic features. These include content and formal schemata for genres, the interpersonal dimension of text, textual organization, and stylistic appropriateness. In order to avoid an overly prescriptive approach that might lead to a stereotypical view of genres, this chapter has stressed the need for students to be exposed to different example texts from the same genre and across different genres, in order to sensitize them to the notion of generic variation.

In a process-oriented syllabus (Breen, 1989), where the syllabus is considered as a posthoc check-list rather than a prescriptive blueprint, the sort of generic description presented here would still be very useful. Used in this context, without unduly manipulating learners, the description would provide a means for teachers to monitor learning in such a way as to ensure that the various aspects of target genres were mastered.

Ultimately, classroom application depends on the teacher, who will be responsible for the methodology. It is up to individual teachers to decide what part the generic description provided by a linguistic approach to genre plays in their classes and how it is manipulated in the various classroom learning tasks. The success or failure of the linguistic approach to genre presented in this article depends very much, therefore, on teachers who are well prepared.

Part III

English for Specific Purposes

5

Teaching the Literature Review to International Graduate Students

John M. Swales & Stephanie Lindemann
The University of Michigan

From a rhetorical perspective, doctoral education in the U.S. can be seen as a cumulative, if untidy, acquiring of expertise in the academic genre set that orchestrates a graduate student's chosen field. We can see this as a kind of generic escalation, marked by steps that impose increasing levels of communicative demand on the student. Thus, in terms of academic speaking, the student progresses from class participation to presentation, and from there to internal colloquia, regional conferences, and finally, to speaking at national and international conferences. The student's instructional trajectory might well take the steps of first working as a tutor or as an assistant in the lab, then as a teaching assistant running discussion sections attached to a lecture course, and on to having sole responsibility for a small class. A typical writing sequence might show a cumulative demonstration of expertise in course assignments, term papers, independent research papers, research proposals, publications, and finally a dissertation.

Although we believe that this account has a certain kind of clarity that might especially appeal to those interested in genre-based approaches to advanced literacy and oracy development, we also acknowledge that it is oversimplified and idealized in a number of ways. First, it ignores the fact that much of contemporary doctoral writing (like faculty writing) is avowedly or prospectively multipurpose. A particular piece might serve to satisfy a program requirement (such as a preliminary examination), set the groundwork for a publication, be a follow-up to a presentation, or be projected to form part of a dissertation. This last is particularly common in the science and engineering fields with their preference for an "anthology" dissertation, the central chapters of which consist of a small number of published or accepted papers. Second, the simple account leaves out all those semihidden genres that are, in fact, strong determinants of a student's degree of success (Swales, 1996); these are genres like *fellowship applications, curricula vitae, responses to reviewers' comments, meetings with advisors, discussions with visitors,* and the like. Third, recent investigators have shown that the process of putting together a plausible Ph.D. student persona is much more complicated than might be supposed from the foregoing. Belcher (1994), Casanave (1995) and especially Prior (1998) have provided evidence of the complex two-way interactions of students and faculty, of the importance of local defining moments in relationships, and of the "up and down" character of progress toward goals. The progress of the doctoral pilgrim is undoubtedly beset by thickets, Sloughs of Despond, and stony ground. Finally, the very nature of those genre goals are often themselves discovered and coconstructed over time. As long ago as 1984, Miller crucially observed that when we learn a genre set, we can also learn to do things that we did not know we could do, such as asking for a second opinion, questioning an editorial decision, or inserting an epigraph. Boxer and Pickering (1995) showed, for example, that international students do not always know that when their colleagues complain about a particular department, instructor, or assignment, this is, as much as anything else, an opening for commiseration, sharing of woes, and hence rapport building.

Even with all these concerns and caveats, viewing doctoral education as a generic ladder makes a fair amount of pragmatic sense. Indeed, at the English Language Institute at Michigan, we have developed a "longitudinal" EAP syllabus designed to help international students with these jumps in communicative demand. The first author has been responsible during the last decade for the two most advanced graduate student writing courses in a four-level sequence: Research Paper Writing (ELI 520, Fall semester) and Dissertation and Prospectus Writing (ELI 600, Winter semester). The participants in these courses are all volunteers (although sometimes "leaned on" by their departmental advisors) and can come from any of the university's 19 colleges. Although there may be an occasional student from, say, music or theater, most are working in the broadly quantitative areas of science, social science, and engineering. They can also come from any country (the university's lone student from Albania attended in 1997), but most come from East Asia, particularly from China, Taiwan, Korea, Japan, and Thailand. There is usually a faculty member or postdoctoral researcher in the class. On average, about 20 attend ELI 520 and 15 take ELI 600. They enjoy, toward the end of their student careers, the social atmosphere of an across-the-campus class and its weird revelations of how things can be so different elsewhere. For example, they come to realize that some departments and programs are much less or much more supportive of their students than their own. They relish academic stories and scandals, and academic humor and parody, as in:

- Recommendation letter: "I am pleased to say that this candidate is a former colleague of mine."

- Joke: "How many doctoral students does it take to change a lightbulb?" "Only one, but it takes five years."

- Dissertation acknowledgments: "Finally, I would like to thank the chair of my committee without whose help and immense attention to detail this dissertation would have been completed years ago."

The classes meet once a week for two hours and are supported by individual consultations, and by help provided by the ELI's Writing Lab, staffed in 1997–1998 by the second author.

The ELI 600 material includes attention to those semihidden—or occluded—genres mentioned earlier, such as *curricula vitae*, *job application letters*, *journal correspondence,* and *fellowship applications*. Other topics include titles, acknowledgments and conclusions. One special focus involves metadiscourse (e.g., Mauranen, 1993) because of its strong relevance to the successful composition of long texts such as dissertations. (For example, nearly all dissertation opening chapters contain a substantial outline of the whole work.) In these classes, the amount of homework and for-class writing is deliberately kept light because the students are all busily engaged on their own research projects and the audience for their writing is not directly the ELI instructor but departmental advisors and instructors, screening panels for conferences, or journal editors and reviewers. In ELI 600, the major exceptions to this stance occur with the *conference abstract*, the *conference poster* (a recent addition), and the *literature review*. This last is the topic of this chapter.

THE LITERATURE REVIEW REVIEWED

The Literature Review (LR) is a part-genre or sub-genre of wide significance in the academic world and in graduate education. It may occupy an eponymous and separate section of a thesis or dissertation, or it may be incorporated within an article introduction, a prospectus outline, or a proposal. University faculty often complain that their students do not write impressive LRs, not so much because they have not done the requisite readings, but because of the poor organization of the material. Typical complaints include the following: LRs are "not sufficiently theme-based," "not structured according to the issues," "insufficiently informed by the research hypotheses," "merely a list," "boringly chronological," or "just describes each piece of research one by one without adequate linkage." Even at a prestigious research university, doctoral student anxiety on this topic can run high. In December 1998, the first author was asked to offer a workshop on this topic for both native and non-native speakers. Instead of the 30 to 40 expected, more than 200 showed up; clearly, professional expectations in this regard can be threatening, perhaps especially for those working in interdisciplinary areas.

However, for a number of reasons, the LR is one of the more difficult part-genres for an EAP writing instructor to teach. First, as we shall attempt to show, the

LR is not really susceptible to the kinds of move analysis that have proved popular for introductions (e.g., Swales, 1990), abstracts (e.g., Melander, Swales, & Fredrickson, 1997), results (e.g., Brett, 1994; Thompson, 1993), discussions (e.g., Hopkins & Dudley-Evans, 1988; Peng, 1987), and many kinds of professional documents. The second important reason is that our current information on the LR is bifurcated toward the extremes of specificity and generality with little of substance in the middle. On the one side, we know a lot about tense (Malcolm, 1987), citation (Bloch & Chi, 1995), reporting verbs (Hyland, 2000; Thompson & Ye, 1991), and adjuncts of reporting (Tadros, 1985), all on the lexico-syntactic level. Some of this knowledge is reflected in writing guides, which contain instructions on (for example) the placement and form citations should take (Biddle & Holland, 1987; Day, 1998; Kronick, 1985; Michaelson, 1986). On the other, there is a subtantial amount of advice with regard to macro features such as aims and purposes, library searches, and taking notes (Biddle & Holland, 1987; Bond & Magistrale, 1987; Michaelson, 1986).

In contrast, we find very little information about how writers get from the macro level to the micro level. Manuals do exist that deal with midlevel functions such as how to use citations (Becker, 1986), what and how much to cite (Woodford, 1976), paraphrasing and synthesis (Biddle & Holland, 1987; Hamp-Lyons & Courter, 1984), or even possible ways of organizing the LR (Rudestam & Newton, 1992; Weissberg & Buker, 1990). However, advice given on organizing an LR is often so brief and general as to be unlikely to enlighten the potential writer who is trying to find out what to include and in what order. For example, Day's (1998) ambitiously titled chapter "How to write the introduction" is a mere three pages; The *APA Publication Manual* (1994) advises the writer to both "assume that the reader has knowledge in the field for which you are writing and does not require a complete digest" (p. 11) and "develop the problem with enough breadth and clarity to make it generally understood by as wide a professional audience as possible" (p. 12). As students might say, "Go figure"! Although some (especially Rudestam & Newton, 1992; Weissberg & Buker, 1990) suggest possible ways of organizing LRs, they only mention a few candidate structures. What this chapter hopes to provide by illustration, then, is how to negotiate a solid middle between the macro and micro levels in a relatively small-scale case study context.

TEACHING THE LITERATURE REVIEW

True to the spirit of this volume, we now offer some actual genre-based teaching materials for consideration and possible adaptation. What immediately follow are the handouts given to the ELI 600 class about a third of the way through the 14-week course. Although they are somewhat lengthy, we include them here because (a) the material is currently "freeware" and (b) some grasp of it is essential for the subsequent analysis and commentary.

ELI 600. LITERATURE REVIEW

Fulan A. Fulani is writing his prospectus. The proposed topic for his dissertation is:

A Formative Evaluation
of
Current Problems in Engineering Education

He is now at work on the Literature Review. He has divided this into six sections. He has reached Section Five, which deals with the teaching of communication skills to Engineers.

He has managed to find nine items for this section. This was hard work as the papers were scattered across a wide range of journals. He has made notes on the articles and has assembled photocopies of the abstracts on separate pieces of paper.

He is now looking at the abstracts and trying to puzzle out which studies go with which, and for what kind of reason. As an ex-student of ELI writing classes, he knows that he cannot just describe or summarize each one separately.

He knows that he has to: a) *impose some order* on the material in order to demonstrate that there is an *organizing mind* at work, and b) exhibit some appropriate level of *evaluation.*

He recollects his advisor's comment, but he is not quite sure if he fully understands it: "One final thing, Fulani. Either you control the previous literature, or it will control you."

But what order and organization? This is his first problem.

What can you suggest? Draw a tree-diagram of the nine abstracts that follow (using number or first author's name) outlining your proposed scheme. Come with your diagram on an overhead or a handout for the next class. Be prepared to explain the thinking processes behind your choices.

1. Van Hoek, J. (1990). Information in Manufacturing Systems and the Needs of the Graduating Engineer. *European Journal of Professional Education*, 17: 67–77.

Few opportunities for developing communication skills exist in the crowded curricula of most B.S. Engineering courses in Western Europe. It is thus important that those few available are spent on fundamental aspects of the most relevant areas. The course developed at the University of Amsterdam is built around case studies of actual manufacturing problems. Students are required to form engineer-manager groups as task forces to solve problems as they arise. In this way they become socialized into the engineering community. Evidence is presented from student evaluations as to the success of this approach.

2. Scott, J. (1989). The Logical Structure of Technical Reports: Software Support. *Journal of Technical Documentation*, 11: 273–282.

The "expression" problem in writing engineering technical reports is secondary to the "comprehension" problem—i.e., the ability to perceive relevance, organize material into sections, and then organize sections into a logical order. This paper begins by considering the question of efficiency and the contributions that "logical sections in logical order" can make to the effectiveness of reports. It then presents an algorithmic IBM-compatible software program which encourages the kind of analysis and organisation underlying effective report writing.

3. McWrath, A. (1984). Communication Skills for Engineering Undergraduates: An Engineer's Response. *The Professional Engineer*, 47: 21–23.

The growing employment of "specialists" in communication skills has recently become problematic in many Engineering Schools. As a professor of Engineering, I am committed to helping my undergraduates improve their writing and speaking abilities. I argue that this is best achieved in the context of real Engineering courses taught by real engineers, not by "outsiders" to the profession who often fail to understand the nature and purpose of engineering communications.

4. Leon, A. & Deng, W. (1993). Developing Communication Skills in Civil Engineering Students. *The Civil Engineer*, 73: 507–519.

Civil Engineers are responsible for devising economic practical solutions to satisfy the needs of the community for roads, bridges, water supplies and other major works. Throughout their education and training it is unlikely that they will receive much formal training in effective communication. To remedy this, a new course of communication studies was introduced two years ago at Manchester University. The essential feature is to have all the communication topics set in the context of civil engineering practice. Thus, a large civil engineering contract is simulated and all aspects of communication skills are related to the simulation. Preliminary results suggest that the students have appreciated the linking of communication studies with civil engineering work.

5. Ahmed, S. & Williams, B. (1991). Content in Engineering Courses for Engineering Students. *Studies in Higher Education*, 33: 74–92.

Communication courses for Engineering undergraduates vary widely in content, from mass media on the one hand to the social responsibility of the engineer on the other. As a rule, students find little interest in such courses because of their distance from their immediate concerns (Olsen, 1987). In contrast, our research shows good responses—as measured by interview and questionnaire—for courses that focus on the day-to-day communication problems of engineers, both with their colleagues and the general public.

6. Lo, C. and Li, C-S. (1993). Empowering Female Students in Engineering Education. *Cross Currents*, 24: 96–109.

Many reports speak of a "chilly climate" toward women engineering students (EEGR Survey [1991] for an overview). Our experimental program provides opportunities for women students to develop their communication skills in sheltered, women-only environments and then apply their new-found confidence in mainstream situations. Follow-up studies report improved grades, more effective participation in class, and increased job offers ($p = 0.5$; QZ = 4.78; ff = X4+ on the Fittori scoring rule).

7. Pradip, S. & Rahim, R. (1992). Moving from National to International Prominence: Computer Engineering in Bombay. *UNESCO Journal of Technical Education*, 23: 2–14.

There has been much talk of the "Bombay Miracle" (e.g., *Time* 8/3/92), but rather less of the communication failures of the computer engineers and scientists in the city. We have developed training courses for engineering graduates stressing cross-cultural differences in negotiation, writing styles, patent laws and contractual obligations among Indian, Japanese and North American leaders in technological change. Although no empirical evidence is yet available, there are signs that the case approach to success and failure in Indian computer engineering initiatives for export is having beneficial results.

8. Sullivan, P. (1991). Problems in Communication Skills Courses. *Journal of Technical Education*, 24: 23–40.

A survey of undergraduate technical communication programs in the US (n = 77) suggests that the acceptability of the program to both students and faculty does not depend on the quality of the program (as measured by staff profiles, curriculum analysis, and level of integration with engineering courses). Rather, the prime determinant is engineering faculty support (or otherwise) for the program. The study suggests that the way forward lies more in canvassing for faculty support than in internal improvements.

9. Fredrickson, K. (1993). Provision for the Non-native Speaker in Graduate Engineering Programs. *English for Specific Purposes*, 12: 222–233.

The increasing numbers of NNS in US graduate Engineering programs have caused various kinds of strain, including faculty burn-out (Perillo 1986), tension between NS and NNS populations for financial support (Luebs 1990) and dissatisfaction with NNS after graduation when their English skills are shown to be less than promised (Swales 1990). An experimental program of "English internships" with US research associates and scientists has proved highly effective in helping NNS students develop their technical writing skills in English. The conclusions suggest that such programs should be expanded to other campuses.[1]

In 1998 we recorded the class presentations and explanations of the schemes (or architectures) the students had devised and the subsequent discussions of their approaches. There were eventually 13 offerings in all, 11 by students and two by visiting scholars attending the class (one a German in philosophy and the other a Brazilian in applied linguistics). Three of the overheads (or handouts) are reproduced: those of a Puerto Rican student from Public Health (B2), a Korean student from Social Psychology (S2), and a Thai student from S. E. Asian Studies (S5).

The public health student offered a general–specific model. The psychology student, at the time writing his dissertation and with a tenure-track job offer from a major research university already in his pocket, said that he "tried to create [his] own story" and wanted to show this at the outset by contrasting a "bad example" and

[1] In case readers are curious, the nine abstracts were specially constructed for this activity. Nearly all participants, however, believed that they were authentic.

a "good example." The student from S. E. Asian studies, in contrast, offered a problem–solution format, and one uncannily similar to the classic schema of Hoey (1983): situation —> problem —> solution —> evaluation. A further clear difference among the three architectures can be seen in their handling of Abstract 8, the one where the author basically argues that nothing can be done in this area without the support of the engineering faculty. The public-health student put it first because of its greatest generality; the S. E. Asian Studies student put it last. The psychology student, however, dropped it altogether, ending his presentation with: "... that's my story. So, I dropped study 8, which doesn't have anything to do with this claim."

Table 5.1
Literature Reviews: Initial Individual Architectures

Social Sciences:	
S1 Organizational Psychology (Korea)	[3 5 1 4 7] [6 2] [9 7] [8]
S2 Social Psychology (Korea)	[3 2 5] [4] [6] [1 7] [9]
S3 Social Work (Japan)	[5] [8 9 3 4] [7 9 2 6]
S4 Urban Planning (Korea)	[1 5 3 4] [7 6 9 2 8]
S5 S. E. Asian Studies (Thailand)	[1 4] [2 3 6 7 9] [2 3 4 6 9] [5 8]
Humanities:	
H1 Vis. Sch., Applied Linguistics (Brazil)	[8] [5 6 9 7] [3 1 4 2]
H2 Vis. Sch., Philosophy (Germany)	[1 5 8] [4 6 3] [2 3 9]
H3 Latin-American Literature (Mexico)	[1 4 7 8 9] [6] [2 3 4 5 8]
H4 Theater (Thailand)	[5] [8 3] [4 1] [6] [9] [7] [2]
Biological & Health Sciences:	
B1 Dental Public Health (Thailand)	[3 5 8] [1 4 7] [9 2 6]
B2 Public Health (Puerto Rico)	[8] [3 2] [1 4 5] [6 9 7]
B3 Cellular Biology (China)	[8] [5 3 4 2] [1 6 7 9]
Physical Sciences & Engineering:	
E1 IOE (Korea)	[5 1 8] [3 4 9 6]

The full panoply of "intelligent variation" is shown in Table 5.1. We have subclassified the students' provenance using the graduate school's four divisions. The numbers refer to the numbers of the abstracts listed on the handout, which are then given in the order in which they appeared on the diagrams. The square brackets refer to their schematic groupings; in previous classes these groupings have tended to be closely correlated with paragraphs in the subsequent write-ups.

As the table shows, the number of groupings ranged from two (E1) to seven (H4), which is likely to be reflected later in variation in the number of paragraphs. Visual scan of the features in the table shows few overall tendencies, although several combinations appear together frequently (e.g., Abstract 4 appears with either 3 or 1 in all but two LR structures). However, readers may have noted that all groups except the social sciences group consistently placed Abstract 8 near the beginning, almost always in the first grouping. In contrast, the social scientists tended to place Abstract 8 at the end; one student (S2) resolved its problematic nature by boldly dropping it. Another detectable trend is quite understandable in that a majority of students placed the three "special cases" (6, 7, and 9) toward the end; the two most obvious exceptions to this were H1 and H3. Finally, S5's structure is more complex, in that she repeated a number of citations.

However, these tendencies may be deceptive. For example, when we checked the four biological and health sciences students from the previous year with a particular view to seeing how they had handled Abstract 8, we found these patterns:

[1 4 5] [3 8] [9 6] [7 2]
[5 4 1] [6 9] [8 3 2]
[5 3 8] [1 4 7] [6 2 9]
[5 4 1 9] [6 7] [8 3 2]

As can be seen, only one of these four placed Abstract 8 in the first group.

In the 1998 class discussion, one of the most debated versions was that of H3, a Mexican student in Latin American literature. Her primary opening category was "engineering student populations by geographical region." One of the social scientists (S1) observed that this choice was "not the major thing," and the instructor noted that it would be "difficult to write up." In response, in the intervening period before the next class, the student wrote an impassioned defense of her scheme, arguing that in different educational locations, needs and solutions could well be different and that these need to be taken into account. Here is her opening paragraph (unedited):

> My last assignment reflected the categories I, as a student of literature, would have chosen, not what an engineering student would. I think I did not see the relevance of other choices, and the biased side of mine. Maybe the tendency to classify by country the literary production comes, among other things, from the awareness of territory that I see in post colonial countries such as mine. So, this explains, in a way, my inclination to do what I did in my classification. Maybe that also explains the devotion of one category for considering engineering women. I see that this classification was not really a "scientific" one as the other approaches showed in class where the categories were the result of a very different way of thinking. Personally, doing this exercise was important to me mainly because it showed me the way that I am used to thinking, the ideas I have about other fields and my criteria for forming categories.

No EAP instructor could wish for a more eloquent or perceptive response, and when the class read it the next week, the others were happy to retract their criticisms and to acknowledge that they too had learned something new about the academic world from H3's justification of her "post-colonial" thinking.

Overall, two general precepts emerge from this first phase of this LR exercise. The first is that the *imposition of order* on this recalcitrant material can take many plausible forms, even when the literature available for review and the dissertation topic are preset. Secondly, the nature of that order seems to be partly affected by the participants' disciplinary training and education. The literature student, as we have seen, focused on territory; in contrast, B3, a biochemist who spends much of his day performing laboratory experiments, said that he organized his literature review "following the steps of science research." In 1996, a Peruvian systematic botanist produced, as part of his disciplinary tradition, a complex multilayered taxonomy. Intellectual confidence may also play a part, at least evidenced by the fact that S2, a brilliant and highly successful student, was the only individual in 1998 to deliberately exclude an abstract because it did not fit his argument. On the other hand, in these groups of well-acculturated students, we have not been able to find any influences from the participants' first language and culture. We suspect that any remaining traces of national–cultural proclivities have been overlaid by disciplinary conventions.

At the end of this first session, participants are asked to send their first draft LRs to the instructor before the next class. They are reminded that there may well have been something to learn from the class discussion and are warned that, irrespective of the merits or otherwise of a particular scheme, some approaches may be harder to write up than others. In fact, a number of the class did make adjustments. Here is the attached commentary from H1, the visiting scholar in applied linguistics (unedited):

> Brief comments on why I changed my framework:
>
> When I first thought of the framework to be used in the section, I imagined it would be easier to start it using the "bad-news-first, light-at-the-end-of-the-tunnel-last" approach. Two things, however, made me change. The first was the group discussion (particularly [S1's] argument of that as issue of further consideration). The second one, was your foresight of how tricky that construction could be. I even tried to keep my original framework, but eventually gave up. Concerning Sullivan (1991), as you will easily realize, I didn't know where to put it (neither now, nor at the time I tried to set up my framework). It didn't fit the logical structure of my argument, but I felt compelled to use it anyway.
>
> You will also realize that I made some other changes in structure of paragraphs. These were much more related to making both my writing and the flowing of the argument an easier task.

In the second session, the drafts are returned with comments on organization, transitions, and flow, and with suggested textual emendations. Attention then focuses on several issues of various kinds. The first concerns questions of metadiscourse, which had already been extensively aired in pre-LR sessions; more particularly, what might be said to link Section Five of the review with the preceding and following ones. For this, a number of opening paragraphs are photocopied for review, each identified by a letter. The class is first asked to try to work out who the authors were. Although this activity might appear to be a rather trivial game, it does have the serious underlying purpose of making the participants cast their minds back to what had been shown and said the previous week. Then certain points are taken up, as in the italicized pieces of this opening sentence:

> This section *provides* several case studies *concerning about* the teaching of communication skills to engineering students.

Next, openings are reviewed for the claims made. Consider these two extracts:

> For this reason, the area of teaching communications skills has received considerable attention in terms of its development.
> Given the growing importance of communication skills in Engineering not much research about it has been carried out.

Who is right? And how might their judgments be affected by home disciplines?

Another major topic involves "copying," paraphrase, generalization, and summary (Hyland, 2000). However, for this, extracts from the drafts written by a previous class are used because class questions and challenges concerning excessive "copying" or "lifting" from the original can be embarrassing or confrontational. Here is a shortened version of the current handout for this:

> Here is Abstract 7 [not given here]
>
> On the second sheet you will find a number of "treatments" of Pradip & Rahim. As you look at them in pairs, view them in terms of these parameters. Write your codes in the margin.
> Information (or the amount of detail in P & R that is retained)
> I o (the amount is about right)
> I + (more information is retained that really necessary)
> I - (the information is insufficient)
>
> Paraphrase (or the amount of rewriting/summarizing of the original)
> P o (nicely done; captures the essence of the original in partly different words)
> P + (perhaps too much changed; doesn't accurately represent the original)
> P - (too much lifted from the original; raises issues of plagiarism)
>
> Linkage & Commentary
> LC o (adequately relates and evaluates P & R in terms of other work)
> LC + (is overly concerned with evaluation)
> LC - (merely describes P & R in terms of itself)
>
> Finally, of the 8 versions, which two would you *most* have wanted to write? And which two would you *least* have wanted to write?
> A.
> Another communication program is developed by Pradip and Rahim (1992) for engineering graduates. All of these programs show appreciable results.

> B.
> Pradip & Rahim have developed training courses for engineering graduates stressing cross-cultural differences via a case study approach of success and failure in Indian computer engineering initiatives for export, and again find signs of beneficial results.
>
> C.
> In their article Pradip and Rahim (1992) talk about the successes in Indian computer engineering and also point out its weakness as a result of communication failures. They relate this with cross-cultural differences in negotiations, writing, laws and contractual obligations among Indian, Japanese and North American leaders in technology.
>
> D.
> Finally, there is one paper that deals with the communication problems of practicing engineers rather than students; once again, the case study approach appears to have been beneficial—this time for computer engineers in Bombay (Pradip & Rahim, 1992).

The final element in the second class session concerns the role, if any, of evaluative comments and how any of these might need to be related to the goals of Fulani's dissertation. Participants are then asked to revise their LRs and resubmit them.

The original nine abstracts, including the citational information, amount to a little more than 900 words. In 1998 the revised drafts varied in length from about 350 words (H2, the German visiting scholar in philosophy) to about 750 words (S1, a Korean in organizational psychology). Most of these are now pretty impressive scholarly documents. For example, here is how H1, the Brazilian applied linguist, eventually dealt with the "tricky" problem of Sullivan (1991):

> The only large-scale study ... (Sullivan, 1991) suggests that the key factor to the acceptability of the program (and by inference to its success) is not the quality of the program itself, but faculty support for it... The issues ... deserve further consideration, not only because of its intrinsic importance, but also because of its implications for the formative evaluation purported by this study. That discussion belongs, however, to the next section of this chapter. [!]

Another example consists of S1's closing paragraph and demonstrates, we believe, a *convincing* level of evaluation, excellent cohesion, and smoothness of argument:

> Overall, researchers seem to agree with the importance of using real-life context in engineering communication courses. Despite the apparent consensus about *what* to teach, there still remains the problem of *how* to teach. Researchers have tried various methods to teach engineers how to communicate and each method appears to be successful for a specific purpose and a special population. Considering that effectiveness of a specific method depends on some moderating variables, future studies should focus on the effects of these moderating parameters, such as purposes of the course, educational and cultural settings, and target population. [original emphases]

The third and final session is largely given over to celebration and congratulations on jobs well done, as well as dealing with some minor editing. It seems to us that Fulan A. Fulani is well on his way to writing a successful dissertation prospectus!

DISCUSSION

Several stages of reading as well as writing are involved in the process of composing a literature review. At the outset, there is the business of finding relevant items or literature, often involving database searches, increasingly on the web, and taking notes on these items. As it happens, this aspect of obtaining the relevant references is well documented in various literatures and regularly demonstrated in workshops run by library staff. Transforming those separate readings into a succinct and coherent account of a disciplinary or interdisciplinary line of research demands a particular kind of reading–writing connection which, inter alia, needs to take intertextual account of citation and paraphrase. Beyond that, there are questions of sequencing and focus in terms of the researcher's goals. Overall, the LR is rhetorically a highly demanding part-genre that generally presents greater rhetorical problems than methods and results sections.

Although some writing manuals discuss several of the rhetorical demands mentioned, and a few suggest different possible ways of ordering studies in a literature review, most have little to say on how or why a writer should choose a particular approach when constructing the review. The non-native speakers who participated in the activity described in this chapter not only came up with a greater number of intelligent structures than are typically proposed in the literature, but also were able to elucidate much about the reasoning behind the various approaches. They noted that these structures were often related to the discipline of the author, and that some structures that they might not have previously considered (such as H3's geographical organization) might be appropriate in some cases. These sorts of valuable observations can be enhanced by the fact that participants not only have to manage the original abstracts, but also must pay attention to and co-negotiate the observations and preferences of others. This, then, is an intertextual exercise rich in perspectives, which may, as H3 noted, show "the way that [they are] used to thinking, the ideas [they] have about other fields and [their] criteria for forming categories." The participants' observations and perceptions will now, in an effort to develop *transfer of learning* (c.f. Wolfson & Willinsky, 1998), be directed toward their readings in their own disciplines, so that they will be more aware of how and why authors might put a literature review together in a particular way.

A further positive aspect of the exercise is its product-oriented emphasis. Issues of organization, metadiscourse, claims made, paraphrase, generalization, summary, and evaluation, as well as the finer language points associated with them, are often treated separately; here they are all addressed in a cohesive activity that brings them together in a meaningful and practical way. Students are thus able to see how these aspects work together to build literature reviews that are integrated into their papers and address their own research questions.

The instructor's role in EAP writing classes, perhaps especially those that are not discipline-specific, has long been a contentious issue (Johns, 1997; Spack, 1988). However, when Spack wrote in 1988, "To suggest that an ESL/EFL instructor can unlock the door to the entire academic universe of discourse is to overlook the complexity and diversity among and within disciplines" (p. 708), she started from an odd premise. No instructor, however polymathic and experienced, can ever really hope to unlock that huge door; what she or he *can* do is help the participants unlock that door for themselves. At least in the case of the junior scholars attending ELI 520 and ELI 600, they can be helped to become more observant readers of the discoursal conventions of their fields and thereby deepen their rhetorical perspectives on their own disciplines. They can be persuaded to help in the instructor's own investigations of academic discourse by conducting mini-studies in their own fields. Indeed, their highly developed analytical skills in their own fields and their commitment to empirical evidence make them surprisingly useful and willing collaborators in various kinds of linguistic analysis. They can also be led to recognize that, if and when they return to their own countries, they will likely have to help some of their own conationals with academic or professional writing in English.

This has been a practitioner paper, written by practitioners for practitioners. Not unexpectedly, writing in this sub-genre, constructing this account of what happens in about five hours of class time, has had its proactive aspects as well as its reflective ones. On one level, we can now see how it would be profitable to give more attention to reporting verbs, especially as Hyland (2000) has recently shown how these vary greatly from discipline to discipline. We can also in hindsight now conceive of methodological refinements, much bolstered by Gosden (1998). For example, with e-mail now widely available, we would like to experiment with having at least some of the "architectures" constructed by disciplinarily close pairs rather than by single individuals. More importantly, the act of writing up this story has both uncovered a weakness in the original design and produced a promising solution. We would be the first to concede that the current LR exercise is very much a *sui generis* activity and only lightly connected to Fulani's major rhetorical purpose/primary hypothesis, which we do not in fact know. The closest we come to those larger communicative purposes is the brief discussion of the claims made, that is, whether we "know" quite a lot or remarkably little about the teaching of communication skills to engineering students. As it happens, the LR in a prospectus or dissertation proposal can probably get away with being agnostic about such assessments. No so in the dissertation itself; not so after the research findings are in. This sea change is, of course, one important reason why students discover (often to their chagrin) that they cannot simply "import" their prospectus LRs into their dissertations. In the future, the LR unit will extend to a fourth week. Participants will be told to fast-forward to 12 months later, to a time when Fulani is writing the second chapter of his dissertation. Let us imagine that his research, among other things, has pointed to these two conclusions:

1. The rapid spread of computer technology has radically changed the communication skills needed by engineering students;

2. Both engineering education and practice are becoming more globalized, with increasing focus on binational and multinational projects.

How would participants *now* write up the nine abstracts? (And perhaps two later pieces of research that need to be incorporated, including one by Fulani himself!)

Finally, on the broader front, the advanced non-native speaking writers who figure prominently in this chapter are not the novice writers with "their often simplistic sterile theories of texts" described by Johns in this volume. But they, too, can be helped both to become better genre theorists and to acquire a finer appreciation of intertextuality, with all this last might imply for appropriate paraphrase (Currie, 1998). For these purposes, there is considerable "modeling" in the activities we have described. However, because of the exigencies of the LR part-genre, this has not taken the form of "traditional" genre analysis with its focus on instructor-presented cycles of "moves" (for example, Swales, 1990). Instead, the modeled architectures are devised by the participants and are then presented, discussed, and perhaps modified. In this sociocognitive process, the demonstrated heterogeneity of responses to a shared task, probably influenced in subtle ways by disciplinary approach and outlook, actually turns out to be a source of enlightenment rather than confusion.

6
Genre and ESL Reading: A Classroom Study

Sunny Hyon
California State University, San Bernardino

Amid interest in genre for various L1 and L2 literacy contexts, there have been few investigations of effects of genre-based pedagogy on students' reading and writing development. Evaluation of different approaches to teaching genres is particularly germane in light of recent debates over the efficacy of such instruction (Cope & Kalantzis, 1993; Fahnestock, 1993; Freedman, 1993, 1994; Reid, 1987; Williams & Colomb, 1993). In a 1993 issue of *Research in the Teaching of English*, L1 composition researcher Aviva Freedman has suggested that, at best, explicit teaching of genres has only restricted value in improving students' writing. She hypothesized that although such instruction may be useful for some students whose learning style is in concert, it is generally unnecessary because students acquire genre knowledge tacitly, and it can even be dangerous if an instructor has inaccurate knowledge of the genres taught (Freedman, 1993; see also Freedman, 1994). Disagreeing with Freedman, Williams and Colomb (1993) asserted that writing, like other skills, can be learned at least in part through direct guidance. They argued that "the harm [of teaching genres] is illusory and that the benefits are many and exceed their costs" (p. 253). Similar debates over the efficacy of genre-based teaching have developed between genre and "process" proponents in Australian educational circles (see discussions in Cope & Kalantzis, 1993; Reid, 1987).

These controversies, along with the continued development of genre-based teaching applications, highlight the need for examining the effects of such instruction on students' reading and writing development. Indeed, in discussing her own skepticism, Freedman (1993) acknowledged that "the research evidence concerning genre acquisition is limited" (p. 226) and called for "more focused research and theoretic consideration of this question" (p. 222). She urged educators to resist the impulse to teach about genres without first asking "what grounds we have for believing that such explication will in fact enhance their learning" (Freedman, 1994, p. 193).

As approaches to genre-based pedagogy vary significantly (Hyon, 1996), investigations need to be conducted of different approaches to such teaching in a variety of classroom contexts. This chapter addresses the need for such studies by evaluating one instance of genre-based instruction in an ESL reading course at a large, midwestern research university. The researcher examined student exams and oral interviews to assess the effects of the course on building students' genre knowledge and developing their L2 reading abilities. The chapter begins by reviewing recent scholarship on the role of genre knowledge in L2 reading and then argues for more investigations of genre-based reading instruction. This section is followed by a description of the approach to instruction and the design of the exams and student interviews. The findings from the exams and interviews are then discussed, highlighting their implications for L2 reading and genre scholarship.

THE ROLE OF GENRE IN ESL READING INSTRUCTION

In the last thirty years, Goodman's (1967) theory of reading as a "psycholinguistic guessing game" has been a prominent framework for conceptualizing both L1 and L2 text processing. In his model, efficient reading is seen as a process in which readers make predictions about text meaning based on only partial decoding of graphic cues. Within this framework, background knowledge is key for helping readers anticipate and construct meaning: "The reader has available to him and brings to his reading the sum total of his experience and his language and thought development" (Goodman, 1967, p. 130).

Since this early research, other work on text processing has framed readers' background knowledge in terms of schemata, or "knowledge structures" in the mind, which shape readers' interpretations of texts (Carrell & Eisterhold, 1983, p. 556; see also Carrell, 1984; Reid, 1993, for discussions of schema and L2 reading). Several types of schemata have been proposed for effective reading comprehension: content schemata, "background knowledge of the content area of a text" (Carrell & Eisterhold, 1983, p. 560); formal schemata, "background knowledge of the formal, rhetorical organizational structures of different types of texts" (Carrell & Eisterhold, 1983, p. 560); and linguistic schemata, "prior linguistic knowledge" (Carrell, 1988, p. 4). Focusing on the first two global types of knowledge, a number of studies have shown that readers' prior awareness of text content or rhetorical organization facilitates comprehension and recall (Carrell, 1985, 1992; Floyd & Carrell, 1987; Hewings & Henderson, 1987; see also reviews in Floyd & Carrell, 1987; Grabe, 1991, and this volume).

Some scholars have discussed the importance of prior knowledge about texts in terms of genre knowledge, a concept that includes, although goes beyond, awareness of organizational structure, or formal schemata (Johns, 1997; Nystrand,

1986). L1 composition researcher Martin Nystrand (1986), for example, suggested that genre, or "what sort of text is under way" (p. 61), is the first element shaping readers' interpretations of a text, guiding their expectations about the text's topic and the author's comment on that topic. Similarly, Johns (1997) contends that knowledge about genres, including awareness of their names, communicative purposes, formal features, reader and writer roles, content, and contexts, is key for effective reading: "Genre knowledge provides a shortcut for the initiated to the processing and production of familiar written texts" (p. 21).

Some schema and genre researchers have highlighted the role of instruction in building L2 readers' understanding of genre structure (formal schemata) to enhance reading effectiveness (Carrell, 1985; Davis, Lange, & Samuels, 1988; Hewings & Henderson, 1987; see also discussion in Grabe, this volume). Focusing on the effects of instruction in discipline-specific genres, Hewings and Henderson (1987), for example, discovered that teaching ESL social science students the organization of economics bank review articles helped them to comprehend and evaluate article content and "to perceive a difference in form and function between economics textbooks and bank review articles" (p. 174).

These studies have provided both experimental and anecdotal evidence that explicit instruction in the formal features of texts builds schemata and enhances L2 reading abilities. However, additional research is needed in order to assess more fully the effects of genre-based instruction on ESL reading, as previous investigations have been limited in the kinds of rhetorically based instruction studied. That is, schema research has generally focused on the impact of teaching text structure to the exclusion of other genre features such as content type, stylistic features, and communicative purposes. These studies have also generally confined measures of training effects to reading recall tests and have not considered other kinds of data, such as open-ended text descriptions and student interviews, in evaluating the effects of genre-based teaching on reading.[1]

This research extends previous investigations of genre-based reading instruction in both the type of teaching examined and the measures used in evaluation. The present study focuses on the impact of teaching genres along several dimensions, including content, structure, language style, and purpose. The researcher analyzes data from both text description exams and oral interviews to assess the instruction's effects on students' genre knowledge and their L2 reading. It is recognized that verbal reports are limited in what they reveal about actual learning experiences, as they only capture students' conscious knowledge and may only elicit what students "expect people [e.g. the experimenter] to want to hear instead of what they actually believe" (Cook, 1993, p. 132). Despite these limitations, however, the interview reports, together with the text description exams, provide useful data about potential effects of genre-based teaching on L2 reading.

---

[1]In one training study, however, Carrell (1985) briefly discusses students' reflections on improvement in their L2 reading abilities.

DESIGN AND IMPLEMENTATION OF INSTRUCTION

The course, ELI 310: Reading and Vocabulary Development, was taught by the researcher during the Winter semester (January–April) 1993 at the University of Michigan's English Language Institute (ELI), a center that provides EAP courses to non-native undergraduate and graduate students as well as to university staff and visiting scholars. The class met for twelve weeks for one hour and twenty minutes each week. To test the methodology, the researcher had also taught a pilot version of the course during the previous semester.

The Students

The eleven students in the course consisted of eight graduate students, two undergraduates, and one university staff person. They represented a range of linguistic and cultural backgrounds, with five from East Asia, three from the Middle East, one from Latin America, one from Puerto Rico, and one from Africa. The undergraduate and graduate students were pursuing degrees in the fields of dentistry, nursing, engineering, anthropology, and marketing.

The Course Genres

Four genres—a hard news story, a feature article, a textbook, and a research article—were chosen as focal points for the course based on their relevance to students' reading needs in English. Although the two news genres may not be assigned reading in students' courses, they are texts that ESL students may want to read more proficiently while living in the U.S. (Mokhtari & Sheorey, 1994). The two academic genres, textbook and research article, are required in many undergraduate and graduate courses.

The course reflected an ESP approach to genre theory and genre-based pedagogy in the features taught. Like other ESP analyses and applications of genre (Bhatia, 1993; Flowerdew, 1993; Johns, 1997; Love, 1991; Swales, 1981, 1990), the course was concerned with raising students' awareness of the formal and functional features of written texts. As shown in Fig. 6.1, the four genres were discussed in terms of content, structure, language style, and purpose. In this way, the course reflected Swales' (1990) definition of genre as a category of texts sharing "some set of communicative purposes" as well as "various patterns of similarity in terms of structure, style, content and intended audience" (p. 58).

	Hard News	Feature Article	Textbook	Research Article
Content	Recent events of some importance or interest	Various factors involved in a large current issue	Concepts in a particular field	A new scientific investigation carried out by the author(s)
Structure	Inverted pyramid strucstructure (information presented in descending order of importance)	1. Anecdotal lead 2. Connection of anecdote to larger issue 3. Discussion of various factors involved in the issue	Cyclical patterns for presenting concepts	1. Introduction a) establishing research area importance b) indicating a gap c) filling the gap 2. Method 3. Results 4. Discussion
Language Style	"Objective": writer attributes opinions to other sources using quotations and citations; balanced with dramatic and emotional language	Subjective: writer may express opinion to appeal readers' emotions and to offer an interpretation of the issue	Sure and authoritative: characterized by lack of reference to evidence or controversy	Cautious: characterized by hedging and reference to experimental evidence
Purpose	To report newsworthy events in the most efficient and objective way	To draw readers into the whole article; to entertain readers and offer an interpretation of the issue	To present the "facts" of a particular field in a patterned manner	To present an interpretation of a timely investigation

FIG 6.1 The Course Genres

In this course, *content* referred to the typical topic focus of the genre, which Berkenkotter and Huckin (1995) argued to be an important defining text element. The topical focus of hard news stories, for instance, was described as interesting or important recent events. Feature articles, on the other hand, were said to concentrate on factors involved in a major current issue not necessarily tied to a single recent occurrence.

Structure referred to a genre's global organizational patterns (formal schemata) central to many ESP and Australian systemic functional genre analyses (Christie, 1991b; Feez, this volume; Joyce, 1992; Love, 1991; Macken-Horarik, this volume; Nwogu, 1991; Swales, 1981, 1990). Love's (1991) analysis provided the basis for the class model of cyclical textbook organization, whereby concepts and sequences may be repeated in different parts of a book. Analyzing two introductory geology textbooks, she found that these texts reflected discourse cycles highlighting relationships between geological processes and products. Following Love, it was hypothesized that academic textbooks in other fields use structural cycles that each reflect a "cognitive model of enquiry" (Love, p. 91) for the discipline, with the cycles varying across fields. Swales (1990) provided the organizational framework for the research article, with his "move analysis" of the article introduction, simplified somewhat for the purposes of the class. With respect to the news genres, the course discussed the inverted pyramid structure of hard news stories, a well-known journalistic framework for organizing information in descending order of importance (Berner, 1992). The less-rushed framework of the feature article (Cappon, 1991), characterized by an anecdotal lead, was presented as a structure found in many (though certainly not all) exemplars of this genre.

As used in this class, *language style* referred to linguistic features that convey the writer's stance toward the text content or audience. For the two news genres, the course considered how features such as quotations, source citations, and dramatic, biased language are used to express degrees of author objectivity or subjectivity toward the material. The language style descriptions for textbooks and research articles, on the other hand, focused on the degree of authority or caution writers express about their claims through the presence or absence of hedging or reference to evidence or controversy (Myers, 1992; Swales, 1990, 1993).

Finally, the course genres were described in terms of their "communicative purposes." Considering, as Johns (1997) argued that "we need to be very careful about attributing single purposes to texts from a genre" (p. 24), the researcher recognizes that the purposes outlined in Fig. 6.1 are not exhaustive. However, the ones listed were considered salient for these genres, providing rationales for some of the texts' formal features.

Methods of Instruction

In its approach to teaching these features, the course resembled other ESP and Australian systemic functional genre applications in its use of explicit discussion, modeling, and analyses of genres (Bhatia, 1993; Callaghan, Knapp, & Noble, 1993; Flowerdew, 1993; Johns, 1997; Joyce, 1992). Each genre unit contained tasks that elicited students' observations about text features. In examining the structure of the research article genre, for example, students were given a modified introduction of an article on ESL listening comprehension (Cervantes & Gainer, 1992), with the numbers 1, 2, and 3 in the margin, and discussed in pairs what the author was doing in each of the three segments. In the following class, students worked in groups to recreate an appropriate structural sequence for the pieces of a cut-up research article. Students' findings from such in-class analyses were discussed as a class, providing a springboard for some of the feature descriptions the instructor later wrote on the board.

In addition to these in-class activities, students analyzed instances of the course genres on their own. For homework, they were often asked to find an example of the genre being studied and to describe evidence of some of the features discussed in class. In one unit, for instance, students found research articles from their own fields and underlined the different moves in the introductions. For the news genres, students were given a hard news story and a feature article on AIDS and asked to write an essay contrasting the content, structures, language styles, and purposes of these texts.

For each of the genres, the class also focused on connections between genre knowledge and students' reading in English. The instructor sometimes asked students to consider how the class model of one of the genres could facilitate their reading. In discussing the textbook, one Japanese undergraduate said that "it just reminds me that I better be critical when I read a book . . . It might be false information . . . unless they provide examples of other side of the story." Students also participated in exercises using rhetorical knowledge to extract information quickly from texts. They were handed one or two texts face down and given just a short time to turn the text(s) over and find the answer to each question the instructor asked orally about the text(s). In an exercise with a modified research article passage, for example, students were asked to identify the purpose of the study, the instruments used in the experiment, the rationale for the study, the outcome of the experiment, the explanations for the results, and the study's general research area. After the allotted time for each question, students shared their answers and the textual clues that had led them to the appropriate information. Through these activities, it was hoped that students would recognize how genre knowledge could provide "shortcuts" for finding important pieces of information and for recognizing the authors' attitudes toward the material.

EVALUATING THE EFFECTS OF THE COURSE: TEXT DESCRIPTION EXAM

Design

For their final exam, students were given a text description exercise that aimed to assess their recognition of genre features covered in the course using a new set of genre exemplars. The exam was divided into three parts, involving five texts. The first two parts of the exam presented students with pairs of texts representing the genres that had been covered in the course, and, for each pair, asked students to describe, using examples, the differences that they saw between the two articles or passages. Passages A and B consisted of a feature article and hard news story, both on the topic of women's transition from homemaking to work. Passages C and D were texts from a research article and a textbook passage, both on parasites in farm animals. In each pair, the genres were ordered in the opposite sequence from their presentation in class (for example, the feature article was placed before the hard news story). These first four exam passages were made up of excerpts from four source texts in *The New York Times* (Kilborn, 1991; Lewin, 1990), *Journal of the Helminthological Society of Washington* (Lyons, Tolliver, Drudge, Grantrom, Stamper, & Collins, 1991), and a textbook called *Parasitology:The Biology of Animal Parasites* (Noble & Noble, 1971). Although the exam passages were substantially shorter than the original texts, they maintained the general sequencing of information in the originals.[2]

Analysis

The exams were coded for whether students labeled the passages as representing particular genres, whether they described the content, structure, language style, and purpose features of the texts, whether their descriptions reflected feature descriptions from the class, and whether they gave examples of these features by referring to specific segments from the texts. A comment was considered a feature description if it referred to at least some aspect of a text feature. For example, one student's comment that Passage A (feature article) "begins with an anecdote" was counted as a description of this text's structure, even though it only described the introductory section of the structure. A comment was coded as a feature example if it illustrated a feature by quoting, paraphrasing, or in some other way referring to segment(s) of the text. For example, a reference to "Katie Rollins case" discussed in the anecdotal opening of Passage A was counted as an example of the structure of this passage. Examples were considered important indicators that a student had actually identified a feature in a text and was not just repeating a feature description remembered from class.

Although only descriptions and examples considered appropriate for the texts were counted, they did not necessarily have to refer to features taught in the class. For example, one student's description of Passage D (textbook) structure as proceeding from general to specific information was counted because it fit the text, even though it did not allude to the cyclical structure discussed in class. The large majority of the students' comments, however, did refer to features the class had studied. After the coding was completed, the researcher rechecked the analysis against the exam papers and then calculated the numbers of students offering genre labels and descriptions and examples of the genre features.

Table 6.1 shows the numbers of students who appropriately labeled the genres of the four texts, described their content, structure, language style, and purpose

---

[2]After the open-ended description tasks in the first two parts, the exam also included a few short answer questions about the main ideas of the news texts and the purposes of the textbook and research articles, as well as a third section on a genre that had not been covered in the course—an academic book review. The purpose of this last part was to determine whether students transferred knowledge about the four course genres in their descriptions of this new genre. This chapter, however, focuses on students' responses on the first two open-ended description tasks.

features, and gave examples from the texts illustrating these features. In the responses cited, students' grammatical and spelling errors have not been corrected.

Table 6.1
Numbers of Students Correctly Naming the Four Text Genres and Appropriately Describing and Exemplifying Their Features on the Final Exam (n = 11)

Genre	Features Described/Exemplified								
	Genre Named	*Content*		*Structure*		*Language Style*		*Purpose*	
		Desc	Ex	Desc	Ex	Desc	Ex	Desc	Ex
FA	10	8	3	11	9	10	5	5	2
HN	10	7	5	11	8	10	9	6	2
RA	9	5	2	11	10	9	9	4	1
TB	9	8	4	7	3	10	5	5	2

Legend:

FA = Feature articule
HN = Hard news story
RA = Research article
TB = Textbook
Desc = Description
Ex = Example

Exam Results

Student Comments on Genre Name, Structure, and Language Style. As shown in Table 6.1, ten of the eleven students correctly named the genres of the feature article and hard-news passages, and nine of the eleven correctly named the genres of the research article and textbook passages. This result indicates that by the end of the course, most of the students were able to recognize instances of the course genres in new exemplars. In fact, the few students who did not give genre labels for the texts described them in ways that suggested that they were aware of their genre differences. Of the four features taught in the class, students most frequently offered appropriate text descriptions and examples of the structures and language styles of the exam texts. As seen in the table, all eleven students described aspects of the feature article, hard news, and research article structures, referring, for example, to the hard news' inverted pyramid framework, the feature article's anecdotal opening, the research article's introductory moves, or other structural aspects of these texts. Nine students also gave appropriate examples of their structural descriptions for these three genres by paraphrasing or quoting from text segments that illustrated different organizational components. This indicated that they truly recognized these features in the texts and were not just repeating the structural descriptions from class. Similarly, most students described the language styles of the four passages in terms of their degree of apparent objectivity or subjectivity (for the news texts) and certainty or caution/hedging (for the textbook and research article texts). Many (between five and nine) also illustrated these features by quoting or referring to specific segments from these texts.

Linguistic Elements as Cues for Genre Structure and Style. The large numbers of students exemplifying these formal elements may be attributed to the fact that some features corresponded with linguistic signals similar to those discussed in class, thus helping students to identify them. For example, the three moves of the research article introduction in Passage C were signaled by such phrases as "Knowledge . . . is important"; "of special interest," "Particularly lacking are . . . ." and "The purpose of the present research." The method, results, and discussion elements were also marked respectively by such cues as "material," "were found," and "Possibly, this is related." Some students included similar cues in their descriptions and examples of the passages' structures. Koichi, a Japanese graduate student, for example, just listed phrases next to his descriptions of the article structure. Next to "gap" he wrote "lacking," by "instruments," "microscope" and by "further research," "Further research is necessary."

In a similar manner, the components of the feature article structure were signaled by linguistic cues, perhaps facilitating their recognition. The woman's name "Katie Rollins" and phrases describing her life, for instance, marked the opening as an anecdotal segment taught in the class for this genre. The description of Katie Rollins differing "only in the details from those of many other Appalachian women" also reflected a phrase type (that is, this is one story of many like it) that the class discussed as a transition between the anecdote and the article's larger issue. Of the nine students who exemplified the structure of this passage, three illustrated it by referring to the anecdote alone. Six, however, offered examples of the anecdote portion as well as some other part of the structure, such as the presentation of the main idea and relevant factors in the issue. One Puerto Rican graduate student, Daniela, wrote:

> The structure of article A starts with an anecdote of Katie Rollins case in the first paragraph. The third paragraph serve as connection to the larger problem already mentioned toward continued in paragraph 4.
>
> Then it starts to cover some other factors. For example, the factor 1 can be the types of jobs, factor two the relationship with the husband when she work using the case of Betsy Van Winkle and so on.

Many students also offered appropriate illustrations of the language styles of the passages. These again corresponded with cues such as hedges and quotations that may have made them readily identifiable. For example, nine of the students offered examples of the more objective style of the hard news story, noting the writer's use of quotations and source citations. Ahmed, a Turkish graduate student, wrote "In the hard news story example, writer is more objective and gives more reliable information by using quotes and cites, such as 'According to the Bureau of Labor Statistic, 43 percent of all women . . .' " With the research article as well, nine of the students described and gave examples of the more cautious style of this text by highlighting the use of the hedge "possibly" in the discussion and/or the final statement that "further research is necessary."

Five students appropriately illustrated the more subjective style of the feature article by noting nonattributed comments in the texts that directly conveyed the writer's opinion. Daniela, for example, referred to "when the author uses the word 'chronically ailing economy'" as an example of a narrative style which appeals to the reader's "feelings toward the problem." With respect to the textbook passage, five students also exemplified the more "sure" style of this text. A Chinese university employee, Suyin, referred to phrases in the passage such as "so called" and "known as" to illustrate how "the language is so sure." Hitoshi, a Japanese undergraduate, also noted language that communicated the text's certainty:

> Everything in this article sounds correct. This is because there is no hedging in the article. Is, are, are used often. One more example is "In the spring or summer, the grubs, or maggots emerge through the holes. . . ." as opposed to using, for example, "It is believed that they emerge though . . ." The non-existence of hedging and avoidance of controversy help the writer be authoritative, credible.

The somewhat fewer numbers of students illustrating the textbook style than the research article style may be due to the fact that it was more difficult to exemplify the absence rather than presence of hedging.

Difficulty with Describing Textbook Structure. Of all of the formal features, the organization of the textbook passage was appropriately illustrated by the smallest number of students (n - 3), suggesting that it was the most difficult for students to recognize and/or explain by the end of the course. Indeed, only one student, Hitoshi, related his examples to cyclical structure discussed in class: "Article D, an abstract from a textbook, has a cyclical patterns. First the writer explains about insects' names, and then goes on to the life cycle. This pattern is repeated twice even in this kind of tiny piece of articles." A textbook's cycle may be difficult to recognize because of a lack of cycle cues shared across exemplars of the genre. As Love (1991) suggested, cycles used in textbooks reflect the cognitive models of their disciplines. Readers may thus need to understand concepts important within a discipline in order to recognize their cyclical patterning in a textbook in that field. In addition, clear cyclical patterns may not exist in some textbooks, perhaps especially outside of the sciences.

Student Comments on Genre Content and Purpose. Across the four genres, fewer students also described and illustrated the content types and purposes of the passages, a finding that may be attributed to several factors. First, some of the content and purpose features overlapped with structural and stylistic elements in the texts. For example, the content focus of the research article—a new scientific investigation—was also suggested in the third move of the article introduction structure, where the purpose of the investigation was stated. Thus, students may have thought their comments on formal text features illustrated text content and purpose as well. Students may also have paid less attention to content and purpose in their responses because they perceived them to be less important in the course curriculum. More time in the class sessions had, in fact, been given to the structural and stylistic elements of the four genres. Finally, content and purpose are perhaps more abstract than structure and language style and thus less easily exemplified by references to particular lexical signals, organizational moves, or other linguistic elements such as hedges or quotations.

Summary of Exam Results. The exam responses suggest what genre features students were most and least able to recognize by the end of the course and the degree to which the course had sensitized students to certain features as they read. Although most of the students holistically identified the genres represented, they seemed better at identifying and illustrating organizational and stylistic features corresponding with familiar linguistic signals than at explaining more abstract elements such as content or purpose, or elements such as textbook cyclical structure, that vary across texts and require substantial content understanding to identify. These patterns indicate that although this short course may have built students' understanding of some genre features and their linguistic realizations, it may have been limited in helping students recognize other rhetorical elements as they read, particularly those that are not as overtly signaled across genre exemplars.

INTERVIEWS

Design

During the week after the course ended, each of the eleven students was also interviewed about the course and its influence on his or her reading. The interview was divided into two parts. In the first part, students were asked to describe passages from the final exam in order to further assess their recognition of the passages' genre features; the second half of the interview focused on students' perceptions of the course and its effects on their reading. This section focuses on the second half of the interview.

Students were asked whether they thought their reading skills or habits had changed since the beginning of the semester, how or why they had or had not changed, what classes and assignments had been particularly useful or not useful to them, and whether the course work in the four genres had influenced their reading of other types of materials. Students were also asked if they had achieved their goals for the course, if they had acquired other skills that they had not expected to, if the course was what they expected, if they felt there was anything lacking from the course, and what skills they still wanted to work on. The interview also contained a number of individualized questions about students' homework assignments and their comments on a midsemester questionnaire and a beginning-of-semester interview.[3] (See sample interview questions in Appendix.)

Elicitation and Analysis

In order to remove some of the bias in verbal reports toward pleasing the instructor/ researcher, the interviews were elicited by another lecturer at the ELI. This lecturer had served as a research assistant for the course and had attended and tape-recorded the class sessions. Before the students signed up for the interviews, the instructor/ researcher assured them that she would not listen to the interview tapes until after turning in the course grades.

The interviews were transcribed and analyzed by the researcher who identified common or noteworthy themes in the transcripts and then categorized students' comments accordingly. If the meaning of a comment was unclear, the researcher relistened to the tape recording and then made a final decision about how to categorize the response.

Interview Results

Like the examination, the student reports shed light on the potential as well as limitations of the course for building genre knowledge and facilitating L2 reading. The responses that students gave with respect to different outcomes of the course are discussed next. Although false starts and hesitations have been omitted from their comments, grammatical errors have not been corrected. Throughout this chapter, the students' names have been changed.

Better Recognition of Genre. Several students (n = 4) indicated that after the course, they were more aware of the genres of texts. One Angolan undergraduate student, José, commented that the distinctions between the various genres were new for him: "I had never studied stuff like that, seeing the difference between newspaper article. Because when you open the newspaper, just newspaper, but there is a difference between those articles . . . Now I know what is a hard news story or feature article." Similarly, regarding textbooks and research articles: "Before I didn't see any difference. . . any book. . . it's a book, book, book. Now I know it's a textbook and research articles. And I can tell you by the language they use; like textbook they have authoritative language and sure language than research article . . . more unsure hedges." Other students, as well, reported improvement in genre recognition. One Saudi Arabian graduate student, Maryam, commented, "If I'm reading the *Time* magazine now I can say 'Oh this is hard news.' 'This is feature article.'"

Greater Attention to Rhetorical Features in Texts. Many students (n=6) mentioned that the course had heightened their attention to formal rhetorical features as they read. Suyin emphasized, "I will pay more attention to the structure and the language style." Some students, in fact, noted that structure was an aspect of texts that they had never focused on in other English classes. One Colombian graduate student, Maria, asserted, "I took many English course, especially reading course in Colombia and here in the United State [sic]. And this course were only focus in to read any materials and say what is the comprehension of these materials. But nobody explain that there are . . . a structure that you can read quickly . . . For me this is new."

Understanding Where to Locate Key Information. According to several students (n = 4), knowledge gained in the course about rhetorical features had increased their awareness of where to locate key ideas in texts. Focusing on the news genres, José indicated that he could distinguish between main idea placement between these two types: "Now I know what is a hard news story or feature article. If it's a hard news story say the most important things first paragraph, and if it's a feature article, you just look for the transition between the anecdote and the connection to large issue that they are talking about." In a similar vein, Suyin remarked, "I used to read just read through and sometimes I don't get the point. And now I know where to look."

Increased Reading Speed. Some students reported that knowledge about genres enhanced their L2 reading efficiency. Maryam, for example, said, "By knowing the steps I'm looking for in the research article or in the textbook that make it a little bit easier for me to like speed it up my reading." Similarly, Ahmed noted that because of the awareness gained about the news genres, "if I saw any article like those I can read efficiently and more quickly . . . if I want to get some specific information that kind of article I can pick it up easily."

Greater Confidence and Enjoyment in Reading. In addition to improving students' reading efficiency, the genre-based approach may have had affective benefits for these ESL readers. Suyin reported that the course had significantly improved her confidence and enjoyment in reading English-language newspapers: "After I know all these, I feel very confident to read *The New York Times*." She suggested that her recognition of news genres gave her an advantage over some native speakers without genre awareness: "I will say 'Oh, this is hard news story.' Even some American student, they don't know hard news story and feature story." Similarly, at the end of an essay assignment comparing two news genre exemplars, she commented, "It is much easier and much fun to read the newspaper especially for foreigners when they know the different structures and their different purposes." In her interview, she suggested that her positive reading attitudes would lead to more frequent reading and thus build her English vocabulary: "You have the good habit; then you feel more interesting to read more; then you will gain more vocabulary in the future, even you're not taking the classes."

Transfer of Course Knowledge to Varied Texts. A number of students (n = 6) indicated that the course effects extended to reading texts that fell outside the class genres. Specifically, some mentioned that awareness of genre-specific organizational patterns and accompanying signaling devices improved their ability to focus on or locate information in other texts. Suyin commented, "It's just a habit when you read. Before that it's just like a white paper. . . You don't know where to pay attention and where you need to concentrate on. Right now, the paper, they're similar; as long as you pay attention to the structure you can figure out somewhere, somehow." Similarly, Daniela indicated that her sensitivity to lexical cues ("some words") for different structural components could help her identify author interpretation in articles that deviated from the organizational models taught in class. Ahmed also observed that although the research papers in his field did not always reflect the class genre features, his new rhetorical awareness transferred to reading these texts: "Before taking course I had no any idea about the language style, contents, or purpose . . . That kind of examination point can help the person who wants to understand any paper or textbook or research paper."

Help with Writing. A few students observed that the course had not only enhanced their text processing but their academic writing as well. Daniela said, "I have to write many papers and it have helped me to write a lot." She remarked that the research article structure had been especially useful: "I'm doing weekly papers for one of my class and other classes and has help me. I just put one of the paper that you gave to us, and just follow the steps . . . in my papers: the first step, the second and third step." In a similar manner, one Korean graduate student, Jahwan, said that from the class he had learned the importance of written organization: "Writing must need some structure. The writer must recognize the structure. And when he write some essays, he must outline the structures and what kind of language styles, where is my main opinion. That's the somethings learned in class."

Difficulty With Comprehending Main Ideas. In addition to these positive outcomes, students reported several shortcomings of the course for developing their reading effectiveness. Two students, for example, suggested that after the course they still lacked adequate strategies or knowledge for comprehending important ideas in texts. Jahwan expressed that although the course helped him *locate* the "main idea part" in texts, this was not sufficient for figuring out the main idea: "Still I have some problems in the reading what's the point. . .. That's not structural problems . . . I know this is a main idea part but where is the main idea?" Similarly, Koichi said that he still needed to improve his understanding, or "gripping" of key ideas in texts:"I don't know exactly how to get information exactly. So I didn't get that information or that strategy in class. So how to get, how to grip the essential part of the article. It's very difficult for me still now."

Lack of Attention to Vocabulary and Need for More Reading Practice. Five students remarked that they wished that the course had focused more on building vocabulary. However, some acknowledged that this short course was naturally limited in what it could address. Koichi asserted that long-term reading improvement depended on extended practice: "From class I learned many kind of knowledge about strategy or kind of knowledge about some aspect of article or textbook... But I think knowledge is just only knowledge... So I think I need more practice just read. And in reading maybe I can apply that knowledge."

DISCUSSION

Although this study is limited in its generalizability to other ESL learners, it can contribute to the field's understanding of the efficacy of genre-based teaching for building learners' genre knowledge and improving their L2 reading abilities. This discussion considers the research implications of the study's findings and offers recommendations for combining a focus on genre with content and vocabulary instruction in L2 reading classrooms.

Potential of Instruction for Building Genre Awareness

The final exams and oral interviews indicate that genre-based instruction may be able to help students holistically recognize instances of genres in new texts and attend to genre features when they read. However, the exam findings also suggest that at least some forms of genre-based pedagogy are more effective for teaching certain features than others. Specifically, a short genre-based course may be best able to raise students' awareness of rhetorical elements that correspond to readily identifiable linguistic cues, as opposed to features such as textbook cyclical structure, which vary substantially in their realization across texts and which require a large amount of field-specific content understanding to identify.

Whether the present instruction was *necessary* for building students' genre sensitivity or whether they would have eventually developed such awareness tacitly on their own (Freedman, 1993, 1994) is not certain. However, for these ESL students, explicit teaching may have facilitated at least a more rapid acquisition of genre knowledge than would have been experienced in the absence of instruction. Composition researcher Richard Coe (1994b) argued that for at least some students, explicit training in various contexts enhances learning. With respect to swimming, for example, he observes that although "people learned to swim for millennia before coaches explicitly articulated our knowledge of how to swim, ... kids today learn to swim better (and in less time) on the basis of that explicit knowledge." With respect to writing he muses, "Might explicit genre knowledge help some students, perhaps especially some of *those who presently fail*?" (p. 159; Coe's emphasis). ESL university students may be among the "some" for whom explicit genre-based teaching is helpful, as they have often not had as much tacit exposure to English-language genres as their L1 counterparts.

Benefits of Genre Sensitivity for L2 Reading

The interviews and exam results highlight that by building students' genre sensitivity, explicit instruction facilitates L2 reading in a variety of ways. For instance, students may develop awareness of where to locate key information in texts. This finding supports Shih's (1992) assertion that "knowledge of the organization of a particular text and of common textual signals can help a reader identify important information as well as relationships between ideas in the text" (p. 302). In addition, the interviews indicate that familiarizing students with genre features improves their reading speed.

According to one student, learning about genres may also increase reading confidence and enjoyment. Indeed, Johns (1997) found that sharing in the "names" of genres "enables [people] to begin their reading and writing of a text with considerable confidence and to comprehend effectively the discourses that are important to them" (p. 23). Imparting these affective benefits has important consequences for students' overall reading proficiency. According to Nuttall (1982), enjoyment in reading helps lead students out of a "vicious circle" of slow, uncomprehending, infrequent reading into a "virtuous circle" of efficient, comprehending, frequent reading (pp. 167–68).

Transferability of Genre Knowledge to Reading and Writing L2 Texts

Swales (1990) asked "whether, to what extent and under what conditions skills acquired within one genre are transferable to another" (p. 233). In response, the present interviews suggest that knowledge gained about specific genres develops rhetorical sensitivity that students can apply to processing various texts. Moreover, according to some students' comments, genre-based reading instruction transfers to L2 writing abilities as well, as it provides students with frameworks for composing their own texts. These findings support recent scholarship highlighting parallels between text processing and production and the usefulness of genre-based instruction for both areas (Davis, Lange, & Samuels, 1988; Johns, 1995; Reid, 1993). According to Reid (1993), for example, "genre analysis, the study of how different kinds of writing are organized and presented for a reader, has been found to help both NSs and ESL students read and write more effectively" (p. 42).

Limitations of Genre-Based Instruction

Like the text description exams, however, the interviews also highlight shortcomings of genre-based pedagogy for enhancing L2 literacy. They indicate that a largely singular focus on rhetorical features may side-step other kinds of reading strategies or content and lexical schemata important for text comprehension for specific purposes. Although the course discussed typical topic focuses of some genres (for example, recent event, timely investigation), it paid limited attention to unpacking many of the concepts or vocabulary items in the genre exemplars discussed in class. Much L2 reading scholarship has emphasized the importance of building and activating readers' content schemata, that is, knowledge of a text's conceptual material (Floyd & Carrell, 1987; Kasper, 1995; Shih, 1992), as well as lexical and syntactic knowledge (Eskey & Grabe, 1988; Grabe, 1991). Shih (1992) remarked, "In academic content reading, the difficulty is that so much of the content of a text may be new and unfamiliar" (p. 292). Similarly, Johns (1997) reported, "Many students argue that content, especially vocabulary understanding, is their greatest obstacle to developing academic literacies" (p. 32).

The student interviews also remind researchers and practitioners that genre-based instruction, or any other kind of skill- or strategy-training, is not a substitute for individual reading practice (Eskey & Grabe, 1988; Grabe, 1991; Nuttall, 1982; Williams, 1986). As Grabe (1991) observed, "Reading *develops gradually*; the reader does not become fluent suddenly, or immediately following a reading development course. Rather, fluent reading is the product of long-term effort and gradual improvement" (p. 379; Grabe's emphasis). Thus, although a genre-based course may help ESL students enter Nuttall's (1982) "virtuous circle" of motivated and frequent reading, students will need to continue reading on their own to develop long-term proficiency in L2 text processing.

Indeed, students' reading experiences prior to a genre-based course will also likely influence the degree to which students benefit from such instruction. Those who have had some experience with reading the course genres (or ones similar to them) will perhaps be better primed for analyzing their features in a classroom setting and for connecting such instruction meaningfully to their reading needs. Ideally, experience with reading relevant genres should precede as well as succeed genre-based instruction.

Combining Rhetoric, Content, and Language in L2 Reading Curricula

In the present course, genre was a useful, though perhaps "one-legged,"[4] approach to L2 reading instruction. In light of the student exams and interviews, a "three-legged" curriculum might include attention to rhetorical text features, content knowledge, and linguistic schemata. All three components of such a tripartite curriculum might still fall under a genre-based approach, as text purpose, structure, content, vocabulary, and syntax all characterize individual genres (Johns, 1997). However, in a short course there is limited time to build schemata on all these levels. In designing reading curricula, therefore, practitioners could cut down on the number of genres discussed in a given course to allow for fuller attention to building

[4]John Swales (personal communication, November 1994) noted that Kenneth Goodman described genre analysis as a one-legged approach to curriculum at the November 1994 NCTE conference.

content and linguistic knowledge relevant to their students' reading needs. Curriculum planners might also consider developing a two or three course sequence, with one course focusing on rhetorical features, such as organizational structures, stylistic features, and purposes of genres, and with the other one or two courses attending to specific content and language required for comprehending texts in students' specific fields of study. These classes could perhaps be linked with content courses in the disciplines to provide greater meaning and authenticity to the texts in focus (Deverell, 1993; Johns, 1997; Kasper, 1995).

CONCLUSION

This chapter has offered one evaluation of genre-based instruction. The students' text description exams and interviews suggest that explicit teaching about genre features can be useful for building ESL students' genre awareness and for facilitating their text processing and production. Specifically, such teaching may improve students' genre sensitivity, their ability to identify important text information, their reading speed and confidence, and the organization of their writing. Genre-based instruction, at least in its present form, however, may not be able to effectively teach all genre features or address other kinds of knowledge or skills that students need for effective L2 reading. In developing a more balanced reading curriculum, practitioners may consider combining instruction about rhetorical genre features with a focus on content and linguistic knowledge. Because the present study examined only one type of genre-based pedagogy in a small ESL reading class, more research is needed on the efficacy of genre as a literacy-building framework.

APPENDIX: INTERVIEW QUESTIONS

Note: Questions in italics are sample individualized questions about students' beginning-of-semester interviews, midsemester questionnaires, and homework assignments.

For the second part of the interview, I'm going to ask you some questions about your reading skills and the course this semester. I'm going to pull those questions from a variety of sources, including the first interview we did at the beginning of the semester, the midterm questionnaire, and the homework assignments.

1. Do you think your reading skills or habits have changed at all since the beginning of the semester or not? Could you explain how they have changed? Could you explain why you think they haven't changed?

a. In your first interview, you said that political articles in the newspaper were the most difficult types of material for you to read. Is this still true or has this changed at all over the semester?

b. You also said that you didn't pay much attention to the structure of a passage when you read. Would you say that this is still true or has this changed at all over the semester?

I also have a question about one of your homework assignments.

c. In your essay comparing the two AIDS articles, you made a comment at the end of your essay. You said, "After all, it is much easier and much fun to read the newspaper especially for foreigners when they know the different structures and their different purposes." Could you explain a little more what you meant by that?

2. Were there any classes and assignments in this course that were particularly useful to you?

3. Were there any classes and assignments in this course that were not particularly useful to you?

4. On the midsemester questionnaire, you said that the newspaper classes and assignments had helped you improve your academic reading. Could you comment a bit more on that?

5. Do you think the work you have done on newspaper articles, textbooks, or research articles has influenced the way you read other types of materials as well, types of reading which you did not cover in class? Could you explain how?

6. In your first interview, you said that one of your goals for this course was to develop different strategies for approaching different types of reading. You also said that you wanted to be able to understand the ideas in what you read and be able to identify why or why not the writer is expressing an opinion. Have you been able to achieve any of these goals in the course or not?

7. Have you acquired any other skills which you were not expecting to?

8. Was the course what you expected it would be or was it different from what you expected?

9. Is there anything you feel was lacking in the course, anything you wished the course had covered but did not?

10. What kinds of skills would you still like to work on in your reading?

Part IV

Bridging Text and Context

7
Textual Analysis and Contextual Awareness Building: A Comparison of Two Approaches to Teaching Genre

Terence T. T. Pang
Lingnan University, Hong Kong

Recent studies on genre privilege the real-life intent of the speaker (See Berkenkotter & Huckin, 1995; Bhatia, 1997a; Yunik, 1997, for example). According to this view, context determines speaker intent. Yunik (1997) remarked:

> Context sets the stage where particular meanings unfold, where individuals learn to create themselves, and where societal traditions are recreated and contested.... The application of theory to teaching ... means *raising awareness* of the processes of making meanings, making identities and making ideologies, in order to empower learners to make informed choices. (p. 321; italics mine)

However, previous approaches to teaching genre focus on the text rather than the context and the social action resulting from awareness of the context. They are based on a belief that genre is driven by rhetorical functions like "description," "exposition," "narration," and "argumentation," which are mode-based and text-oriented, instead of by communicative intent, which is probably field- and tenor-based (Halliday, 1985). Genre is thus more a text-type rather than a speech event (see Paltridge, this volume) and associated with certain grammatical and textual features, which form the focus of ESL instruction. Using this assumption, Hammond, Burns, Joyce, Brosnan, & Gerot (1992) found that the past tense, "action verbs," "verbs of saying," and adverbs of time and place are commonly associated with news reports. With this information in mind, the teacher either points out the grammatical features explicitly to the learners (see Kalantzis & Wignell, 1988, and to a certain extent, Drury & Gollin, 1986), or requires learners to "discover" them through analysis (see

Holborow, 1991, for example). In stark contrast to textual analysis is a contextual awareness-building approach, more parallel to Yunik (1997), which highlights speaker intent and encourages learners to analyze the speech event and the situational variables underlying genres. Both approaches are elaborated next.

TEXTUAL AND CONTEXTUAL ANALYSIS

As mentioned, teaching genres with a focus on language features and textual organization has been a traditional practice (see Flowerdew, this volume). Drury and Gollin (1986) and Jones, Gollin, Drury, & Economou (1989) are examples in which the "exposition genres" (*field* or *laboratory reports*, *essays*, *assignments*, *seminar papers*, *examination answers*, *dissertations*, and *theses*) are given priority because the genres in learners' L1 are thought to be in conflict with those in English (Drury & Gollin, 1986, p. 290; Jones et al., 1989, p. 226).

This approach privileges the study of lexico-grammatical features, as evidenced by a comprehensive coverage of major grammatical points and errors in student texts (Jones et al., 1989). "Textuality" (theme, reference, lexical cohesion, and conjunction), which is mode-oriented and purportedly language-specific, is stressed for ESL learners. "Discourse structure" is regarded as textual structure and often simplified. The three-stage structure of expository writing offered by Drury & Gollins (1986) and the three-part structure for the introduction of a scientific paper in Jones et al., (1989, p. 293) are simplified reflections of findings identified in the research (see Swales, 1990, for example).

Contextual analysis, by contrast, begins with topics outside the text itself, configuring communicative intent, that is, speaker motive and other factors. Some recent approaches have been distancing from register-analytic practices of teaching linguistic features and involving students in analysis of socializing situations (Boswood & Marriot, 1994). As Johns (1997) put it, the context, as "the sphere of human activity," allows writers and readers to "identify texts by name and establish their purposes and reader and writer roles" (p. 27). *Context* is a broad term. It refers to "all the nonlinguistic and nontextual elements that contribute to the situation in which reading and writing are accomplished" (Johns, p. 27) and not always to a physical place or a publication. To function well in a genre, one needs "situated" or genre knowledge, grounded in both the activities and the situation in which the text is produced (Berkenkotter & Huckin, 1995). Knowledge of the activities includes knowledge of the tools, methods, and interpretative framework used in a discipline or workplace, whereas knowledge of the situation refers to familiarity with the rhetorical and conceptual context (Bhatia, 1997b). Thus, for example, a professional film reviewer possesses knowledge of films as an institution from which the genre of film reviews arises. He or she also possesses the approach and interpretative framework for writing them.

Two examples of the approach are reported here: Holborow (1991) and Ventola (1994). The former approach still carries a strong register-analysis flavor, whereas the latter represents a full-fledged contextual-awareness-raising approach focusing on the genre. Holborow's primary concern was to enable learners to write in an appropriate *register*, correcting their "inappropriate style and formulation[s]" (p. 24). She incorporates three distinct elements in her program: analyzing the situation from the text, for example, asking students to infer the situations from two different menus; predicting language from the situations; and rewriting a text for a slightly different situation demanding a change in register. Though the relevance of the context of situation is made explicit to the learners, the approach is largely text-based because the students have to infer the context from the text, instead of predicting textual features from the context. They rewrite a text from a slightly different situation requiring a change in register instead of writing a new text based on different situational variables. Because the ideational and interpersonal factors of context do not feature prominently in her approach, the focus is on register rather than genre.

By contrast, Ventola (1994) provided an example of the contextual-awareness-building approach strongly featuring speaker intent. By viewing genre as the product of interactions in context (Kress, 1987), and communicative intent as of primary significance, Ventola stresses moves and speech acts, which reinforce the intent, instead of clauses, as the basic *structural* constituents of genre. *Moves* are purposeful functional units sustaining the communicative intent of the speaker, whereas *speech acts* denote functions at the discourse level (Swales, 1990). Ventola saw genre as a dynamic event, with interactants continuously engaged in negotiation of meaning, and in the process, making subtle choices in field, mode, and tenor, and realizing such choices through register and moves (p. 279). Her genre flow chart "represents the total potentials of the options open to the interactants for developing the social process within the limits of ... register and genre features" (p. 279). Summarizing the contextual features, the chart indicates possible moves in a genre and accompanying register choices realizing such choices. Cultural differences in the generic structure can be highlighted in this approach. The ultimate criterion for deciding whether texts belong to the same genre is to examine "if they include all the obligatory elements ... and ... some or all of the optional elements in the sequence" (p. 277). Learners can use the flow chart to predict the next step in the discourse. They also learn that texts may display the same register, but not be in the same genre.

THE FILM REVIEW AS A PEDAGOGICAL GENRE

One known, and contextualized, genre is the *film review*. When teaching film reviews, an instructor can focus on the language and the textual structure, or on the speaker intent realized through moves and register (Ventola, 1984). The most obvious intent of the film review is to recommend or not recommend a film to the reader. The obligatory moves are a title, often with an evaluative touch to attract reader attention; an introduction to compare the film with other films; an incomplete synopsis to arouse interest in the film; and an evaluation to comment on the quality of the film, informing the reader whether it is worth viewing. There are optional moves such as discussion of the insides of film production, comments on detailed features of the film, and a conclusion.

The Hong Kong postsecondary students selected for the research reported here need to be aware of how genres operate in contexts. Their course, "Models of Speech and Writing," adopts a genre-based syllabus using contextual analysis. The genres taught–*interview*, *film review*, *narrative*, *editorial*, *TV documentary*, and *casual conversation*—are chosen for their "nonspecialist" nature, as the course aims at enhancing student awareness of a broad range of genres. After graduation, the students may have to translate texts from a variety of genres. By becoming aware of how context influences text, they may develop strategies to analyze a variety of genres. The film review is nonacademic by nature, but is nonetheless a professional genre.

The film review is discussed here for several reasons. The most obvious is that most learners in the class (38 out of 39) did not have experience as producers of the genre, so that changes in the quality of their writing could be ascribed to the teaching. Even though learners would have come across the genre as consumers in casual reading, they had not formulated very strong preconceptions regarding its schematic or linguistic structures. Any differences between the pre- and post-"tests" could be safely attributed to teacher input or classroom experience. The author of a film review speaks in the voice of an expert, showing lay persons his or her knowledge about the actors, the director, and about the shooting of the film, and above all, saying whether the film is worth seeing. The reviewer may even show readers how to appreciate the film. This variety of functions is useful for classroom teaching. In addition, the film review encompasses several modes of discourse or text types: a narrative in the summary of the plot, description in the orientation stage of the narrative, factual exposition in the background of production and in the discussion of the director or actor(s), and persuasion in the evaluation and coda of the narrative, if any, as well as the evaluation of the film.

THE SUBJECTS

Two groups (one with 19 students; the other with 20) of the Year 1 English course, "Models of Speech and Writing," in the B.A. in Translation at Lingnan University, Hong Kong, took part in the study. These Cantonese speakers had obtained grade D or above in the Use of English Examination (Advanced Supplementary Level), which means that they possessed "the minimum standard for coping with university education using English as the medium of instruction," according to the secretary of the Hong Kong Examinations Authority (Choi, 1997). The course exposes students to a variety of nontechnical genres and guides them to analyze their contextual, linguistic, and discoursal features, so that they will be able to analyze other genres.

It is worth noting that though the subjects possessed a reasonable level of proficiency, they had been exposed to prescriptive, even rote, examination-oriented approaches to language learning. Some even treated learning English as learning an academic subject like economics or physics, that is, learning formulas and vocabulary while overlooking the skills aspect and real-life applications of language, not to mention communicative intent and the sociocultural variables in context. With this group, it was decided to determine whether the textual/register analysis approach or the contextual awareness building approach would yield better results.

RESEARCH QUESTIONS

The interrelatedness of context and text is one of the most powerful constructs of the functional systemic model (Halliday, 1985). The *context* functions as a semantic frame for the "use of the verbal symbolic system" within which linguistic features functioning as signs acquire meanings both "in the system" and "in the world of active experience" (Hasan, 1985, p. 34). The *text*, on the other hand, acts as the intermediary between the context and the language system. It provides both an intratextual and an extratextual environment for the interpretation of sentences (Hasan, 1985). Another systemic construct vital to the theoretical underpinning of the present study is the systematicity of language in context. According to Hasan (1985), "the creation of semantic competence depends entirely on the systematic operation of language in social context" (p. 35). To become members of a discourse community (Swales, 1990), learners have to master not just the language, but rather the systematicity of language use in context. Indeed, the register components, field, mode and tenor, representing components in the context of situation, are realized through elements in the lexico-grammatical system (Halliday, 1985, p. 9; Martin, 1984).

The systematicity of language in context includes the discourse features of the text and lexico-grammatical features, the major components of the learning experience of the textual/register analysis group in this study. Kress (1985) noted, "Competent users of language are entirely familiar with and very sensitive to the forms and meanings of genre . . ." (pp. 21–22). It is therefore hypothesised that by learning to study the lexico-grammatical features of texts of a certain genre, learners should be more capable of writing in that genre.

Malinowski's view of the social context as the enabling element for language to be passed down the generations means major factors underlying language use lie in the context, and not just the system. Speaker intent determines the ideational, interpersonal, and textual choices, which are then realized through selected syntactic and lexico-grammatical features. Thus, the context of situation determines "the range of semantic options" (Halliday, 1981, p. 123), and the text represents "semantic choice in social contexts" (Gregory, 1985, p. 122). The second, contradictory hypothesis is that given the context, learners of a relatively high proficiency trained in contextual analysis should be able to generate texts for a genre, using appropriate language from the system.

The two hypotheses are two sides of the same coin, with genre being the mediating element. Nonetheless, they both presume a certain degree of maturity and competence in users. Learners are either capable of generating appropriate language given the context, or developing a "feel" for the genre as a result of textual analysis. Hence, tertiary students with a reasonable level of proficiency were chosen as subjects.

METHODS

The Lessons and the Worksheets

The research took place in the second cycle of the course "Models of Speech and Writing," during a unit on film reviews. The intervention was so posited that students would not have been affected by other learning experiences. In this cycle, for the sake of this study, one group was introduced to genre through contextual awareness building, and another through textual analysis. To evaluate progress, learners were required to write a film review before the unit began and also at the end of the unit.

Both groups went through the same activities before branching off to different tasks:

- ACTIVITY 1. As a pretest, learners wrote a film review, without instruction, of about 300 words on a film they chose, to be compared with the posttest written at the end of the unit.
- ACTIVITY 2. Learners were asked to discuss different movie genres and elements of such genres. They had to think of another cultural product that can be classified into genres. Some examples of English movie genres like James Bond and Western were given, and learners were asked to cite more, including local ones. For the purpose of this research, no discussion of film review as a genre was initially held with the students.
- ACTIVITY 3. Learners read a synopsis of the film *Dead Poets Society*, the review of which was to be used as the focus text of the unit. They then watched the movie and were given the option of watching it again in the Self-Access Center. They were told to retell the story in groups, jot down main points, and discuss whether they liked the movie, the characters they liked and disliked most, and the meaning behind the plot. In the discussion, they also compared the society and culture in the film with local society. Finally, they deliberated about which movie genre the film belonged to.

CONTEXTUAL AWARENESS BUILDING

The learning experience of the experimental group focused on discussing the key elements of the context of situation discussed by Hymes (1972b): that is, situation, participants, ends and goals, act sequence and message form, register, channel, forms of speech, norms of interaction, and genres (and sub-genres). A colleague of the author who had extensive experience of teaching the course taught this group. She was briefed on the approach and went through the worksheets with the author in detail. She also wrote evaluative remarks on the lessons and was interviewed by the author afterwards.

ACTIVITY A1, for the contextual awareness group, featured "general" questions that focused learner attention on contextual variables in writing:

- channel of message (where they found film reviews, spoken or written),
- purpose of communication (reasons for writing film reviews),
- writer role (who writes film reviews),
- audience (who reads film reviews), and audience motives (why they read film reviews);
- register (what style—formal, casual, or technica— are film reviews written in).

For the last aspect, the teacher gave prompts in the form of questions such as "Do you think the film review should be written in an academic style like laboratory reports?" "Would the writer use terms that the audience would find difficult to follow?" "Do you think the writer would use some colloquial expressions?" The teacher reported that in discussing the contextual variables, learners inferred how a professional reviewer would engage in the production of the review, for example, researching the movie production, the director, screenplay, and actors; and viewing the film critically and perhaps watching it more than once. Learners were encouraged to consider these questions when they wrote their film reviews. The teacher observed that the discussion "gave them some chance to use language related to film reviews but not extensively. They did become interested, though. Some brought film magazines to the class." It is interesting to note that appropriate field-related language—that is, expressions related to films such as "camera," "acting," "action," "cast," "box office," "soundtrack," and so on—was generated in a discussion on contextual variables.

ACTIVITY A2 - Learners studied three texts: two movie guides and a film review. They hypothesized about the publications in which the two movie guides were found, and about the publication for the review on *Dead Poets Society* used as the teaching text (drawn from a movie magazine and hence more detailed and specialized). Learners deduced which types of publication the magazines were; the writer roles and purposes; and the target readers, their gender, age, education, interests, and reader purpose. They also studied the register (affectionate, clichéd, academic, and so on); the channel (written, spoken, written to be spoken, written with colloquialisms); and other features typical of the genre.

Inferring contextual components from the text is essential to contextual awareness building. Instead of seeing film reviews as a fixed genre, learners were led to discover that there were significant differences among sub-genres, for example, movie guides, film criticism, and reviews, under the umbrella of "film reviews." The subjects remarked that the film review contained a stronger evaluative element and included more information on the background of production and details about the movie, whereas the much shorter movie guide provided only a brief synopsis and an overall indication of the "viewability" of the film, often in the form of ratings.

ACTIVITY A3 used a movie guide—that is, a text that mainly focuses on the synopsis of the movie and general comments as to whether the film is worth seeing—as the focus text. Learners compared the film review of *Dead Poets Society* they read for A2 and a movie guide appearing as an incomplete synopsis (one with the ending left out) without any evaluation or background of movie production in terms of schematic structure. They focused on contextual differences (publication, writer role and purpose, target readers, channel, and register). Learners concluded that the focus text was not a film review because the element of review was not included. They realized that, as in all cases, the communicative intent determines the genre. Activities A2 and A3 brought home the point that each text could be situated in relation to other texts in the notion of intertextuality.

The activities shared a common goal: to expose learners to a variety of related texts in the target culture institutions out of which the genres and sub-genres arise. The institutions are represented in this case by the cinema and the publications. Discussions of linguistic features and schematic structure were included specifically to show learners that these features are conditioned by the configurations of the context. Though these were the only parts that dealt with such features in the whole unit for the contextual awareness building group, the learners recognized the differences in register between the sub-genres readily.

ACTIVITY A4 learners, having realized differences between genres and sub-genres by analyzing texts, were required to examine differences across genres from another end. They were given descriptions of a variety of genres about film—that is, the movie review, the theoretical essay, and the film essay—and asked to identify the possible discourse purposes underlying each genre and to select moves appropriate to each purpose. They realized the communicative intents and the moves that distinguish one genre from another.

TEXTUAL ANALYSIS

The second group undertook activities that provided them a thorough treatment in schematic structure and grammar, especially in the marked aspects of the texts. The researcher taught this group of students.

ACTIVITY B1 learners rearranged moves appearing as paragraphs in the plot summary. The task was intended to help them understand the schematic structure of plot summaries in film reviews, and the fact that the ending is usually not given so as not to spoil the fun of the would-be movie viewer when he or she actually watches the film. Learners mapped some of the paragraphs onto the moves that are (as was explained to them) typical of stories, that is, orientation, action, complication, resolution, coda, and evaluation. They were then asked to identify the missing move in the plot summary, that is, the resolution, and to explain the reason for the omission.

ACTIVITY B2 learners identified the more general features of the film review: title, introduction, plot summary, evaluation of film, insides of film production, details of film, and conclusion. They discussed which features are essential and which are not.

ACTIVITY B3 used detailed lexical, grammatical, and syntactic analyses to help learners understand how the register in the review is constructed. The features analyzed were: writer attitudes and opinions (positive, neutral, and negative) shown in the use of words and expressions; meanings conveyed by conjunctions; stylistic effects of embedded structures, and the use of tenses in moves (the present tense in the synopsis and evaluation, the past tense in the insides of movie production).

ACTIVITY B4 learners read a text about genetic engineering inspired by the film *Jurassic Park,* and identified and labeled moves and other features in the text. They also studied the tenses and compared the register with that in the focus text, the film review. They concluded that the *Jurassic Park* text was not a film review.

The learners not only completed the tasks successfully, but showed excitement in discovering the fact that different genres are characterized by different grammatical features and organizational structure.

For both groups, the lessons lasted altogether six class hours, spanning three weeks. In addition, other activities were held outside class like watching movies, analyzing more film reviews, and planning, composing, and revising the film review. At the end of the unit, students were again asked to write a film review based on another film they had watched. After each writing, they answered a questionnaire aimed at finding out their writing process and strategies, for example, where and when they watched the film, the purpose of watching the film, the time gap between watching the film and writing the review, the target publication, target readership, and whether they followed a model when writing (See Appendix A).

ASSESSMENT: CRITICAL RATING

In addition to evaluating through a writing-strategy questionnaire, the researchers marked the film reviews both holistically and also according to certain criteria grounded on the functional systemic model (Appendix B; see also Jones et al., 1989). A criterial rating was administered by the writer/researcher and a colleague. A criterial assessment form (Appendix B), covering major aspects of schematic structure, lexis, and grammar was devised for the research (Drury & Gollin, 1986; Jones et al., 1989). The criteria found in the criterial assessment form are divided into three parts (for details under each section, please refer to Appendix B), that is, thematic and discourse functions, moves, and the overall schematic structure, and lexico-grammatical features in the realization of field, mode, and tenor of discourse. These criteria are significant in the realization of both textual and contextual meanings, as underpinned in the systemic functional model. The awareness of context is evident in the answers given in the writing-strategy questionnaire; however, the ultimate judgment on whether a genre has been mastered rests with discoursal and linguistic realizations in the text of a target genre. For example, a competent writer should be able to represent register via the mood system (item 3a in Appendix B) and attitudes through modality markers (item 3b).

The scores in the criterial rating were derived impressionistically along a scale of "very competent," "competent," "limited competence," and "not yet," adopted from Nunan (1991). Because it was difficult to determine the relative weighting of each score, instead of adding up the scores in the criterial rating, the overall impression derived was transformed into a ten-point scale allowing half marks. Criteria not in the assessment form were also taken into account. The procedure may not be very "scientific;" nevertheless, it may be a more accurate indication of the text's proximity to the target genre.

A second procedure, awarding scores according to appropriateness in ideational, interpersonal, and textual meanings, was used to analyze three student texts in the study: one high score, one medium score, and one low score to show the differences and the subtle representations of the meanings of the scores on the criterial rating. The second procedure is not reported at length here because of the cumbersome details involved, but it does confirm the scores given in the criterial rating.

Holistic rating was also used to strengthen the validity of the assessment. Because the two groups of subjects had been exposed to different approaches to genre, it was designed to test whether the criterial-assessment approach favors the textual analysis group. Students may be able to score higher simply by modeling the linguistic features without being fully aware of the reasons behind their use, which, according to functional systemics, is to make meaning. Holistic rating is supposed to be a more accurate reader response to the total impact of the text (Couture, 1985, p. 69), taking into account the interpersonal relationship between writer and audience, and should favor the contextual awareness building group. The one holistic rater was advised to base the assessment on an overall impression of the writing quality and on an overall impression (whether the text resembled a real film review), and allocate marks on a wider range instead of clustering around the middle. The results of the criterial rating and holistic rating were correlated for analysis.

THE WRITING-STRATEGY QUESTIONNAIRE

Whereas the completed Criterial Assessment Form and holistic score represent the researchers' evaluation of the learners' writing products, the writing-strategy questionnaire is the learners' self-report of their composing process in the context of situation. The purpose behind the adoption of this assessment instrument is to see how closely learners adopted strategies as "good apprentices" in composing their film reviews, and whether they were aware of the context. These two factors represent the two aspects of genre knowledge, that is, knowledge of activities and knowledge of the situation. The questionnaire was distributed to the learners when they submitted their work for both the pretest and the posttest. The following topics are covered by the questions:

1. the actual situation of watching the film and the time gap between the viewing and the writing (Qs 1 and 2);
2. exposure to film reviews and previous learning (Qs 10, 11, 14, and 15);
3. awareness of purpose, of audience, and of target publication (Qs 3, 6, 7, 8, and 19);
4. actual planning, focus, and strategies in writing (Qs 4, 12, 13, 16, 17, 20, and 21).

The questions were grouped into 10 categories representing situational variables governing the strategies of the writer in the composing process. The ten categories are **T** (time and place of watching film); **G** (goal of watching the film and purpose of writing); **PL** (planning); **A** (audience awareness); **PU** (publication awareness); **EX** (previous exposure to film reviews); **GW** (groundwork on information); **M** (model for writing); **L** (previous learning); **F** (focus of writing); and **STR** (awareness of schematic structure).

Marks were awarded according to how similarly the learner composed the film review into what might be the process of the professional reviewer. A full mark was awarded if the learner did so; 0 mark if he or she deviated entirely from professional practice; and a half mark if somewhere in between. For example, a full mark was awarded for having a very clear publication in mind, for example, the Saturday Review of the *South China Morning Post*; no mark for having no idea where to publish the piece; and a half mark if the channel was not entirely appropriate, for example, in the *Campus Newsletter,* a quarterly publication devoted to campus news. A total of ten marks could be awarded, and the highest actual score was 8.5. Modeling was not penalized but rewarded as it was not regarded as an undesirable strategy for apprentice writers. They needed to conform to generic conventions and to use technical terms found in similar texts. Thus, the use of relevant texts for information and previous exposure to texts in the target genre were positive factors. Kress (1985, p. 47) provided a sound justification for doing so: ". . . the function of the writer is not that of a *creator* of text, but of an assembler of text. That is, out of her or his experience of other texts, he or she creates a new text which meets the demand of a particular social situation."

Interviews were conducted with subjects who showed considerable or little progress, or whose texts displayed interesting features, for example, very competent use of technical vocabulary relating to film production or inappropriate schematic structure in the post-test.

It should be mentioned that the learners were encouraged to revise their texts after the posttest was assessed, especially if they scored low marks. They were given individualized guidance on the alternative method; that is, a learner originally in the textual analysis group would be counseled on contextual awareness. The resubmitted texts were again assessed but subject to a 10 % discount in the marks gained. The revised marks were not taken into account for the purpose of this research.The scores of the pre- and posttests were calculated for difference. The criterial and holistic ratings were correlated, and both criterial and holistic ratings were correlated with the writing-questionnaire scores separately.

RESULTS

Similar Progress

The relative effectiveness of the two approaches is reported here, though no hard and fast conclusion regarding genre acquisition can be drawn because of the limited sample size, the particular genre used, and the special environment in which the research was conducted.

The assessment procedures seem to be reliable, as the scores obtained from the criterial rating (C rating) and holistic rating (H rating) of the pre- and posttests of the two groups display high correlations, ranging from .77 to over .92. The correlations between the test scores and those of the writing-strategy questionnaire are also high, between .6180 and .7278 except that for the pretest of the contextual-awareness-building group (CAB), which was .4207. This is significant because it reveals that improvement in the quality of texts correlates highly with enhancement in learner awareness of writer intent and professional-like practice in the production of the genre.

Both groups made considerable progress, as is evident in the difference between the marks in the pre- and posttests. CAB improved by 1.79 and 1.89 out of a possible maximum of 10 in the C and H ratings, respectively, and those for the textual-analysis group (TA) improved by 1.825 and 2.15, respectively. This seems to suggest that the subjects are more amenable to the textual-analysis approach. However, when the subjects were classified into three sectors according to their initial scores (low initial scores ranging from 1 to 3; medium initial scores, 3.5 to 5.5; and high initial scores, 6 and above), both C and H ratings revealed that the textual-analysis approach worked better with subjects with low or high initial scores, but not those with a medium initial score.

By contrast, CAB subjects with low and medium initial scores made considerable progress, but those with high initial scores actually displayed slightly negative progress (- 0.25 out of 10 marks for both C and H ratings). Analysis of individual cases reveals that the textual-analysis approach benefited a majority of subjects with low initial scores, whereas the contextual-awareness-building approach served a few subjects in that category well while the rest did not make much progress.

Other Observations

The TA group performed better in the "mechanistic" aspects of writing. Most film reviews written by this group in the posttests use an attractive title different from the title of the film itself. The formats are also better, for example, bracketing the actor's name after the character role name in the plot summary. The obligatory moves and features are all present and sequenced appropriately. A small minority display improvement in format and content, but not in the use of person and mood. One subject was unable to master the role relation of the writer, as is evident in the use of the pronoun "I" and rhetorical questions and exclamations, showing a subjective tone. Only one managed to rise by 4 points according to C rating, and two by 4.5 according to H rating. According to H and C ratings, respectively, one and two subjects did not show any progress.

The CAB subjects seemed able to master the real-life intent and practices of the film reviewer. Their film reviews in the posttests are much longer than those produced by the TA subjects. Most reviews include all obligatory moves. Instead of introducing the story, most mention in the introduction the film's location as compared with other films currently showing, or the historical setting of the film, though this was not a teaching point in the approach. The plot summaries are shorter and end before the complication. All these reveal a higher awareness of the overall discourse functions and moves of the film review: to evaluate the film for potential viewers. However, the reviews displayed weaknesses in the "mechanical" aspects not emphasized in the approach. In addition, most reviews did not use an attractive title, which was also not a teaching point.

One subject did not include a plot summary, even though she handled the linguistic features very well. This may be due to an awareness of discourse function, but indicative of a lack of awareness of the ideational content or the schematic structure. Although the mean progress in both CAB ratings was lower than that of TA, more made considerable progress—one subject each improved by 4, 4.5, and 5 out of 10 in C ratings and one by 5 and two by 4 in H ratings. However, three made no progress, and one showed regression according to C rating, and two and one, respectively, according to H rating. The results show that the approach benefits some considerably, whereas some are not amenable to it at all. This may be due to the fact that most subjects were used to learning English by rote and rules. One candidly remarked that "old habits die hard." There were also subjects in both groups who confessed that they resorted to modeling the superficial features of the "model text," even though they had been advised to choose structures and features that best suited the meanings they had in mind.

In both groups, there were learners who produced excellent film reviews even in the pretest. They already possessed good writing skills before coming to the course. Even though they did not show much improvement in the posttest, they admitted in the interview that the unit did enhance their awareness of either textual or contextual factors in writing. Another observation is that probably as a result of the experience, learners were capable of following the cultural norms of the target language. The film reviews in the posttest mainly focus on the viewability of the movies in the evaluation, as most film reviews in the English press do, instead of moralizing on the story, which is prominent in traditional Chinese film reviews.

CONCLUSIONS

The results show that both approaches yielded almost equal results in the quality of the subjects' writing products and their use of strategies to compose film reviews, despite a slight variation in the patterns of progress of the two groups, especially regarding differing pretest levels of competence. It seems that the hypotheses underlying the research are both valid to some extent; that is, "By learning to study the lexico-grammatical features of texts of a certain genre, learners should be more capable to write in that genre" and "Given the context, learners of a relatively high proficiency and trained in contextual analysis should be able to generate appropriate texts, using appropriate language from the system." Halliday (1991) suggested asking students to "predict the text from the context, and to predict the context from the text" (cited in Johns, 1997, p. 27). This juxtaposition would reduce the artificiality arising from "dichotomising the two approaches" in the design of the present study. After all, both approaches are adopted by writers in real life and, in actuality, are used for the rest of the Hong Kong course.

Both approaches in the study avoid the learning of formulae. Instead, learners were encouraged to formulate their own "rules." Above all, learners needed to familiarize themselves with the idea of choice, of making choices based on informed judgments of the wider sociocultural context, and identifying the interpersonal, ideational/experiential, and textual variables in the immediate situation of communication, as much as tapping their own grammatical, lexical, and syntactic resources in making and negotiating meaning.

APPENDIX A: QUESTIONNAIRE ON WRITING PROCESS

Pre-test

1. Where did you watch the film?
   a. at home
   b. in the cinema
2. How long after viewing the film did you start writing the review?
   a. same day
   b. within a week
   c. more than a week
3. When you watched the film, did you bear in mind the fact that you were watching for the purpose of writing the review?
   a. yes
   b. no
4. Did you do any planning before you wrote the review?
   a. yes
   b. no
5. When you planned or when you wrote, did you bear in mind who your reader was?
   a. yes
   b. no
6. If your answer to question 5 is "yes," who was the reader you had in mind? (You can choose more than one answer.)
   a. the teacher
   b. someone who wants to know whether the film is worth watching
   c. someone who has watched the film and would like to see how others comment on it.
7. When you planned or when you wrote, did you bear in mind where this review might be published?
   a. yes
   b. no
8. If your answer to question 7 is yes, what publication did you have in mind? (You can give as answer a Chinese publication.)
9. How interested are you in films?
   a. very interested
   b. quite interested
   c. not very interested
   d. not interested at all
10. Do you read film reviews in English?
    a. often
    b. sometimes
    c. rarely d. never
11. Do you read film reviews in Chinese?
    a. often

b. sometimes
c. rarely d. never

12. Before you wrote the film review, did you read up published film reviews on the film you were writing on for information?
    a. yes
    b. no
13. Did you follow any model in writing the film review?
    a. yes
    b. no
14. Have you written film reviews before coming to the course?
    a. yes
    b. no
15. Have you been taught to write film reviews before coming to the course?
    a. yes
    b. no
16. When you wrote the film review, which aspect did you pay primary attention to?
    a. the story
    b. the acting
    c. the production of the film
17. When you wrote the film review, which was your primary focus? (Choose ONLY one answer.)
    a. evaluating the film
    b. using correct grammar and expressions
18. What factors influenced you to write the film review as you did? (This is an open-ended question. You may include things like previous learning at school; past examination practice; your own writing style, but please explain in detail what you write.)
19. When you wrote the film review, did you write it as an assignment for the course, or did you treat it as a real film review?
20. When you planned or when you wrote, did you have an idea about the possible structure of the film review?
    a. yes
    b. no
21. If your answer to question 20 is "yes," what parts in the structure did you have in mind?

(The questionnaire for the pretest finishes here.)

<u>Post-test</u>

22. What improvements have you made in the posttest from the pretest?
23. What caused you to make such improvements?
24. Do you agree with the scores given?
    a. yes
    b. no

25. Do you agree with the comments given by the teacher?
    a. yes
    b. no

APPENDIX B: ASSESSMENT SHEET FILM REVIEW

Word Count:		**1 2 3 4**
A.1	Displaying overall functional and thematic unity	
A.2	Use of appropriate speech acts in the moves	
B.1.a	Incorporation of obligatory moves (I, S, E, & C)	
B.1.b	Inclusion of optional moves (BF & BW)	
B.2	Sequence moves in an inductive pattern	
C.1.a	Use of topic-related lexis	
C.1.b	Use of verbs to represent transitivity options	
C.1.c	Use of appropriate participant form (generic/specific)	
C.2.a	Appropriate use of cohesive devices—conjunctions (int. & ext.); references; lexical chains.	
C.2.b	Mastery of theme-rheme relations	
C.2.c	Appropriate format	
C.3.a	Use of appropriate moods	
C.3.b	Use of appropriate modals	
C.3.c	Display appropriate level of formality	

Global Rating:

Comments:

1. Very competent 2. Competent 3. Limited competence 4. Not yet

8

Texts and Contextual Layers: Academic Writing in Content Courses

Betty Samraj
San Diego State University

English for Academic Purposes (EAP) curricula have increasingly been influenced by the results of needs analysis. The sorts of needs analyses conducted within EAP undoubtedly have been influenced by our understanding of genres and the production of genres. Within the EAP tradition, a close relationship between purpose and text structure has been established (Hyon, 1996) and the rhetorical and linguistic features of various types of academic writing have been studied. Thus, different genres, such as introductions of research articles, have been characterized by their constituent moves (Swales, 1990). In addition, lexico-grammatical features, such as passives (Tarone, Dwyer, Gillette, & Icke, 1981) and authorial comment (Adams Smith, 1984) have also been studied. Studies of academic writing, mainly in Australia (for example, Drury & Webb, 1991; Adams Smith, 1990; and Rothery, 1980), have used Martin's (1984, p. 25) definition of genre as a "staged, goal-oriented purposeful activity" and his description of genre as representing "at an abstract level the verbal strategies used to accomplish social purposes of many kinds" (Martin, 1985, p. 251). These studies have isolated the schematic structure of texts and have also specified the generic structure potential of particular genres.

The notion of genre, especially within ESP and New Rhetoric (Hyon, 1996), has evolved over the last several years, moving from a consideration of genres characterized by the presence of certain formal features to a view of genres as "typical rhetorical engagements with recurring situations" (Freedman & Medway, 1994a, p. 3). These recent discussions of genre have also paid special attention to "the complex interplay between texts and their social contexts" (Freedman & Medway, 1994a, p. 8). The relationship has been argued to be not just unidirectional with social contexts affecting texts; texts are also seen to have a bearing on social contexts.

Paralleling the changing notions of genre in ESP and New Rhetoric has been a shift in the view of context from merely rhetorical to a broader conceptualization including both rhetorical situation and context of situation (Coe, 1994b, p. 161), in which the former includes purpose, audience, and occasion and the latter the sociocultural context. Context has also been described to include "social, cultural, political, ideological and discursive dimensions" (Freedman, 1994a, p. 194) and does not refer just to physical place (Johns, 1997, p. 27). Because the context that impinges on the text is seen to be multifaceted and complex, composition experts have wondered whether genres can be taught outside their native contexts (Coe, 1994b, p. 163; Freedman & Medway, 1994c, p. 11). The question has been whether it is feasible or useful to teach the structure of a workplace or academic genre in a writing classroom, definitely not the context in which it is usually produced.[1] Our ability to be able to satisfactorily answer this question no doubt depends on our understanding of the ways in which the context shapes the text.

Studies on academic discourse have sought to relate textual features to broader facets of the context, such as discipline, writing task, and student background. Recent research on writing in different disciplines can be viewed as attempts to connect textual features to disciplinary values, contextual factors that have been posited to influence text (Cheseri-Strater, 1991; Herrington, 1985, 1988; Walvoord & McCarthy, 1990). Another contextual variable is the writing task. For example, Greene (1993) asked whether texts written for different tasks vary in their overall organization. A report task and a problem-based task in a history course were shown to result in texts that have a "loose pattern of organization" (p. 62) and a "problem–solution structure" (p. 63), respectively. In his studies of writing produced by graduate students, Prior (1992, 1994, 1995) went further in the analysis of the context surrounding text production in an academic setting. Employing an ethnographic methodology, he explored the sociohistorical dimensions of the context of writing in an academic institution by focusing on the experiences of individual students and individual instructors, concluding that "academic discourse and academic environments are complex, constructed and unfolding events" (Prior, 1995, p. 77).

This chapter reports on a needs analysis of academic writing grounded in current understanding of genre that includes not just patterns in textual features but also the relationship of the text to the context in which it is produced, where context is broadly construed to include much more than physical context. The context will be analyzed in terms of levels ranging from the general level of the academic institution to the more specific level of the writing task. Previous studies of academic writing by students have focused on various contextual elements but have not necessarily explored the relationship among these elements. In order to explore more fully the relationship among various contextual features surrounding academic writing produced by students, a taxonomy of contextual layers constructed

---

[1]This question appears not to be as important within the Sydney School because context is analyzed in terms of the uncomplicated dimensions of field, mode, and tenor.

by the author will be presented. These layers have been arranged into levels as shown in Fig. 8.1 to depict how various contextual elements may be related one to another. This taxonomy will also be used to explain how context as a whole interacts with text. As shown in Fig. 8.1, the highest level of context that appears to influence the writing is the academic institution. The academic discipline forms a contextual level below this. At another level below, we have the context of the course, which does not completely overlap with the discipline in terms of its values. A more specific context within the course is that of task, and finally we have the context of each individual student in terms of his or her background and choices influencing the text produced.

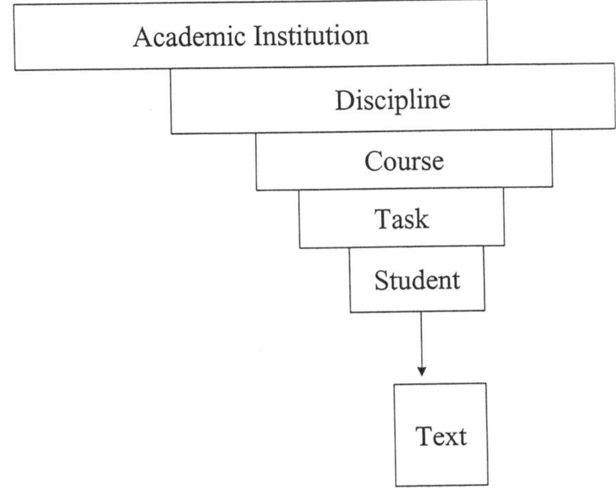

FIG. 8.1: Layers of Contexts

The context and purposes of each (student) writer will not be considered in this chapter, though they would undoubtedly reveal interesting information. The textual features considered here will include overall organization, grammatical and lexical features, and intertextual links. The results of a needs analysis with a broad perspective of context presented in this chapter could enable us to better answer the question of the feasibility and manner of teaching disciplinary writing in EAP programs, a question acknowledged to be problematic (Coe, 1994b, p. 163; Freedman & Medway, 1994a, p. 11).

In this study, the types of writing produced by students in a Master's program in environmental science in a School of Natural Resources and the Environment (SNRE) at a Midwestern university in the United States were explored. Environmental science was chosen because it is an interdisciplinary field, with a complex context, and growing in importance worldwide. The writing in three courses—Wildlife Behavior, Conservation Biology, and Resource Policy—were selected because they captured, to a certain extent, the broad spectrum of courses and subdisciplines included in environmental science. Conservation Biology is an interdisciplinary course in which biological science provides "principles and tools for preserving biological diversity" (Soule, 1985, p. 727). Wildlife Behavior, which deals with how environmental factors influence the ways in which organisms live and behave, and Resource Policy, concerned with United States resource and environmental policy formation and implementation, were selected as representative of the science-based and social-science-based courses included in the Master's-level curriculum.

The study incorporated certain elements of naturalistic investigations of writing conducted by composition specialists such as Walvoord and McCarthy (1990). Because the primary aim was to explore the relationship between text and context, the researcher attended the courses for the semester during which the data were collected, enabling her to become familiar with their subject matter and the types of meaning-making valued in each class. Being present in the classes also provided the researcher with access to oral discussions of the writing tasks and hence allowed her to have a better understanding of the context in which they were assigned. The grades, end comments, and marginal comments given by the subject instructors on each paper served as guides to the textual features that were important in the three contexts. A comparison of the papers deemed successful and less successful by the instructors enabled the researcher to better understand the textual features favored in these different contextual situations. Discussions with the instructors and some of the students in the courses further informed the analysis of the relationship between the textual patterns that emerged from the various discourse analyses performed (see Samraj, 1995, for more detailed account of analyses) and the contexts of production.

Though writing from the three courses was analyzed in the original study (Samraj, 1995), this chapter presents issues in writing from two courses, Wildlife Behavior and Resource Policy.[2] These two courses were chosen because they gave rise to writing activities that were most different from each other. In Wildlife Behavior, students had to produce a term paper that reviewed the literature on a certain wildlife-behavior topic chosen by the students themselves. Resource Policy focused on the process of environmental-policy formation and implementation. Three of the four written assignments were significantly different from those from the other courses as they sought to simulate workplace writing. Students wrote two short memos and a longer memo based on a research paper. I will discuss one of the short memos in this chapter instead of the research paper in order to explore the case of producing a workplace genre within an academic institution. Though the texts produced in both these courses shared one context, that of an M.A. program in environmental science at a large Midwestern university, there were differences in the other contextual layers that surrounded the texts.

In the context hierarchy, the context of the course shares some values with the context of the academic institution, as well as the context of the discipline. However,

[2]The number of texts analyzed from each course was determined by the number of students who agreed to be part of the study: eight from Wildlife Behavior and 40 from Resource Policy.

the course need not include all the values of the discipline because it is molded to a certain extent by the instructor or by departmental decisions and includes the class discussions as well as the readings and other activities that are part of the course requirements. The context of the course undoubtedly varied in a number of ways for Resource Policy and Wildlife Behavior, as will be discussed later. Within this context, we find the writing task. The context of the task can be said to include the communicative purpose of the written text, the audience invoked, and the roles taken by the students in producing the text. In the case of writing the memo in the Resource Policy course, the context of the task is further complicated by the simulated situation within which the text has to be produced. In Wildlife Behavior, by contrast, students produced a form of academic writing, a review paper, as a course requirement.

WILDLIFE BEHAVIOR

The context of the task within this course perhaps had the most obvious influence on the texts produced. The Wildlife Behavior paper was designated as a review paper and did not require reporting on original research. This paper was to include a report of previous research as well as a discussion of competing hypotheses and suggestions for future research. The communicative purpose of the text, to review and integrate studies on a particular animal behavior, is manifested in the overall organization of the student papers. In these, the research is reported either chronologically, with older studies and theories of animal behavior preceding newer ones, or nonchronologically, where the previous research is organized around constituent factors with regard to a particular animal behavior. For example, in one paper on infanticide in langurs, the author discusses older theories of this behavior before moving on to more current theories. In another paper, on chimpanzee maternal care, the student author organizes the paper around various factors such as parental care in general, maternal care versus male care, and alloparenting.[3]

The context of task and the genre can also explain the structure of the introductions in the Wildlife Behavior papers, which are quite unlike those found in research article introductions (Swales, 1990). Many of the introductions begin with a discussion of the animal behavior that is the focus of the paper and include some background research on the topic. In most cases, certain terms are also defined. Only three of the eight papers analyzed include some sort of problematization or indication of a gap at the beginning of the paper, as in the following example (italics added):

> The concept of natural selection as a process of "survival of the fittest" implies that competition occurs between individuals (Darwin, 1859). *Although many* have assumed that competition regularly occurs between individuals of one species due to their completely overlapping life requirements, *the alternate possibility of interspecific*

[3]*Alloparenting* is the mother-like behavior of females who care for offspring not their own.

> *competition has not always been so well received* (Arthur, 1987). Interspecific competition has been defined as interactions between individuals of two species which result in reduced reproductive success for individuals of at least one species (Arthur, 1987). The term asymmetric competition is often applied if such competition favors one species over the other. *To what degree is interspecific competition exhibited in the field? How could such competition evolve, given that intraspecific competition is the main source of competition for a given species?* This paper attempts to answer such questions through relevant studies of raptors.

As the papers were produced in response to a specific task, students did not appear to see the need to justify the literature review being provided; neither did the instructor appear to desire such a justification inasmuch as the absence of any rhetorical effort to establish the significance of the topic did not seem to adversely affect the evaluation of the paper.

The textual structure of the conclusions of the papers can also be related to the task description, which asked for suggestions for future research. The conclusions are not mere summaries of what is discussed in the papers. In all but one paper, the conclusions, which range in length from a few lines to a couple of pages, include a statement of future areas of research.

Writing tasks presented to students in the academic context also assign the students a particular role. In the Wildlife Behavior writing task, most students just filled the role of a "student" displaying knowledge and understanding of the field. The definition of terms in the beginning of some papers is a textual correlate of this role certain students see themselves playing. However, some writers of the Wildlife Behavior papers can also be said to be presenting themselves as potential research assistants by identifying an important gap in the research. In fact, one successful Wildlife Behavior paper received a response from the instructor encouraging the student to fill the gap in the research area.

There was a considerable overlap of the contexts of discipline and course in Wildlife Behavior, and these will be discussed together. Wildlife Behavior is a component of ecology and is concerned with hypothesis-testing and observable animal behavior. The classroom discourse manifested values of the discipline and included predictions based on various hypotheses about animal behavior in certain situations. For example, when discussing patchiness in spatial distribution of resources, the implications of movement from one patch to another were discussed for different scenarios, such as "If the two patches are similar," "If the two patches are different" (lecture notes, Oct. 17, 1992). Previous research (Walvoord & McCarthy, 1990) has shown the structure of classroom discourse to be closely related to the written discourse produced by students. In the Wildlife Behavior course, students who produced texts that were considered successful by the instructor contained "If–then" implication sequences that were present in the lectures:

> In addition, the sex ratio at birth may be biased in favor of the more expensive sex, as more of this sex will die before independence. If, for example, more male offspring than female offspring die prior to weaning in mammals, the sex ratio at birth might be male biased, but by the time of weaning would be biased toward the less expensive females.

Another clear influence of disciplinary values on the texts produced in Wildlife Behavior is in the intertextual links established with prior texts. "Far from being self-contained, far from being fixed, every text incorporates within itself an intersection, a dialogue, a network among writers and readers and other texts" (Selzer, 1993, p. 173). Intertextual links in the Wildlife Behavior papers are mostly restricted to biological and ecological studies of wildlife, scientific texts, and experiments. Many of the titles of books and articles include Latin names for the species being discussed, such as "Harem-male replacement and infanticide in the blue monkey (*Cercoithecus mitis stuhlmanni*) in the Kibule Forest, Uganda." This seems to be a means for the writers to align themselves with the biological discourse community. The date of publication of the materials referred to also seems to bear disciplinary influence. It is not uncommon for students to refer to the works of Darwin published in the 1800s, though these references are made only in the more successful papers from this course. Miller and Halloran (1993, p. 113) have pointed to the historical depth in the rhetoric of the evolutionary biology (a closely related field) essay, which is also manifested in some of the student texts from Wildlife Behavior.

Thus, a particular textual feature can be shaped by several contextual layers because each context is directly or indirectly influenced by the other contexts to which it is related. For example, the role assigned to students in the context of the task is partly a result of the task being embedded within a course in a discipline and academic context. Therefore, it is not always easy to delineate completely the parts of a multifaceted context that give rise to different aspects of a text.

RESOURCE POLICY

The context of the task in Resource Policy was more complex than in Wildlife Behavior because the students had to produce a text within an embedded simulated context of the workplace. The students were assigned a three-page memo to Governor Sargent of Massachusetts, advising him on how to go about implementing an extremely difficult transportation control plan. In this case, the task was carefully constructed in terms of writer's role, audience, topic, and, to some extent, content.[4] The students were given a case to read and instructed to use material from a reading assignment and lecture notes in writing the memo. Students were to take the role of a policy staff person working for a governor and assume they were in the context of advising the governor about a line of action concerning the previously mentioned bill. Because of this complex context of task, there are significant textual differences

---

[4]A copy of the assignment is provided in the appendix.

between the Resource Policy memos and the "review papers" produced in Wildlife Behavior.

The texts produced for this task have formal features that resemble those in workplace contexts. For instance, all the memos begin with the "To," "From," and "Subject" headings that characterize the beginnings of memos. Some of the students also tried to fit the text more into the simulated context by dating the memo appropriately to 1973 instead of 1992 (when the memos were written), by referring to supposed previous correspondence between Governor Sargent and themselves ("Thank you for requesting my analysis of the TCP decision") or making reference to hoped-for future communication with the Governor.

An important textual feature of the memos is placement of the recommended line of action in the introduction, as in the following excerpt:

> I suggest, Governor Sargent, that you select the only politically feasible option currently available to you—selective implementation of the EPA plan. Your primary concern at this moment is the 1974 election. You must, therefore, ensure your political survival through this crisis. Since conflict is inevitable, the key to your re-election is choosing the "safest" political route through this crisis. Strategic implementation of the EPA plan will result in the greatest potential for political gains and the least risk of political costs. One possible option is the EPA–State Cooperative plan minus politically sensitive programs such as the retrofit program.

Although the macrostructure of the memo was not specified in the assignment, students were told that the Governor had a busy agenda and did not have the time to read long memos. Given such a situation, we can perhaps say that the macrostructure placing the recommendation at the beginning of the memo was invoked by the specified audience.

Another textual feature that can be related to the simulated workplace context is the absence of explicit intertextual links. As mentioned earlier, the students were given materials such as cases to read and, though reference is made to the information from these materials, the intertextual links are not made explicit by the use of citations characteristic of academic writing. The student writers appear to have accurately estimated that shared knowledge is different in this simulated workplace context.

The communicative purpose of the memo, which was established by the writing task, is not just to inform the Governor about the recommended line of action but also to persuade him of its viability. As such, justifications are an important component of the memo. Most memos contain a number of recommendations in addition to the recommendation that the Governor give partial support for the Transportation Control Plan. These are all followed by justifications in the successful memos, resulting in a cyclical pattern as shown below:

Background
Main Recommendation
Extended Justification
[Minor Recommendation (1)]
[Justification (1)]
[Minor Recommendation (2)]
[Justification (2)]

Because of the genre and rhetorical context, students in this course adopted a role quite different from that adopted by those in the other course. Here the students took on the persona of a policy staff member within the Massachusetts Governor's office advising an elected official. In this simulated context, the student's persona is most clearly seen in the recommendations given. Some of these recommendations are very direct imperatives such as "Enforce those aspects of the TCP that are similar to the plan negotiated with the EPA officials in September." Here these students as officials do not seem to adopt the norms for academic writing of mitigating face-threatening acts when making new claims (Myers, 1989). The use of hedging devices such as modals and conditionals prevalent in academic discourse (Hyland, 1996) is conspicuously absent in the recommendations found in the memos.

A textual strategy that the students used that appears to be most misaligned with the simulated context, but in consonance with the larger academic context, is the conclusion. In Huckin and Olsen's (1991) description of professional memos, no mention is made of a conclusion. The structure of memos is given as one of movement from most crucial information in the Foreword and Summary to more detailed information in the rest of the memo. Conclusions, a general characteristic of academic papers, are found in several of the less successful student memos, revealing that conflicting values in different contexts, the context of the task and the context of the academic institution, can pose a problem for novice writers in simulated contexts.

The most obvious effect of the contexts of the discipline and the course relates to the social, economic, and political issues that are the focus of the memos. Unlike the writing in Wildlife Behavior, academic biological matters do not appear in the memos at all. Instead,the topics of focus are the environment and its preservation.

The discussions in the policy course also influenced the writing task. The professor conducted discussions of decision making similar to what the students had to produce in writing. In fact, students were told in the instructions for this writing assignment to "think through the political analysis framework we have been developing in class . . . and go over your notes from the lecture on elected executives" (see Appendix). This course made extensive use of cases, and students were given ample opportunity during class sessions to participate in discussions that involved making policy decisions within the context of simulated situations. During such discussions, students adopted the roles of policymakers in various politically challenging situations and provided relevant justifications for the courses of action advocated. As a result, the context of the writing task can be said to be squarely embedded in the context of the course.

DISCUSSION

When textual features are related to contextual elements in this study, a complex picture of the nature of writing practices in an academic institution appears. In particular, some of the varying contextual influences of the texts were identified. The world of work that the students were being prepared for formed an overarching context that had some indirect effect on the writing students produced. Discussions with administrators and senior faculty members in the school revealed that most of these students working on a Master's degree, within Environmental Science, in Resource Ecology and Management and especially Resource Policy and Behavior, would pursue professional careers in government agencies, such as the State Department of Natural Resources, environmental consulting firms, nonprofit organizations such as the World Wildlife Fund, or even doing field research. As a consequence, the curriculum of the school was developed and structured to meet the needs of these students and society. The writing task in Resource Policy can be seen as an instance of this larger context beyond the school affecting the writing experiences of the students.

The writing tasks faced by Master's-level students in SNRE can also be argued to be influenced, in some cases, by the context of the school: its values, and traditions. The school describes itself as being interdisciplinary in its focus. The curriculum is described as "interdisciplinary coursework in natural resources" (Bryant, Gregerman, Crowfoot, Kaplan, Nowak, & Stapp, 1987, p. 198) in an issue of the *Environmental Professional* devoted to descriptions of various environmental programs in the United States and Canada. This aim to be interdisciplinary has affected the types of courses students have to take in a particular program, and as a result, the range of writing experiences they have, including the writing of memos and review papers.

The values of the two fields, Resource Policy and Wildlife Behavior, also formed a contextual layer around the texts produced. The foci of the texts produced, political in the former, and biological/ecological in the latter, can be traced to this contextual layer. The context of the course including the class discussions also was a clear influence on the texts produced. The type of inferencing, "if–then sequences," produced in the oral discussions in the Wildlife Behavior classroom, is evident in the written texts. In the Resource Policy course, oral discussions of recommendations and their justifications were an important contextual layer that influenced the writing task. Finally, the context of the task containing within it the communicative purpose of a text, the role the student had to adopt, and the audience involved were seen to be powerful influences on the text.

The analysis also indicates that textual features cannot always be traced back to one layer of the context, as these levels or layers of context are themselves connected to one another. For example, the contexts of course and discipline were seen to be closely connected in Wildlife Behavior. The intertextual links established in the student papers are related to values that belong to both the contexts of the course and discipline in this case. However, these two contexts, though related, are not identical, which can be used to explain differences in textual norms in student writing compared to published academic writing (see Samraj, 1995). This broad view of the context as multilayered also shows that features of different contextual layers can be in dissonance. This was perhaps most clearly seen in the writing of the memo in Resource Policy. As discussed earlier, a workplace context was embedded within the context of the task in this course, and, consequently, features of the simulated context were not always in alignment with the overarching context of the academic institution.

This analysis of student writing also reveals that some of the graduate students experienced difficulty producing writing that was valued by the instructors of the different courses. Some of the problematic aspects of student writing could be explained through the students' failure to consider the importance of certain layers of context that had a bearing on the writing. For example, in Resource Policy, some students' papers were not as successful as others because they failed to place as much value as expected on the context of the task. Freedman (1995, p. 141) claimed that students in disciplinary courses can learn to write "extraordinarily well" by being immersed in the "extraordinarily rich discursive contexts provided in disciplinary classrooms" (Freedman, 1995, p. 134). Though students in my study wrote in a rich context with many layers, they did not always succeed in responding appropriately to the relevant values of the contexts.

The results of this needs analysis in which genre is related to context lead to two central questions. First, should there be separate instruction for writing in the disciplines? Second, if so, how should the instruction be carried out? The following discussion seeks to address both questions.

Some composition teachers and scholars have taken a stance against teaching disciplinary writing in the composition classroom. One reason offered for this is that this writing is complex, and that the rules are too complex and too numerous to be understood and articulated by an outsider to a specific discourse community (Freedman,1994). The teaching of workplace writing has also been discouraged, for similar reasons. Hill and Resnick (1995) argued that simulations of workplace writing in the composition classroom are deficient because they provide simplified writing situations that students are unlikely to meet in the real workplace. These authors state that these simulations specify the mode of communication to be used and the purpose and audience for the text, which are often different from experiences in workplace sites.

Recent studies on writing in the disciplines and in the workplace (such as Beaufort, 1997) have shown us how complex the writing activities are; there are no simple formulae for writing success in these contexts. It has been shown that teachers will not be able to completely replicate workplace (see Freedman, Adam, & Smart, 1994) or disciplinary writing in the composition classroom because it is impossible to replicate all the necessary workplace and disciplinary settings to meet the needs of all the students.

However, research has not shown if students' learning to write in simulated contexts has actually been detrimental to their eventual writing in these workplace and disciplinary contexts. By learning to write in simulated contexts, students can learn at least some of the textual features that are favored in those contexts, which can facilitate acculturation into the target context. The simulated writing assignment in Resource Policy is a case in point, for students did learn some of the norms of writing that were connected to the workplace setting (for example, the need to state the recommendation at the beginning of the memo) that they would not have otherwise acquired.

Some recent work (Henry & Roseberry, 1998; Hyon, 1995; Madden & Myers, 1998) has indicated that the explicit teaching of genres within composition classrooms has led to learning. Though not studies on the teaching of complex disciplinary or workplace writing, they have still indicated that students can usefully be made aware of the structures of genres. Future studies need to trace the writing experiences and successes of students in content courses and the workplace after they have been given explicit genre instruction in composition courses.

Composition experts (such as Coe, 1994b) have asserted the need for teachers to provide contextual information when discussing different genres with their students. The results of studies such as the present one can be used by EAP teachers to discuss the ways in which writing can vary across contexts. EAP teachers need to stress that academic writing varies not just along disciplinary lines. Instead, they need to help students understand the multiplicity of the contextual layers surrounding the texts produced in content classes or professional contexts.

The results of this study suggest that it is not sufficient for EAP teachers to present to their students different "packages" of textual features that belong to different genres, because students may not be producing identifiable genres in their content courses. Rather, as Johns (1997) and others have advocated, EAP teachers need to enable their students to become ethnographers of the writing practices of their disciplinary communities. In making their students ethnographers, EAP teachers should also pay considerable attention to the ways in which contextual dimensions or layers of context can be brought together to give rise to various kinds of texts.

Strategies that have been suggested for teaching the process of genre production (such as Flowerdew, 1993) can be modified by EAP teachers to focus more on the role of context. Flowerdew (1993), Johns (1997), and Bhatia (1993) suggested that teachers can use the results of previous genre analyses to make their students aware of variation across and within genres. EAP teachers could also draw from previous studies on the relationship of text and context to discuss with their students the variation found in the contextual layers surrounding texts. Class discussion could also then center on the different textual values that parallel certain contextual features. As a result, EAP teachers can hope to increase students' awareness not only of the discursive features found in texts, but also the levels of contexts that have a bearing on text structure in academic writing. In other words, students can learn to "metacommunicate" (Flowerdew, 1993) not just about text, but also about context.

This study illustrates in concrete terms the complexity of the contexts in which students write in the disciplines, even within a single major. It adds to previous studies on student writing in the disciplines not just by showing how texts produced in various courses vary in terms of their textual features, but also by proposing a taxonomy of context layering to explain these textual differences in terms of the contexts that surround the texts. It demonstrates how layers of contexts can be juxtaposed and together can reinforce a particular textual feature or how various layers can be in dissonance. Moreover, it reveals the complex ways in which writing in different academic courses are related.

APPENDIX: DECISION MEMO ASSIGNMENT, EPA AND TRANSPORATION CONTROLS

It is late November 1973. On November 8, EPA published the final transportation control plan (TCP) for the Boston metropolitan area. It is a plan that has shocked Massachusetts officials for it calls on them to implement a series of fairly drastic measures in a very short time period. State officials are concerned both about the "absurd time schedules" contained in the plan and the likelihood that the plan would impose enormous burdens on the state budget. For example, the plan mandates that a system for inspecting and maintaining emission controls on all gasoline-powered vehicles has to be developed and adopted by the state legislature in less than five months. Having worked for a number of months with the EPA to develop a feasible TCP, Massachusetts Governor Frank Sargent is surprised by the provisions contained in the final TCP and concerned about its impact on the state, yet is ostensibly required by law to carry out this plan. In his view, the state has several ways in which it could respond to the federal mandate, none of which are overwhelmingly attractive: He could try to enforce the plan; he could enforce it selectively; he could try to continue to negotiate with the EPA; or he could refuse to enforce the plan.

As a member of Governor Sargent's policy staff, you have been asked to advise the Governor on the way in which the State should respond to the EPA's plan. You should outline your recommendation clearly, documenting the reasons you chose your selected strategy. (Your proposal may be one of the options listed in the previous paragraph or another approach, if you think it would be more feasible). Your memo should concentrate on *an explicit evaluation of the political feasibility of taking the action you prescribe*, that is, its political benefits and costs given the political environment described in the case, and considering the Governor's policy and political stakes in the issue and the resources he has to make and implement his decision.

Your memo should be no more than three double-spaced typed pages (approx. 750 words). Take the time to write a clear, concise memo. The Governor's agenda is full; he has little time to read lengthy memos. To assist you in preparing the memo, you should probably think through the political analysis framework we have been developing in class, read the background material on Governor Sargent contained in the Weinberg reading (assigned 10/1). You may work in groups to analyze the case and discuss Governor Sargent's options, but your memo should be an individual effort. (original emphases)

Part V

The New Rhetoric

9

Writing Instruction in English for Academic Purposes (EAP) Classes: Introducing Second Language Learners to the Academic Community

Christine Adam
Natasha Artemeva
Carleton University, Canada

This chapter examines implications of current research and theory in the field of first language writing, specifically theories of genre and situated learning for the instruction of English as a second language for academic purposes (EAP). We wish to enter the discussion as researchers of first language writing and as teachers who teach writing in EAP classes to international students. In fact, this chapter arises out of a dissonance we feel in our experiences as both researchers and teachers of writing. We will review some of the key developments in composition theory and research and look at some issues that arise when these are applied in a second-language classroom setting. In doing so, we will draw on one of our EAP classrooms to illustrate how carefully constructed language instruction and the use of electronic discussion groups allow students to learn both content and appropriate response to the rhetorical situations they will meet in disciplinary classrooms.

In a 1995 article in *College Composition and Communication*, Muchiri, Mulamba, Myers, and Ndoloi stressed the important contributions of first language composition research to the EAP community but warned us that it has necessary, and crucial, limitations. They wrote that EAP "works in multilingual settings by narrowing the range of English until it is considered teachable. Its researchers and teachers have something to learn from the broader range of English use considered in composition research and literacy studies" (p. 190). They suggested beginning a discussion among composition researchers and EAP writing teachers.

Although Muchiri et al. (1995) saw the need for second language teachers and composition researchers to examine the pedagogical usefulness of current writing theory and research, we must keep in mind that such a discussion has only recently begun in the field of first language writing instruction. In the introduction to *Reconceiving Writing, Rethinking Writing Instruction*, Joseph Petraglia (1995) wrote that "to date, there has been relatively little concerted discussion within the writing field that concentrated specifically on the fundamentally awkward relationship of writing theory and most writing instruction" (p. xiii). Petraglia's edited collection focuses primarily on the (mainly American) practice of teaching first-year composition (what he refers to as "general writing skills instruction") in university. This discussion, though it obviously will have important differences, can provide us with valuable insights into EAP pedagogy. Our intentions here are to examine some of the ways in which composition theory and research are being considered in first language (L1) writing pedagogy and to analyze the usefulness and limitations of some of these discussions for the EAP classroom.

WRITING THEORY AND RESEARCH

It goes without saying that L1 writing theory and research are increasingly rich, both because of the range of disciplines they draw on (literary theory, social and cognitive psychology, education, linguistics) and the diversity of research settings (varying levels of formal education, work sites, and so on). As researchers, our work has been enriched by this diversity. In what follows, we review some of the key theoretical and research issues that have shaped our thinking about writing pedagogy in the EAP classroom.

THEORIES OF GENRE

One of the most important catalysts for, and consequences of, this academic field has been a redefinition, or reconceptualization, of what we understand as genre. Previously seen as a means of categorizing text types (primarily literary ones) on the basis of surface features or formats, genre has been expanded to encompass all there is that causes those features and that makes them recognizable. Carolyn Miller (1984), in a seminal article "Genre as Social Action," called us to look at genres as typified responses to situations we socially construct or recognize as recurrent. Viewed in this way, genre includes a multitude of things—the exigencies which bring about the need for some form of discourse, the ways in which we actually compose it, whether we collaborate in order to do so, when we read it, why, how, and where. John Swales (1990), looking at genre from a teacher's perspective, proposed a somewhat different definition. He defined genre as a class of communicative events that share a common communicative purpose. Swales located genres within discourse communities, (that is, groups of people who share certain language-using practices) which develop, use, and modify written genres in response to the recurrent rhetorical situations they face. By thus locating genres, Swales provided a useful means for looking at how they work in educational settings, in a way clearly distinguishable from the so-called Sydney School of genre-based literacy instruction (see Freedman & Medway, 1994c; and Feez, this volume, & Macken-Horarik, this volume, for further discussion of this distinction).

Redefinitions of genre also recognize the plasticity and flexibility of texts and the rhetor's ability to reshape and manipulate genres to suit certain rhetorical situations. See, for example, Schryer's (1995) use of "genre" as a verb: we genre our way through social interactions, choosing the correct form in response to each communicative situation we encounter (and with varying degrees of mastery).

Bakhtinian Notions of Utterance and Addressivity

The writings of Bakhtin have enhanced our understanding of the social embeddedness of genre and the acquisition of genres (both written and oral) within communities of language users. In "The Problem of Speech Genres" (1986), Bakhtin provided two useful concepts for understanding the nature of genre: the utterance as the analyzable unit of speech, and the addressive nature of speech. First, Bakhtin proposed that we regard the utterance as the analyzable unit of discourse because it "occupies a particular definite position in a given sphere of communication" (p. 91). Words and sentences acquire meaning through the utterance. Bakhtin claimed that speakers are able to choose the generic form of utterance that best accomplishes their speech plan (or intention) within the communicative situations in which they find themselves interacting with others. Second, as a link in a chain of discourse, the utterance is fundamentally dual in nature—it simultaneously responds to past utterances while also anticipating future utterances; it is at the same time responsive and response-driven.

Bakhtin also pointed to a general awareness of the presence of "the other" in language as well as the more specific awareness of a partner in a communicative situation:

> ...from the very beginning, the utterance is constructed while taking into account possible responsive reactions, for whose sake, in essence, it is actually created. As we know, the role of the *others* for whom the utterance is constructed is extremely great.... From the very beginning the speaker expects a response from them, an active responsive understanding. The entire utterance is constructed, as it were, in anticipation of encountering this response. (p. 94, emphasis in original)

Because speakers and writers anticipate response, we can see how their texts are in fact shaped by an awareness (however tacit) of the addressivity of speech. Equally important to Bakhtin is the role of earlier utterances, arising out of both oral and literate "conversations," which provide speakers with a rich store to draw on as they shape their own utterance.

> Each utterance is filled with echoes and reverberations of other utterances to which it is related by the communality of the sphere of speech communication. Each utterance refutes, affirms, supplements, and relies on the others, presupposes them to be known, and somehow takes them into account. (p. 91)

Another Bakhtinian notion important to this discussion is the distinction between primary genres, which are most akin to forms of spoken communication, and secondary genres, more complex written forms. He refers to the relationship between these, asserting that "primary genres are altered and assume a special characteristic when they enter into complex ones" (p. 62). Recognizing how these various genres intertwine and enrich one another can become a key issue in writing pedagogy, particularly in EAP classrooms where students are required to master secondary genres while, in many cases, they have not yet mastered primary genres in the target language.

SITUATED LEARNING

Berkenkotter & Huckin wrote in a 1993 article in *Written Communication* that an important feature of genres is that they are situated in, and learned through, social processes. The enculturation of the writer (academic or workplace) into the appropriate discourse of a new setting is paramount to his or her becoming a member of that community. The field of situated learning, most usefully outlined in *Everyday Cognition: Its Development in Social Context* (Rogoff & Lave, 1984), has significantly contributed to our understanding of how it is that genres are learned and mastered. Although processes of "situated learning" or "situated cognition" may be interpreted and applied in a number of ways, there are these important similarities:

1. A central tenet is that learning is not something that goes on solely in the head of the learner or as the transference of "knowledge" from one head to another. Rather, learning is understood to take place through performance or engagement.
2. Learning is viewed as social. Within communities of practice, there is collaboration among relative old-timers (or "guides") and newcomers (or "learners").
3. The learner's participation in community practices is attenuated; the guide very often models and then gradually gives over more and more of a task to the learner (Freedman & Adam, 1996; Hanks, 1991).

A separate emphasis in the study of situated cognition is put on the question of transferability of acquired skills to other, usually more complex, contexts. This is an especially important issue in the study of genre learning in educational settings—ones in which students move from one "community" to another as they leave one class and go on to the next.

RECENT TRENDS IN GENRE RESEARCH

The reconceptualization of genre has been complemented and extended by a range of writing research that has moved away from a solely text-based agenda to one that explores the complex and shifting relations between textual features and rhetorical situations. When writing is viewed as situated within the social, and the features of writing are viewed as constituents of social motives and responses, writing researchers find themselves increasingly using the texts as artifacts from which they can infer functions, determine strategies, and relate them to rhetorical contexts (Coe, 1994b). Additionally, researchers' interests have extended beyond the university classroom to such diverse sites as tax accountants' offices (Devitt, 1991), high technology companies (Artemeva, 1998), social work agencies (Paré, 1991), central banks (Smart, 1993), and industry (Yates & Orlinkowski, 1992).

Of course, there is a continued interest in writing in academic settings, but through a social lens. Rather than focusing on the ways in which individual writers, skilled and unskilled, tackle simulated, experimental writing tasks, researchers have begun to investigate academic writing "in situ"—going into classrooms, studying how writing plays a role in learning, how it differs not only from discipline to discipline (McCarthy, 1987, and Walvoord & McCarthy, 1990) but also from classroom to classroom within the same discipline (Samraj, this volume).

This growth in research both inside and outside the university has led to a number of important points for consideration in our understanding of writing and the learning of genres:

- Genres arise out of, and reflect, a rich discursive environment (Hunt, 1994a, 1998b; Yates & Orlikowski, 1992);
- Genre research is characterized by more than just textual features, including composing processes, modes of collaboration, and reading processes, among others (Freedman, Adam, & Smart, 1994; Paré & Smart, 1994);
- Much of the rhetor's knowledge of genres is tacit, even, or especially, for expert writers (Freedman, 1987, 1993, and Medway, 1993);
- One's ability to "genre" in a community is almost always a necessary part of his or her socialization/acceptance into a community (Berkenkotter, Huckin, & Ackerman, 1991; Freedman & Adam, 1996); and
- People learn to use genres (at home, in the community, in classrooms, at work) very often without explicit instruction (Dias, Freedman, Medway, & Paré, 1999; Freedman & Adam, 1996; Freedman, Adam, & Smart, 1994; Heath, 1983).

This last point is important because it leads us to look at how it is that genres are learned and, conversely, taught. When we look beyond our own educational contexts—where we rarely question the fact that we need to "teach" students how to write the genres that are expected of them, and we look at the many other settings in which people write, and do so with considerable skill—we encounter a radically different perspective on genre learning. Studies such as Freedman and Adam (1996) pointed to the usefulness of theories of situated learning in "illuminating what happens in both university and workplace settings as members of both communities set out on the business of writing and learning to write" (p. 396). Drawing on and adapting analysis presented by Lave and Wenger (1991), these authors suggested that the following areas are key in determining successful genre learning: the goals, authenticity, and attenuation of the writing task; the roles assumed by guides and learners; the nature of evaluation; and the sites for learning.

IMPLICATIONS FOR EAP WRITING INSTRUCTION

Research that examines the ways students, or new employees, learn to write in new situations and that considers classrooms and worksites as new "cultures," that the newcomer must navigate has been useful for us as second language teachers—for our students are indeed journeying through many layers of enculturation as they begin to study in English-language universities. We have been able to draw on first language research and theory, particularly from the areas of genre theory and situated learning, to question assumptions in our teaching and to find explanations for pedagogical ineffectiveness. However, our enthusiasm for direct applications of theories of genre and situated learning to the EAP classroom is tempered by an awareness that there are important cultural, linguistic, and social factors that have a bearing on a writer's movement into any community. In EAP classes, students often face totally different relationships between self and others than the ones they were used to in their own cultures; they go through processes of negotiating and acquiring new social identities and appropriating the objects and goals of a new community (A. Lee, personal communication, January 17, 1998). All of these factors may, in fact, impede the second language student's enculturation into a North American academic setting.

In what follows, we will highlight a number of issues that have arisen as we ourselves have gone about attempting to apply recent writing research and theory in our EAP classroom teaching. First, we examine the popular and well-established movement toward content-based language instruction (Johns, 1997). In doing so, we argue for a rethinking of the nature of the content used in the EAP classroom if the EAP course is not attached to a subject-matter course. We then examine an EAP course in which the content is language-learning itself. A key component of the communication used by students in this course is the electronic newsgroup—a recent pedagogical innovation that we also study in light of reconceived notions of genre and genre learning.

WHAT GETS TAUGHT IN EAP WRITING CLASSES

In this section, we examine the selection of content for EAP courses that are taught to students who come from a variety of disciplines and that are not linked to or "sheltered" by a disciplinary course (for definitions of these EAP models, see Johns, 1997). As we see it, there are two potential hazards in applying current writing research and theory to this type of EAP classroom:

1. that a language instruction curriculum is implemented in which we are in danger of equating "accuracy" with "authenticity," (Petraglia, 1995, p. 93) by importing pared-down, "real" situations and texts into our classrooms from other parts of the university; and/or
2. that we conclude that the social nature of academic writing is simply too complex and shifting and decide to focus on teaching the more stable concepts of text structures and language forms, and/or encouraging students to develop their "sense of themselves as writers," inventing their own particular rhetorical situations.[2]

In the first case, we refer to the popularity of a variation of content-based language instruction, in which

> the language instructor is responsible for teaching both content and language, usually doing so without the collaboration of content-area faculty as the course is not taught in conjunction with a sister academic course. Replacing the subject matter and academic processes and tasks associated with a sister content course, then, are one or more mini-topics or themes. Themes are chosen to best meet the interests of the students, who come from a variety of disciplines, or no discipline at all, and form the basis of the integrated and contextualized language instruction. (Meyer, 1994, p. 10)

This model is based on the assumption that in order to provide "authentic" tasks for the EAP classroom, teachers need to find "academic" input and stimulate relevant output to fill the pedagogical space in the classroom. With little concern for their real world pedagogical purposes or importance, samples of texts and tasks are taken from disciplines around the university and presented to the students in order to facilitate their performance "as" particular types of students. Russell Hunt (1993) referred to such sample texts as *textoids*—those in which the reader (or writer) is passively decoding (or coding) language and in which "interpretation and response tend to wander...." He described a situation in which students wrote in response to Hemingway's "Hills Like White Elephants" as part of an in-class assignment: "They [the students] didn't read for meaning, or write to convey it. Nor, not at all incidentally, did I read what they wrote for its meaning: I read it to find out what they knew—a completely different matter—*and to assess their ability to write*." (emphasis ours).

The importation of disciplinary content into the EAP classroom is an enterprise admirable for the intricacy with which it concocts roles for students and teachers, texts and assignments. But at its base, that is all it is—a mélange of stripped-down, rhetorically simplified events. The sampling of "real" themes (for example, topics like "Desertification" or "Global Warming"), texts, and tasks from a disciplinary classroom into the EAP classroom "misrepresents and oversimplifies academic

[2]A useful initial discussion on the second issue—writing instruction that attempts to situate itself outside of the complexities and power-relationships of much other academic writing—can be found in Bartholomae (1995) and Elbow (1995).

discourse and reduces it to some stable and autonomous phenomenon that does not reflect reality" (Zamel, 1995, p. 515). Themes, texts, and tasks are imported from disciplinary classrooms to a very different context and, therefore, the focus of teachers' and students' attention is changed dramatically from the original rhetorical context. Unlike in a disciplinary classroom, the EAP instructor cannot respond authentically to the content of the students' writing and is left to comment on textual features and use of language. There is, in fact, a pseudo-exigence to the rhetorical activity that results in both students and teachers performing in an "as-if" setting.

The obvious questions arise: How can we as teachers assist our students in developing their English language skills and, at the same time, work toward their mastery of pedagogical genres? What, therefore, can be the subject matter in the EAP course that is taught to students who come from a variety of disciplines? Our response is actually a series of (rhetorical) questions: Inasmuch as the students really are learning to develop their language/writing skills, why not make that the subject? Why bother approximating disciplinary genres that are, in fact, far from being stable entities and that continue to evolve (Kamberelis, 1995) according to the individual teacher's idiosyncrasies, world view, time constraints, teaching goals, values, and so on? Why not simply have the students engage, *as EAP students*, in the study of English and of learning English and use or develop classroom genres to reach that end?

How Do We Determine "Authenticity" in the EAP Classroom?

EAP students *do* need to address authentic tasks, for we know that successful language acquisition takes place through genuine communicative need (Brinton, Snow, & Wesche, 1989), but as second language teachers we often overlook the fact that we can quite legitimately provide and shape those tasks within their own classroom contexts and from our own areas of expertise. In fact, the more that we are able to provide input that we ourselves understand and to respond to student writing as ourselves, the more "authentic" a learning environment we create for our students—an environment that acknowledges who the students are, why they are there, what the teacher's role is, and where that classroom is situated within the context of an academic institution. In the same way that other courses in the university are "busy noisy, intertextual space[s]" (Bartholomae, 1995, p. 64) to which students are expected to respond, we too need to establish classroom contexts which are messy, rhetorically sophisticated ones—places where students are required to negotiate by managing rhetorical tasks. Bartholomae (1995) stated that students need to see themselves inside an event: "a practice—linguistic, rhetorical, cultural, [and] historical" (p. 65).

Acknowledging the importance of authenticity for classroom tasks has consequences for our students' learning. In fact, the face validity of the content our students learn and the tasks they perform can play an important role in their motivation. In this respect, Russell Hunt (1998b) referred to Carolyn Miller's distinction between Bitzer's "exigency" and Burke's "motive." The exigency, according to Miller, has to be recognized by the actor to become a motive. EAP students need to perceive what they are doing as real and of consequence, rather than viewing their tasks as dummy runs or simulations of something "out there" in the rest of the university. Hunt (1993) wrote that "the way to create a context in which students are writing and reading for meaning is to put the writing and reading into situations where they serve purposes which the students can see as real and which they can adopt as their own." The danger in an EAP classroom that attempts to import tasks from various disciplines is that the students may not view these tasks as relevant and/or real.

Our point is this: We believe that content is important, but not content for content's sake. Rather, we are making an argument for pedagogical content that acknowledges what the student is there for.[3] In developing language curricula, EAP teachers and curriculum developers have turned to experts in other academic fields to find out how they teach and what they require students to write (Johns, 1997). In doing so, however, some of them have been mistaken in assuming that they should adopt into EAP curricula other disciplines' tasks and texts. A pendulum's swing in the other direction, and EAP teachers decide that all that the academy demands cannot possibly be taught, and so they turn away from any type of classroom subject matter and have students write "writing"—choosing their own chosen topics with the impression that anything that helps them to write will assist them in their future experiences at university. What EAP teachers miss in this case, however, is the second-language students' development of their sense of themselves *as members of an academic community.*

What Do EAP Teachers Focus On?

The general practice of teaching "virtually any of the forms of discourse used by any discourse system which functions in English" (Scollon & Wong-Scollon, 1995, p. 200) in the EAP classroom leads to the situation in which EAP teachers teach forms of discourse they themselves rarely or never use outside of the classroom. Therefore, for these EAP teachers, the primary function of a specific genre is not its authentic use, but use as an example in the class (Scollon & Wong-Scollon, 1995). Whereas in a disciplinary classroom language is considered a vehicle for mastering subject matter, in an EAP classroom, content is often treated as a convenient vehicle for teaching language. EAP teachers—with their focus on the features of written discourse—often do not, or cannot (as they have little factual knowledge of the

---

[3]Jolliffe (1995) cited Kaufer and Young's distinction between "content" and "subject matter," content being of the "What I did on my summer vacation" variety, and subject matter referring to content that has been discussed in recurrent rhetorical situations, has a publicly shared history, and a theory to be learned (p.200). He pointed out that there are typically three pedagogical approaches to "content" in the general writing skills instruction classroom: (a) student-centered, expressive; (b) teacher-mandated (e.g., thematic units); and (c) a "blended compromise" in which the students write on a specific topic but draw on their own personal experience with, and response to, that topic.

content), pay much attention to the accuracy of the content of a written piece produced by a student (Zamel, 1985).

THEORY IN PRACTICE: WHAT CAN BE TAUGHT IN EAP CLASSES?

There is no reason why EAP teachers cannot teach language skills in the context of a course in which they can act as experts in disciplinary content. For example, EAP teachers can teach their students important factual data and theories about language-learning that will make students more aware of the process they are going through, and that they as second language learners can benefit from. At the same time, EAP teachers can grade papers according to the quality of their content *and* their use of language, both of which indicate a student's ability to participate appropriately in the discourse of the classroom.

Designing a Course

The second author of this chapter has attempted to apply principles of theories of genre and situated learning to the teaching of an intermediate EAP credit course offered at a Canadian university. The goal of the course was to engage students in a series of logically connected writing activities to allow them to begin their acculturation into the genres of North American academic writing. The course was organized around thematic units, with the emphasis on the area of the teacher's professional expertise: the teacher selected and presented units in such a way that the course followed a continuous theme—language learning.

The course was designed around various writing activities that would culminate in a final assignment. The requirement was that the topic of the final assignment relate to the umbrella theme of the course—language learning—and at the same time raise a question that was important for the student as a member of an academic community. The final assignment consisted of several interconnected activities that preceded the submission of the final paper. Students were asked to review each other's "proposals" for the final paper posted to the electronic course newsgroup and to provide feedback to their classmates; to make the final choice of their topic based on the feedback received from peers and the teacher; to select relevant sources from those considered in class and to do some independent library search; to make an oral presentation on the chosen topic in class; and, finally, to write and submit the final paper.

The teacher felt competent responding to the content of student writing, as she was able to focus legitimately on both content and language use. Rogoff (1990) stated in her discussion of one model of situated learning (guided participation) that one of its most important characteristics is that it engages learners and experts in a collaborative process of building bridges from the novices' present understanding and skills to arranging and structuring novices' participation in activities. This, of course, resonates with Vygotsky's (1978) notion Zone of Proximal Development, which he defined as "the distance between the actual developmental level as determined by independent problem solving and the level of potential development as determined through the problem solving under adult guidance or in collaboration with more capable peers" (p. 86).

Using an Electronic Medium

As the use of computers in language classrooms has increased dramatically over the past years, second language teachers have started to recognize and acknowledge the social aspect of computing as a tool that creates a medium for student communication in the target language (Savignon & Van Patten, reported in Beauvois, 1995). Recent second language acquisition research that focuses on the social aspects of second language learning emphasizes the need to use the target language in meaningful communicative activities in EAP. In the EAP class, the typical student is often trying to improve his or her abilities in producing what Bakhtin (1986) referred to as secondary genres (and EAP courses are almost always explicitly about that), when very often his or her control of primary genres is weak or nonexistent. In fact, for many students, their only contact with English, their only sense of themselves as being a part of an English-language community, is in the EAP classroom. In the course we describe in this chapter, students were asked to participate in an electronic newsgroup[4] discussion throughout the term, post their journals, comment on other students' postings, and raise questions. The purpose of the electronic newsgroup was threefold: to provoke discussion on topics related to the theme of the course, to provide opportunities for "regulated improvisations" (Schryer, 1998), and to allow for an easier transition from informal "conversation" on topics related to classroom discussions to formal academic writing. By introducing the newsgroup into the EAP classroom, the teacher creates a space "in which the context of utterances is immediately and perceptibly available to the participant in a useful and accessible form, offering more functional information for planning and shaping the discourse: offering ... back pressure that is very similar to what a conversational dialogic situation offers to the creation of an oral utterance" (Hunt, 1998a). Such "dialogic situations" on newsgroups can be considered a hybrid of spoken and informal written language, that is, a mix of primary and secondary genres in the Bakhtinian sense.

Helping EAP students to view writing to the newsgroup as a turn in the classroom conversation may be difficult when the students have little experience participating in any other real conversation in English outside of the classroom. As

[4]Electronic course newsgroups, or discussion groups, are automatically created for all courses taught in the University. These newsgroups are used in conjunction with an internal university network called CHAT, or with common newsreader programs such as Netscape Newsreader, Microsoft Outlook Express, and others. All students are permitted to have accounts on the system and can have access to the newsgroups from on-campus computer labs and home PCs. Any message posted to the course newsgroup can be read by anyone in the class.

we discussed earlier, Bakhtin (1986) wrote that each utterance we make is filled with the voices of others and made in anticipation of the response of others. This is further complicated for the student who is accustomed to voices in other languages, and responses that adhere to different cultural conventions. Researchers (for example, Beauvois, 1995) have found that participation in a newsgroup discussion improves students' oral conversational skills, and therefore their mastery of primary genres in the target language because it stimulates quick responses to other students' postings while not requiring formal academic writing. Kress (1995) stressed that communication through the electronic medium "brings ... the social proximity of speech into what is still a written interaction—except that this writing now begins to unravel in terms of its most writing-like characteristics, and begins to look much more speech-like in its grammatical and syntactic form" (p. 23).

Hunt (1998a) illustrated how the use of collaborative electronic discussion can create opportunities for learning (learning about writing and rhetorical persuasion or other subjects). Classes that incorporate a collaborative investigation teaching method on-line allow for teaching that engages students in the activity. The teacher observes closely what the students can do, "what they actually do, what as Vygotsky (1986) insisted—they can almost do, and can do with a little help from their friends; and then finds ways to promote learning that's specific to where each learner is and to where she or he needs to be" (Hunt, 1994b, p. 227). This is the type of teaching that Fuller and Lee (1997) called "the pedagogy of here and now," an approach that allows students to master genres within specific social context and through a direct involvement and collaborative effort.

Discussing the topics of their papers in a conversational mode on the course newsgroup allowed students to exercise their knowledge of primary genres in English and provided a necessary bridge to writing in a secondary genre—the academic paper for a course on language learning. The teacher hoped that as the term progressed, students would be able to use the newsgroup to exchange ideas and opinions, give suggestions and/or provide critiques of each other's selection of topics for the final paper. She hoped that they would, therefore, be able to produce better, more informed, pieces of writing. As Hunt (1998a) pointed out, student writing on the newsgroup becomes more intertextual and multivocal as the term progressed. Earlier writing tends to be a summary of events and other people's remarks. Later, the writing becomes less of a summary and more reflexive. When facing an audience drastically different from the readership they were so used to (their teacher), students could learn to adapt their writing to meet the needs of other readers—in this case, their peers.

We will now look at one example of collaborative learning and problem solving that happened on the electronic newsgroup. One of the students (Jay) initially chose to write his final paper to seek an answer to the question: "Why are universities forcing students to study ESL?" We present a printout of a small part of the electronic discussion that took place on the course newsgroup. The unedited messages are presented in the original sequence. Only the names and e-mail addresses of the students have been changed.

[1] THE FINAL.....ESSAY!!

jchen@canada.ca

Hi! My fellow classmates! I am going to introduce my "FINAL ESSAY" topic. The topic is: Why are universities forcing students to study ESL? There is one thing I don't understand, why are we paying for education that we can get in highschool?

Every year many of friends said they got into university but they must be intensive for English. And I think why? That will be the same as highschool except that we are paying for it. Some people might say that the teaching methods are better since it is university professors that are teaching these courses. But that is not always the case, although the students are university students. Sometimes they are still treated as highschool students. Also, when one person has spoken their mother tongue for more than 18 years. It might be hard for them to learn English at the pace that the school wants them to. I think what is most important is the students' study habit. Tell me what you think of these topic, or what ideas you have towards this topic... I know a lot of you have opinions towards ESL, tell me!
Thanks!

In this provocative posting, Jay demonstrated quite sophisticated rhetorical strategies—rhetorical questions, invitations for the exchange of opinions, explicit encouragement to respond to his message—that attracted the attention of his classmates and resulted in a thread of follow-ups to Jay's original message.

[2] Re: THE FINAL.....ESSAY!! Follow-up 1

akwong@canada.ca

This topic is very interesting. As far as I know, a international student in Canada usually take at least one year ESL courses in order to improve his/her English no matter he/she is in high school or in university, if his/her English is not "excellent".

Take an example, in Vancouver, an international student have to take an ESL test before he/she goes into a high school. If he/she has placed into an ESL class, he/she needs to take the ESL test every year or so to see if his/her English is good enough to become a regular student. Sometimes a student may need a few years to complete the ESL classes before he/she can go into a regular classroom, no matter he/she is a VISA student or a "landed."[5] However, in the case of university, most of universities don't accept an international student whose TOEFL result is below 550 or so, for those school thinks a student's English is an most important factor of learning. By the way, even a native speaker, who didn't pass his/her English course in high school level, cannot go to post-education at all.

I think, if your essay can prove that students, who don't have enough TOEFL score, can do well in school just like most of the native speaker; that will be excellent. And I believe this too!!!! And that's why some schools such as, Carleton U., York U. and Ryerson have an English test for student whose TOEFL score is not high enough. Anyway, ESL class is kind of helpful in some way though. You may find some

[5]The landed immigrant status in Canada is similar to the permanent resident status in the U.S.

information about this ... in the library, look up "Canadian Academic English Language Assessment" or "CAEL"[6] in the library index.

Anyway, I hope this will be helpful for you.

Alan

[3] Re: THE FINAL.....ESSAY!! Follow-up 2

lfu@canada.ca

Interesting! As a ESL student. I've the same question as you, however, I don't understand it, 'cos we're in university now, and the courses we take in U require a higher level of English to understand what the text book wrote and what the prof. said. By the way, there is a full credit for this ESL course, it is a good deal, right?

Leshin

[4] Re: THE FINAL.....ESSAY!! Follow-up 3

bjoikic@canada.ca

I don't understand your question "Why universities force students to study ESL?". As I know, no one didn't force me as same as you, I suppose for you, to come here with poor English. All of us had a chance to wait a year more and study ESL somewhere else, to show a high level of English at the test or to be in one of ESL classes here at University, as we chose.

Bojko

[5] Re: THE FINAL.....ESSAY!! Follow-up 4

svinayag@canada.ca

Jay,

You have choosen interesting topic. But your question is not realistic because there is a huge gap between high-school and university. In high school teachers are always concerned about students, but in university no ones cares about students and students are responsible all of their moves. That is why universities really concerned about immigrants students English knowledge.

The second thing you were talking about 'why we are paying tution fees.' Because high school is totally depends on government, but universities are not totally depend on government. Also there are several reasons can be explained.

---

[6]The Canadian Academic English Language (CAEL) Assessment is a topic-based test of English frequently submitted by second-language applicants to Canadian universities to prove that their English is at the level required for academic study. The CAEL is comprised of an integrated set of language tasks and activities, systematically sampled from first-year university classes.

SATHYA

[6] Re: THE FINAL.....ESSAY!! Follow-up 5

akwong@canada.ca

>The second thing you were talking about 'why we are paying tution fees.' >Because high school is totally depends on government, but universities are >not totally depend on government. Also there are several reasons can be >explained.

Sathya,

I think what he [Jay] meant was the tution fees for international (VISA) student; it is from CAD$7,647.10 to CAD$8,392.10 a year (*include compulsory miscellaneous fees). Well! This is really a huge amount of money for a student—even his/her parents, isn't it? As I know, unfortunely, there are still some parents don't ever consider ESL courses as a "regular" course like, such as, Arts, Commerce, Science or Engineering courses. For this reason, those parents may not be happy if they know their boy/girl is using that large amount of tution fees, to attend a "non-regular" course, like ESL.

Anyway, this is only some parents opinion. How's you guys' opinion?

Alan

The newsgroup discussion proved to be a good site for student learning. Students' familiarity with the subject of the discussion allowed them to become involved in collaborative problem solving while they were helping each other to come to terms with the topics for the final papers. Each message shows that students were well-informed on the subject (not only did they express their personal opinions but also supported them with facts or references to sources[7]) and full of genuine interest. The newsgroup discussion represented a well-developed dialogue in which students demonstrated sophisticated rhetorical strategies.

Interestingly, the electronic discussion reprinted here made Jay change his original position and argue against it in the final paper. The electronic newsgroup discussion provided scaffolding for writing an academic paper in a way similar to that in which group discussion provides scaffolding for students' essays in a disciplinary classroom (Faigley, 1990) and allowed them to learn to use codes that are intelligible for discourse communities beyond their EAP classroom (Faigley, reported in Beauvois, 1995). With the help of his classmates and the teacher, Jay was able to find more sources related to the topic. Using and developing his classmates' arguments presented on the newsgroup, he was able to reconsider his initial position and wrote his final paper justifying the necessity of EAP courses for second-language university students. The newsgroup discussion gave a new direction to Jay's thoughts and shaped his final paper.

The teacher was an active participant in the discussion. The electronic newsgroup, supplemented by personal e-mail messages that the students and teacher exchanged,

[7]See Message [2] from Alan.

allowed the teacher to detect individual problems and help students much more quickly and in ways not possible in a traditional EAP classroom. A common situation in which a student panics and decides to change the topic because he or she cannot find enough sources could be resolved via on-line conferencing within a couple of hours, even if the teacher was unavailable for a personal consultation. The teacher was able to suggest additional research strategies often more quickly and conveniently than by phone or in person (Olsen & Lepeintre, 1995), and could thus provide opportunities for the student to learn in collaboration with an expert, as is described in the theories of situated learning (Lave & Wenger, 1991; Rogoff, 1990).

By using options that the electronic system offers—such as posting follow-ups to original messages and posting follow-ups to follow-ups—students are able to collaborate on the tasks and learn from each other. Beauvois (1995) notes that such cooperative efforts "provide students with the occasion for 'real' communication, that is, negotiation for meaning and clarification of ideas" (p.178). Hunt (1998a) described student postings on a course newsgroup as texts to which the only response is instrumental. It is a comment on the content of the message, not on the structure of the other student's writing. This is the type of response students will most likely receive in disciplinary classes where professors often tolerate errors in language if these errors do not impede understanding of the ideas or lose focus on the content (Fuller & Lee, 1997; Giltrow, 1998; Giltrow & Valiquette, 1994).

In his discussion of newsgroups in the classroom, Partee (1996) noted that an electronic classroom "never closes" (p. 81). He said:

> like being in a dormitory (except probably a lot quieter), all students in a class can share an insight or enthusiasm with their colleagues at any time of day or night. Response may come within a few minutes or a few hours, but each student can feel the satisfaction of being heard immediately (at least by the computer). Physical proximity simply is no longer the determining factor for direct and immediate intellectual interaction. (p. 81)

It has also been noted by many authors (Beauvois, 1995; Hunt, 1994, 1998; Manning, 1996; Partee, 1996) that beyond the fact that electronic newsgroups promote group discussion, such discussion can be more inclusive than in a classroom environment and can encourage students who are otherwise silenced in the classroom because of their status, race, handicap, or gender to "speak up" and to contribute profound insights and questions in ways that they avoid in traditional class settings (Manning, 1996). Jay, for example, was a very shy and quiet student who never spoke in class unless spoken to by the teacher. However, on the newsgroup he succeeded in provoking a fruitful discussion. In addition to this, the electronic discussion provided students with the unique opportunity to tap into "expertise" that would not be available to them in a traditional classroom: "Instead of relying on a student in an adjacent seat for information, one command sends a plea for help to the entire class, usually resulting in at least a handful of responses within hours" (Manning, 1996, p. 203).

In EAP classes, students often tend to sit with those who share their mother tongue, thus relying a lot on interaction in their first language. Speaking in the target language is often not seen as a means of communication, but rather as an academic endeavor, and the classroom is not perceived as a place for "real" conversation (Beauvois, 1995). Thus, students do not view speaking in English as part of mastering the primary genres that will serve as a basis for the development of secondary—in this case, academic—genres necessary for their careers at university. Here again, classroom reality can lead to the divorce of primary and secondary genres rather than provide a context for their development and mutual enrichment. On the newsgroup, students cannot rely any longer on their first language, and they learn how to request and interpret information relevant to classroom discussions by interacting with other students in English, that is, "they use the target language exclusively to accomplish a task" (Beauvois, 1995, p. 178). Students use and develop both their resources in primary genres in English, as the exchange of postings is very informal on the newsgroup, and their mastery of academic genres, as the discussion that takes place on the newsgroup is devoted to academic matters (for example, the topics of their final assignments in our EAP classroom).

Faigley (1990) described the discourse of electronic discussions as "wavelike, with topics ebbing and flowing intermingled with many currents. Not only do many voices act out Bakhtin's principle of dialogism, but the movement recalls the opposition he described between the monologic centripetal forces of unity, authority, and truth, and the dialogic centrifugal forces of multiplicity, equality, and uncertainty" (p. 308). If, as Anne Freadman (1987) defined it, "learning to write ... is learning to appropriate and occupy a place in relation to other texts" (p. 122), then by creating space and opportunities for students to hear other voices and incorporate them in their writing and thinking (as Alan, for example, did in the follow-up message [7] by pulling Sathya's text into his posting, or as Jay did by changing the focus of his final paper), we allow them to discover that meaning is not fixed but socially reconstructed each time language is used (Faigley, 1990).

CONCLUSION

In this chapter, we reviewed recent key developments in composition theory and research and investigated their applicability to a second language, content-based classroom setting. Using one of our EAP classrooms as an illustration, we attempted to demonstrate how a shared theme and the use of electronic discussion groups allowed students to master content and learn how to provide appropriate responses to the rhetorical situation in a university classroom.

The students described in this chapter participated in an EAP class where the content of the course was language learning and where the teacher was not only able to assist them with the features of the English language, and, therefore, with the development of primary genres, but was, in fact, an expert on the content. By using a dialogic medium of communication—an electronic newsgroup—the students for the first time in their lives were able to create a discourse community of North American university students, participate in an academic discussion, and incorporate the results of this discussion in their academic writing. It was a true example of the acquisition of strategies necessary for a successful mastery of academic genres through enculturation into a discourse community.

Hanks (1991) said that learning happens "in the process of coparticipation, not in the heads of individuals" (p. 13). Learning can, then, be perceived as a collective endeavor that takes place in a participatory framework, not in an individual mind. Theories of situated learning allow educators to focus on the relationship between learning and the social situations in which learning occurs in classrooms, and to interpret learning as distributed among participants. Peer interaction in these models is seen as enhancing, motivating, and channeling the choice of activities (Lave & Wenger, 1991; Rogoff, 1990). As we have demonstrated in this chapter, genuine peer interaction in the EAP classroom leads to insightful solutions to unforeseen problems and allows for enculturation into academic discourses to happen. As Bakhtin (1986) brilliantly expressed it:

> [T]he unique speech experience of each individual is shaped and developed in continuous and constant interaction with others' individual utterances. This experience can be characterized to some degree as the process of assimilation—more or less creative—of others' words.... Our speech, that is, all our utterances (including creative work) is filled with others' words, varying degrees of otherness or varying degrees of "our-own-ness," varying degrees of awareness and detachment. These words of others carry with them their own expression, their own evaluative tone, which we assimilate, rework, and reaccentuate. (p.89)

By freely engaging in collaborative problem solving and discussion of final assignment topics for the course, students in our EAP class demonstrated that they are able to get "a sense of text as dynamic and situated, as 'itself,' located in a specific place and time, indeed multiply located in a complex of discursive positionings" (Fuller & Lee, 1997, p. 412).

10

The New Rhetoric of Genre: Writing Political Briefs

Richard M. Coe
Simon Fraser University, Canada

Although it does finally offer a specific writing assignment I hope you will adapt and use with your students, this chapter does not use genre theory to generate a more effective pedagogy for achieving traditional objectives of English composition. Rather, it suggests something more radical: that the new genre theories, in addition to helping us achieve existing objectives, also require us to reexamine certain basic assumptions that have long underpinned how we teach writing and what sorts of writing abilities we encourage our students to develop.

THE THEORY

As I understand it, the crux of the new genre theories is this: "A genre is a socially standard strategy, embodied in a typical form of discourse, that has evolved for responding to a recurring type of rhetorical situation" (Coe & Freedman, 1998). Although this emphasis may seem to place me among those genre theorists Flowerdew (this volume) calls "contextual" or "social," I see myself as urging an understanding of genre as the motivated, functional relationship between text type and rhetorical situation. That is to say, a genre is neither a text type nor a situation, but rather the functional relationship between a type of text and a type of situation. Text types survive because they work, because they respond effectively to recurring situations. I have grave doubts about research and pedagogical practices that, after defining genre as the relationship between text type and recurring situation, proceed by inferring situation from textual features. If we are to confirm the relationship between text and situation, we need independent information about situation. Just as in biology one explains the development of a species as an adaption to a niche in an ecosystem, so one should explain a recurring text type as a functional response to a recurring rhetorical situation. Thus, I believe both researchers and students should study both "the lexico-grammatical features of texts" (Pang, this volume) and also the rhetorical features of the recurring situation to which the texts are a response. Linguistic and rhetorical text analysis should be paralleled by analysis of the rhetorical situation and its broader contexts[1] because we and our students need to understand the interrelationships.

Principle: Genres embody socially established strategies for achieving purposes in rhetorical situations.

Although we usually recognize genres by their formal features, genres are, in fact, "typified rhetorical *actions* based in recurrent situations" (Miller, 1984, p. 159, emphasis added). Genres strategically "size up the situations, name them in a way that contains an attitude toward them" and suggest an appropriate response (Burke, 1973, p. 1). To explain generic structures, we should restore to consciousness the strategies they embody and the ends they are structured to serve. We should help students (who tend to focus on the tyranny of genre) to understand that genres are not only constraining, but also generative (heuristic). Even the *five-paragraph essay* has the virtue of motivating students to "support" generalizations and to invent *three* reasons or examples (instead of just one). Genres constitute "configurations of semantic resources that the member of the culture associates with a situation type ... the meaning potential that is accessible in a given social context" (Halliday, 1978, p. 111). But "genres must be fully mastered in order to be manipulated freely" (Bakhtin, 1986, p. 80). There is an important distinction between mastering a genre and being mastered by it. This distinction of Bakhtin's is the basis for my strong agreement with Johns (this volume) that we should destabilize the reductive conceptions of school genres as rigid text formats, which our students typically bring to our classes, especially in relation to the pedagogical genres known as *the research paper* (Johns, this volume), *the essay* (Fort, 1971), and *the paragraph* (Coe, 1990b, pp. 197-84).

The new theories share an understanding of genres in particular and writing in general as situated and motivated social action (Miller, 1984). That said, we should understand the various versions of genre theory are themselves motivated and situated. The new genre theories vary significantly, especially in size of text type they associate with genre, in large part because they were developed in different sites to serve different pedagogical and social purposes. As Johns notes in her introduction to this volume, for some *exposition* is a genre (Grabe, this volume), for others *science writing* is a genre (Halliday & Martin, 1993), for yet others, the

[1]In striving to relate to the discussion already ongoing in this volume, I have mixed my usage of *situation* and *context* in this paragraph; generally, I use *context* to refer to the broader social context and *situation* to refer to the more immediate rhetorical situation. These contexts should include what Malinowski (1923) called "context of situation" and "context of culture."

literature review is a genre (Swales & Lindemann, this volume). Myself, I sometimes want to focus on the differences that distinguish various sub-genres of literature review as they differ from one academic or professional discipline to another. How wide a set of text types one wants to call a *genre* seems to vary with the purposes that motivate one's study or pedagogy (Johns, "Introduction," note 8). The Sydney School in Australia, for instance, developed very much among educators concerned with elementary schools; its defining purpose was to introduce nontraditional pupils to the dominant culture's "genres of power," hence its focus on relatively broad genres like science writing. North American rhetorical genre theorists, by contrast, focused on postsecondary students and workplace writers; their defining purpose was to help students and professionals adapt to the varieties of academic and professional writing. As a specialist in rhetoric and advanced composition at a Canadian university, I myself fall into this group, hence my sometime desire to make fine distinctions among what others call subgenres. Applied linguists who focus on ESL students need to work with a version of genre theory adapted to their particular purposes; I suspect this should mean a midrange notion of genre, defined more by cultural than disciplinary differences.

Principle: Genres are not just text types; they imply/invoke/create/(re)construct situations (and contexts), communities, writers and readers (that is, subject positions).

Part of what defines a discourse community is the genre system it sanctions and empowers. Indeed, mastery of this genre system is a key distinction used by members to distinguish themselves from outsiders.[2] Using the formal features of a genre usually means adopting a subject position implicit in the genre and invoking and/or reconstructing both the community's values and its view of the rhetorical situation (and contexts). How can one write a five-paragraph essay without accepting empiricism and rationality (that is, the value that opinions should be supported by evidence, examples, and reasons)? How can one write a traditional academic paper without accepting the value of traditional objectivity (that is, without excluding the personal)? Even school genres are political and often ideological: learners who adopt a dominant culture's genres may gain access to

---

[2]Reviewers' responses to an earlier version of this chapter are relevant in this context, I think. I am grateful for their comments, which guided my revision, in large part by making me aware that I am, at least in some ways, an outsider here. One suggested that, while it conveyed my meaning effectively, "the unconventional rhetorical form ... might compromise readability" for some of this book's intended readers and suggested I should inform readers at the beginning that I had adopted a distinct style (which I hereby do, though I see it as a somewhat normal style in my own field). Similarly, reviewers suggested I didn't supply enough explanation of my theoretical claims, nor enough evidence and examples—which I take to indicate that I made false assumptions about the background knowledge of this book's readers. Given the assertions I am making in this chapter, I was both embarrassed and grateful for the opportunity to correct or offset errors created by my own failure to think adequately about what is, for me, a somewhat unusual rhetorical situation.

power and opportunity; they also learn to adopt the subject positions validated by that culture, to dance the attitudes (Burke, 1973, p. 9) and participate in the ongoing reconstruction of that culture. In Bartholmae's (1985) sense, they are (re) "inventing the university." In any particular instance, this may or may not, on balance, serve their own interests (Fort, 1971; Lee & Fuller, 1997).

Principle: Understanding genre will help students become versatile writers, able to adapt to the wide variety of types of writing tasks they are likely to encounter in their lives.

Much of the pedagogy of teaching academic writing focuses on what supposedly remains the same from discipline to discipline (for example, opinions should be supported by facts, sources should be referenced, theses should be stated in introductions, endings should summarize). To some extent, especially with "underprepared" students or students from a different culture, such generalizations are useful; they are also, however, based on many English instructors' opinion that the English "essay" (whatever exactly that variable term may mean to each individual instructor) epitomizes "good writing" (or at least, good academic writing). Even within academia, however, "good writing" is quite different in psychology, history, English, engineering, and business courses. In the world of professional work, "good writing" varies significantly from company to company within one type of business (for example, Freed & Broadhead, 1987). Although there are specialist writers who are good only in one genre or discourse (for example, spy thrillers, journalism, technical writing), we should be developing the sort of good writers who are versatile, who can adapt to a wide variety of writing tasks and situations (National Council of Teachers of English, 1979). Decontextualized generalizations about structure do not achieve this aim.

If we recognize the principle of *différance* asserted by the new genre theories and confirmed by empirical studies of academic and professional writing (see, for example, Dias, Freedman, Medway, & Pare, 1999; Freedman & Medway, 1994, Part III; Spilka, 1993), we must recognize that different writing situations require different types of writing, that what is good in a piece of academic literary criticism may not be good in a newspaper book review and will very likely not be good in a brochure. And we must recognize, in keeping with Derrida's pun, that difference is often related to deference, that is, to power. This is perhaps clearest when such differences serve a gatekeeping function, excluding those who haven't mastered certain conventions from a disciplinary or discursive community.

IMPLICATIONS

The preceding principles call into question several assumptions about writing that underlie traditional English composition instruction and thus suggest revisions not only to that instruction but also to its objectives. Developing certain abilities neglected in traditional writing instruction may be crucial to students' success in advanced academic, professional, political, and personal writing situations. Knowledge of the textual structures of school genres like the English essay and research paper may act much like first-language interference when our students approach professional, political, and personal writing.

Traditionally, composition teachers talk and think in terms of "good writing." We may not accept the modernist preferences canonized by Strunk & White's (1959) *Elements of Style*. We may question some of the usage conventions listed in the handbooks, and we certainly do not agree fully with each other about the stylistic qualities of good writing. But we still talk about writing as if there were a Platonic ideal, as if all good writing shared certain qualities, as if we can judge how "good" a piece of writing is on the basis of certain observable textual qualities. This often leads us to decry as "bad" writing that is highly successful in the world.

As Bakhtin (1986, p. 80) noted, "Many people who have an excellent command of a language often feel quite helpless in certain spheres of communication precisely because they do not have a practical command of the generic forms used in the given spheres." Rhetorically allowing myself a bit of hyperbole, I often tell my students, "There ain't no such thing as 'Good Writing.'" What I mean is that effective writing is rhetorically situated, is good for *something,* achieves *situated* purposes. If we can't say what a piece of writing is *good for,* on what basis do we declare it good? Although there is some room for generalizing, "good writing" is a situated variable that should be understood in relation to what classical rhetoricians called "purpose, audience, and occasion."

I do believe there are principles of good writing, but their application varies with situation and subculture. They are on a higher level of generality than "prefer concrete to abstract noun" (Ohmann, 1979). Although I myself can think of no academic or professional writing situation in which it is okay to use possessive nouns without apostrophes, I can think of situations (for example, much legal writing) in which semicolons are eschewed and comma splices are normative—no matter what the handbooks say. True principles of punctuation are both rhetorical and situated (for example, use punctuation conventions that will help your primary readers chunk and read your sentences as you intend). Similarly, there are many academic and professional writing situations in which a thesis statement may not appear in the introduction and/or in which unity of purpose is signified without using a thesis statement; our students need to understand that unity of purpose is what matters. They need to perceive that thesis statements are only one possible device—and often not an appropriate one—for asserting that unity.

Similarly, where traditional composition teachers referred to the "general educated reader" or, at best, to audience, we should remind ourselves that "audience" is a reductive metaphor when extended from speech to writing. Readerships are far more diverse (and often more hierarchical) than the term "audience" suggests. The term "audience" is unfortunately singular (Paré, 1991; Park, 1982) and consequently leads, at best, to exercises in which a student writer is asked to analyze "your audience" (taken as a *singular* mass noun). Moreover, this sort of analysis tends, for reasons I have never quite understood, to focus on demographic characteristics (for example, how old are they?) rather than on the rhetorical factors that matter: For example, what knowledge, beliefs, and vested interests do these readers have in relation to your purpose and subject matter (Coe, 1990b, pp. 150–152)? Quite unlike student papers, most public, corporate, and professional writing must address multiple, heterogeneous readerships.

Although composition specialists routinely assert that students should learn to write for a wide variety of purposes and audiences (for example, NCTE, 1979), most university composition courses teach, at best, a rather narrow range. Often without any explicit discussion of the nature of academic audiences, composition instructors teach students structures appropriate for writing with intellectual rigor to well-educated audiences, often specialists, that is, readers who probably are more literate and more knowledgeable than the student writer. At least in its incarnation as a service course, freshman composition is primarily or ultimately instruction in academic writing. For all our references to "the general reader," we do not ordinarily teach students how to communicate technical subject matter to general readers of average education. Both these types of writing are important and difficult—and involve drastically different applications of the general principles of composition.

If we accept new genre theories and empirical studies of workplace writing, we must also recognize that, rhetorically speaking, *academic writing is atypical*. Students who have learned how to get As on course papers may have developed a "trained incapacity"[3] that interferes with their doing more rhetorical writing effectively. Although practice in writing academically does in some ways prepare students for the writing they may do as citizens, professional workers, consumers, and so on, in other ways it deflects their attention away from crucial aspects of most worldly writing tasks. Because of its peculiar readers and purposes, academic writing is organized primarily by its subject matter, by its argument. At least on one level of analysis, its primary purpose is to present its subject matter convincingly, to explain clearly, to represent knowledge.

Traditionally, composition teachers have dealt with persuasion by teaching some variant of classical argument. Argument is one form of persuasion, but not the only one and often not the most effective. I first came to understand this as a

[3]Burke (1969) used Veblen's terms to argue that any training, education, or socialization teaches us to focus our attention to certain aspects of what we are perceiving, interpreting, or responding to. Inevitably, therefore, it deflects our attention from other aspects. Teaching students or other people to pay attention to what is important in a situation, task, or text inevitably involves a judgment about what is less important or not important, and inevitably deflects their attention away from what has been judged less relevant, sometimes to the point where they no longer even notice it. If these people then move to another situation, task, or text, the mode of perception, interpretation, and response they have so carefully learned sometimes produces an inadequate perception and thus an incompetent response. Consider traditional English teachers, so focused on "correctness" that they don't notice their students' writing is disengaged and boring, or traditional doctors, so focused on the body of the "patient" as object, as site of symptoms, that they barely listen to anything the sick person says (and usually interrupt long before the person finishes explaining the problem). In the extreme, trained incapacities may become so dysfunctional as to justify the term "occupational psychosis."

principle of written composition in relation to Rogerian persuasion (Teich, 1992; Young, Becker, & Pike, 1970, Chapter 12). Once stated, humanistic psychologist Carl Rogers's persuasive axiom—that, if you want to persuade people to change anything important, threatening them (which tends to make them defensive)—seems obvious. If, to put it in St. Augustine's Christian terms, the purpose is not to win the argument, but actually to persuade your parishioners to live Christian lives, then achieving one's purpose must be understood in relation to what readers understand, believe, and do after your persuasion. If, following Malinowski (1923), Burke (1973), and Richards (1936), we think of writing as symbolic *action* and ask what a particular text or genre *does* (as distinguished from what it says), we must judge writing in terms of purpose or function, that is, in terms of how well it does what it is supposed to do. In some cases, often academic, all a text does is try to persuade readers that what it says is true—but most worldly writing makes truth claims primarily to achieve purposes, not vice versa.

Imagining realistic rhetorical situations usually means confronting contradictory purposes and audiences, which are quite common in real writing situations. Confronted, for instance, with this sentence from a government brochure on conjugal violence "—Abused women can seek help from establishments in the health and social services network, namely the local community service centers and the social service centers"—students should be led to see the contradiction between the writer's overt purpose (encouraging battered women to seek help) and the writer's tacit purpose (satisfying a supervisor by emphasizing a verbose description of the department's network). Can we rewrite to achieve both purposes, or must this writer make the hard choice? Our textbooks talk about writing with *a* purpose, for *the* audience; they do not give much advice about multiple and conflicting purposes, audiences, occasions.

Unlike traditional English composition assignments, but like all writing tasks I assign, the task presented in this chapter requires students to address a very specific rhetorical situation. My students come out of high school expecting to write "on a topic" and understanding writing tasks as *topic + format + word length.* To this I add *purpose(s) + readership, + occasion*. I also redefine "format" as genre (that is, as the strategic, functional relationship between what they call format and rhetorical situation) and I tell them "word length" is a code that indicates what size writing task they should undertake.

THE ASSIGNMENT IN ITS CONTEXT(S)

To exemplify some of the ways I think the new genre theories should modify how we frame and teach writing, this chapter presents an innovative persuasive writing task. This assignment works well in Simon Fraser University's advanced writing course, which is defined not only as "advanced," but also by its focus on preparing students for nonacademic writing, for the worldly writing tasks they will face after graduation. (For a fuller discussion of the entire course, at least as it existed a decade ago, see Coe, 1990a). This course is the last of a series that exists in relation to our innovative Writing Centre.[4] Our other writing courses focus specifically on academic writing; the advanced course is designed to embody the ultimate objectives of our program and to help students move beyond that narrow focus in preparation for life after graduation.[5] If your course comes earlier in your writing program and/or if your students are not fluent in English or are less "advanced," you will probably want to adapt this assignment to your students' situation. I present it here primarily to exemplify concretely how one might put into practice the principles discussed in the earlier parts of this chapter. I am claiming not that it is better than traditional persuasive writing assignments, but that it embodies a different judgment about what students should learn in order to persuade effectively.

Students should understand writing as a social, communicative process that takes place in diverse discourse communities, that engages *différance.* They should come to understand the implications of rhetorical situations by writing for widely divergent purposes, audiences, and occasions (including nonspecialist audiences with no better than average—say, Grade 8—reading abilities, a.k.a., the North American general public). Sometime before they have finished with us, they should learn to deal with complex rhetorical situations (for example, contradictory purposes, multiple and/or hostile audiences). They should understand the relationship between form and process, structure and strategy. Thus, they should learn how to initiate themselves into new discourse communities by analyzing discourses to reveal the functions of formal continuities. Ideally, they should also learn how to invent new forms for new purposes.

[4]Simon Fraser University's Writing Centre is founded, at least in my view, on four defining principles (which we strive to embody, albeit not always successfully). The first, and most relevant here, is that the Centre uses a genre-based approach, promotes what we call "genre awareness" among students, and presents genre as a social memory of a rhetorical/discursive strategy. Second, the Centre puts a lot of emphasis on difference and diversity among the various academic disciplines and, more generally, among discourse communities and rhetorical situations. This means, among other things, teaching rhetorically situated genre awareness instead of some decontextualized Platonic notion of "Good Writing" or "The Essay." Third, the Writing Centre strives to operate not as a service centre for "defective students" but in partnership with the various disciplines. We see the Writing Centre as having expertise on writing, rhetoric, and discourse; but each academic discipline is expert in its own disciplinary discourses and genres. Fourth, pedagogy and research are tied: No one works in the Writing Centre without being involved in its research projects. Even students seeking help are directed to research the practices of the disciplinary discourse they are trying to use. The notion that teaching and research intertwine is a foundational value of universities; our goal at SFU has been to apply that value to writing instruction (even when carried out by teaching assistants and peer tutors).

[5]One broader context is Canada. In relation to this particular writing task, it matters at least a bit that Canada is a parliamentary democracy in the British tradition; that Canada is a more decentralized federation than, say, the United States; that Canada allows more cultural difference than, say, the United States; that civility is honored almost as much in Canada as liberty is in the United States. In part because of what Canadians call "the French fact" and in part because the aboriginal population has not been erased to the same extent as in some other settler states, for example, the U.S., Canada has always imagined itself as a "cultural mosaic," not a "melting pot;" multiculturalism is another fact (and government policy). It is unimaginable that the Canadian parliament would establish an "Un-Canadian Activities Committee"—in part because it would be too hard to agree on an exclusionary definition of "Canadian." Arguably, no other multinational, multicultural country works as well as Canada. (See Coe, 1988, and works cited therein.)

One way to focus students' attention is to insist that each piece of writing have a specifically defined rhetorical situation, and to respond and grade accordingly. The mechanism I use to assure this is to have students state the situation on the cover sheet of each piece of writing. I then evaluate each student's manuscript as an editor does—not a judge, a critic, or some mythical educated reader—by imagining how well it would work, how well it would achieve its purpose(s) with its intended readers on the likely occasion(s) when it would be read—and then by giving advice about how it might be revised to better achieve its purposes with its readers. (This, of course, assumes they will have the opportunity to revise, which I create by reducing the number of individual writing tasks.)

In keeping with my own argument (Coe, 1987) that students best come to appreciate genre as choice if exposed to two or more forms for any general purpose, this unit on persuasive writing introduces classical argument, Rogerian persuasion, and political briefs. Ordinarily, it comes after they have written a brochure (a genre I choose because it is so far different from academic writing), addressed to readers who know much less than they do about the subject of the brochure and who read less fluently than average North Americans. Ordinarily it is followed by a large assignment in which they analyze and explain how to write in an unfamiliar genre of their choice. That is to say, instead of confining ourselves to teaching particular special types of writing—there are, after all, so many, and the world is changing too quickly to allow us to predict accurately which types our students will need five or ten years hence—we teach students how to analyze particular types of writing in order to learn them.

Because this is nowadays merely a three- or four-week unit in a broader course, students no longer practice all three forms of persuasion, only the last. As preparation for this writing, students read and discuss in class a textbook chapter contrasting classical argument and Rogerian persuasion, passages on evaluating rhetorical situations and analyzing audiences, and instructions on writing "reader-based" prose (Coe, 1990b, Chapter 9, and pp. 146–169). They also read and discuss Giltrow's seminal article (1988) on briefs. Sometimes, I also have them read the opening section of Burke's *Philosophy* (1973), which I see as antecedent to the new genre theories. The assignment itself is as follows:

> Your task in this set of writings is to produce a brief proposing a solution to some public problem. After reading your brief, your primary readers should perceive the problem in your terms and believe your proposed solution is worthy, feasible, politic—and definitely better than the alternatives. Length of the completed brief: approximately 1,000 words (not counting appendices).

Students who choose to write in small groups and do this assignment collaboratively get to use more than a thousand words (if they so desire), as can students who persuade me that the rhetorical situation they have chosen requires a longer brief. I have assigned a genre, a type of writing task, but each student (or sometimes a collaborative group of students) selects the specific topic and specific rhetorical situation.

A political brief is not an academic but a worldly task in which understanding the subject matter is not a sufficient condition for success; understanding readers (and antagonists) and their motives is crucial. The writer's subject position is citizen and stakeholder, not employee (or student). It does require writers to address one primary audience—but those readers are highly motivated to find an outcome that will make happy as many stakeholders as possible; thus the competing stakeholders become crucial secondary audiences. It also distinguishes between symbolic action and symbolic representation of knowledge by using a rhetorical situation where "winning the argument" often means failing to achieve one's purpose (precisely because it creates antagonism rather than consensus, because it treats a potential win–win situation as a zero–sum, win–lose situation).

The general rhetorical situation for any brief is that a public decision-making body has asked for public input to help it understand a situation, make a decision, or devise a new policy. A brief, in this context, means a piece of writing (perhaps written to supplement a shorter oral presentation) designed to influence a public decision-making body. It could be addressed to a parliamentary commission but is more frequently local, addressed to a police, parks, or school board, or community organization. One such brief written for English 371 involved a small city park that was used by neighbors, young children, bocce players, and frisbee and ball players, among others. The bocce players, for the most part retired Italian immigrant men, tended to dominate (and even dug shallow drainage trenches that tended to trip the frisbee and ball players). Neighbors with small children wanted expanded playground facilities. The Vancouver Parks Board set up a subcommittee to resolve the conflict.

As Giltrow (1988) argued, when they are not merely being used by politicians as stalling devices, public commissions are politically motivated to find solutions that will antagonize as few voters and stakeholders as possible. Thus, the primary readers of a political brief are often more concerned with finding a consensus than with finding out who is right. Giltrow suggested that most briefs are written as traditional arguments, but that the most effective briefs are more conciliatory. Just as legal briefs offer judges arguments and precedents to "plagiarize" in their decisions, so effective political briefs reframe what their authors desire as serving stakeholders generally. To write an effective political brief, it helps to understand the positions and arguments of all stakeholders so that one can present one's solution as taking all stakeholders into account. For the student writing about "bocce park," this meant researching the various groups of stakeholders—and ultimately presenting not the proposal/argument she originally planned, but one that genuinely did satisfy all stakeholders. Thus she was able to address the motives of each stakeholder group and also the political motive of her primary audience.

Like many of the assignments I devise, this one requires students to produce a series of writings. Although they receive feedback on each writing (sometimes from peers, sometimes from me), only the last is formally marked. In this case, all I ask at first is that students describe the problem, state the rhetorical situation, and propose a draft solution. To help them describe the problem and devise a solution, I often have them use a heuristic like the Utopian U (Coe, 1990b, pp. 66–69; Shor, 1980, Chapter 5). This heuristic helps writers move from problem through analysis to solution by contrasting various aspects of the existing reality to a proposed solution. Especially for this assignment, the crucial part is the base of the U, the diagnosis that explains why the status quo exists (despite its defects). Without this diagnosis, students tend to invent solutions that are utopian in the derogatory sense. (In Shor's example, one does not find a workable solution to the terrible food in the student cafeteria if one ignores money, resources, and students' food preferences.) In my Advanced Writing class, students write notes based on what the U helps them discover, then present and discuss this in small groups. (All I do is to check that everyone has done the writing and then move among the small groups making occasional suggestions.)

For the next week, I ask each student to "imagine a rhetorical situation in which an action or policy proposal could be presented as a written brief to a public decision-making body, list the stakeholders, and do an 'audience analysis.'" Each student or collaborative group has begun by writing a single sentence that defines her or his own purpose, that is, the desired outcome. But the main part of the week's work is to write an analysis of the readers to whom the brief will be presented (especially their motives). Each student must list the other positions (including the status quo) likely to be presented or considered and explain how each position is justified by those who hold it. Most importantly, students must indicate areas of common ground and mutual purpose and then outline proposed rhetorical tactics. Once again, these are brought to class and presented and discussed in small groups. Only after all this is done do I ask for a draft of the brief itself.

This three- or four-week unit includes four pieces of writing: an analysis of the problem/solution, an analysis of the rhetorical situation, a fully developed draft, and a revision. My major "marking" load comes between the first finished version in week three and the revision. I write long comments—response plus instructions about how to revise. (Once the revision is done, I just reread quickly to see if the revision merits an improved grade.)

This segment of the course exposes students to three persuasive genres (traditional argument, Rogerian persuasion, and political brief) and then has them practice the one that is most rhetorically complex. Not only do they learn they have multiple options, not only do they practice evaluating rhetorical situations, analyzing audiences, and writing "reader-based prose," but they also learn how to write for complex and diverse readerships. In part because of what they do, in part because I theorize it for them, most students also come to understand generic structures as rhetorical strategies and genres as social processes.

Part VI

Pedagogical Quandaries

11

Approaching Genre: Pre-Writing as Apprenticeship to Communities of Practice

Virginia Guleff
San Diego City College

Since the mid-1980s when Psycholinguistic–Cognitive views of learning began to directly influence composition pedagogy, writing classes have been dominated by "The Process Approach." This approach, which incorporates a workshop environment in the classroom (Silva, 1990), an emphasis on finding individual meaning through writing (Zamel, 1994) and prewriting, drafting, and peer editing before production of a final text (Leki, 1992), has assisted writing instructors in moving away from the traditional, positivistic approach previously used in classrooms. Writing classes which were once dominated by the perfecting of form in a single text now allow for multiple opportunities of invention. Clearly, this acknowledgement of process in the classroom has created a rich environment for students to develop as writers.

However, an unfortunate outcome has been the codification of the "writing process." In many composition classrooms at all levels throughout the United States, students are asked to follow the now obligatory steps of prewriting, drafting, and revising. For each assignment, students are instructed to use "free-writing" or "brainstorming" or "clustering" as invention strategies in preparation for writing. They may complete "bubble charts" in their textbooks or "graphic organizers" as a means to develop and organize their ideas before they write. These prewriting techniques are undoubtedly useful in helping students overcome emotional barriers to writing and in promoting creativity and voice, but a routine observance of them in a writing class is troublesome in several ways.

First, students are often encouraged to use the same prewriting techniques in the same way for every writing assignment they complete. Perhaps this is because most second-language composition classrooms are, as Johns (1997) termed them, "monogeneric." In a monogeneric writing class, the dominant assignment is the *essay*, and so students are taught to approach this assignment in the same way time after time. But, as writing teachers know and as current theory has indicated, rarely are students repeatedly faced with exactly the same kinds of writing tasks during the course of their academic and professional lives. In fact, as Bartholomae (1985) has stated, "Every time a student sits down to write for us, he has to invent the university for the occasion . . . he has to learn to speak our language . . . to try on particular ways of knowing, selecting, evaluating, reporting, concluding and arguing that define the discourse of our community" (p. 134).

This issue leads to the second problem: Most prewriting strategies focus on the individual writer, not on the social context in which texts are produced. However, in many of the writing situations that students face outside the composition classroom, it is rare that students be asked to give their opinion, find individual meaning, or develop their voice. Instead, they are engaged in exactly what Bartholomae has articulated: they are grappling with the kinds of information they should include and exclude in their writing, and they are inventing themselves as novice members of the various academic communities they encounter on their campuses.

Many composition teachers have acknowledged the need for developing the kind of literacy techniques that students can carry with them to a variety of situations to help them deal with the problem Bartholomae has identified; many teachers now talk of having their students write for different audiences and for different purposes. This usually translates, however, into a "letter to the editor" assignment where students write a letter to a local newspaper and learn something about the business letter format. This assignment is not necessarily a bad one, but what is of concern, and most relevant for this chapter, is that students who are given the "letter to the editor" assignment are often encouraged to approach the assignment in the same way as they would an essay, using exactly the same prewriting techniques for their letter as they would for an essay. Students are not encouraged to think about how and when a letter to the editor might be written (on the spur of the moment, or when a topic in the newspaper is extremely compelling) and are not given the opportunity to think about how strange it is to write a cluster, to brainstorm, or to write repeated drafts of this kind of text.

A codification of the writing process implies that there is only one process to follow when students write. When students have writing processes that differ from the steps prescribed by the codified "Process Approach," they may become concerned and abandon strategies that were useful to them in the past. They may also become unwilling to accept variations in the writing process, leading them to be inflexible writers in other contexts. Finally, a rigid adherence to specific steps in a writing process makes it difficult for students to see the connections between the writing they do in their composition classes and the writing they do in other classes. The writing process becomes an isolated technique for their composition classes, and they may not be able to see how they are building a repertoire of writing strategies that they can choose to apply or not apply in other writing situations.

This is certainly not to fault composition teachers, for many are constrained by the curriculum in which they teach or by tests that are administered by their institutions. Additionally, textbooks often present an obstacle for teachers in that they may be heavily based on one approach, usually the codified "Process Approach," and the teachers may have little time, means, or opportunity to supplement their texts with materials based on other approaches. However, to introduce our students to a narrow view of prewriting, when in fact they will need a much broader notion to be successful writers, both academically and professionally, is a disservice to them. We need to help them develop a repertoire of prewriting strategies, ones that include consideration of both individual invention and social context and ones that will help them cope with the varied and complex writing tasks they face.

SOME CURRENT SUGGESTIONS

There has been a shift during the past 15 years in the literacy paradigm at the theoretical level—as mentioned in the introduction to this volume—which would help reframe the notion of prewriting tasks, but this information has been slow in reaching composition classes. Consideration of an individual's genre knowledge, as well as shared genre knowledge by communities of practice as central to the understanding of text processing and production, has not been fully realized and integrated into what we know about the writing process. So, what are some ways to expand the notion of the writing process in general and prewriting in particular to include the situated nature of texts? Johns (1997) suggested literacy teachers consider a "socioliterate view." In a socioliterate view, traditional and process approaches are developed further to include issues raised by genre theory. For instance, a traditionalist view of writing is broadened from considering language as a set of "formal facts" to considering form as used to serve a purpose. Likewise, elements of the "Process Approach" such as schema, strategies, and metacognition are expanded and viewed as socially mediated. Finally, a socioliterate view sees literacy as socially constructed. Issues of roles, purposes, topics, conventions, and histories of readers and writers are all taken into consideration in this view of literacy.

As Johns (1997) also noted, a teacher in a socioliterate classroom would exploit these views and would carefully craft assignments that require students to write texts from different genres: from *summaries*, to *abstracts*, to *love letters* and *recipes*. Additionally, students could be asked to write for various purposes, such as to complain, to request, or to compliment. Writing assignments in a socioliterate classroom would also include assignments based on different contexts, such as taking notes on a lecture or writing under various time constraints. Finally, students in a socioliterate classroom should be exposed to writing assignments that involve varied conventions and values from reading and writing poetry to reading and writing lab reports. Consideration of these elements in a writing assignment would help the students work toward such goals as being able to "draw from knowledge of genres and apply this knowledge to analysis and critique of known and new texts," to "perpetually revise theories of genre," and to "assess, expand upon and revise strategies for approaching literacy tasks" (Johns, 1997, p. 129).

Coe (1994b) also urged teachers to consider genre when working with students. He stated that we should teach genre "as social process, archaeologically and ecologically" (p. 163). He defined teaching "archaeologically" as directing students to observe structures in the texts. From these structural artifacts, students should be guided to guess the functions and strategies and to then relate the artifacts to the context of the situation in which the text was written. Teaching "ecologically" would include an exploration of how genres fit into the context in which they are situated. Ultimately, the goal of this approach would be to teach students the process of genre analysis so that "When they join a community ... and someone presents a genre in which they will have to write, they should know how to figure out what's going on. We should never talk with them about genres without providing (or helping them discover) contextual explanations" (Coe, 1994b, p. 163).

What Johns and Coe both speak to are the social elements that exist within the writing process. An acknowledgement of these social elements in a composition classroom creates opportunities to prepare students for what Lave & Wegner (1991) called "communities of practice." According to them, as students experience the university, they begin to understand the distinct communities that are held together or separated by not only genres and vocabulary but also by practices and values. A composition class, then, could be seen as an opportunity to support students as they write their way through the university and uncover these distinct community practices. Specifically, Johns's paradigm of socioliteracy and Coe's of teaching "archaeologically" and "ecologically" can be integrated with what we know about the writing process to further inform our use of this process in our classrooms, particularly in terms of prewriting.

If the various stages of the writing process are viewed as socially situated, that is, if students learn particular writing processes from the social environment that surrounds the text, then prewriting can be viewed as a crucial step—for it is in prewriting that students decide how to approach a text. This kind of expansion of prewriting would then need to include not only reading texts from a specific genre and looking for artifacts but also a mechanism for discovering the practices of the community for which the students are writing, practices that may include a variety of data collection methods—from interviewing, to surveying, to quantitative experimentation, or practices which may include reading a variety of sources and reflecting on them. An understanding of the practices different communities use to approach a text is an essential component to students' genre knowledge if they are to develop effective theories that they can expand or revise in future writing situations.

What is argued in this chapter, then, is that prewriting activities can and should be exploited to provide apprenticeship for students in the various communities of practice they experience at the university. Specifically, prewriting activities need to include not only reading and locating artifacts in texts of the genre in which they will write, but also opportunities for students to learn the kinds of practices the communities engage in before they approach a text. This is a challenging goal for most classrooms, and the extended prewriting project presented in the next part of this chapter was successful primarily because the design of the program in which it was taught created unique opportunities. It is presented as one way to incorporate a socioliterate view of pre-writing, with the hope that it will provide a springboard for reconsidering prewriting in a variety of writing situations.

THE CONTEXT

This extended prewriting project was assigned in a freshman composition class taught on the campus of a California State University. The students in the class were part of the Freshman Success Program. In this program, students are enrolled in a block of classes during their first semester. Usually, this block consists of a General Education course, a writing course that is linked to the GE course, a study group for the GE course, and a University Seminar of 6 to 8 students that is designed to help students become accustomed to university life. The students who participated in the extended pre-writing project were enrolled in Sociology 101 for their GE class. In conjunction, they were also enrolled in the Rhetoric and Writing 97A writing class, which I taught.

The students in the 97A class were primarily Spanish/English bilingual students, although there were also speakers of Vietnamese, Farsi, and Mandarin. In addition, there were several bi-dialect students who spoke Ebonics or Chicano English. Most of the students in the class were economically disadvantaged and were the first in their families to attend college. Additionally, the 97A students had very unclear expectations of college life. From an anonymous, informal survey, most students stated that they thought college assignments would be "harder" and that there would be "more reading" and "longer papers" but did not really know how many hours they would need to prepare for their classes or what specifically would be required of them.

THE ETHNOGRAPHIC PAPER

The major project for the Sociology 101 course in which my 97A students were enrolled was an ethnographic paper that used participant observation as its primary method of data collection. This ethnographic project was based on the students' experiences volunteering at the Child Development Center on campus. The students had to spend a minimum of 8 hours working in the center, and they were expected to take field notes on what they observed and did there. Afterwards they needed to compile their notes and describe their experiences at the Center. In addition, they were asked to analyze their experiences in light of what they had been learning in their Sociology 101 course.

In support of this assignment, the Sociology 101 instructor created a detailed handout for the students which reminded them of the number of hours they needed to complete in the Child Development Center and which explained his expectations for both the content and the format of their papers. Also, the instructor provided class time for discussion of field notes and for clarification of the assignment. As he expressed to me, his primary motivation was to give the students an opportunity to act sociologists. He wanted to provide as much support as possible so that the students' worries about the writing of their papers would not detract from their experiences at the Center.

Although the 97A students were excited about doing what "real" sociologists do, they were also somewhat intimidated by the project. To begin with, they were completely unfamiliar with qualitative research methods. Most were accustomed to quantitative methods, which pose a hypothesis first and then look for data to prove or disprove it. None of the students had previous experience in using a qualitative method, by which hypotheses are derived from the data collected. Additionally, the students had limited experience with reading ethnographies (although they did have a primary source packet for their Sociology 101 class), and they had never taken field notes, much less attempted to organize and then analyze them. Of course, many of these issues, especially building familiarity with ethnographic studies, were addressed in the Sociology 101 class as the semester progressed. But even though the students were aware of this and were enthusiastic, they still had many concerns about completing this project.

THE EXTENDED PREWRITING PROJECT

In support of the Sociology 101 assignment, I designed a series of assignments for the 97A class. First, we read and analyzed sections of an ethnographic study, *A Place on the Corner* by Elijah Anderson (1975), which used participant observation as its primary means of research. Next, the 97A students were asked to observe their Sociology 101 class for 2 days. They were asked to take field notes (see Appendix A) on each of those days and were given a particular focus for each day. This exercise was designed to give students an opportunity to more fully understand the difficulties of balancing the tasks of participating (by taking class notes and discussing concepts in class) and of observing (by preparing field notes for their 97A assignment). Additionally, they were asked to organize their data and work with it in a qualitative way. Finally, they were to write up their findings in a short report. Each part of the extended prewriting assignment was designed to support these students as they entered a specific community of practice—in this case sociology—and to present an opportunity for students to be apprenticed in a particular way of being.

READING A TEXT AND LOCATING ARTIFACTS

As previously mentioned, in order to introduce students to an ethnographic study that relied on participant observation, we read sections of Elijah Anderson's *A Place on the Corner*. During the early 1970s, Anderson conducted his study at Jelly's, a bar and liquor store located on Chicago's South Side. This particular ethnographic study was chosen for its interest value and for the vivid and engaging descriptions Anderson provides of the patrons of Jelly's. Additionally, it was chosen because of its clear organization and accessible use of sociological terms and theories.

As a class, we read and discussed *A Place on the Corner* in several ways. First we discussed the content, noting particular characters that we liked or disliked and building an idea of what a night at Jelly's would be like. Next, we considered why Anderson chose Jelly's, and what he was trying to tell his readers about the social order he observed among those who frequented the bar.

The 97A students then reread the Anderson text in search of specific artifacts related to text organization. They noticed that Anderson began with a brief preface telling how and why he conducted his study. They also observed that Anderson described the setting in more detail and discussed two key sociological points before moving to a discussion of the people at Jelly's. Finally, they found that Anderson returned to sociological theory in the last part of his book.

One artifact of particular interest to the students was the way that Anderson organized his discussion of the people at Jelly's. In this part of his text, Anderson created three groups for the people who frequent the bar: The Regulars, The Wineheads, and The Hoodlums. The students were especially struck by the way that Anderson had created his own categories based on his data and had not relied on categories created by other sociologists to explain what he had observed.

The final phase of our discussion of *A Place on the Corner* involved group work in which students were asked to find and highlight any instance where Anderson specifically cited the work of another sociologist or where Anderson had used a sociological term with which they were familiar. One especially useful passage in Anderson's work was where he relates his findings at Jelly's to the work of Charles Horton Cooley:

> We can make some headway toward understanding the life situations of the men at Jelly's in relation to their self-identities and their statuses in the group by considering the concept of the extended primary group. For Charles Horton Cooley, the primary group was defined as a small ongoing, close-knit gathering of individuals engaged in face-to-face social interaction. Its members possess a "we" feeling, which they gain through their social interaction with one another and through their intimate involvements in the group as distinct from the external social world. (p. 33)

The students were interested in this passage because it contains the work of Charles Horton Cooley, a sociologist with whom they were familiar from their class work.

They were familiar with Cooley's definition of primary groups and were proud that they could understand the reference. The students also noted how Anderson introduced Cooley's concept of primary groups and identified this concept as relevant to understanding his data from Jelly's. They next noticed how Anderson explained Cooley's concept in his own words. Then they continued their group work by looking at the next section of Anderson's work:

> Although the group at Jelly's possesses these basic characteristics of a primary group, it is really something more than a primary group is ordinarily conceived to be. It is a large and loosely interrelated group of men who, despite their loose association "keep up" with one another. They all know one another, at least by sight or by name, and they all matter to one another... But the large, encompassing group is socially stratified and segmented, especially when certain issues involving individual status and identity come to the fore. (p. 34)

The students were intrigued by this passage, for in it Anderson presented ideas and data which expanded on and differed slightly from Cooley's original definition. Some students commented that they were surprised that Anderson didn't pick a quote from Cooley which fit exactly with his findings. They were also surprised that Anderson could expand upon or revise Cooley's definition of primary groups. An important discussion then occurred about the nature of working with qualitative data and the ways in which data from this kind of method doesn't always fit neatly into previously articulated categories or definitions.

WORKING WITH COMMUNITY PRACTICES

In this extended prewriting assignment, the students were given a handout detailing the focus of their field notes during the participant observation of their Sociology 101 class (see appendix). On the first day, they were asked to make notes about the physical setting of the class and on the participants in the class, including their sociology instructor. On the second day of taking field notes, the students were asked to comment on the way the teacher organized the class. They were also asked to note any goals or views the instructor expressed through lecture or class activities. Additionally, the 97A students were asked to pay particular attention to the content of the other Sociology 101 students' comments. They were asked to look for evidence that the students understood the organization of the class or the goals and view of their professor.

In class, as we discussed the field notes, the students were often surprised at the details some of their classmates had noticed which they had not included in their own notes. There were variations in descriptions and in the amount of time that particular activities in the 101 class had taken. There were lively discussions about what really had occurred in each class session they had observed. Some students began to realize that they had not taken enough notes; others realized that they had taken more notes than they could manage. Some realized that they had written in such haste that their handwriting was now indecipherable. After reflecting on these issues related to their field notes, the students decided that each one needed to rely on what he or she had recorded at the time of the observation and not try to second guess or doubt their notes. They also concluded that taking field notes was a messy process.

CONNECTING ARTIFACTS AND PRACTICES TO APPROACH TEXTS

When the students began to work on ways to shape their classroom notes into a paper, they returned to Anderson's ethnography and revisited the ways in which he had organized his own study. The students then decided to organize their notes by separating information about the setting of the class from information about the participants in the class. Some also decided to use Anderson's method of creating original names for the groups of people they had observed and wrote brief descriptive paragraphs in class categorizing each group. One student created groups called EOPS, Anglos, Loners, and Latecomers. About the EOPS students (of which she considered herself a member) she wrote:

> The first group I saw were the EOPS. It was impossible to ignore and not notice this huge group. This group of students consisted of Filipinos, Chinese, Hispanics and African-Americans. Basically, the EOPS consisted of minorities and were all starting freshmen.... Everybody who was in the group was familiar with each other's faces. We called each other by our first names. We shared the same opinions and talked about the same topics. For example, one girl I saw was concerned about one of the readings in class. In seconds almost everyone in the group shared their thoughts and feelings about it. As the EOPS students dominated the social world, many of the other students began to tilt their heads slightly to listen for the latest scoop of the day.

Another student called her groups Sleepers, Talkers, and Pay Attention People. In describing the Sleepers she wrote:

> Sleepers are people who sit in the back that don't take notes and don't listen to the professor. There are at least five people who sleep everyday, and three of them are female. These particular students are non-participants of the lectures and the discussions that take place in class, so it is understood that they don't study at all or study too much for other subjects. For the Sleepers, it is easily understood why they take little snoozes in class. Sociology is not always going to be interesting to some students, and it tends to fail to zap their interests. The professor does the best he can to keep the students' attention. He often lectures on topics that the book may not even discuss, and if you sleep, of course you will not get the important concepts; and meanings of what you have read. But the sleepers continue to sleep anyway.

Others students decided to separate information about the Sociology 101 instructor from information about the sociology students. One student even organized her data around verbal and nonverbal participation. About the nonverbal participants she wrote:

> The professor continued his lecture on the seven step development of a hypothesis that is incorporated into a research paper. . . . The reaction of the class was not that big due to the fact that some of the students were sleeping, eating reading the newspaper, and doing other homework in class. You could also see that (the professor) was not too happy with the class by his facial expressions.

After the 97A students had created categories and written descriptive paragraphs, they were prompted to analyze their work. This was, by far, the most challenging aspect of the sequence for the 97A students. To approach this task, we first revisited Anderson and reviewed how he had incorporated sociological concepts and terms into his own work. The students were then asked to review the materials from their Sociology 101 class as possible sources to help with the analysis. As a class, we compiled a list of possible concepts, terms, quotations, and ideas to incorporate in their papers. From their textbook, the students identified the three sociological paradigms (Structural–Functional, Social–Conflict and Symbolic–Interaction) as being particularly useful. Also, passages from *The Little Prince*, a novel they had read for their sociology class, provided important insights on the nature of learning that they could relate to their field notes. Finally, from their primary source packet, the students identified several works such as Goffman's article on the dramaturgical approach, Gracey's article on kindergarten as boot camp, and Robertson's article on education as potentially useful in an analysis of what they had observed in their Sociology 101 class. After we had compiled a list of these works, the students then reviewed their notes and descriptions to make connections with the sources.

As students visited and revisited these source materials, they began to pull kernels from their field notes and descriptions to form an argument about what they had observed in their Sociology 101 class. They soon realized that they did not need to write about everything that they had seen or noted during their participant observation. In fact, many found that they could richly describe one aspect of their participant observation and that they could focus on one argument to present in their final paper. For example, one student who decided to work with the Gracey article wrote this short paragraph in class:

> The article "Learning the Student Role: Kindergarten as Academic Boot Camp" by Gracey suggests that while attending Kindergarten we were set up as "us and them," in which we still portray in university life. In my observation I found that socialization is a major factor that takes place in sociology class. Because of socialization, students have learned their status and roles in society.

Another student began to work with the Gracey article in this way:

> As Gracey points out, "children are learning the student role ... that will play for many more years of their lives." In kindergarten, children are taught how to "behave" in class.

> They are taught that when the teacher enters the room that is when the work shall begin. "They learn how to fit in with a social system, how to follow rules, how to be punctual, how to respect authority..." All of these learned practices are embedded into the child's mind and is carried on until they reach higher education where they will apply it. This, I feel, is where the students I refer to as the "regulars" come in. They are the ones who are always on time and ready to take notes when the professor steps through the threshold.

Finally, one student began to work with a sociological paradigm in this way:

> The Structural-Functional paradigm is defined as the base of society to form stability. Sociology 101 is the introduction of the course to help you understand the field of sociology, and the way you see the world. (The professor) is expected to give lectures and meaning to the topic of study and the student is expected to read the text and participate in class. This is just like how the government is expected to make laws and the people are expected to follow them.

Although these examples represent first attempts and clearly need revision and further consideration, they also provided an important first opportunity for students to make connections between the artifacts they had uncovered during text analysis and the data they had gathered on their own while practicing as a community member. Later, the students were able to incorporate and rely on the paragraphs they created as well as the artifacts they had uncovered as they worked to write their larger texts. Ultimately, the experiences they had while completing this extended prewriting sequence helped to equip them with many resources for approaching their Child Development Center project for their 101 class.

CONCLUSION

The extended prewriting project presented here is a complex expansion of an important part of the writing process and seeks to create opportunities for apprenticeship into a particular community of practice. It is also a project that has implications for both pedagogy and genre theory. In terms of pedagogy, the extended prewriting project suggests that instructors rethink the writing process as socially situated and expand notions of prewriting and invention to include opportunities for discovering community practices and to acknowledge the socially mediated nature of these writing processes. This includes an understanding that different writing situations offer different prewriting opportunities and chances to seek out and learn about what writers in specific communities of practice do before approaching their writing tasks. This also includes creating multiple opportunities to practice community-specific ways of being, as in the example presented in this chapter of creating smaller assignments in support of larger projects.

In terms of genre theory, this chapter suggests that the focus in the literature, which is often on the text that is produced, should be expanded to include the processes that occur before text production. It locates genre knowledge not only within the text but also within the activities that lead to a text. In this way, the social construction of texts could be expanded to include both the intertextual knowledge as well as the process knowledge that writers bring to a text. The approach to a text used by various communities of practice, then, is revealed as an essential element of genre knowledge. It is this crucial information that we must pass along to our writing students to help them with the variety of writing challenges they face in their academic and professional lives.

APPENDIX: ETHNOGRAPHIC PROJECT

For this writing assignment you will be asked to gather data about your Sociology 101 class by acting as a participant observer on two different days. On both of these days you should collect field notes in class using the questions listed below.

Write your field notes on pieces of paper separate from your class notes. Remember, these are field notes, so you do not have to write in complete sentences and it's okay if they are a little messy. However, they should be detailed enough so that you can use them when you write up your final paper. Use the following questions to guide your note taking:

DAY 1

1. Describe the physical setting of the Sociology 101 class. (What does the room look like? Where is it? How many people are there? Is the room crowded? Is the room well-lit or is it dark? Is there a blackboard? Is it easy to read?)

2. Take notes on the participants in the class. (What is your professor for Sociology 101 like? How does he present his lecture materials? What are the students in the class like? Do many participate? In what ways do they participate?)

DAY 2

1. Pay careful attention to the content of the lecture. How does the professor organize it? What can you tell about his goals for your class by the organization of his lecture? What can you tell about his views of Sociology by the lecture?

2. Pay careful attention to the content of the participation by the students in the class. Do the students understand the organization of the lecture? Do the

students understand the goals of the class? What can you tell about the students' views of Sociology by their responses?

12
The Teaching of the Academic Essay: Is a Genre Approach Possible?

Tony Dudley-Evans
University of Birmingham
United Kingdom

The increased prominence of genre-based approaches to the teaching of academic or professional writing has been a feature of English for Specific Purposes courses in the last ten years. The influential research of Swales (1981; 1990) on the introduction to the academic article and that of Bhatia (1993) on promotional genres have been translated into teaching materials (for example, Swales & Feak, 1994; Weissberg & Buker, 1990), that provide valuable insights for students into the ways of structuring research reports and articles. There are no doubt numerous other sets of in-house materials that also make use of this research. The academic article, in particular, has a regularity in its discourse structure that lends itself to an analysis that makes use of "moves" that typically occur in a more or less fixed order. Although there have been concerns about the dangers of an overprescriptive approach to the academic writing resulting from a genre approach (Paltridge, 1996; Prior, 1995) and about the absence of research into other faculty genres such as the master's or doctoral dissertation (Dudley-Evans, 1997), there is little doubt that the existing research into genre has enriched and broadened the teaching of academic writing. Similarly, the awareness that much nonliterary writing involves the mixing of genres, and the need to manipulate the generic conventions (Bhatia, 1997a), has led to increased sophistication in the teaching of professional writing.

THE ESSAY

In this chapter, however, I wish to discuss the problems and challenges of developing a genre approach to the teaching of a typical classroom genre (Johns, 1997) that does not lend itself to a move analysis along the lines of the work on the academic article and promotional genres referred to earlier. This is the essay or, as it is more precisely called in the university in which I teach (the University of Birmingham, England), "The 2000- or 3000-Word Assignment." The experiences that I wish to draw upon come from teaching international students on various master's courses related to business, finance, banking, and accountancy at the University of Birmingham. The particular courses that I refer to are the MBA in International Banking and Finance and two master's courses, one in Accounting and Finance, the other in Money, Banking, and Finance. These are all one-year courses that follow a heavy lecture program from late September through to May, at which time the examinations take place. In the final part of the course, the students carry out a small-scale research project over the summer period, which is written up in a 10,000- to 15,000-word dissertation.

During the year, students have to write between ten and 12 assignments (the number varies according to which course they follow and which options they take within the course). The length of these assignments is usually between 2,000 and 3,000 words.

The courses themselves are very much designed for international students and are followed by very few home students. They are postexperience courses designed for young professionals with some experience in the areas of business, accounting, banking, portfolio management in investment, and so on, and aim to provide a mix of practical training in these areas supported by an introduction to the relevant literature in the field. The aims of the course thus differ significantly from those of other master's courses in humanities, science, and engineering, which are more academically oriented. The business, accountancy, and finance courses are very much geared toward the needs of the international students and are seemingly quite successful in blending elements of training with more traditional academic requirements. To give an example, assignments may ask students to adopt the position of an investment counselor advising a client on the desirability of investing in different markets, thus reflecting closely the type of professional activity that they might engage in once they have obtained the master's qualifications. They will, however, be expected to justify their recommendations in the assignment by reference to appropriate sources, thus satisfying the academic side of the course. In fact, the courses, in my experience, face similar challenges to master's courses in TEFL/TESL run in my own department where there is a constant and stimulating need to balance aspects of theory and practice in training teachers.

The students thus have to write in three main academic or classroom genres throughout the course: the *assignment* (or essay), the *examination answer*, and the *dissertation*. Of these, the assignment is the most difficult to prepare students for. The dissertation follows something like the traditional IMRAD format (introduction, method, results, and discussion) and lends itself to an approach that introduces students—flexibly!—to the various moves that they will need to use in the different sections of the dissertation. Students are prepared for examination questions through team-taught sessions in which subject and language teachers work together to demystify the meaning of questions and to develop appropriate strategies for answers. Assignments are much trickier for a variety of reasons. First, they vary quite considerably in what they expect students to do. Some are basically reviews of the literature, others present case studies, and others mirror professional documents presenting advice for clients. They thus also vary in the amount of "knowledge-telling" or "knowledge-transformation" expected (Bereiter & Scardamalia, 1987); the reviews of the literature will mostly involve knowledge-telling, but the case studies and the simulation of professional documents will combine knowledge-telling and knowledge-transformation in that they draw on the relevant sources, but the student is expected to develop a critique of past or current practice in the subject area and to simulate documents providing recommendations for clients. Second, they do not lend themselves to a straightforward move analysis, partly because they do not usually have a number of delineated sections in the way that an article or dissertation will normally have, and even where there is a delineated section, such as the introduction or conclusion, there does not seem to be a predictable structure for these sections in the same way there is in the academic article. The writer may adopt a number of strategies in introducing or concluding the essay, and thus the move approach that seems so relevant to the writing of articles, theses, and reports is of limited value.

RESEARCH INTO ESSAYS

Research into the discourse structure of assignments, or essays as they will generally be called, is limited. Jordan (1997, p. 7) reported on the various study skills required in essay writing, listing the following skills:

1. planning, writing drafts, revising;
2. summarising, paraphrasing and synthesising;
3. continuous writing in an academic style organized appropriately;
4. using quotations, footnotes, bibliography;
5. finding and analysing evidence, using data appropriately.

These are clearly important skills and are likely to be taught as part of a process approach to the teaching of writing. But, as Jordan noted, they relate to all the genres that students have to write and certainly do not help distinguish what is particular to the essay.

Jordan (1997, p. 9) also listed a number of specific academic concepts/functions: describe, define, exemplify, classify, assume, hypothesize, compare, express, caution, and so on. The teaching of these functions is the basis of many English for Academic Purposes textbooks, but again does not help sort out what is directly involved in writing an essay as opposed to other classroom genres.

The one attempt to devise a set of moves that I am familiar with is that of Hyland (1990, p. 69), who suggested that the argumentative essay has three stages: thesis, argument, and conclusion. Within each stage there are a number of moves, as shown in Table 12.1. Many of the moves are optional, and these are indicated in parentheses.

TABLE 12.1

Genre of the Argumentative Essay

Stage	*Move*
Thesis	(Gambit) controversial or dramatic statement (Information) background material (Proposition) states writer's position and delimits topic (Evaluation) brief support of proposition (Marker) introduces and/or identifies a list
Argument	(Marker) signals the claim and relates it to the text (Restatement) rephrasing or repetition of proposition (Claim) reason for acceptance of the proposition. Either a. strength of perceived shared assumptions; b. generalization based on evidence; or c. force of conviction (Support) grounds that underpin the claim: either a. assumptions used to make the claim; or b. data or references
Conclusion	(Marker) signals conclusion boundary (Consolidation) relates argument to the proposition (Affirmation) restates proposition (Close) widens context or perspective of proposition

This set of moves is useful; it is quite revealing about the development of an argument in an essay, but the number of optional moves is problematic. One solution to this might be to think of elements not as *moves* as in the Swales and Bhatia models, but as what Young (1994), in analyzing university lectures, describes as *phases*. Phases are "strands of discourse that recur discontinuously throughout a particular language event and, taken together, structure that event. These strands recur and are interspersed with others resulting in an interweaving of threads as the discourse progresses" (p. 165).

But the main problem, at least in the use of the model, is that it fails to account for the fact that there is considerable variation among the essays required by different disciplines or even within one discipline among different subject lecturers. As Horowitz (1986a, p. 447) stated, in essays there is "a specific range of acceptable writing behaviours dictated not by the individual but by the academic community." Similarly, Kusel (1992, cited in Jordan, 1997, p. 237) concluded from a study of the structure of essay introductions and conclusions from six different subject areas that the discourse of these sections varies considerably across disciplines. However potentially useful it may be, Hyland's model is essentially rather limited and seems based more on intuition about what an essay should include than on detailed analysis of a suitable corpus of essays.

Another approach to the analysis of the essay is that of O'Brien (1995), who noted that the Rhetorical Structure Theory (RST) presented by Mann and Thompson (1986; 1988) provided a useful means of understanding why "weak" texts are incoherent. RST analysis involves the establishment of linkages between different spans of text, which might involve relations such as Claim and Evidence, or Cause and Result. O'Brien shows that lack of coherence in a section can be explicitly highlighted by indicating the absence of linkages between different sections of the text. By analogy, the RST approach can also be used to help writers strengthen the coherence of their text by increasing the number of specific links. Although this research is clearly relevant and deals with a key aspect of academic writing, its weakness is that it does not address the more general problem of presenting and developing in the essay an argument supported by evidence and citation in the style expected by the subject department.

THE WRITING COURSE

The failure to identify any text analysis immediately and directly applicable to the teaching of writing essays has led to various conclusions. The main one is that the writing course should concentrate on introducing students to the academic stance expected of a postgraduate student in these departments, notably the "rhetoric of objectivity," or the "rhetoric of no rhetoric." The two constituents of the course are (a) a focus on certain relevant features of the essay, notably the use of an appropriate style in writing, the presentation and discussion of data, the use of hedging devices in the making of claims, the use of sources and (b) one-to-one tutorials in which students are helped to structure the essays coherently and to adopt the appropriate stance expected by the department.

It might be thought that a more extensive team-taught program along the lines of similar programs run with other departments at Birmingham (Johns & Dudley-Evans, 1980) would be appropriate with the particular aim of helping students understand the expectations and requirements of subject lecturers with regard to the assignments that they set. This indeed would be extremely desirable, but the nature of the staff in the Business School is such that it has not been possible to set up more than a limited number of team-taught classes on examination questions in the period leading up to the examinations at the end of the first and second terms. There are two reasons for this. First, many of the courses are options, and students select their own program from a large number of options available. This means that it is impractical to concentrate on a particular essay as many in the group will not, in fact, be writing that essay. Second, many of the courses are taught by visiting lecturers, and it is therefore difficult to ask them to participate in further classes related to English and study skills. The team-taught sessions that are run concentrate on general examination skills and strategies for answers.

The part of the English course that focuses on linguistic features of the essay concentrates on introducing aspects of English style, particularly the choice of lexis and grammatical features that are more formal and "academic" in style. Many international students are unaware of the differences between informal spoken English and the more formal style expected in an essay, and this lack of awareness may have been increased by the otherwise desirable concentration in general English courses on spoken language and on a communicative approach to the teaching of that language. The course[1] emphasizes features such as the following:

1. the preference for more formal verbs such as *investigate* rather than *look into, fluctuate* rather than *go up and down, obtain* rather than *get,* and so on;

2. the need to avoid colloquial expressions such as *sort of negative, the future is up in the air, pretty good*;

3. the need to avoid contracted forms such as *isn't, can't,* and so on;

4. the preference for nominalized forms, for example, *the cooperation of IBM and Apple led to the establishment of a new factory* rather than *IBM and Apple have been cooperating, and this has led to the setting up of a new factory*;

5. the avoidance of "run on" expressions such as *etc.,* and *and so forth*;

6. the careful and selective use of the personal forms *I*, *we*, and *you* and the avoidance of *one*; and

7. the avoidance of direct questions and the preference for indirect questions.

These issues are taught through short exercises comparing informal and formal language, and activities in which students are asked to revise passages written in an inappropriate style.

[1]These materials were developed by my colleague Martin Hewings.

The focus on these aspects of language serves two purposes: It helps students remove the kind of basic stylistic errors that make their writing appear "foreign" and that may take the attention away from the content of the essay. It also helps to introduce students to the stance as an academic writer expected of them by the departments. This effort is taken a stage further in the subsequent units, which deal with the need for caution in academic writing and the need for the use of hedging devices, particularly when making claims based on data collected. Students are taught to present data appropriately and to use modal verbs, appropriate reporting verbs such as *indicate* and *suggest,* and other hedging devices such as the use of vague expressions like *a significant amount, slightly higher* (Channel, 1994; Hyland, 1996) in making generalizations from the data.

These two units on linguistic features and hedging work well and are popular with students, particularly as they deal with the actual problems that they seem to face in the first period of the one-year course when they are having to write these other assignments for the first time. There is, however, one main danger with the approach. Because of the lack of extensive contact between EAP and the departmental staff (faculty) mentioned earlier, the materials are general in nature and do not relate directly to particular assignments. This can be compensated for to some extent in the one-to-one tutorials where students are helped with the actual structure of the essay that they are writing, particularly the introduction and the conclusion. But only certain students with particular problems will have the opportunity of having a tutorial, and there is the consequent danger that the strategies taught in the writing class will not, in fact, be transferred to the writing of the actual assignments required by the departments.

USE OF SOURCES

As a result of these misgivings about the pedagogical materials, a major effort has been made to ensure that the final part of the writing course, the use of sources and quotation or citation, reflects the actual practice in the departments and the expectations of the lecturers marking assignments.

There is a considerable amount of confusion about the rights and wrongs of using sources, on the part of both students and lecturers in these courses. The concept of plagiarism indeed has been much discussed in the literature in recent years with interesting contributions by Pennycook (1996), Scollon (1995), and Widdowson (1993), among many others. Many of these contributions suggest that the definition of plagiarism is very difficult to pin down and will vary from culture to culture. Pennycook (1996) argued that the extensive quotation of others' actual words without attribution of the source is acceptable behavior in Chinese society, and Widdowson (1993) seemed to suggest that we all plagiarize one another all the time. While accepting that plagiarism is a difficult concept to define and that we academics do steal one another's ideas, I feel that too much philosophizing can confuse the issues. It is my experience that most international students are either aware of or quickly understand the issues of plagiarism, provided that they are discussed fully in class time. They know that to copy extensively and widely from essays written by the previous year's students or from the Internet is dishonest, and that to quote directly from a source without attribution is wrong. They also know (or quickly understand) that in most cases they will need to convert the original words from a source into their own words and that the key criterion of successful and correct citation is whether they have shown understanding of the source. It is my experience that once the basic purpose of making use of sources is understood, it is the techniques of quotation and citation that really cause the problems. Students are worried by questions such as how many quotations can be used in an essay, how far the original text needs to be changed, and how one actually shows understanding of the text.

In this regard I have found the emphasis on the "sin" of plagiarism that is frequently placed in university regulations and departmental handouts unhelpful. In one of the departments whose students I teach, a handout on plagiarism is distributed at the beginning of the academic year. The following quotes are extracts from this handout:

> Plagiarism is considered by the University as a serious offence. It is a form of cheating and as such is penalised by the examiners according to its extent and gravity.
>
> Plagiarism is a form of cheating in which the student tries to pass off someone else's work as his or her own. When it occurs it is usually found in dissertations, theses or assessed essays. Typically substantial passages are "lifted" verbatim from a particular source without proper attribution having been made.
>
> Do not copy from other students. Staff can easily detect copying.

It is difficult to disagree with anything in these quotes, but the tone and emphasis of the document seem less than helpful. Clearly, copying from other students or the Internet is cheating and deserves punishment if discovered. But is a failure to attribute sources so sinful? In many cases it will result from a lack of knowledge about the techniques of attribution and unwillingness to alter the original rather than from a preparedness to take risks through cheating.

It is my experience that most students are uncertain about how far to go in changing the original text of a source. In the "knowledge-telling" part of assignments where the focus is on, for example, an accountancy technique or an investment procedure, it is actually difficult to change the original wording that much. The key thing is to include a reference and to show that one has understood the source. Swales and Feak (1994, p. 126) get down to the real nub of the matter when they ask in the exercise quoted next to draw the line between what is acceptable and what is not:

1. copying a paragraph as it is from the source without any acknowledgment;

2. copying a paragraph making only small changes, such as replacing a few verbs or adjectives with synonyms;
3. cutting and pasting a paragraph by using the sentences of the original but leaving one or two out, or by putting one or two sentences in a different order;
4. composing a paragraph by taking short standard phrases from a number of sources and putting them together with some words of your own;
5. paraphrasing a paragraph by rewriting with substantial changes in language and organization, amount of detail and examples; and
6. quoting a paragraph by placing it in block format with the source cited.

As Swales and Feak acknowledged in their teachers' book (Swales & Feak, 1994, p. 68), it is difficult to decide whether Option 4 constitutes acceptable behavior or not. In my survey of five key established lecturers in the MBA in International Banking and Finance course, only one regarded Option 3 as acceptable, but three found Option 4 acceptable.

There is the same problem with the use of data taken from the Internet. Many students in business, banking, and finance courses look up reports posted by companies on the Internet and make effective use of data they find there about turnover, profits, and sales. Again, it is very difficult to change the wording very much as it consists of basic description and presentation of data. The key thing is to acknowledge the source.

By contrast, when students engage in "knowledge-transformation," that is, in evaluating techniques or models, or in making recommendations for action, the issues are clearer. It is much easier for students to use their own words because they are evaluating rather than reporting, and the expectation is that they will do so.

In teaching students what is and what is not acceptable in the use of sources, it has been found that a full discussion of all the issues and a detailed examination of the techniques of referencing, both in the text and in the bibliography, are more effective than a focus on the techniques of paraphrasing. It is useful to discuss examples of paraphrasing to see whether it has been done adequately, but this is not enough in itself. We have found that teaching the technique of making a reference in the text is particularly important; it is surprising how often handbooks and textbooks focus only on the bibliography. The questions addressed in the course are the advantages and disadvantages of integral or nonintegral citation (Swales, 1990), the preferences within the departments for either the APA or number style of referencing in the text, and a discussion of whether limited direct quotation from sources is desirable. It is my experience that the amount of referencing that different disciplines favor varies considerably: political science seems to favor a larger amount of direct quotation than other social sciences, whereas the sciences and engineering use very little, if any, quotation.

The question of what is acceptable behavior in the use of sources and how far the source really needs to be adapted and paraphrased ultimately comes down to what is accepted by subject lecturers marking the assignments. There is evidence that lecturers supervising dissertations or marking assignments for international students in applied linguistics often do not, in fact, pick up cases where the student has taken *verbatim* quite long chunks from the original text, and certainly option 4 in the exercise from Swales and Feak quoted earlier is regarded as acceptable. Whether this is a result of the widespread use of continuous assessment and the consequent increase in the amount of marking that has to be done, or an acceptance of the difficulty of changing the behavior of international students remains a question that is difficult to answer. It is certainly a case, I would argue, where we as EAP teachers need to be aware of and act upon what Graves (1975) referred to as the "informal order" or practical system of what is actually accepted by subject lecturers as compared with the "formal order," which is set down in the institution's regulations. Graves' example of the informal order comes from the Third World, but the same phenomenon can be observed, I would suggest, in First World universities.

Wilson (1997) has indeed suggested that the limited use of copying from sources may be a useful stage on the way to developing the appropriate academic style for the use of references to support an argument. Drawing on work by Chanock (1996) and Whitaker (1993), she suggested that when students are learning to write classroom genres, they develop "interdiscourse," which is formed from their hypotheses about what is required in a new classroom genre. She also suggested that there are four stages in the development of academic writing. These are: *repetition*, which involves extensive copying without citation; *patching*, which also involves extensive copying but with the appropriate citations; *plagiphrasing*, in which students blend copied sections, quotations, paraphrases, and their own words; and, finally, *conventional academic writing*. She suggested that the third stage, plagiphrasing, shows that students are beginning to speak with their own voices, and is an important stage on the way to developing the appropriate academic writing style.

DISCUSSION

The course described differs from many genre-based courses in its focus on the appropriate academic stance for a master's course and the appropriate strategy for the use of sources. Many EAP writing courses (for example, Weissberg & Buker, 1990), assume that non-native speaking writers are essentially familiar with the conventions of the genres that they have to write, but need help with translating that familiarity with the conventions into appropriate language. This is by now a very familiar move-based type of course based on Swales' research into the academic article and other similar work. The course described here assumes that learners have had relatively little experience with the writing required of them at the University of Birmingham and need help with adjusting to the appropriate stance, that is, the mixing of academic and professional writing expected of them in what are postexperience and essentially practical courses. In its focus on stance and strategies, the course has certain similarities with the approach adopted in Swales and Feak's *Academic Writing for Graduate Students* (1994); the difference is that it is concerned not with the reporting of research findings but with the process of showing that the writer has understood and can summarize the relevant sources. The course also deals with a major academic area that causes difficulty for international students at the University of Birmingham: the appropriate use and citation of sources.

I believe this description of the writing course for master's students has a number of implications for genre teaching. It is now widely accepted that text analysis attempting only to establish a set of moves for a given genre or part-genre (a particular section of the academic article, say) is insufficient. The move analysis needs to be supplemented by analysis of sociological features of the context within which the text is used and of the discourse community that will read and judge the text.

In the same way, the teaching of moves as part of an academic writing course for graduate students needs to be supplemented by consideration of the appropriate academic stance expected by the department. As Swales and Feak (1994, p. 3) stated in the introduction to their textbook, it is important to stress the concept of "positioning." This involves asking students to assess what they are writing in terms of how well it is positioning them as junior members of their chosen academic "communities." The stances that the students taking the courses at the University of Birmingham described here have to adopt are rather diverse, but the basic point made by Swales and Feak holds true.

There is a particular danger in any kind of genre teaching: The writing teacher may find the teaching of a set of generalized moves a straightforward and popular method that may lead to a certain comfortable isolation from the actual discipline. The risk is that such an approach will not confront many of the day-to-day problems students encounter when writing the actual genres required by the department. As always in English for Specific Purposes work, there is a need to find out what the actual problems are and come up with innovative solutions rather than settle unquestioningly for accepted procedures.

The genre of the assessed essay or the 2,000- or 3,000-word assignment is much less predictable than the research report and dissertation. The teaching of issues related to stance or positioning is, I have argued, much more feasible and more relevant than an attempt to establish and teach a pattern of moves. It is thus essential for the writing teacher to find out as much as possible about the expectations of the department through dialogue and the examination of actual texts that students write and subject lecturers' reactions to them. Such an approach—especially where it attempts to find out how one or more aspects of academic writing (for example, using sources) is regarded by subject lecturers—is as much a genre approach to the teaching of writing as a course focusing on the moves in the introduction or discussion sections of a research article.

13

Destabilizing and Enriching Novice Students' Genre Theories

Ann M. Johns
San Diego State University

At the 1996 International Association of Applied Linguistics (AILA) Conference in Finland, John Swales hosted a 3-day symposium entitled Genre and Thick Description, in which valuable discussions of genre theory, text evolution, and research were presented. Few of the papers were devoted specifically to pedagogy, and when the distinguished group was asked to suggest the implications of their work for pedagogical practice, they were, for the most part, silent. At the Second International Genre Conference in Vancouver (January, 1998), hosted by Rick Coe, there was more discussion of pedagogy, particularly of the establishment at Simon Fraser University of a genre-based writing center in which teaching and research are integrated (see Coe, this volume). However, the important, invited papers, did not focus on teaching. Again, some of the essential pedagogical issues were sidestepped or downplayed during most of the conference. Why is this? Why do some[1] of the finest minds in genre theory eschew discussion of the pedagogical implications of their work?

Here is one hypothesis: There are direct contradictions between what the theoreticians and researchers continue to discover about the nature of genres and the everyday requirements of the classroom. The experts point out that genres are complex mental abstractions,[2] perpetually subject to change (see especially Kent, 1993), socially situated, and revised to respond to varied audiences or purposes. An individual's genre theory and experiences can present possibilities for text production but not absolutes, invitations but not templates. Fowler (1982) made these remarks about the writer in a specific rhetorical situation:

---

[1]Not everyone attempts to avoid this discussion, of course. See Freedman and Medway, 1994c.

[2]See Johns (1997), pp. 20–37.

> The writer is invited to match experience and form in a specific yet undetermined way. Accepting the invitation does not solve his [sic] problems of expression . . . But it gives him access to formal ideas as to how a variety of constituents might be suitably combined. (Folwer, 1982, p. 31 cited in Kamberelis, 1995)

Thus, as Berkenkotter and Huckin (1995) explained, there are the centripedal forces that contribute to a particular text's prototypicality within a genre (and thus, Fowler's "access to formal ideas"), and conversely, there are the centrifugal forces within a specific situation requiring the revision of an individual's genre theory in the production of a suitable text. Berkenkotter and Huckin warned that "recurring situations resemble each other only in certain ways and only to a certain degree" (1995, p. 6). Thus genres are both repeated and constantly revised.

Yet, in classrooms, we literacy teachers must simplify and make generalizations, and so we are tempted to provide templates in order to teach and test our students. Our curricular tendencies are to emphasize regularities and to search for stability so that students can learn some concrete facts about texts. My experience indicates that in many classrooms throughout the world, if issues of writing are discussed at all, the emphasis tends to be on what have been determined to be fixed forms, or organizational modes, "including illustration, example, exemplification, comparison, contrast, partition, classification, definition, causal analysis, and so on" (Silva, 1990, pp. 14–15). In my own state, The English Standards for the State of California public schools emphasize the importance of writing narratives and expository essays that define, inform, explain, or analyze. (*California Academic Standards Commission: Language Arts*, October 1, 1997). Thus, we teachers are often encouraged to focus almost exclusively on the importance of text type (see Paltridge, this volume), to the detriment of the many other features of texts and contexts that influence successful genre processing and production.

There is another important contradiction between theory and pedagogical practice, relating to the broader elements of rhetorical situations. Much of the genre literature includes mention of the relationship between genres and what have been called *discourse communities* (Swales, 1990, 1998) or *communities of practice* (Brown & Duguid, 1989). These terms refer to groups of individuals who "own genres and . . . specific lexis" (Swales, 1990, p. 52), and who are central in determining, through their community membership and text ownership, how important genres will evolve. In *Situated learning: Legitimate peripheral participation*,[3] (1991), Lave and Wenger argued the following:

> To be able to participate legitimately in a mature way [in communities of practice] entails that newcomers have broad access to areas of mature practice. (p. 110).

However, if we choose to examine or write texts within our literacy classrooms from academic or professional genres created within communities of practice, we remove

[3]See, for an important, but complicating discussion, Swales' (1998) definition of a Place Discourse Community. (pp. 201–208)

them from the authentic situations in which they have been employed and from the very individuals who are community insiders. Texts then become artifacts for study rather than tools for achieving "repeated social action" (Miller, 1984). Freedman and Medway (1994b), who have written extensively about genre and pedagogy, made this comment:

> According to our new, more rhetorically informed view...producing an example of a genre is a matter not just of generating a text with certain formal characteristics but of using generic resources to act effectively in a situation through a text. While a learned structure provides a crude framework as well as a set of constraints, achieving an effective text involves innumerable local decisions for which the decontextualized formal rules learned in advance will provide no guidance. What has to be attended to, rather, are features of the situation, which is to be defined not only as immediate circumstances (participants, specific purposes, recent history), but also in terms of more general and diffuse elements such as pervasive values, priorities, and expectations prevailing within the larger field of the discipline, the profession, or whatever. (p. 10)

Thus, conventionalized text types, or modes, may provide "an invitation" (Fowler) or a "crude framework" (Freedman & Medway). They may also provide "critical strategies" for achieving specific purposes within a rhetorical situation (Kiniry & Rose, 1993). In addition, the study of texts from target contexts may give us some sense of text variation and content. However, producing a successful text within a professional or academic discourse community requires much, much more.[4] (See, for example, Purves, 1991; Swales, 1998.)

In a paper that argued for a reevaluation of the teaching of composition, Ramanathan and Kaplan (2000, pp. 180-83) asked us to keep these points in mind about genres, discourse communities, and dynamism:

1. Genres evolve and change to meet the growing and changing sociocognitive needs of discourse communities;
2. Genres evolve and develop to meet the needs of changing technology; and
3. Genres evolve to adapt to changes in ideology and world-view in discourse communities.
4. Genres change as individuals take liberties with textual conventions.

A COMMON DILEMMA

Like many teachers throughout the world whose students are novices, I have come to understand that student theories of academic texts are often in direct opposition to the genre theorists' complex ideas. My students see texts they read, particularly textbooks, as autonomous, uncontested and unnegotiated, unencumbered by the

[4]Unless, of course, we create our own discourse communities, ignoring those in which the studentswill be processing texts in the future. (See e.g., Spack, 1988)

values and oppositions that they may freely recognize in their out-of-school lives and textual experiences. Most view their traditional writing class essays as sites for expressing their (often unsupported) opinions, organized according to the five-paragraph essay template that exploits particular preassigned modes, such as comparison and contrast and cause and effect.[5] Because they have practiced the same school paper (the five-paragraph essay) structure many times, my students can tell me how many sentences should be part of each paragraph, where the thesis goes, and even what kinds of conjunctions should be employed with each mode selected. What my university colleagues and I have seen over the years, then, are very limited and constricting theories of written academic genres.

Given these informal, but persistent, findings, what are our responsibilities as pedagogues? As I see it, our major responsibility is to help students to become genre theorists in the true sense: to destabilize their often simplistic and sterile theories of texts and enrich their views of the complexity of text processing, negotiation, and production within communities of practice.

A LITERACY CONTEXT

For the past decade or so, I have been teaching in the Freshman Success Program at my university, a linked (adjunct)[6] class curriculum enrolling more than 1300 students each year. This program for first-year students is designed to provide a bridge between their secondary school experiences and university academic life. The students' schedule includes a general education (breadth) or major course, a writing class, a study group, and an orientation class, combined in what we call an academic "package." In this chapter, I will draw from research in a specific package designed to motivate and engage the students, destabilize their theories of genre, and involve them in evolving conceptions of academic requirements and texts.[7] In the particular class discussed here, the students were "remedial." They had attained low scores on the university writing examination, and yet they were otherwise qualified for entrance. In this class were 23 17- and 18-year-old students, mostly immigrants to the United States or children of immigrants, none of whose parents had attended university. The majority were Latino (17), but there was a smattering of students from other ethnic groups: two African-Americans, and one student from each of these ethic groups: Vietnamese, Hmong, Philippino, and Anglo. This is a typical "remedial" class at my large, public university, and it may be somewhat typical of writing classes in high school and universities throughout the American Southwest.

In this particular package, the writing class was linked to an introductory history class. The history instructor and I had worked together for several semesters,

---

[5]School essays are, in many other parts of the world, much more academic, I realize (see Dudley-Evans, this volume). But the "personal essay" is endemic in many parts of the United States.

[6]For a discussion of the organization and management of adjunct-based classes, see Iancu, 1997.

[7]For a more complete discussion of this program and its goals, see Johns, 1997.

and had developed some jointly held goals for the students. Among our goals were the following:

1. *To evoke student interest.* We were very much concerned with motivating the students in this group to perform, and thus we chose a theme, "Human Migration," for both classes (writing and history), a topic with which the students were familiar and in which many were interested because of their family backgrounds.
2. *To draw from students' own life histories.* We wanted to draw from the students' own rich historical experiences and from those of their families. I was also interested in drawing from students' pedagogical histories, particularly their theories of genre developed in secondary school classrooms.
3. *To provide "empowering" experiences.* Because our students were considered "remedial" by the university and were sometimes subject to discrimination because of their bilingualism and ethnicities, we wanted to give them textual and other experiences in which they had the powerful roles, in which they were the authorities. To accomplish this, we linked our academic package with a first-year class in a nearby secondary school that also enrolls a large number of immigrants. Throughout the term, our students interviewed, advised, listened to, and presented talks to their secondary-school partners. In this way, our students became models, not only of university entrants, but of researchers and of genre theorists.
4. *To destabilize students' theories of history and their theories of genre.* At first, these two goals do not seem to be parallel, but they proved to have a great deal in common. Students' theories about history were static: in high school, they approached the subject as a group of names and facts to be memorized and repeated on examinations. They believed that there existed "facts" and (personal) "opinions," with nothing else in between. Students also had static theories of genre, thinking of texts, for example, as formally organized essays. It was the history instructor's goal to destabilize the students' "facts" theories and to help them to understand that history is constructed by those who are reporting it. For example, students found that reports of migratory histories might vary among members of a family or ethnic group, depending upon speaker and writer purposes and experiences. Among other reading texts, the history instructor required a volume entitled *Unsettling Europe*, in which case histories of migrants within the European context were reported.[8]

It was my parallel aim to help students to understand that all written texts are socially constructed and are often sites of negotiation and controversy.

5. *To provide sufficient "scaffolding," or "assisted performance," that is, for students to be supported, critiqued, and encouraged as their theories were*

[8]See Johns, 1997, p. 144, for the other goals outlined by the history instructor.

destabilized. In pursuing this goal, the work of Vygotsky and his followers became important. The famous "Zone of Proximal Development," which is the theme when discussing Vygotsky's views of pedagogy, refers to assisting students in a specific social/pedagogical situation, "associated with the . . . discourse, and with potential consequences for developing new forms of thinking" (Moll, 1990, p. 2). In discussing how pedagogic tasks should be organized, Vygotsky argued for "whole" activities, which could be partitioned into "units" that contain essential characteristics of the whole, not "skills" per se, but elements that assist the student to construct, or process, meaningful and socially appropriate tasks for specific contexts. As students work toward a complex task, these "units" are completed and integrated. Students may then be able to see how "genre sets" or "systems" (Yates & Orlikowski, 1998) contribute to the production of a complex task.

In addition to organizing the task into meaningful units, neo-Vygotskian theorists discuss issues of "assisted performance," that is, the ways in which the instructor, or student peers, provide assistance in working toward a complex task. Methods for assisted performance have been categorized into the following by Gallimore and Tharp (1990): *modeling* an activity or process for imitation, *contingency management* through rewards and punishment, *feeding back* through peer or instructor critique and evaluation, *questioning* to guide the students toward their goals, *cognitive structuring* through structures of explanation or structures of cognitive activities, and *instructing* through giving directives. Instructing and contingency management appear to be most common and transparent in classrooms. For this reason, I will concentrate here on conscious use of the other concepts: modeling, feeding back, and cognitive structuring within the history package. It should be noted that we could not divide literacy tasks from assisted performance, or, in more common parlance, we could not separate the text products from the processes for reading or writing texts, for the two are intertwined in our classrooms, and in the histories of most genres (see Coe, and Guleff, this volume).

THE APPROACH

It would be impossible to discuss everything we attempted, so I have focused here on certain goals within the classroom framework: drawing upon students' genre histories and their discussions of their evolving theories of genre generated by their university classrooms, the resultant destabilization of those theories, and our efforts to provide assisted performance throughout the process of accomplishing assigned tasks.

Students' Genre Theories

Reading. Reflection was a dominant element in our classrooms, and drawing from student reflections was essential to our research. Generally, the students were asked to reflect in writing as they encountered new experiences or completed a task. In one written text of this type, I asked the students to compare the reading required in high school with reading in university. I received a variety of answers, but there were several themes that wove themselves throughout most of the reflective texts. One of these was "the difficult style of university texts." Claudia made this comment about style: "(In college) I am expected to read material that is either written in an old style or has words you have never heard of before." Universally, students found the college reading "boring" for a number of reasons. Angie explained one reason why students were bored: "We don't get to pick the books that we want to read, and we're not interested in writing about them."

Most students' experiences with reading in high school had been limited. For the most part, they had read only self-selected literature, but "now we read histories, and original sources, and stuff" (Rocio). This genre variety demanded a number of approaches to reading, one of which was critical analysis. Mario recognized this requirement and viewed it as distinctly different from what was required in his earlier education:

> In high school, I didn't have to do alot of analysis of the content and structure of a reading. Here in college, I have to look for why and what the author is trying to say, for his or her argument. The point and the meaning is more important than the characters, plot, and that work I had to do in high school.

As can be seen, the students were expected to be much more responsible as readers than they had been in the past. One of the most insightful students, Sal, had this to say:

> Upon entering college, I experienced that difficulty of adjusting to the requirements of a professor. Your assignments are do [sic] the next class day. The reading is difficult to understand at times. The professor doesn't read to you. The student is given a list of the required reading and is expected to follow it. No one tells you if you are falling behind.

In their history package, the students were confronted with a number of new challenges: independent reading, processing a number of genres, and analyzing the required texts for argumentation and other features.

Writing. In many secondary school classrooms in North America, The Writing Process[9] has become standard and routinized. The written product is predictable:

[9]I have put The Writing Process in caps because this complex activity has become, in many cases, as routinized as the text products. The first day, students "brainstorm," then they draft and peer review papers, then they revise, and finally they edit for errors.

The Five Paragraph Essay, organized according to an assigned mode. Because of these past literacy experiences, our students brought a few templates for writing, and most attempted to apply these templates to every text, no matter what the task required. Many students claimed to have conducted research using sources in secondary school, but when I asked them about the purposes and forms of a research paper, they said that their papers were "just essays with some outside stuff put in."[10] What they commented upon most in their reflections were the requirements of the final products in their history package. Students were amazed by the fact that they were expected to proofread the final drafts of their papers, that they were actually required to turn in near-perfect products after the long writing process was completed. Marco spoke of this difference with his high school experience in the following way: "The writing has to be more collegiate than in high school, meaning, that the material must be good in presentation, typed, and must be proofread." Patricia wrote that "In college the writing needs to be well done, you can't have spelling errors. Instructors get mad when students have bad grammar and when they are plagiarizing."

[At this point, the reader may be thinking, "Well, the 'remedial' students in California may have these limited theories and experiences; however, my students have a much broader repertoire." Before making this claim, I suggest that you spend some time exploring your students' genre theories through reflections or other methods. Their theories may not be parallel to my students', but they may be fully as limited and constricting.]

DESTABILIZING STUDENTS' GENRE THEORIES

What could we do to destabilize these theories, to enable students to broaden their concepts of genre and their genre repertoire? In the section that follows, I will discuss some of our attempts in this Freshman Success package, not all of which were successful. The history instructor assigned novels, but expected students to read them for their authors' constructions of history. She assigned original sources, texts in which a number of writers presented the same event in a variety of ways. The textbook was to be read only for details, such as dates, and the instructor never examined the students on any of these details.[11] From these experiences came the students' comments about reading.

In my composition classroom, I concentrated as much as possible on writing, particularly upon destabilizing and enriching students' theories about "the research paper." Unfortunately for literacy teachers, the pedagogical research paper is very poorly defined within academic contexts, for

---

[10]I recently discovered that in at least one local high school, a research paper looks exactly like a five-paragraph essay in that it begins with a thesis, etc.

[11]One of her take-home final examination questions was: "Was the history of Western Civilization a story of progress—or not?"

> Research can inform virtually any writing or speaking . . . There is nothing of substance or content that differentiates one paper that draws on data from outside the author's own self from another such paper—nothing that can enable one to say "this is a research paper and that paper is not." I would assert, therefore, that the so-called research paper as a generic, cross- disciplinary term, has no conceptual or substantive identity. (Larson, 1982, p. 813)

As Swales (1988, 1990) and others have indicated, professional research papers are also specific to rhetorical situations. The features that distinguish one discipline, or one academic journal, from another, are the various elements that contribute to research: What kinds of questions are asked or hypotheses posed; what type of data is collected; how the data is displayed within the text; and, not incidentally, how the text is organized.

In order to introduce students to some of the variety within research processes and products, we required two papers, one based on interview data about the family migratory experiences of the secondary students with whom our students were paired, and one on a more narrow topic related to migration[12] for which research on the Web and in the library was required. The papers were to look very different from each other (for example, the interview paper used quotes and quote analysis; the topic paper required a purpose statement and research questions). However, they had one characteristic in common: The heavily hedged "thesis" or argument had to appear in the conclusion, and, to be acceptable, it had to result from an analysis and presentation of the data and sources. The thesis could no longer be an opinion stated in the first paragraph and supported by a few outside sources, as had been the case in most of their high school experiences.

Providing Assisted Performance

If we are to destabilize, and enrich, students' genre theories, we must provide for them the kind of assisted performance that will enable them to succeed. One of the most common causes of undergraduate student failure in universities is that most discipline-specific faculty (in biology, history, economics, etc.) have implicit expectations for student work, yet they provide little assistance to students in completing their literacy tasks. By their very nature, students are novices and apprentices, and we, as teachers, have an obligation to initiate them. As I mentioned earlier, Vygotsky and his followers suggest that we organize teaching into "whole" activities, which, in turn, can be partitioned into "units" that contain essential characteristics of the whole. Because research papers of all types are intertextual in that they draw from sources outside of the writer's own text, our first inclination was to organize the students' "units" into the various texts that they would collect to provide the data for their papers. However, after some experimentation and

[12]Students selected topics such as affirmative action, denying immigrant women obstetrical care, the effects of migration upon the economy, child/immigrant parent conflicts, and migrant students and gangs.

discussion, we decided to organize the "units" around the various processes (and products) that contributed to their final papers. Their writing portfolios (see Johns, 1997) thus became Migration Project Manuals (MPMs), divided into a number of sections entitled "Notes," "Interviews," "Sources," "Drafts," "Reflections," and "Final Papers." Though there was some overlap between the sections, we found that these divisions, and due dates for each entry (for example, "Notes from the interviews, November 2," "Reflections on Discovering Sources," December 4.") assisted the students in managing the two rather difficult research papers that they were assigned *and* in beginning to understand the differences between the two papers, in terms of both processes and written products. At the end of the semester, the students were required to turn in their MPMs along with the final papers in order to be graded in both their history and writing classes.

CONCLUSION

One of the issues about which genre theorists and pedagogues should be more concerned, in my view, is the nature of the genre theories that our students bring with them to class. Some of these theories, particularly the rich, complete ones about the "homely" genres of their own families and cultures, can assist them to apply social constructionist views to academic and professional genres (see Johns, 1997). However, other theories, such as the limited ones they may have acquired in school, need to be destabilized, enriched, and expanded. A general theme in our students' final portfolio reflections related to their new experiences at university, experiences that caused them to review their theories about texts and to become more aware of the interaction between process, intertextuality, and products, and the variation among texts even within what is assumed to be a single pedagogical genre such as the research paper or five-paragraph essay.

Part VII

Conclusion and Responses

14

Narrative and Expository Macro-Genres

William Grabe
Northern Arizona University

To say that all human thinking is essentially of two kinds—reasoning on the one hand, and narrative, descriptive, contemplative thinking on the other—is to say only what every reader's experience will corroborate.
—William James (from Bruner, 1986)

There are two modes of cognitive functioning, two modes of thought, each providing distinctive ways of ordering experience, of constructing reality. The two (though complementary) are irreducible to one another. Efforts to reduce one mode to the other or to ignore one mode at the expense of the other inevitably fail to capture the rich diversity of thought.
—Bruner, 1986, p. 11

In this chapter, I would like to argue for a view of genre types that, in some respects, has a long rhetorical tradition, though I will not call on that tradition for my arguments. Rather, I want to explore a range of arguments that establish the validity of narrative and expository macro-genres as ways of talking about texts and as ways of constructing texts. Of course, such a position, to the extent that it is persuasive, has important implications for any theory of genre. It also has implications for approaches to reading and writing instruction and what students are able to do, or are not able to do, with respect to learning through text.

The arguments presented here cross a number of disciplinary boundaries and, in some respect, provide converging evidence for two ways of constructing and interpreting text (or two ways of constructing knowledge). After a brief commentary on a definition of genres (and macro-genres), this paper will offer arguments from cultural psychology, learning theory, educational psychology, discourse comprehension research, literacy development research, and corpus linguistics. This survey will close with consequences for a theory of genres and implications for instruction.

A VIEW OF GENRES

For various historical, theoretical, and instructional reasons, we no longer want to be seen as endorsing traditional notions (which do include much unwanted baggage). But we have, perhaps, become captive to certain newer simplistic terminology, dichotomies, and conceptualizations that constrain our thinking. It has now become an important part of our professional credentials to decry a simplistically specified "current traditional" approach to writing, to deny value to models of writing (Charney & Carlson, 1995; Smagorinski, 1992), to belittle the potential of outlining (Kellogg, 1994; Walvoord, Anderson, Breihan, McCarthy, Robinson, & Sherman, 1995), and to see notions of narrative and expository as passé (see Paltridge, this volume). In these efforts to develop modern views of composition/writing theory and practice, certain resources for teaching and learning are labeled as inappropriate or ineffective without sufficiently exploring ways to make such resources effective components of a more broadly conceived view of learning to write (from a student's perspective) and writing instruction (from a teacher's perspective).

With respect to the term genre, significant advances have been made in the ways we discuss this notion, in the theorizing that supports purposes and uses of language, and in the opportunities this notion provides for effective teaching and learning. Following explorations and theorizing by Atkinson (1991), Berkenkotter and Huckin (1995), Bhatia (1993), Johns (1997), Martin (1993a), and Swales (1990), among others, it is now possible to see genre as a central concept determining how discourse is organized and used for various purposes—how it both constitutes and is constituted by recurring social situations that lead to recognizable and shared conventions and expectations. Although there is certainly much room for debate and contestation over specific ways to understand and define genres (Berkenkotter & Huckin, 1995; Johns, 1997; Martin, 1993a; Swales, 1990), it is also clear that the concept of genre has evolved in ways to reflect real uses of written (and oral) discourse among cultures, social groups, and communities of users.

It is not the goal here to review these advances in theorizing and their accompanying opportunities for instruction; there is no question that these advances have been powerful catalysts for rethinking the role of discourse structuring in writing in relation to social contexts and purposes for writing. Rather, I want to argue that this movement in genre research has left behind some important notions that need to be given their place within the broader conceptualization of genre—in particular, the notions of narrative and expository forms as macro-genres with distinct purposes, uses, and demands on writers.[1]

Current interpretations of genre typically assume a functional "naming" perspective; that is, they discuss forms of discourse that reflect the situation of use in which such forms arise. Thus, we discuss the purposes and uses of the scientific research paper and its subsections, the *abstract*, the *research proposal*, the *sermon*, the *academic lecture*, the *interview*, the *questionnaire*, the *job application*, the *classified ad*, the *marriage announcement*, the *letter of recommendation*, the *letter of invitation*, and so on. In all of these cases, formal features become conventionally established within a range of options that are recognizable by social groups who share such knowledge of use in appropriate contexts.

At the same time, we also recognize a range of academic instructional genres that consistently arise, at least by name, across a wide range of academic contexts. These instructional genres are typically, though not always, more loosely defined and incorporate within themselves considerable variation. Johns (1997), for example, discussed the *research paper*, the *take-home exam*, and the *in-class essay* as three instructional genres that are assumed to fit certain expectations by the assigning teachers but which are sufficiently loose with respect to purpose, reader-writer roles, content, formal structure, register, and cultural expectations that students should be taught to "negotiate" these expectations with each teacher.

From a different perspective, taking a somewhat more formalist than functionalist starting point, the Australian genre approach to literacy instruction similarly engages students in exploring and using a range of "loose" instructional genres. However, in these cases, the functionalist interpretations derive less from "named" use than from a Hallidayan theory of functional language use (Halliday, 1993). Derewianka (1990) and Martin (1993a), among others, identified this range of "loose" instructional genres with respect to elementary-school literacy instruction as including *recounts*, *procedures*, *descriptions*, *reports*, *explanations*, and *expositions*. Much like the academic instructional genres noted by Johns, these genres need to serve as a source of metalinguistic awareness on the part of students, particularly in the K–12 setting, and students must learn how to negotiate the expectations of these curriculum genres with teachers.

The Australian view of genres—that basic curriculum genre types need to be part of a student's metalinguistic awareness if the student is to appropriate and use potentially powerful genres—leads to the argument of this paper. In addition to a range of loose educational genres that conventionally arise in many education settings (whether identified by functional names or by functional structuring), there is also a need more generally for students to recognize and explore the many (distinct) ways that narrative and expository texts can be used to construct knowledge and serve important communicative purposes.

The family of narrative discourse structures represent text types that are typically episodic in nature and include a set of identifying criteria that bear family

[1]There may be other macro-genres, or genre families, beyond narrative and expository texts. In this chapter, it's enough to make the argument for these basic macro-genres.

resemblances to one another. All narratives involve characterization and a protagonist's perspective; they involve sequences of events, some events being out of the ordinary and requiring explanation, typically presented as a causal chaining of events. It makes more sense to speak of narratives in terms of "What happened?" than in terms of "What is the main idea?" Types of narratives include, among others, recounts, forecounts, historical events, (auto)biographies, tales, and fictions. To the extent that we talk about or analyze narratives, we discuss settings, characters, initiating events, episodes, conflicts, emotional feelings, outcomes, resolutions, and evaluations (Labov & Waletzsky, 1967). Most narratives are centrally driven by an assumption of causal sequences chaining together to provide a coherent interpretation. There are also a number of purposes and formal linguistic features associated with most common narratives, as will be noted in the brief section on applied linguistics corpora research.

The family of expository discourse structures represent text types that offer conceptualizations of knowledge or ways to build knowledge (Kucan & Beck, 1996). Expository texts provide ways of framing our knowledge of the world, synthesizing diverse sources of knowledge, classifying and categorizing our knowledge in various hierarchical (rather than strictly sequential) forms, and representing what we have come to know in conventionalized discourse structures—they allow us to reflect on our knowledge in ways distinct from narratives and (hi)stories. From this perspective, summarizing main ideas of an expository text becomes a different task from summarizing a plot sequence, and synthesizing information to construct new knowledge relations becomes a task quite distinct from drawing inferences from a story or evaluating aspects of a narrative with respect to moral lessons, emotional evocation, or protagonist actions.

It is certainly true that there is a long rhetorical tradition of modes of discourse going back to the eighteenth century, and taking on preeminent status in the 19th century with Bain's (1877) formulation of expository, descriptive, narrative, and argumentative modes of discourse (see also Patridge on text types, this volume). It is also true that such a scheme has been conventionalized as a generic instructional format with unrealistic models that artificially highlight each mode (as well as patterns of arrangement such as comparison and contrast, cause and effect, classification, definition, and so on). One can certainly point out, and rightly so, that causal sequences are central to both narrative discourses and most problem–solution texts, that descriptions are potentially important in both narrative and expository writing, and that narratives can occur in expository discourse and vice versa. One can even say that narratives construct and frame knowledge of the world, though typically in an indirect manner (Eco, 1989). Nevertheless, we need to reconsider if the distinction between narrative and expository macro-genres provides a productive means for understanding different purposes for texts. Are there conventionalizations basic to each type of macro-genre that offer insights into the ways that texts operate in the world and in educational institutions? Are there important instructional insights that students can be made aware of and that can lead to more effective student writing? In the following sections, I will present arguments external to rhetoric for maintaining a general two-part distinction between narrative and expository types of discourse.

ARGUMENTS FOR THE TWO-PART DISTINCTION

Cultural Psychology

In a series of recent arguments, Bruner (1986, 1990) has claimed that there are two fundamental ways of learning to understand the world, or "two modes of thought" (Bruner, 1986). Bruner argued that narrative thought and paradigmatic thought (or expository thought) represent two ways of interpreting the world and of drawing meaning from interactions with the world. The strength of a narrative is determined by the drama, believability, and goodness of a story. It can be defined in terms of its sequentiality, its factual indifferences, its unique way of departing from the canonical, its dramatism, and its dual control of a putative real world alongside the mental events of a protagonist (Bruner, 1990, pp. 43–52). Its primary structural mechanisms are plot, character, and perspective. Narratives typically deal with human potential, human action, and human intentionality; as such, their most forceful applications involve recognizing universal ideas through the telling of a particular story, and it is by recognizing the importance of the particular that narratives suggest more generalizing tropes such as metonymy, metaphor, synecdoche, and inference, allowing us to discuss one person's story in relation to other peoples' stories. In this way, narratives invite interpretation of the story rather than asking logically what a story means (Bruner, 1990, pp. 54–61). Narratives also invite the reader to consider alternative versions of a story in ways that are not as openly possible with explanations of concepts and phenomena.

Bruner further extended his analysis of narratives as a foundation for individual understanding by suggesting that typical narratives have four essential features (not components of narrative structure—Labov & Waletzsky, 1967): (a) agentivity, (b) sequential order, (c) sensitivity to the canonical (canonical event-structuring preferred), and (d) a narrator's perspective (a voice). These features are essential not only for understanding narrative structure but also for understanding early language acquisition and the development of "self" at an early age. In analyses of young children learning the functional uses of language at early ages, examining data from 18 months to four years, Bruner (1990, pp. 83–93) argued that young children are constantly exposed to short typical narratives from mothers and begin to internalize basic narrative forms in interpreting the world from as young as 18 months of age.

Paradigmatic or expository texts, in contrast, are assumed to draw on a frame of logic that is not readily open to a range of interpretations but follows a logic that is displayed by the expository text itself (whether true or not, whether accurate or not). Expository explanations, definitions, and/or descriptions use frames of categorization and conceptualization that evoke a system by which to relate each part to the others (whether done successfully or not). The assumed system is presented by hierarchical classifications, disjunctions, strict implication, and statements that invite generalization. The goal of expository text is consistency, systematicity, and noncontradiction—the paradigmatic text is intended to transcend the particular instance (Bruner, 1986, pp. 12–13).

For Bruner, the paradigmatic (expository) mode also arises out of our experiences with the world, though not necessarily the formulations that guide written discourses of this type. From an early age, children develop paradigmatic discourse. Bruner noted the rise of a problem-solving mode of understanding, initially developed to account for inconsistencies in the evolving narrative reality (Bruner, 1990, pp. 93–94; Newkirk, 1987). At later ages, the paradigmatic shaping of our world knowledge is built up from numerous similar encounters with phenomena to be explained. From these experiences, we generate general models of how the world works quite apart from specific contexts and apart from how we operate in the world. Bruner suggested that this mode of thought allows us to account for an enormous amount of information about the world with a minimum of distraction or attention to detail. These models of the world that we create, however, are likely to be skewed and naïve (Gardner, 1991), indicating that a powerful purpose for curriculum genres of an expository type is to allow us to reconsider our naïve theories of the world and restructure them in more refined ways (even if still not the most appropriate ways; Bruner, 1986, pp. 47–52). Such an argument offers one developmental explanation for why children have greater difficulties working with expository tasks than narrative tasks.

Macro-Genres and Learning Theory

Learning-theory research offers a different approach to textual discourse, one that provides an additional strong argument for an expository prose macro-genre. One of the primary assumptions with respect to school texts is the expectation that students will be able to learn from text resources. Learning from texts is a major concern for education researchers, and for most teachers. Informational (expository) texts,[2] as opposed to narrative texts, are usually seen as the primary input for learning new information in social sciences, science, math, and history. These texts (whether textbooks, specific topical resources, Web sites, trade books, encyclopedias, and so on) are most commonly used in situations in which students do not have a high level of prior topical knowledge, but are expected to increase this knowledge as a result of encounters with these informational texts.

There are many concerns and issues commonly associated with the notion that

[2]A number of authors use the term *informational* rather than expository. By my understanding of the term, it is synonymous with expository prose, broadly defined; that is, it typically includes argumentative and persuasive texts that do not involve narration as the basis for their arguments (cf. historical narratives, which may need their own category as informational texts). I will use the term *informational* text where that is the common use of authors.

students learn from texts. First, there is the concern that informational knowledge will not motivate students when it is presented as text resources outside the immediate interests of students. Second, there is the concern that informational texts assume a "transmission of knowledge" mode of learning rather than the joint construction of knowledge through social interaction. Third, there is the concern that informational resources are often inappropriate resources for learning or that teachers do not know how to use these resources effectively to promote learning. These issues have all been discussed widely, and they are yet to be fully resolved. Nevertheless, it is true that more expert students do read and interpret informational resources better, and they are better able to learn information from these texts.

One of the major drawbacks to discussion of these informational texts has been the recognition that "informational" texts do not have an easily discernible set of organizing frames through which to present information (Cote, Goldmann, & Saul, 1998; Kucan & Beck, 1996; Lorch & Van Den Broek, 1997). Making use of a term proposed by Mohan (1986), we don't have a clear sense of the "knowledge structures" that underlie informational texts, or of how these knowledge structures get translated into text structuring. One goal to promote learning from texts would be to explore the more generic frames or discourse structures that are used by writers and readers to convey and explain knowledge. The more consistent such a frame of reference becomes, the more it is open for generic patterning and instructional uses, and the more it can support learning from texts (Mosenthal & Cavallo, 1998). In this respect, the curriculum genres noted could represent underlying knowledge structures to the extent that: (a) they are open to investigation (verifiable), (b) they are generalizable, and (c) they can be used by students to enhance learning. A further goal of a theory of knowledge structures would be to explain how students would use such structuring to construct their own knowledge (or how text structuring can contribute to learning new information).

There is relatively little research work in this area, though there is much theorizing. There is also relatively little that can be drawn from most instructional contexts and teaching experiences because most teachers have minimal notions of how discourse can structure knowledge or of how one might exploit such resources systematically. One exception is the systematic exploration of learning from informational texts that has been developed and continues in the work of Mosenthal (1985) and his colleagues (Kirsch & Mosenthal, 1991a, 1991b; Mosenthal & Cavallo, 1998; Mosenthal & Kirsch, 1992).

In earlier work, Mosenthal (1985) proposed a rather unique framework for describing expository prose as a set of structures that build on each other to create more complex ways of presenting knowledge. For Mosenthal, expository prose represents a break from narrative prose, not only in terms of structure but also in educational uses. Expository prose is more common in secondary grades and beyond, and its primary purpose is to update knowledge. He sees narratives as distinct from expository prose also in the sense that narratives provide easily recognized common structures for organizing prose, whereas expository prose does not have commonly recognized major frames of reference that could be used to assist students' learning.

Mosenthal first described expository-type texts as "a process of partial, descriptive, and operational specification" (1985, p. 389). He argued that relations between phenomena (actions, states, sets of actions, sets of states) and text representations, or between one text representation and a second one, are built up initially through partial descriptive features and examples on the one hand, and partial operations (actions and events) that use procedures and criteria to identify a process. Simply stated, we create lists of salient and useful features and events that describe phenomena, and we develop various ways to combine and nest list-like structures to derive expository prose texts of various types and complexities. Because specifications in texts are always partial, writers must choose the key features and decide how they interrelate and form hierarchies: This is seen by Mosenthal as the "problem of content organization" (as opposed to the "problem of content selection," 1985, p. 392). The task for the writer, then, is that of creating a "specification hierarchy" to organize the presentation of content and to order information with respect to other information (as propositional relations). As a result, features, examples, procedures, and criteria are organized as simple units available to build more complex knowledge units and more complex expository structures (Mosenthal, 1985).

Using these building blocks for expository prose, Mosenthal then outlined basic types of expository specification hierarchies (much like curriculum genres proposed by Heath, 1986; Martin, 1989; and Mohan, 1986). As Mosenthal stated, "By considering the different combinations of specification function, topic organization, and propositional relations, one can identify six/seven different types of specification hierarchies" (1985, p. 397). These types include: records, reports, generalized record/reports, loose classification, strong classification, speculatives, and theoreticals. Space precludes any extended discussion of this framework, though Mosenthal argued that a continuum runs from "records" to "theoretical," with wider choice, less constraint, and simpler structural hierarchies determining beginning points along the continuum. This incremental approach would seem little different from several other specifications of instructional expository frames. However, Mosenthal has since developed an approach that specifies both how pieces can be fitted together incrementally (and open to such analysis, in reverse) and how learning can follow from such structuring.

In a more recent series of articles, Mosenthal & Kirsch (1991a, 1991b, 1992; Kirsch & Mosenthal, 1991a, b, &c; see exemplary references in the bibliography) described how expository texts provide the means by which knowledge construction, as a theory of learning, can take place. Drawing on learning concepts described by Vosniadou and Brewer (1987), they proposed that learning from text involves the gradual accretion, tuning, and restructuring of information that is drawn from texts and that interacts with prior knowledge. This process of building additional information, they argued, applies to an awareness of expository curriculum genres and their roles in these accretion, tuning, and restructuring processes. In articles covering several years in the *Journal of Reading* (1989–1992), they outlined ways that both documents and texts build knowledge representations in increasingly more complex patterns from initial lists of relatively simple mechanisms (features, examples, actions, criteria). These basic mechanisms of identifying features and their combinations lead to curriculum genres of definition, description, comparison–contrast, classification, time sequence, cause and effect, problem–solution, conditional, and theoretical frames. The key point is that their framework is not simply intended to describe patterns in texts as curriculum genres that exist in learning contexts, but to explain how such genres are created and then used as a means to help learners build their own information structures.

Most recently, Mosenthal & Cavallo (1998) have begun to test the arguments made for this framework through learning studies. In a recent study, they examined the learning processes of students following a series of lessons intended to raise awareness of these knowledge structures, and they explored the learning outcomes of such instruction. Their research centered on a set of lessons involving the process of meiosis to 140 tenth-grade high school students. Students were assessed on their level of knowledge of meiosis prior to the reading and instruction and then reassessed by information recall after instruction. At one level of learning, many students added additional features to descriptions of the process or filled in descriptive information for points of reference in greater detail. This form of learning from texts involves accretion of information. A second group of students added new knowledge through the process of tuning: They added new points of reference, added new steps in the process, generalized across cases to create classes of events and processes, and/or created new classes to differentiate a number of cases. In each case, students changed the frame of reference for the concept, and in several cases they created new levels of concept representation. A final group of students, via restructuring, redefined their ways of understanding the process of meiosis, or recognized that the key goal was to understand the process of change itself rather than identifying features and isolated descriptions of the process. Using Mosenthal's framework for knowledge modeling, the progress these students made in their learning from texts, and the extent of their progress after different stages of instruction, can continue to be identified and explored.

The essential argument from this exploration of one approach to learning theory and the construction of knowledge is that expository texts can be systematically examined, classified, and used for teaching students to learn new knowledge from texts. In this respect, expository prose, as a macro-genre, provides resources to explain how certain learning theories can be operationalized. Such a perspective aligns well with major views on learning from most currently viable general theories of cognition and learning (Anderson, 1995; Bruner, 1986, 1990; Kintsch, 1988, 1998; Vygotsky, 1978).

Educational Psychology and Expository Prose

There is strong evidence that training students to become more aware of the ways that texts are structured, and text organization signaled, leads to better recall of information and better task performance using that information (Pearson & Fielding, 1991). The large majority of this work has been carried out with learning from expository texts because students have difficulty with reading expository material and learning from textbooks (Cote, et al., 1998). Similar problems typically do not occur with narrative texts, particularly fiction, for two reasons. First, most fiction reading in schools is not difficult to understand and interpret. Second, assessment of fiction usually involves interpretation of the text rather than comprehension assessment to see if the material is understood and learned. (Historical narratives in history textbooks, however, pose as many comprehension and application problems as do expository texts in various context areas.) Overall, three areas of research are discussed next as aspects of educational psychology and educational training research on learning from texts: text-structure awareness, top-level text structuring, and graphic organizers.

Considerable educational research in literacy instruction highlights the importance of *text structures* for students' comprehension and learning from texts (Paltridge, this volume; Pearson & Fielding, 1991). In much of this research, there is a clear distinction between expository (informational) texts and narrative texts. Narrative texts represent a much larger portion of texts read (and written) by students in K–12 contexts (Lemke, 1988; Rothery, 1996), and most students have a relatively strong sense of narrative story structure in elementary grades (Taylor & Samuels, 1983). In fact, many efforts to teach story structures to non-disability students provide inconsistent outcome differences because most students already know these story structures, at least intuitively, and other measures are more effective indicators of narrative recall (background knowledge, central-event sequence, causal structure; Pearson & Fielding, 1991; Pressley & Woloshyn, 1995). In general, evidence argues that expository text types are harder for students to learn from than narrative texts (Cote et al., 1998; Crowhurst, 1990; Engelhard , Gordon, & Gabrielson, 1992; Spiro & Taylor, 1987).

In the case of expository prose, research has demonstrated repeatedly that students with a better knowledge of the organizational structures in a given text (comparison–contrast, classification, cause–effect, problem–solution, argument for a position) recall more information from the text and perform better on comprehension tasks (Armbruster et al. 1987; Carrell, 1992; Pearson & Fielding, 1991; Taylor, 1992). Moreover, students who are able to identify and use an author's organizational structuring recall more important information from texts (Carrell, 1992; Taylor & Samuels, 1983). In the words of Pearson and Fielding:

> We have found incredibly positive support for just about any approach to text structure instruction for expository prose. It appears that any sort of systematic attention to clues

> that reveal how authors attempt to relate ideas to one another or any sort of systematic attempt to impose structure upon a text, especially in some sort of visual representation of the relationships among key ideas, facilitates comprehension as well as both short-term and long-term memory for the text (1991, p. 832).

Research on *top-level organizing structure* with expository genres has demonstrated that students with greater awareness of the *major* organizing structure of a text recall information better from the text and learn more from the text in summarizing tasks. These results apply equally for both L1 and L2 readers (Carrell, 1992; Meyer, 1987; Taylor, 1992). In most of this research, the identified top-level structures include the following: description/collection, temporal sequence/process, cause–effect, comparison–contrast, and problem–solution text structures. Although it may not always be the case that students can explicitly describe the text structure being processed, those who follow the text organization in their recalls and summaries perform better.

A number of studies have demonstrated the effectiveness in using *graphic organizers* to teach text structures to students in order to enhance their learning from texts (Griffin & Tulbert, 1995). In most cases, these graphic organizers involved the teaching of graphic representations with expository texts (except historical narratives). The entire notion of graphic organizers as an important way to improve students' learning from text follows from the arguments that expository type texts impose significant learning difficulties on students that do not generally apply with narrative texts. These difficulties are often traceable, in part, to the inability of students to recognize (and then use) the text structuring generated by authors in organizing the information presented. (See also McKenna & Robinson, 1997; Vacca & Vacca, 1996 for applications.) Although it is certainly true that narratives can impose extraordinary difficulties on readers (as with Henry James, William Faulkner, Toni Morrison, and others), it is unlikely that the sources of these difficulties reside with an inability on a reader's part to recognize basic patterns of discourse organization.

In summary, there is considerable evidence from research in educational psychology and literacy training that expository prose genres represent major types of educational texts encountered in K–12 school contexts. They generate distinct learning issues and concerns, they call for distinct instructional practices, and they implicate learning outcomes quite separate from narrative types of text.

Cognitive Psychology and Comprehension Research

Comprehension research in cognitive psychology has its roots in the mid-1970s and it has expanded its influence considerably within the last ten years, particularly with the appearance of Kintsch's (1988) Construction–Integration model of text comprehension (see Lorch & Van Den Broek, 1997 for historical overview). The past ten years has also been a time in which comprehension research has given more attention to the effect of genre variation on comprehension processing. Graesser and

Britton (1996, p. 342) commented that recent research has explored, and continues to explore, processing models and performance differences as they arise across expository, narrative, literary, and conversational texts. In order to discuss research results and processing differences across genres, it will first be necessary briefly to discuss more general research efforts in discourse comprehension.

Easily the most influential approach to discourse comprehension has been the propositional models of Kintsch and Van Dijk (1978), and more recently, Kintsch's Construction–Integration model of text comprehension (Kintsch, 1988, 1998). In his work, and in numerous other studies in the field, the psychological reality of propositional encoding of language has been well established and now is the dominating framework in comprehension research (Britton & Graesser, 1996; Singer, 1990). From the early 1980s, Kintsch has been proposing that text comprehension is comprised of three levels of processing: the surface structure of language, the textbase level, and the situation model. During the past five years, there has been extensive evidence for the independent function of a textbase level of comprehension and a situation-model level of comprehension (Kintsch, 1998; Zwaan, 1996).

Essentially, comprehension of text occurs at two levels (discounting the surface representation for the moment). At the level of a textbase, the reader reconstructs closely the information provided by a text, along with organizing instructions provided by the author. The textbase represents a close summary of the actual information provided with minimal elaboration by background knowledge, reader purpose, or reader attitude. The situation model, in contrast, represents a second version of text comprehension, combined with strong interpretation from prior knowledge, reader purpose, and reader attitude. For Kintsch, the textbase amounts to the memory structure of the text whereas the situation model represents information learned from processing the text (inasmuch as it is integrated with the reader's prior knowledge). There are many implications from such a view of discourse comprehension that extend beyond the scope of this chapter (see Grabe, in press; Kintsch, 1998). One critical result of this two-level notion of comprehension is that, in most cases of successful comprehension, a reader constructs both an efficient propositional network of information indicated by the text and also an appropriate mental model—a personal interpretation of what the text means for that reader. This approach allows, depending on any given reading situation, an opportunity for both comprehension of a text in line with an author's intentions and also a reader interpretation of the text.

Varying the conditions of reading will lead to differing combinations of strengths and limitations in the processing of either the textbase or the situation model. Because the textbase is a propositionally constructed network of text-presented information, it is driven by concerns for coherence-signaling mechanisms in the text itself (and thus coherence is derived, at least in part, from the linguistic elements of the text itself). The situation model, on the other hand, is driven by prior knowledge, thematic representations, and reader goals and attitudes (Kintsch, 1998; McNamara, Kintsch, Songer, & Kintsch, 1996; Voss & Silfes, 1996).

One consequence of this approach is that expository prose texts, under usual conditions in which reader background knowledge is relatively low, will privilege the construction of a strong textbase but a weaker situation model (and hence learning difficulties due to low integration with prior knowledge). Narrative texts, in contrast, tend to exhibit strong situation models, interacting strongly with relevant prior knowledge, and weaker textbase representations because of emphasis on the situation model. As a result, narrative texts lead to strong inferencing and strong integration with prior knowledge (and hence easier and more complete delayed recollection and learning from text).

Not surprisingly, when students read expository texts, they typically perform better on tasks that require textbase knowledge and less well on tasks that emphasize situation model knowledge. In addition, when students carry out comprehension tasks *during reading* that support situation-model building (sorting information into major categories), they will enhance their recall from expository prose because such tasks complement the natural processing emphasis with an expository text. For much the same reason, when students carry out tasks that focus on textbase information (fill in the details), they will enhance their recall for narrative prose because the task complements the tendency to emphasize situation-model processing (the major story line) with narrative texts. Thus, a reader's comprehension is improved by doing tasks that are complementary to the information emphasized by a given genre. This line of research, which has strong implications for instruction, falls within a general theory of comprehension performance variation known as the Material Appropriate Processing (MAP) framework (Einstein, McDaniel, Owen, & Cote, 1990; McDaniel & Einstein, 1989; McDaniel, Hines, Waddill, & Einstein, 1994).

It should be emphasized that Kintsch's Construction–Integration model is not limited in its application to any subset of text types. The same holds true of many other general approaches to text comprehension (Britton & Graesser, 1996; Gernsbacher, 1997; Just & Carpenter, 1992; McDaniels & Einstein, 1989). The current research in cognitive psychology on text comprehension does demonstrate, however, that a number of important variables make independent contributions to text recall and learning from texts, and included among these variables is text type at the level of narrative and expository prose.

Educational Literacy and Writing Development

As a complement to the processing research that draws on cognitive psychology and discourse comprehension, much evidence from a literacy-development perspective exists for making strong distinctions between narrative and expository macro-genres. These arguments are seen in the research comparing elementary-student reading of narrative and expository texts by Kucan & Beck (1996), confirming many of the arguments raised by comprehension researchers; research on persuasive writing by Crowhurst (1990) that shows strong distinctions between narrative and persuasive writing; and research that young children are fully capable of engaging in expository prose writing of various sorts at young ages and engage productively with expository prose as they progress through the school grades (Newkirk, 1987; Pappas, 1993).

Kucan and Beck (1996), in a study of four fourth-grade students reading both narrative and expository texts throughout the school year, found that students read narrative and expository texts in different ways. Narrative texts generated many more hypothesis statements and more inferences, predictions, and interpretations. Students processed actively to synthesize upcoming information. With expository texts, students spent more time elaborating on text information and commented more on details and local text information. In summary-writing tasks, students provided more of the important ideas from the narrative texts whereas they focused more on local details from the expository texts. The researchers found that children's processing behaviors remained consistent in these regards across readings of five different narrative texts and five different expository texts. The authors also noted that students reading the expository texts generated more connections to personal experiences in efforts to make the information more familiar to their own knowledge base, though in the process they also generated misinterpretations of the texts.

Engelhard, Gordon, and Gabrielson (1992) used writing samples from the Georgia statewide writing assessment program to examine writing variation among eighth-grade students. Drawing on a sample of over 125,000 student essays, they scored essays with an analytic scoring rubric across five domains (content, style, sentence formation, usage, and mechanics). Comparing writing quality across three macro-genres (narrative, descriptive, and expository), these researchers found strong evidence that students wrote much higher rated essays when the prompt required a narrative essay, and students consistently wrote lower quality essays when assigned an expository prompt.

In a review of studies on persuasive writing among students, Crowhurst (1990) found that students wrote much better essays when writing narratives and lower quality essays when writing argumentative essays. She outlined reasons why persuasive (and expository) writing appears to create writing problems for students that narrative tasks do not generate. In a range of studies, she noted that students producing argumentative texts write less, do not carry out the prompt task, often reveal poor organization, and use inappropriate style. Crowhurst also noted that children at early ages are capable of engaging in persuasion as an oral genre, but do not develop the skills well in writing (Lemke, 1988). This early appearance of more informational prose is also noted by other researchers.

In a well-known study of early child writing, Newkirk (1987) examined more than 100 writing samples of nonnarrative writing by students from Grades 1 to 3. Validating Bruner's arguments that children make early use of a nonnarrative mode of thought, he found that children produce at least eight types of informational text. He argued that early writing should not simply be viewed as either story or expressive writing. Instead, he developed a strong argument that children's writing evolves out of list making and labeling rather than emerging out of narrative storytelling skills (cf. prior discussion of Mosenthal). In particular, the notion of listing as an expository-text foundation suggests that students recognize distinctions between spoken and written language (and their uses) and between an episodic mode of writing and an informational mode of writing.

Coming from a somewhat different research perspective, Pappas (1991, 1993) drew on Hallidayan systemic perspectives for understanding the functional nature of literacy development; nevertheless, she arrives at conclusions similar to Newkirk. Pappas argued in a series of studies that children develop a semiotic system for discourses that includes a range of spoken and written registers. She argued that children learn both story and information-book genres and they develop them interdependently. She demonstrated ways in which children consistently and correctly distinguish story structures from informational structures in their reenactments from books. She also showed that young children are at least as motivated by reading informational books as they are when reading stories.

It is apparent, then, that the conceptualization of two macro-genres (or perhaps three) is consistent with research findings for emergent writing development. These results point out not only that students appear to create basic generic patterns of text organization under consistent conditions, but also that research studies are consistent in these findings across student groups and writing conditions. Many studies consistently show that students have greater difficulty with expository-writing assignments; these early-learning studies suggest that a more coherent and focused effort to teach expository writing and to practice such writing consistently would improve students' writing abilities. Of course, one could argue that such genres that organize initial writing lose their significance when writing develops into more mature functional and professional uses. However, the following section provides evidence that the basic macro-genres of narrative and expository prose types are readily observable in a range of studies of adult, edited prose.

Applied Linguistics Corpus Analysis

The influence of genre structuring in texts can be seen by examining a corpus of texts that represent a variety of settings. In this way, corpus linguistics adds to the evidence for genre differences, particularly with respect to a research methodology developed by Biber (1988, 1995a). An early example of this method that applied to genre-related issues involved research exploring the textual nature of expository prose. Grabe (1987) analyzed 150 texts belonging to 15 distinct functional categories, including professional natural science, introductory text natural science, popular natural science, professional social science, professional humanities, business reports, professional letters, fictional narratives, and editorials. The key results of the study, based on a factor analysis of 33 different lexical, syntactic, and cohesion features, supported a major separation of narrative texts from all other text types in the corpus.

The interpretation of functional dimensions on the basis of a factor analysis of lexico-syntactic feature counts may seem to be limiting methodology for those unfamiliar with Biber's methodology. However, factor analysis is intended to reveal latent traits in psychological research, a goal equally appropriate for a complex set of linguistic data that is assumed, appropriately so, to be multidimensional in nature. The fact that the resulting dimensions are reasonably interpretable, and that the interpretations receive strong validity support from follow-up analyses, indicates that the methodology can be applied to analyses of genre variation across a textual corpus. The results demonstrate that narratives occupy a multidimensional textual space distinct from all types of nonnarrative prose. A further outcome of this study is that the basic distinctions found to emerge with elementary-grade writers does not disappear when mature writers write within real-world functional genre constraints. The macro-genres of narrative and expository prose remain as strong as ever.

In research involving text analysis on a larger scale, Biber (1988) analyzed 23 functional genres of spoken and written language, using an automated tagging program that he developed. In his study, he used 67 linguistic-feature counts in a factor analysis that generated six strong interpretable factors. His multidimensional approach has since been validated in a number of studies (Biber 1990, 1995b), and his research has provided a number of well-documented insights into discourse variation across spoken and written text types. For purposes of the present chapter, the key result of his study of spoken and written discourse is the generation of a dimension of variation that was strongly driven by narrative texts. His second most powerful dimension across all 23 spoken and written text types was one he labeled, "Narrative versus Nonnarrative Concerns." This dimension strongly separated fiction from all other text types and accounted for a large amount of discourse variation.

Although the research findings from Biber's work have implications that extend beyond the immediate issues of this chapter, they serve to highlight the distinct nature of written narratives as a family group of text-types. Narrative texts appear to be functionally distinct, generating their own functional dimension and influencing other interpretive dimensions of textual variation, even across widely divergent languages.

IMPLICATIONS OF RESEARCH FOR A THEORY OF GENRES

The various arguments assembled here make a case for two macro-genres through which we construct ourselves and our view of the world. Both macro-genres operate interdependently, but they each emphasize different functions and purposes in literate social contexts, and each imposes constraints on formal text production. Moreover, each macro-genre offers unique ways to learn from texts. These arguments, however, are not intended to provide a justification for writing instruction in freshman composition programs through traditional readers that sort texts according to various genres and patterns of organization. In fact, the freshman composition setting is perhaps the least useful place to explore the uses and implications of the macro-genres as proposed in this chapter. Although there are many complexities with the arguments made here that need to be explored further and perhaps qualified, the arguments are not directed specifically towards writing courses.

One can, of course, find ways to counter most arguments, and each of the arguments presented in this chapter can be contested. However, the range of disciplinary arguments, and the converging evidence in line with a notion of narrative and expository macro-genres, should lead us to recognize some appropriateness to these notions. It is usually the case that a traditionally held view which may no longer be in fashion, but which is hard to dislodge, may reflect some aspects of insight that need to be reconsidered. Although the traditional modes of discourse may have outlived their usefulness, there may still be space for the roles of narrative and expository macro-genres. The test of this usefulness should rest more with controlled research, instructional observations, and learning opportunities than with theorizing. It may be the case, much as argued by Johns (1997) with respect to writing-instruction approaches, that macro-genre notions may contribute some aspects to the larger instructional context without needing to be seen as central instructional concepts. Their usefulness may lie with the additional opportunities they provide for metalinguistic reflection and awareness of writing purposes, formal constraints on composing, and typical expectations of readers.

This chapter has been developed as a classification of types of evidence in favor of considering, and teaching, two basic types of textual discourse. After an initial setting section and a linkage to prior topical theory on genres, I explored five areas in turn that contributed to my argument for two distinct macro-genres. Could this presentation have been as readily presented as a narrative, and should it have been? One mark of composing expertise may, in fact, be the ability to transform an expository frame of representation into a narrative one and vice versa. However, I do not believe that such a demonstration would provide an argument against the thesis of this chapter (or even the fact that I can state a thesis for this chapter). Crucially, the arguments being made here do not depend on any bravura performance as much as on whether or not the arguments capture the typical, the conventional, and the teachable.

IMPLICATIONS FOR INSTRUCTION

The instructional implications of the arguments made in this chapter are potentially far reaching. One would be to reexamine the sorts of textual input brought into the classroom under the assumptions that students should learn from these texts or should interpret these texts in insightful ways. Would students' learning from, and use of, these texts be enhanced by knowledge of how discourse is structured and then applying this knowledge to their own writing? There is now sufficient supporting evidence that both graphic representations of text structure and awareness raising of text organization and its signaling improve students' learning from texts.

One obvious connection would be to provide models of texts to explore, not unlike traditional approaches to comprehension, and this approach has been shown in research studies to be effective when done appropriately. However, such a response is not an especially creative suggestion. There are certainly other insightful ways to bring textual awareness to students, and this should be one goal of instruction. For example, certain options for content-based instruction would provide opportunities to use information from many texts for a variety of writing tasks. Students' efforts to synthesize complex sets of information in order to develop arguments or theoretical positions will require them to recognize the overall discourse structure of the texts and will create natural opportunities for teaching students to see the discourse organization. Other more creative options for presenting discourse organization can be developed through transactional strategy instruction, instructional conversations, and "questioning the author" (Beck & Kucan 1997; Kucan & Beck, 1997; Pressley, El-Dinery, Gaskins, Schuder, Bergman, Almasi, & Brown, 1992). These strategy approaches generate discussions that focus on comprehension of the text, and can lead directly to explorations of how the text organization itself supports a reader's interpretation. (See, Grabe, in press.)

There are a number of other ways that students and teachers can explore the structuring provided by texts, not as a prescriptive how-to-do procedure but as patterning and signaling that inform readers, and then use such structuring themselves in their own writing, as appropriate to a given context. Using needs analysis in the classroom (taking stock of students' needs and abilities at the outset) is an important way to analyze the volume of language to be read and/or written, the complexity of text material, the vocabulary demands made, the discourse difficulties to be encountered, and the content to be covered. Unfortunately, most language teachers still do not consider a needs analysis a necessary first step in any course, and content teachers are typically unaware that students' language abilities, or language development, should even be considered in course planning.

At advanced levels of instruction, both Johns (1997) and Swales (1990) addressed needs analysis steps with L2 students and at-risk students. They provided many suggestions that involve students in their own developing awareness of the texts they use and produce for learning purposes. An argument put forward in this chapter is that such needs analysis and metacognitive awareness of literacy acts at the university level can be extended to include recognition and exploration of macro-genre differences when appropriate, as well as their uses in various academic contexts. (Additional instructional ideas for exploring text structure, particularly for expository texts, are presented in Grabe, 1995; Grabe & Gardner, 1995; and various chapters in Miller, 1995).

A number of specific instructional ideas follow directly from the research issues discussed in this chapter. The research of Mosenthal and his colleagues suggests that expository structure may be explored by building up complex structures out of simpler versions, and students can be taught to recognize this incremental complexity in texts. The use of graphic organizers to support text structure awareness, and teach comprehension, supports text structure awareness as well. The research on discourse processing points out the need to understand how different types of tasks support comprehension efforts in different ways, and how teachers can, through appropriate task development, direct students' attention to weaker aspects of their comprehension processing. This research also demonstrates that comprehension is influenced by a complex combination of language difficulty, task type, text complexity, student proficiency, and student background knowledge. For the teacher, the key point is that these variables can be manipulated for instructional purposes.

The research on younger students' learning from texts reveals that students need practice at more difficult or less common assignments such as synthesis, argument, and problem-solution tasks, and students need more practice, in general, with expository and argumentative texts. Although many of these implications seem to apply only to expository texts, that need not be the case. Historical narratives, for example, often demand comprehension beyond timeline reference and main character development. Students need to recognize complex cause and effect relations, inferred options and outcomes, analyses of options taken or not taken, and problem–solution patterns (though with the outcome already established). Literary fictional narratives can make extreme demands on student comprehension, and one source of support is to raisc awarcncss and appreciation of the language organization and structure that comes into play in interpretation.

The issue of instructional implications to be drawn from research on macro-genres is much like the issues surrounding the teaching of grammar. People tend to point to simplistic instructional approaches, and reject them, as if these approaches are handed down as the only solutions. It is important to separate conceptually important insights from potentially poor instructional practices inasmuch as they are two entirely different matters. One can have the right conceptual understanding of some larger notion, such as textual organization, text comprehension, writing processes, or grammar, but not have any way of conveying those insights through instructional practices. Alternatively, one can use a range of instructional practices that seem to satisfy course and curriculum goals without understanding a frame of reference that explains why the practices seem to work. The point, in brief, is that instructional issues involving textual uses and forms of macro-genres, and how students learn through these genres, should be reconsidered without all of the baggage of caricatured traditional instruction and unanchored theorizing.

15
A Universe of Meaning—How Many Practices?

J. R. Martin
University of Sydney, Australia

WHAT IS GENRE?

To begin, I'd better declare what I mean by *genre*, which is a term I use to name configurations of meaning that are recurrently phased together to enact social practices[1] (Martin, 1992, 1997a). As a linguist, I've worked mainly on verbal configurations of meanings in spoken or written discourse; but in multimodal texts, other semiotic systems make an important contribution as well (image, music, action and others; Kress & Van Leeuwen, 1996; Lemke, 1998; Van Leeuwen, 1992).

In these terms, Grabe seems to be suggesting that we can generalize across these recurrent configurations of meanings and recognize two large families of genres, narrative and exposition, which he refers to as macro-genres.[2] I'm not sure whether Grabe agrees with James and Bruner, whose remarks he quotes at the beginning of the chapter and who suggest that there are these two macro-genres (narrative and exposition) and no others. But I can't resist commenting on this strong and remarkably plausible claim.

WHAT'S A FAMILY?

Genre is a term for grouping texts together; for Grabe, macro-genre is a term for grouping genres. This raises the issue of how we group things together. Basically,

[1]Note that I am not distinguishing genre from text-type here,inasmuch as genre, as I use the term, fits into a global model of language in relation to social context informed by systemic functional linguistics (Martin, 1997a, 2000).

[2]I should clarify at this point that in my own work, I have used the term "macro-genre" to refer structurally to texts comprised of more than one "elemental" genre (Martin, 1995, 1997a), not to refer systemically to families of genres.

there are two alternatives. One has to do with classification—the formation of taxonomies on the basis of criteria differentiating one grouping from another. The other has to do with family resemblance—the development of parameters that position groups along a scale of similarity and difference. Technically, we can refer to the first grouping principle as *typological*, and the second as *topological* (Martin, 1997a; Martin & Matthiessen, 1991). Grabe's macro-genres appear to be based on the second principle: "The family of narrative discourse structures represent text types that are *typically* episodic in nature and include a set of identifying criteria that bear *family resemblances* with one another" (italics added). This topological perspective allows for the possibility of fuzzy borders, a notion that is probably critical to the plausibility of narrative and exposition as encompassing macro-genres.

For example, Grabe characterizes narratives as involving sequences of events, some events being out of the ordinary and requiring explanation, typically presented as a causal chaining of events. These parameters would appear to push a number of genres to the borders of the macro-genre. *Personal recounts*, for example, tend to deal with ordinary experience not requiring explanation (Martin, 1985b; Rothery, 1994); *Western news stories* deal with extraordinary experience, but tend not to relate this experience chronologically (Iedema, 1997a; White, 1997); *observation* (Rothery, 1994) and *gossip* (Eggins & Slade, 1997) refer to events in general terms without spelling out the sequences involved. What ties these genres to the narrative family is not so much their sequencing, but the fact that like other narratives (Martin, 1997b; Martin & Plum, 1997), they make their point by evaluating experience (a narrative parameter not specifically mentioned by Grabe but considered central in the work previously cited, as inspired[3] by Labov & Waletzky, 1967).

This is not, of course, to challenge Grabe's macro-genre, but simply to clarify that the notion of family resemblance is critical. If we pursue the complementary typological perspective, then we are forced to establish a set of specific criteria that all members of the narrative macro-genre share, and make decisions at the borders as to whether things are in or out. If sequencing events in time is crucial, then the 19th-century news story will be in (as a kind of recount), but during the 20th century, the Western news will fall out (since chronology fades away); if out-of-the-ordinary events are criterial, then anecdotes and examples (Martin & Plum, 1997) will be in as they deal with remarkable events, but recounts of everyday experience will be out (since they are too flat, too ordinary). If we want a big family, we'll need the elasticity a topological perspective on grouping provides.

FRONTIERS

Even with elasticity, I wonder to what extent the distinction between narrative and expository macro-genres can be secured. Let's explore this through some genres

[3]For a comprehensive overview of Labov and Waletzky's legacy, see the *Journal of Narrative and Life History*, *7*, pp. 1–4 (a special issue edited by Michael Bamberg).

from secondary school history (Coffin, 1996, 1997; Martin, 1997a; Veel & Coffin, 1996). An outline of the genres in question is presented as Table 15.1. They have been arranged from top to bottom along a learner-oriented pathway, bridging from the common sense experience of naive apprentices through to mature construals of history informed by contemporary critical theory. This pathway highlights major steps in learning given the new kinds of semiotic resources that need to be drawn on to construct the genre. For reasons of space, it is not possible to exemplify or discuss this pathway in any detail here (see Feez & Joyce, 1998a, for an accessible introduction).

Table 15.1
An Ontogenetic Topology (Learner Pathway)
for Some Secondary-School History Genres

GENRE	*INFORMAL DESCRIPTION*	*KEY LINGUISTIC FEATURES*
personal recount [Orientation^Record]	agnate to story genres; what happened to me	sequence in time; 1st person; specific participants
autobiographical recount [Orientation^Record]	borderline - agnate to story & factual genres; story of my life [oral history]	setting in time; 1st person; specific participants
biographical recount [Orientation^Record]	story of someone else's life	setting in time; 3rd person (specific); other specific & generic participants
historical recount; [Background^Record]	establishing the time line of the grand narrative	setting in time; 3rd person; mainly generic participants (but specific great 'men')
historical account; [Background^Account]	naturalizing linearization rendering the grand narrative inevitable	incongruent external causal unfolding; 3rd person; mainly generic participants; prosodic judgment
factorial explanation [Outcome^Factors]	complexifying notion of what leads on to/from what	internal organization of factors; factors externally linked to outcome; 3rd person; mainly generic participants
consequential explanation [Input^Consequences]	complexifying notion of what leads on to/from what; hypothetical variant - if x, then these	internal organization of factors; consequences externally linked to input; 3rd person; mainly generic outcomes participants

exposition - one-sided; promote [Thesis^Arguments]	problematic interpretation that needs justifying	internal conjunction keying on thesis
challenge - one-sided; rebut [Position^Rebuttal]	someone else's problematic interpretation that needs demolishing	internal conjunction keying on thesis
discussion - multi-sided; adjudicate [Issue^Sides^Resolution]	more than one interpretation considered	internal conjunction keying on thesis; + internal organization of points of view
deconstruction [Foucault; cf. Ian Hunter]	avoiding reductive temporal & causal linearization into grand narrative, effacing voices of the 'other'...	replace naturalizing time/cause explanation with 'spatial' discursive formation realizing episteme

(Halliday, 1994; Martin, 1992)

Basically, what we have here is a cline of apprenticeship that moves from recounts of personal experience to deconstructive critique, arguably from narrative to exposition in Grabe's terms. The border area involves three key genres—historical recount, historical account, and factorial explanation. *Historical recounts* unfold chronologically, enacting "grand narratives;" *historical accounts* unfold causally, explaining how one event leads to another; *factorial explanations* deal with a complex of factors simultaneously affecting outcomes.

Historical Recount (Setting in Time; Long Time Scale)

> . . . BY THE MID TWENTIES, big changes took place to meet the needs of the fishing industry and government fisheries managers. The Board began to employ full-time scientific staff, and Technological Stations were established in Halifax, Nova Scotia, and Prince Rupert, British Columbia. The staff quickly became multidisciplinary. At the Biological Stations, physics and chemistry were added to zoology in recognition of the importance of understanding fish habitat. At the Technological Stations, zoologists did some initial work on refrigeration of fish, but chemists, bacteriologists, and engineers soon took over responsibility for industrial research and development.
>
> DURING THE DEPRESSION YEARS, the fisheries research and development program was maintained despite constrained budgets. Facilities for volunteer investigators could only be provided to those with independent financing, and the small permanent staff endured a 10% reduction of salaries. DURING THE WORLD WAR II YEARS THAT FOLLOWED, there was the additional setback of loss of some staff to war service . . . [Martin, W. R., 1991, p. 37]

Historical Account (Cause and Effect; "Explaining")

> Man has been making animals rare and even extinct for thousands of years, and one of

the main ways man has achieved this is BY THE DESTRUCTION of their habitat. The destruction of a habitat MEANS THAT the vital balance between an animal and its environment is disturbed. In ancient times the destruction of habitat and the extinction of animals was quite small. Since then it has rapidly increased. People began to make more use of machines and industrialization occurred, bringing with it changes which would destroy the face of the earth's environment forever. As the demands grew, wood and later coal, supplied the resources needed; this in turn RESULTED IN THE DESTRUCTION of forests and habitats. At the same time that industrialization was taking place, humans were settling in new parts of the world. Whenever they settled, nests were cut down and farms established. This destroyed the habitat of many animals.

THE EFFECTS OF INDUSTRIALIZATION and the need of more land DUE TO THE GROWTH OF POPULATION seriously AFFECTED WILDLIFE and still is today. Already half the world's tropical rainforests have already been destroyed or irreversibly damaged. This reckless ravaging of some of the most amazing habitats on earth MEANS THAT by the year 2000 the destruction will be complete and the world will be without these areas.

Factorial Explanation (Explaining Outcomes in Relation to Multiple Factors)

WHY Did the Long March Succeed?

This question has often been raised by historians, and a NUMBER OF FACTORS have been suggested to EXPLAIN the success of the Long March.

1. One of these is the leadership of Mao Zedong. The success of his guerrilla tactics after Zunyi revived the confidence of a demoralised army at a crucial stage.
2. He also had the benefit of the brilliant army commanders such as Zhu De and Peng Duhai, who were able to implement his guerrilla strategies.
3. The courage and toughness of the young members of the Red Army, many of whom were teenagers, also contributed to its success.
4. The discipline of the Red Army, which won the confidence and support of the peasant population, contrasted with the disunity of the enemy. For example the warlord of Yunnan province, Long Yun, was more concerned about Chiang Kai-shek taking over his province than he was about smashing the Communists. [Buggy, 1998]

Of these genres, historical recounts are the most arguably narrative, factorial explanations the more arguably exposition; in between, historical accounts share chaining of events with narrative, and causal explanation with exposition. So the borders[4] of narrative and exposition seem genuinely blurred. This is perhaps predictable once we adopt a topological perspective on genre relations. More troubling is the relatively seamless trajectory through narrative to exposition once we ground ourselves in a discipline (in this case secondary school history). History

[4]For discussion of related "border" issues, see Unsworth, 1997, 1998, and Veel, 1997 on sequential, causal, theoretical and factorial explanations in science; and Iedema, 1994b, 1997a, and White, 1997, on event oriented versus political news stories.

in a sense constructs its own macro-generic assembly, in the service of its discourse-specific goals. I'm not sure the assembly is any less coherent as far as configurations of meaning are concerned than Grabe's macro-genres, once the diversity of narrative and expository texts is considered.

Two points here: (a) the frontiers of narrative and exposition may be more heavily populated than we might predict, and (b) the coherence of a macro-genre depends on our reading position, which raises a question as to whether Grabe's purchase on families of genres is as institutionally neutral as an observer-stance pretends. For further discussion of the family of history genres alluded to here, see Coffin, 1996, 1997; Feez & Joyce, 1998a; Martin, 1997a; Martin, in press. For related work on geography genres, see Humphrey, 1996; Martin, 2000; for English genres, see Rothery, 1994; Martin & Plum, 1997; for science genres, see Veel 1997, 1998; Martin & Veel, 1998.

OTHER FAMILIES

Just two macro-genres? Any other contenders? I'll suggest a few. One group I'm not sure how Grabe would deal with is the *service encounter family* (Hasan, 1985; Ventola, 1987), whereby goods and services are exchanged. Variations include door-to-door sales, market stalls, small shop transactions, purchases in larger stores, buying major items (including bargaining for, say, a house or car), auctions, mail orders, shopping on the Internet, and so on. Another group we might refer to as the *appointment family* (Hasan, 1978), with variations including family scheduling, making a date with friends, party invitations, leave applications, conference announcements, program scheduling, institutional timetabling, medium and long-term planning, and so on. As another group we might consider is *interviewing*, including interrogation, cross examination, talk-back radio, student consultations, oral examinations, counseling, thesis supervision, chat shows, job or promotion interviews, expert panels, in-depth interview with celebrity/expert, and so on. I'm not trying to be exhaustive here, just flagging the possibility of additional macro-genres.

Another family that has been studied in some detail (Iedema, 1995, 1997b; Rose, 1997, 1998; and Rose, McInnes, & Korner, 1992) deals with *control*, including procedures (instructions, recipes, manuals, etc.), giving directions, protocol, directives, and possibly duty statements and hortatory expositions. Rose (e.g., 1998) has studied procedural discourse in the workplace in some detail, and introduces the relevant genres as follows:

> At the top of the industrial ladder, enabling texts are not framed as commands at all, they are simply statements about the manufacturing technology and the roles of workers, i.e., *duty statements*. At the bottom, however, the commanding function is foregrounded, it is realised directly and less negotiably as a series of imperatives—*a simple procedure*. In between, workers at the next level need to make choices about what actions to take.

> These decision-making functions are realized in *conditional procedures*. At this level workers also need to know how the technology operates in order to "select and use appropriate techniques and equipment required to perform tasks of some complexity"—to borrow the National Training Board's terminology. These descriptions of the workings of the technology are realised as *topographic procedures*. Many tasks involve multiple participants, including operators and technicians so the procedure must foreground the identity of the worker to carry out each step in the task. We have called this type a *co-operative procedure.*
>
> Each of these procedures are concerned with operating technology—the field is technological and more or less specialised. They may also involve some knowledge of scientific measurement, but generally limited knowledge of scientific theory. The next level of procedure involves scientific laboratory work—testing products and materials. While this work also involves operating technology, it is generally highly technical and demands significant knowledge of scientific theory—the field is scientific and technical. We have called this genre *technical procedures*. (Rose, McInnes, & Korner, 1992, p. 139)

The genres are outlined by Rose as Fig. 15.1, and arranged in a cline associating

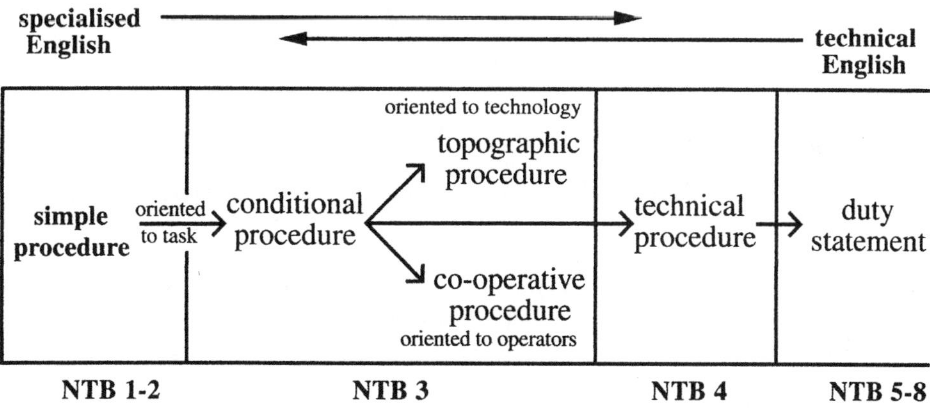

Fig. 15.1: Procedural genres in relation to National Training Board (NTB) levels in science-based industry

control of the genre with Australian National Training Board levels. Note that even if the procedures are collapsed into the narrative family on grounds of event chaining, we still have the problem of a cline including duty statements that do not feature chronological organization. Obviously not included here are the protocol (rules and regulations) genres that circumscribe behavior (Martin, in press) and directive genres that demand changes (Iedema, 1995, 1997b; Martin, 1998a); the way in which directives deploy rationale to motivate change brings them very close in organization to hortatory exposition, the genre that presents arguments in favor of proposals about how the world should be (Martin, 1985a; Martin & Peters, 1985)—blurring perhaps the border between exposition and the procedural family posited here.

The point here then is that there are arguably a number of macro-genres that appear to lie outside the scope of Grabe's proposals, unless his category of exposition is a great deal more elastic than I take it to be (too elastic,[5] perhaps, to function as an abstract label for recurrent configurations of meaning). Of note is the fact that for the most part these families (service encounter, appointment making, interview and procedure) lie outside of Academe—which raises once again the question of Grabe's reading position in relation to his macro-generic claims.

GENRE RELATIONS

I judge from Halliday (1994) and Matthiessen (1995) that the grammar of English is a combinatorial powerhouse whose potential to construe genres has barely been tapped. Our universe of meaning, in other words, is very sparsely populated (much like our physical universe)—how many stars can we find, arranged into how many galaxies, using what technology, from whose point of view? How many genres, arranged in how many macro-genres, using what criteria, from whose reading position? Grabe discusses two galaxies; I suggested a few more, noting as I went the problem of fuzzy borders and the possibility of seeing the genres Grabe considers as grouped differently from alternative perspectives (i.e. secondary school history, science based industry). What Grabe and I share is an interest in grouping genres into large galaxies of meaning, alongside the task of assigning texts to genres (identifying the solar systems out of which the galaxies are composed).

Like Grabe, my interest in macro-genres has been driven by educational concerns—early on to make a place for exposition in the primary school curriculum (Martin, 1985b); later to promote writing for learning across the curriculum in secondary school (Martin, 1993b). In this work, we grouped genres by discipline (English, history, science and so on) and within disciplines we worked on learner pathways that realigned genres as the basis for a spiral curriculum that could start with what students know and guide them into specialized discourse (without always having to start from scratch, term after term, year after year, since nothing could be assumed). In this kind of work genre relations are critical—to understand both the

[5]The use of the cover term "explanation" by Ogburn, Kress, Martins, & McGillicuddy, 1996, illustrates the more than generous elasticity that gives me pause here.

work that is done recontextualizing a discipline for school, and the work done apprenticing students into its discourse. In such interventions, galaxies of genres do matter.

From the perspective of education, one might well argue that narrative and exposition are the heart of the matter (our Milky Way as it were). The texts attracting evaluation in education (Bernstein, 1975, 1990) are largely ones that are *written* rather than spoken, that construct *academic* rather than domestic or workplace discourses, and that make statements about the world rather than proposals for action. From this reading position, the service encounter, appointment making, interrogation, and control macro-genres suggested earlier are far from central—presenting themselves perhaps as single stars stranded here and there in an expanding universe. Upon closer examination, however, as seen perhaps from another world, that's not how they look at all. As naive poststructuralists, we might even begin to question the utility of having any categories at all.

Like Grabe, however, I think that categories do matter (unfashionable neostructuralists that we are). Nothing confirms this more strongly for me that the so-called "mixed genres"[6] often presented in evidence against the utility of classifying genres. Some narratives do the work of scientific explanations, for example, as in the paragraph below, reflecting perhaps the excesses of progressive education and its obsession with the authenticity of story genre. (Chouliarki, 1998; Martin 1985b, 1998b).

> O.K. boys, on the count of three. One, two, three .... Oh no, the ear flaps have caught my vibrations. NOT AGAIN. I shoot through the auditory canal at very high speeds, going along bumps and ridges, through every nook and cranny. Then SMASH. I hit the ear drum, jarring my whole body and making my head spin like a merry-go-round. Then without any rest, I collide with three other bones, all pushing into one another. On again of again here I go. This time to a roundabout which I must add has some greenish-grey, gooey fluid. Oh gross.

There are procedures doing the work of expository challenge, as in the "Terra Nullius Pie" recipe below:

> [5.] INGREDIENTS . . .[7]
> 1 * "Empty" continent (a wide brown one will do nicely)
> 10 * Point Plan, OR

---

[6]The term "mixed genre" has always seemed a contradictory misnomer to me, confusing genres with the texts that instantiate one or more of them; in addition, it unhelpfully groups together radically different kinds of "mixture" —for discussion see Martin, in press.

[7]*Terra nullius* is the doctrine justifying British occupation of Australia on the grounds that no one was living there; the *10 Point Plan* refers to Liberal Prime Minister John Howard's 1997 plan for adjudicating Land Rights; *Sorry Tears* refers to the issue of the stolen generations of Aboriginal children taken from their families by government officials and the grass-roots swelling of remorse in opposition to Howard's ongoing refusal to offer an official government apology. I am grateful to Miriam Corris for drawing this text to my attention.

> 100 Litres "Sorry Tears"
> Some live Cultures
> Plenty of re-written history to garnish
>
> METHOD
> Take the land and thoroughly clean of any people. Remove as much of the forest and minerals as you can. Next liberally pour wastes into waterways until nicely blue-green. At this point you'll be tempted to carve the pie up into 10 big slices, but this may cause heartburn or even armed insurrection later!
> ALTERNATIVELY, sprinkle well with sorry tears and leave to reconcile for a while. When cool, share it out—if no one is too greedy there'll be plenty to go round... [*pulp* student magazine of Southern Cross University, 1998]

My point is that if we find the notion of texts drawing on more than one genre useful, then we have to acknowledge the distinctive recurrent configurations of meaning that are being drawn upon—the distinctive genres. The notion of "mixed genres" depends on having distinct ingredients to mix. And this leaves us with distinguishing these ingredients (the genres) as an important task.[8]

As we compile a list of genres, it does seem important to ask questions about how these genres are related to each other—into how many and what kinds of macro-genre. Early in the 1980s, my colleagues and I revised traditional Hallidayan approaches to modeling social context (field, mode, and tenor) by introducing an additional level of analysis, called genre, to pursue just this work (see Martin, 1992, 2000, and in press for discussion). Our plan was to begin mapping our culture as a network of social practices, one set of genres in relation to another. It's encouraging to have an opportunity to respond to some empathetic research from across the Pacific. Cheers from what you call the "Sydney School"—a term in need of fuzzy borders if family differences be told!

---

[8]In a similar way, recognition of distinct genres underpins our interpretation of generic change, as the meaning potential of our culture evolves. For discussion see Lemke, 1995, and Martin, 2000.

16

Applied Genre Analysis: Analytical Advances and Pedagogical Procedures

Vijay K. Bhatia
City University of Hong Kong

One of the most interesting developments in discourse studies in the past two decades has been the predominant use of genre theory, not only to the description of language in use, but also to the teaching and learning of language in context, where it has been effectively used at various levels of language teaching, from the elementary and secondary school levels to the tertiary and university levels and beyond to workplace and other professional contexts (Candlin, 1993). Whenever a concept has such a range of applications to contexts as diverse as those mentioned, it is only natural that there would be variations in interpretation, use, and values attached to individual interpretations and applications. Grabe's chapter on "Narrative and Expository Macro-Genres" is no exception in this respect. In his comprehensive account of two macro-genres, he identifies two major issues: first, the issue of the direction in which genre research has gone and, second, that of pedagogical application. Let me take up these issues one at a time.

He begins by setting the scene in the following words:

> . . . genre research has left behind some important notions that need to be given their place within the broader conceptualization of genre—in particular, the notions of narrative and expository forms as macro-genres with distinct purposes, uses, and demands on writers.

Grabe points out that genre research has moved away from what he calls the broader conceptualization of genre, which he views in terms of two macro-genres, narrative and expository. He then makes a very strong case for distinguishing narratives from expository texts as two macro-genres, almost entirely based on evidence external to genre theory. He also concedes that the boundaries of narrative and expository genres are flexible and fluid rather than distinct, and that one can legitimately expect aspects of narration in expository writing and vice versa. The same, one may be tempted to conclude, must be true of other so-called macro-genres, which may include descriptive and argumentative discourse. By the same token, it is possible to claim that there are several other types of macro-genres, which also have such fluid boundaries, some of which may be promotional, evaluative, reporting, introductory, and possibly several others. However, one may argue, "To what extent do all these 'so-called' macro-genres share their typicalities, whether conceptual, practical, or applied?" To me, there are problems of ambiguity involved here. These so-called macro-genres potentially represent two different categories. First, some of them, especially narratives, expositions, descriptions, arguments, evaluations, and so on seem to be different from promotional genres, reporting genres, academic genres, and introductory genres. The most important difference in the two is that the first type are rather independent of any grounded and situational context, whereas the others are firmly grounded in specific, though to some extent flexible, rhetorical context. This second type I have also referred to as *genre colonies*. They often have several members, broadly related in terms of the communicative purposes they tend to serve, the rhetorical conventions and contexts they seem to share, and also in terms of the lexico-grammatical and discoursal features they display. The confusion, unfortunately, arises from the fact that when we talk about "narration," we can mean any of three rather different entities: narration as a rhetorical process, or narrative as any specific instance of a narrative genre, or maybe a genre colony, which comprises a number of members such as historical accounts, (auto)biographies, stories, fairy tales, novels, and others, as Grabe quite rightly points out. As a matter of fact, in a broader framework, all these realizations of rather different aspects of genres seem to be part of a versatile system that has generic realizations at a number of levels.

At the top end of the system we have what I would like to call *rhetorical or generic values*, which are realized in terms of a set of typical lexico-grammatical features. Let me emphasize here that the relationship between "generic value" and its lexico-grammatical realization is unlikely to be always one-to-one. A typical generic value may be realized in terms of several different set(s) of lexico-grammatical features, depending upon the nature of the specific genre of which it is a part. What Grabe calls macro-genres, of which he says narratives and expository texts are prime examples, to me can be better conceptualized as colonies of specific genres, of which historical accounts, (auto) biographies, stories, fairy tales, novels, and many others are members. All of them to a large extent share some of the major typicalities in terms of what they intend to communicate, how they do it, and to what extent they are associated with overlapping rhetorical contexts and traditions.

The main difference between the two levels of conceptualization is that generic values are largely decontextualized and, hence, not grounded in a specific rhetorical situation. That is one of the main reasons why these values can be combined in various ways to give rise to any form of situated use of language, forms often identified as individual genres. It is interesting to note here that although these values are, in a sense, independent of any specific generic artifact, they are often used to realize various genres. In other words, for these values to be associated with and realized as identifiable genres, it is necessary that they be firmly grounded in specific rhetorical contexts. Second, they are highly versatile, in the sense that they can realize a number of identifiably different and yet related genres. Narration is often indispensable in the realization of stories, reports, historical events, autobiographies, and newspaper reports. Similarly, expositions are exceptionally useful devices in the construction of textual knowledge in the form of textbooks, scientific articles, encyclopaedic entries, and so on. Descriptions, in the same way, become useful in the textualization of scientific and technical brochures, trade books, technical manuals, science textbooks, and parts of scientific reports. However, in practice these generic values are used in various permutations and combinations to construct a variety of genres. Descriptions and evaluations, for instance, often combine to textualize many of the promotional genres, including advertisements, reviews, brochures, leaflets, and corporate and fundraising genres.

The emerging picture, thus, posits at least three levels of conceptualization. At the top level we see the category of *generic value*, which is essentially independent of any grounded contextual constraints. The second level is that of more general *genre colony*, but these are rather loosely contextualized in terms of socially recognizable situations. Finally, at the third level, we have what we call *individually identifiable generic constructs*. These can be diagrammatically represented as follows:

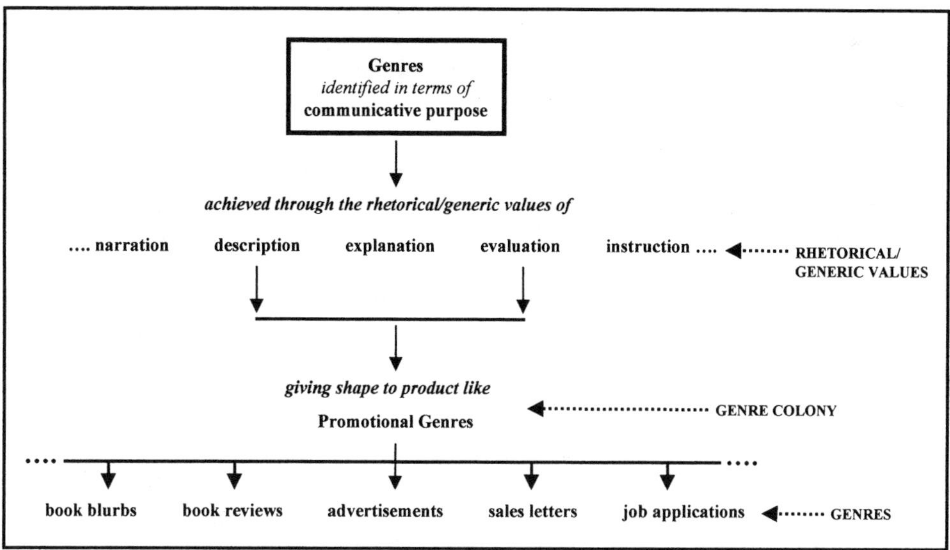

FIG 16.1: Levels of Generic Description

In a similar manner, it is possible to identify several other colonies, some of which may include colonies of "reporting genres," "academic introductions," "letter genres," "instructional genres," "narrative genres," and "expository genres," most of which are rather loosely defined because they show considerable overlap between the various member genres they colonize. It is important to remember that this process of colonization is not necessarily confined within the boundaries of a specific colony; it can be seen across colonies as well, giving rise to what I have elsewhere (Bhatia, 1995, 1997a) referred to as mixed and embedded genres. To sum up, I see three different levels of generic description:

- *generic values*, which are independent of any grounded realities of social context,
- *genre colonies*, which are rather loosely grounded in broad rhetorical contexts and are identified on the basis of flexible and fluid overlapping of generic boundaries, and
- *individual genres*, which are more typically and narrowly grounded in typical sociorhetorical contexts.

I think it is more appropriate to regard narration, description, evaluation, report, and argument as primary generic or rhetorical values, which can combine in various permutations and combinations to realize more specifically situated generic artifacts, depending upon the communicative purpose a particular genre is intended to serve. In the context of the above, I would argue that the status of "narration" and "exposition" is neither undermined nor misunderstood. In actual fact, it would be rather confusing to give them the status of genres, because they are rather difficult to assign any grounded description. Genre-based research draws its strength more from application than from theory, whether it is aimed at school, university, or professional ESP-level application. As such, the analysis is more grounded in rhetorical contexts, communicative purposes, and linguistic structures than in features of style.

Grabe's chapter goes to extreme lengths to establish a claim about the identity, validity, and legitimacy of narrative and expository genres, each of which has a reasonably established basis in classical rhetorical studies. The chapter covers quite an extensive range of evidence, primarily from learning theory, cultural and educational psychology, and discourse comprehension research to give further support to his claim that the two entities are conceptually distinct, which undoubtedly they are. However, in my view, they seem to refer to two rather different generic concepts—a generic process and a loosely grounded generic product—and hence cause confusion. Generic processes are like speech acts, which have functional values but are independent of specifically defined rhetorical contexts. Genre colonies are often situated in somewhat "loosely" defined sociorhetorical context whereas genres are often situated in a narrowly grounded sociorhetorical description. Considered in this light, narration and narrative genres are very different, in terms of theory (that is, conceptualization), practice (that is, configuration and contextualization), and application, which I shall briefly turn to next.

In the area of language teaching, we see at least two distinct applications: one at school level, especially the one pioneered by the Australian systemic school, and the other at the university and professional level, often associated with ESP teaching. The two approaches to these applications are also very distinct. The first one has a clear focus on the generality of genres, indicated by a downward movement from generic value toward genre colony (see Fig. 16.2). The second one, on the other hand, has a much narrower focus on the specificity of genres, indicated by an upward movement from individual genres towards genre colonies.

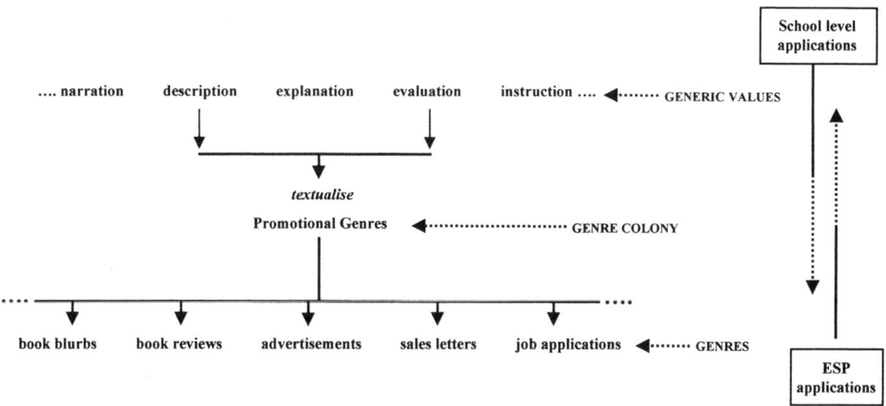

FIG 16.2: Applications of Genre-Based Descriptions

The two applications have developed along these lines for very good reasons. School-level writing tasks are often difficult to contextualize too narrowly as the learners have a rather limited experience of the world and a limited awareness of the contexts in which language is likely to be used. It is also difficult to define the actual needs of the learners at that stage of their sociocognitive development. Hence, the most convenient and productive linguistic exposure for them is likely to be broadly generic rather than specific. At the ESP level, on the other hand, learners are more likely to have the discipline-specific and sociocultural knowledge associated with narrowly defined professional and academic contexts. They may also have other constraints in terms of economy of time and effort, effectiveness, and pragmatic success of the intended communication.

In the light of this discussion, I would like to point out that genre theory has neither ignored the status and reality of narratives or expository genres, nor undermined their usefulness in pedagogic applications. It is, however, true that these macro-genres have been ambiguously interpreted, which is understandable in the context of the historical development of these useful rhetorical concepts.

17

Response(s) to William Grabe's "Narrative and Expository Macro-Genres"

Carol Berkenkotter
Michigan Technological University

Dear Bill,

I hope you don't mind my not addressing you as Professor Grabe; it just seems a bit too formal for this letter. I've written about seven pages of notes while reading your chapter; some questions, some paraphrases, some notes of key points and issues. And now I've come to that moment when I must transform these jottings into a situationally appropriate textual form.

I should mention that I've already made a stab at responding about a half an hour ago, using the discourse conventions I'm most familiar with for writing a response. Below in Text 1 you can see how I began:

Text 1

> Bill Grabe has written an impressive review of the literature in several related fields pertaining to discourse structure, text comprehension, writing development, and applied linguistics corpus analysis. If I were a writing program administrator (which I am not), I would make this essay required reading for graduate students and faculty teaching not only first-year writing courses, but technical and professional writing courses as well. However, I would meet with great resistance from colleagues, not only from my own department, but from other writing program administrators and teachers of graduate training courses in English departments.
>
> Why is this? One would think that Grabe's major argument that "in addition to a range of loose educational genres that conventionally arise in many educational settings (whether identified by functional names or by functional structuring), there is also a need more generally for students to recognize and explore the many (distinct) ways that

> narrative and expository texts can be used to construct knowledge and serve important communicative purposes" (p. 249) represents a view that has been long known in the rhetoric and composition community. One need only to think back to the mid- and late 1980s when at Carnegie Mellon University, Ph.D. students were engaged in federally funded research aimed at understanding the kinds of procedural and declarative knowledge required by "writing from sources" tasks in different disciplines. My colleagues in the AERA Writing and Reading SIGs, Nancy Spivey, Linda Flower, John R. Hayes, and a group of Ph.D. students including John Ackerman, Stuart Greene, Christine Haas, and Karen Shriver were involved in what then was called "reading to write" research. During this short period, a number of faculty and graduate students produced several first-rate empirical studies which were reported in dissertations and published in professional journals.
>
> There were, as well, some first-rate studies conducted by Spivey and others that examined the kinds of difficulties that college students had when summarizing and synthesizing material from source texts into expository classroom genres. This research was published, as were the writing-from-sources dissertation studies conducted by Ackerman (1989), Greene (1990), and other doctoral students. Although cited in educational research journals or composition journals publishing empirical research (e.g., *Research in the Teaching of English, Written Communication*), this research is rarely (if ever) cited in mainstream composition journals such as *College Composition and Communication, College English*, or *Journal of Advanced Composition.*

Then I went to make a quick sandwich and a cup of herbal tea, and came back to the computer only to read what was on the screen with much dissatisfaction. Am I really that stuffy and pedantic? Do I always have to resort to the normative academic register? Do I have to write a formal essay? Does my recent research with Doris Ravotas on psychotherapists' written texts, which demonstrates that *in situ* institutional texts display a mixture of narrative and expository conventions (Ravotas & Berkenkotter, 1998), necessitate my attempting to make this point formally as well as discursively?

So now I am resorting to that oldest of scientific writing genres, the epistolary, because I want to cut to the chase and describe what I see to be both the strengths and problems of the approach you advocate.

There is a fascinating overlap between the studies you cite and some of the research in systemic functional linguistics on variations of "explanatory texts" based on syntactical and grammatical features (Halliday & Martin, 1993; Martin, 1992). This research sheds light on some of the central differences in text structure among several varieties of expository texts and is relevant, I think, for the kind of metalinguistic awareness that you are suggesting that teachers should attempt to inculcate in their students.

However, I'm bothered by what seems to me to be a post hoc fallacy in your reasoning. As you show, there has been a great deal of reading research in which the research design itself was based on researchers using texts that they divided into narrative versus expository text types. However, because this distinction was a key methodological feature of this research, can you then argue that the research also shows that classroom genres fall into these two categories? You do make the point that Biber's corpus analysis of many different kinds of text types presents good empirical evidence for making the expository/narrative distinction across both oral and written genres. On the other hand, these text types were analyzed out of any kind of cultural or rhetorical context. From the research I've conducted with biologists, and more recently with psychotherapists, on writing in institutional contexts—writing which is intertextual and interdiscursive—my conclusion is that texts written in such contexts possess both narrative and expository lexical and syntactical features and rhetorical conventions (See Berkenkotter & Huckin, 1995; Ravotas & Berkenkotter, 1998). Similarly, Journet's (1991, 1995) studies of the use of narrative conventions in texts in the historical biological sciences, such as evolutionary biology, suggest that these texts combine both narrative and expository conventions into a generic hybrid.

There also seems to be some confusion as to what kind of or how many macrogenres researchers have identified—you suggest that for the most part there are two, but then qualify this assertion with the comment that there are perhaps three "macrogenres." Are these the narrative, descriptive, and expository genres, the distinctions made by Engelhard et al. (1992) or Crowhurst's (1990) narrative and argumentative genres? Again, the researcher's decision regarding *how to categorize the unit of analysis* seems to be driving what the respective studies show about differences between these largest categorizations of text type. And you appear to be conflating research decisions with findings.

Now that I've made these caveats, I must tell you that your literature review is an impressive amassing of research in several different fields—to make the point that teachers of writing, whether ESL or L1 instructors, can benefit by reading this research. Very few teachers in writing programs in English departments, who are trained by faculty whose discipline is English studies, are familiar with the studies you describe in the research areas of reading, text comprehension, educational literacy and writing development, or applied linguistics corpus analysis. ESL teachers are probably more receptive to this research because I don't sense that there exists the hostility against empirical research that one finds in composition programs and in mainstream composition journals such as *CCC* and *CE*. In fact, for the last several years, rather than publishing research, both of these journals have published articles in which empirical studies are routinely bashed, and in which autobiographical, impressionistic narratives are described by their authors as "studies," or, worse, as "ethnographies." This distrust or outright xenophobia against social science research methods is also expressed as skepticism toward helping to train students to use the discourse patterns of the sciences and social sciences, as Johns points out in her introduction. There seems to be a prevailing view that *training* in academic genres amounts to *entraining* students in the hegemonic forms of discourse that oppress the powerless, a form of the "if you're not part of the solution, you're part of the problem" reasoning that many of us espoused in the turbulent 1960s. As Tom Huckin and I have argued (1995), however, to withhold from students the broad range and appropriate use of curriculum genres in the interests of fostering a "critique" of the hegemony of academic genres is to foist the predilections of many English faculty on hapless undergraduates.

For these reasons, Bill, I can see why your message—as you seem to understand by your comments on the last few pages—could be misconstrued as an exhortation to return to that obsolete pedagogy of teaching the traditional modes of discourse, the staple of composition textbooks of 30 years ago. The horns of the teacher's dilemma, as you suggest, is to make a goal of instruction bringing textual awareness to students "by exploring the structuring provided by texts, not as a prescriptive how-to-do procedure, but as patterning and signaling that inform readers, and then use such structuring themselves in their own writing, as appropriate to a given context" (p. 264). Your comments here make me think of Francis Christie's (1985) wonderful example of the first grade teacher whose students were learning about the development of chickens by observing an egg hatching in an incubator, recording their observations, and reading expository prose in a science textbook, *Egg to Chick*. When the egg hatched, the teacher asked the children to "write a story" based on their reading and observations. Her instructions resulted in the children producing some weird hybrids, as Christie documents. That teacher's lack of understanding of the relationship between the textbook's text structure, the children's observations, the situationally appropriate generic response, and the activity setting of a science lesson and its genres, has always represented to me the problem of the language arts teacher who does not receive training in reading or applied linguistics research.

Among rhetoric and composition teachers there persists a kind of obdurate resistance to the kind of instruction you propose, and a preference for the field's latest interests, as represented in cultural studies composition textbooks and, more recently, those textbooks that provide instruction for the uses of electronic technology. The presence of new media presents exciting communicative possibilities, especially with regard to examining features of emergent text structures. However, I fear that the interest in the content of a web page supersedes interest in helping students become aware of how electronic media require a knowledge of text structure every bit as much as do print media.

Yours truly,

Carol Berkenkotter

CONTRIBUTORS

Christine Adam is Assistant Director of the Centre for Initiatives in Education at Carleton University (Canada) where she teaches courses in academic language and culture. She has designed and taught ESL courses for academic and business purposes and is a University Writing Consultant. Her current research interests lie in areas of activity theory, North American genre studies, and theories of situated learning. She has published in *Business and Technical Communication*, *Written Communication,* and *Carleton Papers in Applied Language Studies.*

Natasha Artemeva teaches English as a Second Language for academic and business purposes and coordinates the Engineering Communication Program at Carleton University (Canada) and is Vice President of the Canadian Association of Teachers of Technical Writing. She has also taught English as a Foreign Language in Russia. Her current academic interests lie in the areas of comparative rhetoric, North American genre theory, theories of situated learning and distributed cognition, and activity theory. She has published in *Carleton Papers in Applied Linguistics*, *Technostyle*, and *Technical Communications Quarterly.*

Vijay Bhatia is a Professor at the City University of Hong Kong where he teaches postgraduate courses and directs the MA program in the teaching of ESP. He has been involved in a number of research projects, including "Changing Patterns of Genres and Identity in Hong Kong Public Discourse," "Strategies and Competencies in Legal Communication," "Teaching English in Meeting the Needs of Business Education," and "Improving Legal English: Quality Measures for Programme Development and Evaluation." Dr. Bhatia has published widely on genre and discourse analysis, English for Specific Purposes, and law and professional communication. His volume entitled *Analyzing Genre: Language Use in Professional Settings* (Longman) is used in many postgraduate courses. He serves on the editorial boards of several international journals, including *English for Specific Purposes* and *World Englishes.*

Carol Berkenkotter is Professor of Rhetoric and Communication at Michigan Technological University. With T. N. Huckin, she published an internationally recognized volume entitled *Genre Knowledge in Disciplinary Communication:*

Cognition/Culture/Power (Erlbaum, 1995) and has authored numerous articles on academic and professional genres. She is currently working on a book titled *Psychiatry's Rhetorics: The Curious Case of the Case Report.*

Richard M. Coe, Professor of English at Simon Fraser University (Canada), has taught in China and the United States. He founded and chaired the Canadian Council of Teachers of English Commission on Public Doublespeak and was a Director of the British Columbia Plan Language Institute. His *Toward a Grammar of Passages* (Southern Illinois University Press, 1988) introduced an instrument for studying generic structures. In 1990, Prentice-Hall published a thoroughly revised edition of his innovative textbook under the new title, *Process, Form, and Substance: A Rhetoric for Advanced Writers.* He has also published numerous articles on rhetoric, literacy, composition, drama, popular culture, and literary critical method, including the prizewinning essay, "Rhetoric 2000." At present, he is working on *Toward a Better Life: How and Why to Read Kenneth Burke.*

Tony Dudley-Evans is a Senior Lecturer in the English for International Studies Unit at the University of Birmingham (UK), where he specializes in teaching academic writing to international students and ESP and genre analysis to masters students. He has published and presented widely in English for Specific Purposes and discourse and genre analysis. He has extensive experience of ESP both in the UK and around the world, and is the coeditor of *English for Specific Purposes: An International Journal.* With M. J. St John, he wrote *Developments in ESP: A Multi-Disciplinary Approach* (Cambridge, 1998).

Susan Feez works in the Professional Development section of the National Centre for English Language Teaching and Research (NCELTR) at Macquarie University in Sydney, Australia. NCELTR is the key research center for the Adult Migrant English Program, a national initiative responsible for providing immigrants to Australia with English language studies. Feez works mainly in the field of TESOL curriculum development, but she is also involved in language and literacy curriculum development in the schools (K–12).

John Flowerdew has taught, designed curricula, and trained teachers in France, UK, Venezuela, several Arab countries, and Hong Kong. His research interests include discourse analysis, ESP/EAP, curriculum theory, and the use of English in Hong Kong. Currently Professor in the English Department, City University of Hong Kong, he has published widely in leading applied linguistics, language teaching, and discourse analysis journals. He is editor of *Academic Listening: Research Perspectives* (Cambridge).

William Grabe is a Professor of English and Department Chair at Northern Arizona University. He has research interests in reading, writing, and literacy, including L1 and L2, child and adult, theory and practice. He is also interested in written discourse analysis, language policy, and the status of applied linguistics as a discipline. His most recent publication is *Theory and Practice of Writing* (Longman, 1966), coauthored with R. B. Kaplan, and he is currently working on a volume on L2 reading, *Applied Linguistics in Action—Reading* (Longman), coauthored with F. Stoller. He has been working with Educational Testing Service for a number of years on the development of TOEFL 2000, is editor of *Annual Review of Applied Linguistics*, and will be President of the American Association of Applied Linguistics in 2001–2002.

Virginia Guleff is ESL Coordinator at San Diego City College, where she teaches reading and writing to both native and non-native speakers of English. She is coauthor of two ESL textbooks: *Interactions Two: A Multi-Skills Book* (with E. Thrush & D. Poole) and *Authentic Elements* (with M. Sokolik & C. Lowther). Her research interests include the relationship between participant structure and classroom interaction as well as the use of authentic materials as classroom sources for apprenticeship into disciplinary practices.

Sunny Hyon received her Ph.D. in Linguistics from the University of Michigan and is Associate Professor of English at California State University, San Bernardino. In several articles, she has explored ways that genre analysis and genre-based pedagogies vary in English for Specific Purposes, in composition studies, and in systemic functional linguistics. Her current research interests include ESL reading and composition.

Ann M. Johns is a Professor of Linguistics and Writing Studies at San Diego State University where she teaches English for Academic Purposes to bilingual and native-speaking students and a variety of research and pedagogical courses to graduate students. She also directs the campus Center for Teaching and Learning. She has published widely on issues of academic literacy and text coherence. Her 1997 volume, *Text, Role, and Context: Developing Academic Literacies* (Cambridge) incorporates her various research interests: genre analysis, novice student strategies for academic literacy acquisition, and disciplinary values, roles, and discourses.

Stephanie Lindemann is a Ph.D. candidate in the linguistics program at the University of Michigan. Her research interests include second language learning, native–non-native speaker interaction, conversation analysis, and speech perception. She is writing her dissertation on the relationships between listener attitudes towards non-native speakers and perception and comprehension of non-native speech.

Mary Macken-Horarik is a teacher and researcher in the field of language education. She played a pioneering role in the development of genre-based curriculum materials for New South Wales primary schools and, since 1991, has worked to extend the usefulness of the systemic functional model of language to secondary education. Her current research focuses on teachers' views and practices regarding the teaching of knowledge about language and literacy. She currently teaches systemic functional linguistics in the Faculty of Education at the University of Technology, Sydney.

J. R. Martin is Associate Professor in Linguistics at the University of Sydney. His research interests include systemic theory, functional grammar, discourse semantics, register, genre, multimodality, and critical discourse analysis, focusing on English and Tagalog—with special reference to the transdisciplinary fields of educational linguistics and social semiotics. Publications include *English Text: System and Structure* (Benjamins, 1992); *Writing Science: Literacy and Discursive Power* (with M. A. K. Halliday, Falmer, 1993); *Working with Functional Grammar* (with C. Mattiessen & C. Painter, Arnold, 1997); *Genre and Institutions: Social Processes in the Workplace and School* (edited with F. Christie, Cassell, 1997), and *Reading Science: Critical and Functional Perspectives on Discourses of Science* (edited with R. Veel, Routledge, 1998).

Brian Paltridge is a Professor of Applied Linguistics at Auckland University of Technology. He has published in a number of international journals and has contributed to the *New Ways in TESOL* series. He is author of *Genre, Frames and Writing in Research Settings* (Benjamins, 1997) and *Making Sense of Discourse Analysis* (Antipodean Educational Enterprises, Australia). He is an editor of the *Australian Review of Applied Linguistics*, and a member of the *English for Specific Purposes* editorial board.

Terence T. T. Pang is an Assistant Professor in the Department of English at Lingnan University (Hong Kong) where he has established a self-access center and conducted a university-wide study of learning styles. He has been funded by the University Grants Committee to construct the Hong Kong Oral Proficiency Scale and has co-produced a video for the learning of polite English using a cultural approach. His research interests are varied. Using genre analysis, he studied the compilation of local gazetteers in Guangdong during the Qing Dynasty. Recently, he has been working with John Flowerdew to use Critical Discourse Analysis to examine the political discourse of Hong Kong, focusing on the rhetoric of Chief Executive Tung Chee-hwa, and he has been exploring the discourse power struggle centering around a power station. Among his forthcoming publications are three biographical entries in *Political Leaders of Modern China, 1840–99: A Biographical Dictionary* (Westport: Greenwood).

Betty Samraj is an Assistant Professor of Linguistics at San Diego State University. Her research interests include genre analysis and writing in the disciplines, using analytical frameworks from English for Specific Purposes, composition studies and rhetoric, and systemic-functional linguistics. She was awarded a Ph.D. by the University of Michigan (1995) where she conducted dissertation research on writing by graduate students from a number of courses in an interdisciplinary environmental science program. Her further studies dealt with various fields within environmental science, namely conservation biology and wildlife behavior.

John M. Swales has been Professor of Linguistics and Director of the English Language Institute at the University of Michigan since 1987. Previously, he was Reader in ESP and Course Tutor for the MSC in TESP at Aston University, UK. Book-length publications over the last decade include *Genre Analysis* (Cambridge, 1990), *Academic Writing for Graduate Students*, with C. Feak (University of Michigan, 1994), and *Other Floors, Other Voices* (Erlbaum, 1998). A sequel to the academic writing textbook, again with C. Feak, entitled *English in Today's Research World: A Writing Guide*, was published by the University of Michigan Press in 2000. Other current interests include the Michigan Corpus of Academic Speech in English (MICASE) and the relationships between genre and silence.

REFERENCES

Ackerman, J. (1989). *Reading and writing in the academy.* Unpublished doctoral dissertation, Carnegie Mellon University, Pittsburgh, PA.

Adams Smith, D. (1984). Medical discourse: Aspects of author's comment. *English for Specific Purposes, 3,* 25–36.

Adams Smith, D. (1990). Source and derived discourse. In M. A. K. Halliday, J. Gibbons, & H. Nichols (Eds.), *Learning, keeping, and using language* (pp. 415–433). Philadelphia: John Benjamins.

Adamson, H. D. (1990). ESL students' use of academic skills in content courses. *English for Specific Purposes, 9,* 67–87.

American Psychological Association. (1994). *Publication manual of the American Psychological Association* (4th ed.). Washington, DC: APA..

Anderson, E. (1975). *A place on the corner.* Chicago: University of Chicago Press.

Anderson, J. R. (1995). *Learning and memory: An integrated approach.* New York: J. Wiley & Sons.

Anthony, C. P. (1983). *Structure and function of the body.* St. Louis, MO: C. V. Mosby & Co.

Armbruster, B., Anderson, T., & Ostertag, J. (1987). Does text structure/ summarization instruction facilitate learning from expository text? *Reading Research Quarterly, 22,* 331–346.

Artemeva, N. (1998). The writing consultant as cultural interpreter: Bridging cultural perspectives on the genre of the periodic engineering report. *Technical Communications Quarterly, 7,* 285–299.

Atkinson, D. (1991). Discourse analysis and written text conventions. In W. Grabe (Ed.), *Annual Review of Applied Linguistics, 11, Discourse analysis* (pp. 57–79). New York: Cambridge University Press.

Atkinson, D. (1992). The evolution of medical research writing from 1735 to 1985: The case of the *Edinburgh Medical Journal. Applied Linguistics, 13,* 337–374.

Australian Government Publishing Service. (1975). *Situational English for newcomers to Australia.* Canberra: Australia..

Bain, A. (1877). *English composition and rhetoric.* London: Longman, Green & Company.

Bakhtin, M. M. (1986). The problem of speech genres (V. W. McGee, Trans.). In C. Emerson & M. Holquist (Eds.), *Speech genres and other late essays* (pp.66–102). Austin: University of Texas Press.

Ballard, B., & Clanchy, J. (1984). *Study abroad: A manual for Asia students.* Selangor Darul Ehsan: Longman Malaysia.

Bartholomae, D. (1985). Inventing the university. In M. Rose (Ed.), *When a writer can't write: Studies in writer's block and other composing process problems* (pp. 134–165). New York: Guilford Press.

Bartholomae, D. (1995). Writing with teachers: A conversation with Peter Elbow. *College Composition and Communication, 46,* 62–71.

Bazerman, C. (1988). *Shaping written knowledge: The genre and activity of the experimental article in science.* Madison: University of Wisconsin Press.

Bazerman, C. (1994). Systems of genres and the enactment of social intentions. In A. Freedman & P. Medway (Eds.), *Genre and the new rhetoric* (pp. 79–101). London: Taylor and Francis.

Bazerman, C. (1997). Reporting the experiment: The changing account of scientific doings in the philosophical transactions of the Royal Society, 1665–1800. In R. A. Harris (Ed.), *Landmark essays on the rhetoric of science: Case studies* (pp. 169–186). Mahwah, NJ: Lawrence Erlbaum Associates.

Bazerman, C. (1998). Emerging perspectives on the many dimensions of scientific discourse. In J. R. Martin & R. Veel (Eds.), *Reading science: Critical and functional perspectives on discourses of science* (pp. 15–28). London: Routledge.

Beaufort, A. (1997). Operationalizing the concept of discourse community: A case study of one institutional site of composing. *Research in the Teaching of English, 31,* 486–529.

Beauvois, M. H. (1995). E-talk: Attitudes and motivation in computer-assisted classroom discussion. *Computers and the Humanities, 28,* 177–190.

Beck, I., & Kucan, L. (1997). *Questioning the author.* Newark, DE: International Reading Association.

Beck, I., & McKeown, M. (1989). Expository text for young readers: The issue of coherence. In L. Resnick (Ed.), *Knowing, learning, and instruction: Essays in honor of Robert Glaser* (pp. 47–65). Hillsdale, NJ: Lawrence Erlbaum Associates.

Becker, H. S. (1986). *Writing for the social scientist: How to start and finish your thesis, book, or article.* Chicago: University of Chicago Press.

Behrens, L. (1980). Meditations, reminiscences, polemics: Composition readers and the service course. *College English, 41,* 561–570.

Belcher, D. (1994). The apprenticeship approach to advanced academic literacy: Graduate students and their mentors. *English for Specific Purposes, 13,* 23–34.

Benesch, S. (1993). ESL, ideology, and the politics of pragmatism. *TESOL Quarterly, 27,* 705–717.

Bereiter, C., & Scardamalia, M. (1987). *The psychology of written composition.* Hillsdale, NJ: Lawrence Erlbaum Associates.

Berkenkotter, C., & Huckin, T. N. (1993). Rethinking genre from a sociocognitive perspective. *Written Communication, 10,* 475–509.

Berkenkotter, C., & Huckin, T. N. (1995). *Genre knowledge in disciplinary communication: Cognition/culture/power.* Hillsdale, NJ: Lawrence Erlbaum Associates.

Berkenkotter, C., Huckin, T. N., & Ackerman, J. (1991). Social context and socially constructed text: The initiation of a graduate student into a writing research community. In C. Bazerman & J. Paradis (Eds.), *Textual dynamics of the professions* (pp. 191–215). Madison: University of Wisconsin.

Berner, R. T. (1992). *The process of writing news.* Boston: Allyn & Bacon.

Bernhardt, S. A. (1985). Writing across the curriculum at one university: A survey of faculty members and students. *ADE Bulletin, 82,* 55–59.

Bernstein, B. (1975). *Class, codes and control (Vol. 3): Towards a theory of educational transmission.* London: Routledge & Kegan Paul.

Bernstein, B. (1990). *The structuring of pedagogic discourse (Vol. 4): Class, codes and control.* London and Boston: Routledge & Kegan Paul.

Bhatia, V. K. (1993). *Analyzing genre: Language use in professional settings.* London: Longman.

Bhatia, V. K. (1995). Genre-mixing in professional communication: The case of "private intentions" v. "socially recognized purpose."In P. Bruthiaux, T. Boswood, & B. Bortha (Eds.), *Explorations in English for Professional Communication* (pp. 1–19). Hong Kong: City University of Hong Kong.

Bhatia, V. K. (1997a). Genre-mixing in academic introductions. *English for Specific Purposes, 16,* 181–195.

Bhatia, V. K. (1997b). Introduction: Genre analysis and World Englishes. *World Englishes* [Special issue devoted to genre and World Englishes], *16,* 313–320.

Biber, D. (1988). *Variation across speech and writing.* New York: Cambridge University Press.

Biber, D. (1989). A typology of English texts. *Linguistics, 27,* 3–43.

Biber, D. (1990). Methodological issues regarding corpus-based analysis of linguistic variation. *Literary and Linguistic Computing, 5,* 257–269.

Biber, D. (1995a). *Dimensions of register variation: A cross-linguistic comparison.* New York: Cambridge University Press.

Biber, D. (1995b). The multi-dimensional approach to linguistic analyses of genre variation: An overview of methodology and findings. *Computers and the Humanities, 26,* 331–345.

Biddle, A. W., & Holland, K. M. (1987). *Writer's guide: Political science.* Lexington, MA: Heath.

Bloch, J.,& Chi, L. (1995). A comparison of the use of citations in Chinese and English academic discourse. In D. Belcher & G. Braine (Eds.), *Aca-*

demic writing in a second language: Essays on research and pedagogy (pp. 213–274). Norwood, NJ: Ablex Publishing Company.

Bloor, M. (1998). English for specific purposes: The preservation of the species (some notes on a recently evolved species and on the contribution of John Swales to its preservation and protection). *English for Specific Purposes, 17,* 47–66.

Bond, L. A., & Magistrale, A. S. (1987). *Writer's guide: Psychology*. Lexington, MA: D. C. Heath & Company.

Boswood, T., & Marriot, A. (1994). Ethnography for specific purposes: Teaching and training in parallel. *English for Specific Purposes, 13,* 3–21.

Bottomley, Y. (1994). *From proficiencies to competencies: A collaborative approach to curriculum innovation* (Report No. 6). Sydney: National Center for English Language Teaching and Research.

Boxer, D., & Pickering, L. (1995). Problems in the presentation of speech acts in ELT materials: The case of complaints. *ELT Journal, 49,* 44–58.

Braine, G. (1995). Writing in the natural sciences and engineering. In D. Belcher & G. Braine (Eds.), *Academic writing in a second language. Essays on research and pedagogy* (pp. 113–134). Norwood, NJ: Ablex.

Breen, M. (1989). Contemporary paradigms in syllabus design (pt. 2). *Language Teaching, 20,* 157–174.

Brett, P. (1994). A genre analysis of the results section of sociology articles. *English for Specific Purposes, 13,* 47–59.

Bridgeman, B., & Carlson, S. (1983). *Survey of academic writing tasks required of graduate and undergraduate foreign students* (TOEFL Research Rep. No. 15). Princeton, NJ: Educational Testing Service.

Brindley, G. (1984). The role of needs analysis in adult ESL program design. In R. K. Johnson (Ed.), *The second language curriculum.* Cambridge: Cambridge University Press.

Brindley, G. (1985). *The assessment of second language proficiency: Issues and approaches*. Adelaide, Australia: National Curriculum Research Center (NCRC).

Brindley, G., & Hood, S. (1990). Curriculum innovation in adult ESL. In G. Brindley (Ed.), *The second language curriculum in action.* Sydney: National Center for English Language Teaching and Research (NCELTR).

Brinton, D. M., Snow, M. A., & Wesche, M. B. (1989). *Content-based second language instruction.* New York: Newbury House.

Britton, B., & Graesser, A. (Eds.). (1996). *Models of understanding text.* Hillsdale, NJ: Lawrence Erlbaum Associates.

Brown, J. S., & Duguid, P. (1989). Situated cognition and the culture of learning. *Educational Researcher, 18,* 34–42.

Brown, K., & Cornish, S. (1997). *Beach Street 1: An English course for adults.* New South Wales, Australia: AMES Publishing.

Brumfit, C. (Ed.). (1986). *The practice of communicative teaching.* Oxford: Pergamon Press.

Bruner, J. S. (1986). *Actual minds, possible worlds.* Cambridge, MA: Harvard University Press.

Bruner, J. S. (1990). *Acts of meaning.* Cambridge, MA: Harvard University Press.

Bryant, B., Crowfoot, J., Gregerman, S., Kaplan, R., Nowak, P., & Stapp, W. (1987). Environmental education, advocacy, and communication: School of Natural Resources, The University of Michigan. *The Environmental Professional, 9,* 196–201.

Buggy, T. (1988). *The long revolution: A history of modern China* (Modern History Series). Sydney, Australia: Shakespeare Head Press.

Burke, K. (1969). *A rhetoric of motives.* Berkeley: University of California Press.

Burke, K. (1973). *The philosophy of literary form.* Berkeley: University of California Press.

Burns, A. (1990). Genre-based approaches to writing and beginning adult ESL learners. *Prospect: A Journal of Australian TESOL, 5,* 3.

Burns, A., & Hood, S. (Eds.). (1995). *Teachers' voices 2: Exploring course design in changing curriculum.* Sydney: National Center for English Language Teaching and Research.

Burns, A., & Hood, S. (Eds.). (1997). *Teachers' voices 2: Teaching disparate learner groups.* Sydney: National Center for English Language Teaching and Research.

Burns, A., & Hood, S. (Eds.). (1998). *Teachers' voices 3: Teaching critical literacy*. Sydney: National Center for English Language Teaching and Research.

Burns, A., & Joyce, H. (Eds.). (1999). *Teachers' voices 4: Staying learner-centered in a competency based curriculum*. Sydney: National Center for English Language Teaching and Research.

Burns, A., Joyce, H., & Gollin, S. (1996). *I see what you mean: Using spoken discourse in the classroom*. Sydney: National Center for English Language Teaching and Research.

Burton, J., & Nunan, D. (Eds.). (1988). *National curriculum project*. Adelaide, Australia: NCRC.

Cadman, K. (1997). Thesis writing for international students: A question of identity? *English for Specific Purposes, 16,* 3–14.

Callaghan, M., Knapp, P., & Noble, G. (1993). Genre in practice. In B. Cope & M. Kalantzis (Eds.), *The powers of literacy: A genre approach to teaching writing* (Critical Perspectives on Literacy and Education Series) (pp. 179–202). London and Washington, D C: Falmer Press.

Callaghan, M., & Rothery, J. (1988). *Teaching factual writing: Report of the Disadvantaged Schools Program Literacy Project*. Sydney: Metropolitan East Disadvantaged Schools Program.

Campbell, P. (1986). *Towards active voice. Report of the Committee of Review of the AMEP (Adult Migrant English Program)*. Canberra: Australia Government Printing Service.

Candlin, C. N. (1993). General editor's preface. In V. K. Bhatia (Ed.), *Analyzing genre: Language use in professional settings* (pp. ix–xi). London: Longman.

Canseco, G., & Byrd, P. (1989). Writing requirements in graduate courses in business administration. *TESOL Quarterly, 23,* 305–316.

Cappon, R. J. (1991). *The Associated Press guide to news writing* (2nd ed.). New York: Prentice-Hall.

Carrell, P. L. (1984). Evidence for a formal schema in second language comprehension. *Language Learning, 34,* 87–112.

Carrell, P. L. (1985). Facilitating ESL reading by teaching text structure. *TESOL Quarterly, 19,* 727–752.

Carrell, P. L. (1988). Introduction. In P. L. Carrell, J. Devine, & D. E. Eskey (Eds.), *Interactive approaches to second language reading* (pp. 1–7). Cambridge: Cambridge University Press.

Carrell, P. L. (1992). Awareness of text structure: Effects on recall. *Language Learning, 42,* 1–20.

Carrell, P. L., & Eisterhold, J. C. (1983). Schema theory and ESL reading pedagogy. *TESOL Quarterly, 17,* 553–573.

Carson, J., Chase, H. D., Gibson, S. U., & Hargrove, M. F. (1992). Literacy demands of the undergraduate curriculum. *Reading Research and Instruction, 31,* 25–50.

Casanave, C. P. (1995). Local interactions: Constructing context for composing in a graduate sociology program. In D. Belcher & G. Braine (Eds.), *Academic writing in a second language: Essays on research and pedagogy* (pp. 83–110). Norwood, NJ: Ablex Publishing Company.

Casanave, C. P., & Hubbard, P. (1992). The writing assignment and writing problems of doctoral students: Faculty perceptions, pedagogical issues, and needed research. *English for Specific Purposes, 11,* 33–49.

Caudrey, T. (1998). Increasing students' awareness of genre through text transformation exercises: An old classroom activity revisited. *TESL-J* [Online]. Available: http://www.-writing.berkeley.edu/TES-EJ/ej I_1/a2.html.

Celce-Murcia, M. (1990). Discourse analysis and grammar instruction. *Annual Review of Applied Linguistics,* 11, 135–151.

Cervantes, R., & Gainer, G. (1992). The effects of syntactic simplification and repetition on listening comprehension. *TESOL Quarterly, 26,* 767–770.

Channel, J. C. (1990). *Vague language.* Oxford: Oxford University Press.

Chanock, K. (1997). The interdiscourse of essays: Listening one-to-one and telling one-to-one hundred. In K. Chanock, V. Burley, & S. Davies (Eds.), *What do we learn from teaching one-to-one that informs our work with larger numbers?* (pp. 50-55) Proceedings of the Conference held at La Trobe University November 18-19, 1996, pp. 50-55. Bundoora: Language and Academic Skills of La Trobe University

Charney, D., & Carlson, R. (1995). Learning to write in a genre: What student writers take from model text. *Research in the Teachings of English, 29,* 88–125.

Cheseri-Strater, E. (1991). *Academic literacies: The public and private discourse of university students*. Portsmouth, NH: Boynton/Cook.

Choi, C. C. (1997, September 16). Let's be positive about language. *South China Morning Post,* p. 5.

Chouliarki, L. (1998). Regulation in "progressivist" pedagogic discourse: Individualized teacher-pupil talk. *Discourse and Society, 9,* 5–32.

Christie, F. (1985). Language and schooling. In S. Tchudi (Ed.), *Language, schooling, and society*. Portsmouth, NH: Boynton/Cook.

Christie, F. (1990). The changing face of literacy. In F. Christie (Ed.), *Literacy for a changing world: A fresh look at the basics* (pp. 1–25). Melbourne: The Australian Council of Educational Research.

Christie, F. (1991a). Literacy in Australia. *Annual Review of Applied Linguistics, 12,* 142–155.

Christie, F. (Ed.). (1991b). *Teaching critical social literacy: A project of national significance on the preservice preparation of teachers for teaching English literacy*. A report submitted to the Federal Minister for Employment, Education and Training, Canberra, Australia.

Christie, F. (1995). Genre-based approaches to teaching literacy. In M. L. Tickoo (Ed.), *Reading and writing: Theory into practice*. Singapore: SEAMEO Regional Language Center.

Christie, F., & Martin, J. R. (Eds.). (1997). *Genres in institutions: Social processes in the workplace and school*. Herndon, VA: Cassell Academic Press.

Cleheran, R., & Moodie, J. (1997). A systemic approach to the teaching of writing for supervisors of international students: Perspectives from genre theory. In R. Murray Harvey & H. C. Silins (Eds.), *Learning and teaching in higher education: Advancing international perspectives* (pp. 73–89). Adelaide: Flinders University of South Australia.

Clemens, J., & Crawford, J. (1994). *Words will travel: An integrated communicative English language program for intermediate level learners*. Marrickville, New South Wales: ELS.

Cloran, C. (1994). *Rhetorical units and decontextualisation: An enquiry into some relations of context, meaning and grammar* (Monograph in Systemic Functional Linguistics No. 6). Department of English Studies, University of Nottingham, United Kingdom.

Coe, R. M. (1988). Anglo-Canadian rhetoric and identity: A preface. *College English, 50,* 849–860.

Coe, R. M. (1990a). Advanced composition as fishing pole: Principles, processes, practices. In J. L. Adams & K. H. Adams (Eds.), *On teaching advanced writing: Why and how* (pp. 71–87). Portsmouth, NH: Heinemann/ Boynton-Cook.

Coe, R. M. (1990b). *Process, form, and substance: A rhetoric for advanced writers* (2nd ed.). Englewood Cliffs, NJ: Prentice-Hall.

Coe, R. M. (1994a, May 18). *Eco-engineering workplace genres.* Paper presented at the Conference on College Composition and Communication, Nashville, TN.

Coe, R. M. (1994b). Teaching genre as process. In A. Freedman & P. Medway (Eds.), *Learning and teaching genre.* (pp.157–172). Portsmouth, NH: Heinemann/Boynton-Cook.

Coe, R. M., & Freedman, A. (1998). Genre theory: Australian and North American approaches. In M. Kennedy (Ed.), *Theorizing composition* (pp. 136–147). Westport, CT: Greenwood Publishing Company.

Coffin, C. (1996). *Exploring literacy in school history.* Sydney: Metropolitan East Disadvantaged Schools Program.

Coffin, C. (1997). Constructing and giving value to the past: an investigation into secondary school history. In F. Christie & J. R. Martin (Eds.), *Genres and institutions: Social processes in the workplace and school* (Open Linguistics Series) (pp. 196–230). London: Pinter Publishing Company.

Colina, S. (1997). Contrastive rhetoric and text-typological conventions in translation teaching. *Target, 9,* 335–353.

Colman, J. (1988a, May). Curriculum structures in adult language learning: Background studies and the AMEP context. *Prospect: The Journal of the Adult Migrant Education Program, 4,* 1. Sydney: National Center for English Language Teaching and Research. (NCELTR)

Colman, J. (1988b, September). Curriculum structures in adult language learning: Implications for the AMEP. *Prospect: The Journal of the Adult Migrant Education Program, 4,* 1. Sydney: National Center for English Language Teaching and Research. (NCELTR)

Connor, U. (1996). *Contrastive rhetoric: Cross-cultural aspects of second language writing*. Cambridge: Cambridge University Press.

Cook, V. (1993). *Linguistics and second language acquisition*. New York: St. Martin's Press.

Cope, B., & Kalantzis, M. (Eds.). (1993). *The powers of literacy: A genre approach to teaching literacy*. London: Falmer Press; Pittsburgh: University of Pittsburgh Press.

Cope, B., Kalantzis, M., Kress, G., & Martin, J. R. (1993). Bibliographical essay: Developing the theory and practice of genre-based literacy. In B. Cope & M. Kalantzis (Eds.),*The powers of literacy: A genre approach to teaching writing* (pp. 231–247). London: Falmer Press.

Corder, S. P. (1973). *Introducing applied linguistics*. Harmondsworth, England: Penguin.

Corder, S. P. (1981). *Error analysis and interlanguage*. London: Oxford University Press.

Cornish, S. (1992). *Curriculum guidelines*. New South Wales, Australia: AMES.

Cote, N., Goldman, S., & Saul, E. (1998). Students making sense of informational text: Relations between processing and representation. *Discourse Processes, 25,* 1–53.

Couture, B. (1985). Effective ideation in written text: A functional approach to clarity and exigency. In B. Couture (Ed.), *Functional approaches to writing: Research perspectives* (pp. 66–92). Norwood, NJ: Ablex Publishing Company.

Crombie, W. (1985). *Discourse and language learning: A relational approach to syllabus design.* Oxford: Oxford University Press.

Crowhurst, M. (1990). The development of persuasive/argumentative writing. In R. Beach & S. Hynds (Eds.),*Developing discourse practices in adolescence and adulthood* (pp. 200–223). Norwood, NJ: Ablex Publishing Company.

Currie, P. (1998). Staying out of trouble: Apparent plagiarism and academic survival. *Journal of Second Language Writing, 7,* 1–18.

Davies, F. (1994). From writer roles to elements of text. In L. Barbara & M. Scott (Eds.), *Reflections on language learning* (pp. 170–183). Clevedon, UK: Multilingual Matters.

Davies, F. (1995). *Introducing reading*. London: Penguin.

Davies, F., & Greene, T. (1984). *Reading for learning in the sciences*. Edinburgh: Oliver and Boyd.

Davis, J. N., Lange, D. L., & Samuels, S. J. (1988). Effects of text structure instruction on foreign language readers' recall of a scientific journal article. *Journal of Reading Behavior, 20,* 203–214.

Day, R. A. (1998). *How to write and publish a scientific paper* (5th ed.). Phoenix, AZ: Oryx Press.

Delaruelle, S. (1998). *Beach street 2: An English course for adults*. New South Wales, Australia: AMES.

Derewianka, B. (1990). *Exploring how texts work*. Rozelle, New South Wales: Primary English Teaching Association (Dist. by Heinemann, Portsmouth, NH).

Devitt, A. (1991). Intertextuality in tax accounting: Generic, referential, and functional. In C. Bazerman & J. Paradis (Eds.), *Textual dynamics and the professions: Historical and contemporary studies of writing in professional communities* (pp. 336–357). Madison: University of Wisconsin Press.

Deverell, G. (1993, April). *Setting reading component objectives for an integrated EAP course*. Paper presented at the annual meeting of the Southeast Asian Ministers of Education Organization (SEAMEO) Regional Language Center Seminar, Singapore.

Dias, P., Freedman, A., Medway, P., & Paré, A. (1999). *Worlds apart: Acting and writing in academic and workplace contexts.* Mahwah, NJ: Lawrence Erlbaum Associates.

Drury, H. (1992). *Literacy for further studies project report*. Queensland: Department of Education, Adult Education Service.

Drury, H., & Gollin, S. (1986). The use of systemic functional linguistics in the analysis of ESL student writing and recommendations for the teaching situation. In C. Painter & J. R. Martin (Eds.), *Writing to mean: Teaching genres across the curriculum* (Occasional Paper No. 9) (pp. 208–290). Sydney: Applied Linguistics Association of Australia.

Drury, H., & Webb, C. (1991). Literacy at tertiary level: Making explicit the writing of requirements of a new culture. In F. Christie (Ed.), *Literacy in social processes* (pp. 214–227). Australia: Faculty of Education, Northern Territory University.

Dudley-Evans, T. (1993). Variation in communication patterns between discourse communities: The case of highway engineering and plant biology. In G. Blue (Ed.), *Language, learning, and success: Studying through English* (pp. 141–147). London: Modern English Publications in association with The British Council, Macmillan.

Dudley-Evans, T. (1995). Common core and specific approaches to the teaching of academic writing. In D. Belcher & G. Braine (Eds.), *Academic writing in a second language. Essays on research and pedagogy* (pp. 293–312). Norwood, NJ: Ablex Publishing Company.

Dudley-Evans, T. (1997). Genre models for the teaching of academic writing to second language speakers: Advantages and disadvantages. In T. Miller (Ed.), *Functional approaches to written text: Classroom applications* (pp. 150–159). Washington, DC: United States Information Services.

Dudley-Evans, T., & St John, M. J. (1998). *Developments in English for specific purposes: A multi-disciplinary approach.* New York: Cambridge University Press.

Eco, U. (1989). *Foucault's pendulum.* San Diego: Harcourt-Brace.

Eggins, S. (1994). *An introduction to systemic functional linguistics.* London: Pinter Publishing.

Eggins, S., & Slade, D. (1997). *Analyzing casual conversation.* London: Cassell Publishing.

Einstein, G., McDaniel, M., Owen, P., & Cote, N. (1990). Encoding and recall of texts: The importance of material appropriate processing. *Journal of Memory and Language, 29,* 566–581.

Elbow, P. (1995). Being a writer vs. being an academic: A conflict of goals. *College Composition and Communication, 46,* 72–83.

Englehard, G., Gordon, B., & Gabrielson, S. (1992). The influence of mode of discourse, experiential demand, and gender on the quality of student writing. *Research in the Teaching of English, 26,* 315–336.

Eskey, D. E., & Grabe, W. (1988). Interactive models for second language reading: Perspective on instruction. In P. L. Carrell, J. Devine, & D. E. Eskey (Eds.), *Interactive approaches to second language reading* (pp.223–238). Cambridge: Cambridge University Press.

Ewington, E. J., & Moore, O. F. (1971). *Human biology and hygiene.* London: Routledge & Kegan Paul.

Fahnestock, J. (1993). Genre and rhetorical craft. *Research in the Teaching of English, 27,* 265–271.

Faigley, L. (1990). Subverting the electronic workbook: Teaching writing using networked computers. In D. A. Daiker & M. Morenberg (Eds.), *The writing teacher as research* (pp. 290–311). Portsmouth, NH: Boynton/Cook.

Feez, S., & Joyce, H. (1998a). *Text-based syllabus design.* Sydney: National Center for English Language Teaching and Research.

Feez, S., & Joyce, H. (1998b). *Writing skills: Narrative & non-fiction text types.* Sydney: Phoenix Education.

Flowerdew, J. (1990). Problems of speech act theory from an applied perspective. *Language Learning, 40,* 79–105.

Flowerdew, J. (1992). Definitions in science lectures. *Applied Linguistics, 13,* 202–221.

Flowerdew, J. (1993). An educational, or process, approach to the teaching of professional genres. *ELT Journal, 47,* 305–316.

Flowerdew, J., & Miller, L. (1992). Students' perceptions, problems and strategies in L2 lectures. *RELC Journal, 23,* 60–80.

Flowerdew, J., & Miller, L. (1995). On the notion of culture in second language lectures. *TESOL Quarterly, 29,* 345–374.

Flowerdew, J., & Miller, L. (1996a). Lecturer perceptions, problems and strategies in second language lectures. *RELC Journal, 27,* 23–46.

Flowerdew, J., & Miller, L. (1996b). Lectures in a second language: Notes towards a cultural grammar. *English for Specific Purposes, 15,* 345–373.

Flowerdew, J., Li, D., & Miller, L.. (1998). Attitudes towards English and Cantonese among Hong Kong Chinese university lecturers. *TESOL Quarterly, 32,* 201–259.

Floyd, P., & Carrell, P. L. (1987). Effects on ESL reading of teaching cultural content schemata. *Language Learning, 37,* 89–108.

Fort, K. (1971). Form, authority and the critical essay. *College English*, 33, 629-39.

Freed, R. C., & Broadhead, G. J. (1987). Discourse communities, sacred texts, and institutional norms. *College Composition and Communication, 18,* 154–165.

Freadman, A. (1987). Anyone for tennis? In I. Reid (Ed.), *The place of genre in learning: Current debates* (pp. 91–124). Geelong, Victoria: Deakin University Press.

Freedman, A. (1993). Show and tell? The role of explicit teaching in the learning of new genres. *Research in the Teaching of English, 27,* 222–251.

Freedman, A. (1994). "Do as I say": The relationship between teaching and learning new genres. In A. Freedman & P. Medway (Eds.), *Genre and the new rhetoric* (pp. 191–210). London: Taylor & Francis.

Freedman, A. (1995). The what, where, when, why, and how of classroom genres. In J. Petraglia (Ed.), *Reconceiving writing, rethinking writing instruction* (pp. 121–144). Mahwah, NJ: Lawrence Erlbaum Associates.

Freedman, A., & Adam, C. (1996). Learning to write professionally: "Situated learning" and the transition from university to professional discourse. *Journal of Business and Technical Communication, 10,* 395–427.

Freedman, A., Adam, C., & Smart, G. (1994). Wearing suits to class: Simulating genres and simulations as genres. *Written Communication, 11,* 193–226.

Freedman, A., & Medway, P. (Eds.). (1994a). *Genre and the new rhetoric.* London: Taylor & Francis.

Freedman, A., & Medway, P. (1994b). Introduction: New views of genre and their implications for education. In A. Freedman & P. Medway (Eds.), *Learning and teaching genre* (pp. 1–22). Portsmouth, NH: Boynton/Cook.

Freedman, A., & Medway, P. (1994c). *Learning and teaching genre*. Portsmouth, NH: Boynton/Cook.

Freire, P. (1972). *Pedagogy of the oppressed.* London: Penguin.

Fullan, M. (1982). *The meaning of educational change*. Toronto: Ontario Institute for Studies in Education.

Fullan, M. (with Stiegelbauer, S.). (1991). *The new meaning of educational change*. New York: Teachers College Press.

Fuller, G., & Lee, A. (1997). Textual collusions. *Discourse: Studies in the Cultural Politics of Education, 18*, 409–423.

Gallimore, R., & Tharp, R. (1990). Teaching mind in society: Teaching schooling and literate discourse. In L. C. Moll (Ed.), *Vygotsky in education: Institutional applications of sociohistorical psychology* (pp. 175–205). New York: Cambridge University Press.

Gardner, H. (1991). *The unschooled mind*. New York: Basic Books.

Gernsbacher, M. (1990). *Language knowledge as structure building*. Hillsdale, NJ: Lawrence Erlbaum Associates.

Gernsbacher, M. (1997). Two decades of structure building. *Discourse Processes, 23*, 265–304.

Gilbert, P. (1990). Authorizing disadvantages: Authorship and creativity in the language classroom. In F. Christie (Ed.), *Literacy for a changing world: A fresh look at the basics* (pp. 54–78). Hawthorn, Victoria: The Australian Council for Education Research.

Giltrow, J. (1988). Canadian context for public advocacy: Briefs as a genre. *Technostyle, 7*, 17–25.

Giltrow, J. (1998, January). Meta-genre. Paper presented at the Second International Symposium on Genre: Literacy and Literature, Vancouver, BC, Canada.

Giltrow, J., & Valiquette, M. (1994). Genres and knowledge: Students writing in the disciplines. In A. Freedman & P. Medway (Eds.), *Learning and teaching genre* (pp.47–62), Portsmouth, NH: Boynton/Cook.

Goodman, K. S. (1967). Reading: A psycholinguistic guessing game. *Journal of the Reading Specialist, 6*, 126–135.

Gosden, H. (1998). An aspect of holistic modeling in academic writing: Propositional clusters as a heuristic for thematic control. *Journal of Second Language Writing, 7*, 19–41.

Grabe, W. (1987). Contrastive rhetoric and text-type research. In U. Connor & R. B. Kaplan (Eds.), *Writing across languages: Analysis of L2 text* (pp. 115–137). Reading, MA: Addison-Wesley.

Grabe, W. (1991). Current developments in second language reading research. *TESOL Quarterly, 25,* 375–406.

Grabe, W. (1995). Discourse analysis and reading instruction. In T. Miller (Ed.), *Functional approaches to written text* (pp. 5–20). Paris: TESOL France. (Reprinted by the United States Information Service, Washington, DC, 1997)

Grabe, W. (in press). Reading research and its implications for reading assessment. In A. Kunnan & M. Milanovich (Eds.), *Language proficiency assessment.* New York: Cambridge University Press.

Grabe, W., & Gardner, D. (1995). Discourse analysis, coherence, and reading instruction. *Lenguas Modernas, 22,* 69–88.

Grabe, W., & Kaplan, R. (1996). *Theory and practice of writing: An applied linguistic perspective.* London: Longman.

Graesser, A., & Britton, B. (1996). Five metaphors for text understanding. In B. Britton & A. Graesser (Eds.), *Models of understanding text* (pp. 341–351). Hillsdale, NJ: Lawrence Erlbaum Associates.

Graves, G. F. (1975). *Communication and language.* London: British Council. (ETIC Archives 954ox onx)

Gray, B. (1983, May). *Helping children become language learners in the classroom.* Paper given at the Annual Conference of the Meanjin Reading Council, Brisbane, Australia.

Gray, B. (1986). Aboriginal education: Some implications of genre for literacy development. In C. Painter & J. R. Martin (Eds.), *Writing to mean: Teaching genres across the curriculum* (Occasional Paper No. 9) (pp. 188–208). Sydney: Applied Linguistics Association of Australia.

Gray, B. (1987, December). How is "natural" language teaching—Employing wholistic methodology in the classroom. *The Australian Journal of Early Childhood, 12,* 4.

Greene, S. (1990). *Writing from sources: Authority in text and task.* Unpublished doctoral dissertation, Carnegie Mellon University, Pittsburgh, PA.

Greene, S. (1993). The role of task in the development of academic thinking through reading and writing in a college history course. *Research in the Teaching of English, 27,* 46–75.

Gregory, M. (1985). Towards communicative linguistics: A framework. In J. D. Benson & W. S. Greaves (Eds.), *Systemic perspectives on discourse* (Vol. 1, pp. 121–134). Norwood, NJ: Ablex.

Griffin, C., & Tulbert, B. (1995). The effect of graphic organizers on students' comprehension and recall of expository prose: A review of the research and implications for practice. *Teaching & Writing Quarterly, 11,* 73–89.

Hagan, P. (1994, September). Competency-based curriculum: The NSW AMES experience. *Prospect: A Journal of Australian TESOL, 9,* 2.

Hale, G., Taylor, C., Bridgeman, B., Carson J., Kroll, B., & Kantor, R. (1996). *A study of writing tasks assigned in academic degree programs* (TOEFL Research Rep. No. 54). Princeton, NJ: Educational Testing Service.

Halliday, M. A. K. (1975). *Learning how to mean: Exploring in the development of language.* London: Edward Arnold.

Halliday, M. A. K. (1976). *System and function in language.* London: Oxford University Press.

Halliday, M. A. K. (1978). *Language as a social semiotic: The social interpretation of language and meaning.* London: Edward Arnold.

Halliday, M. A. K. (1981). Types of structure. In M. A. K. Halliday & J. Martin (Eds.), *Readings in systemic linguistics* (pp. 29–41). London: Batsford Academic and Educational Press.

Halliday, M. A. K. (1985). *An introduction to functional grammar.* London: Edward Arnold.

Halliday, M. A. K. (1992, October 3). *Towards a language-based theory of learning.* Paper presented at the Phonetic Society of Japan in the context of the Symposium on Language Acquisition, Tokyo.

Halliday, M. A. K. (1993). *Language in a changing world* (Occasional Paper No. 13). Canberra: Applied Linguistics Association of Australia.

Halliday, M. A. K. (1994). *An introduction to functional grammar* (2nd ed.). London: Edward Arnold.

Halliday, M. A. K., & Hasan, R. (1985). *Language, context and text: Aspects of language in a social semiotic perspective*. Geelong, Victoria: Deakin University Press.

Halliday, M. A. K., & Hasan, R. (1989). *Language, context, and text*. London: Oxford University Press. (Original work published 1985)

Halliday, M. A. K., & Martin, J. R. (1993). *Writing science: Literacy and discursive power*. London: Falmer Press; Pittsburgh: University of Pittsburgh Press.

Halliday, M. A. K., McIntosh, A., & Strevens, P. (1964). *The linguistic sciences and language teaching*. London: Longman.

Hammond, J. (1989). The National Center for English Language Teaching and Research literacy project. *Prospect: A Journal of Australian TESOL, 5,* 23–30.

Hammond, J. (1990). Teacher expertise and learner responsibility in literacy development. *Prospect: A Journal of Australian TESOL, 5,* 39–51.

Hammond, J., Burns, A., Joyce, H., Brosnan, D., & Gerot, L. (1992). *English for social purposes: A handbook for teachers of adult literacy.* Sydney: National Center for English Language Teaching and Research.

Hamp-Lyons, L., & Courter, K. B. (1984). *Research matters*. Rowley, MA: Newbury House.

Hanks, W. (1991). Foreword. In J. Lave & E. Wenger (Eds.), *Situated learning: Legitimate peripheral participation* (pp. 11–21). Cambridge: Cambridge University Press.

Hasan, R. (1977). Text in the systemic functional model. In W. U. Dressler (Ed.), *Current trends in text linguistics* (pp. 228–246). Berlin: Walter de Gruyter.

Hasan, R. (1979). On the notion of text. In J. S. Perofi (Ed.), *Test versus sentence: Basic questions of text linguistics* (pp. 369–390). Hamburg: Helmut Buske.

Hasan, R. (1984). The nursery tale as a genre. *Nottingham Linguistic Circular* [Special issue on systemic linguistics], *13,* 71–102.

Hasan, R. (1985). The structure of a text. In M. A. K. Halliday & R. Hasan, *Language, context, and text* (pp. 52–69). Geelong, Victoria: Deakin University Press.

Hasan, R. (1996). Literacy, everyday talk and society. In R. Hasan & G. Williams (Eds.), *Literacy in society* (pp. 394–424). London: Longman Publishing.

Hasan, R., & Martin, J. R. (Eds.). (1989). *Language development: Learning language, learning culture. Meaning and choice in language: Studies for Michael Halliday. Vol. 27: Advances in discourse processes.* Norwood, NJ: Ablex Publishing Company.

Hatim, B., & Mason, I. (1990). *Discourse and the translator.* London: Longman Publishing.

Heath, S. B. (1983). *Ways with words: Language, life and work in communities and classrooms.* Cambridge: Cambridge University Press.

Heath, S. B. (1986). Sociocultural contexts of language development. In California Office on Bilingual Education (Ed.), *Beyond language: Social and cultural factors in schooling language minority children* (pp. 143–186). Los Angeles: California State University.

Henry, A., & Roseberry, R. L. (1998). An evaluation of a genre-based approach to the teaching of EAP/ESP writing. *TESOL Quarterly, 32,* 147–156.

Herndl, C. (1993). Teaching discourse and reproducing culture: A critique of research and pedagogy in professional and non-academic writing. *College Composition and Communication, 44,* 349–363.

Herrington, A. J. (1985). Writing in academic settings: A study of context for writing in two college engineering courses. *Research in the Teaching of English, 19,* 331–359.

Herrington, A. J. (1988). Teaching, writing, learning: A naturalistic study of writing in an undergraduate literature course. In D. M. Jolliffe (Ed.), *Writing in academic disciplines* (pp. 133–166). Norwood, NJ: Ablex.

Hewings, A., & Henderson, W. (1987). A link between genre and schemata: A case study of economics text. *University of Birmingham English Language Research Journal, 1,* 156–175.

Hill, C. A., & Resnick, L. (1995). Creating opportunities for apprenticeship in writing. In J. Petraglia (Ed.), *Reconceiving writing, rethinking writing instruction* (pp.145–158). Mahwah, NJ: Lawrence Erlbaum Associates.

Hoey, M. (1983). *On the surface of discourse.* London: George Allen & Unwin.

Holborrow, M. (1991). Linking language and situation: A course for advanced learners. *ELT Journal, 45,* 24–32.

Holliday, A. (1994). *Appropriate methodology and social context.* Cambridge: Cambridge University Press.

Hood, S. (1995). From curriculum to courses: Why do teachers do what they do? In A. Burns & S. Hood (Eds.), *Teachers' voices: Exploring course design in a changing curriculum* (pp. 21–34). Sydney: National Center for English Language Teaching and Research.

Hood, S. (1996a). *Focus on reading.* Sydney: National Center for English Language Teaching and Research.

Hood, S. (1996b, March). *Linguistics and pedagogy.* Paper presented at the American Association of Applied Linguistics Conference, Chicago, IL.

Hopkins, A., & Dudley-Evans, T. (1988). A genre-based investigation of the discussion sections in articles and dissertations. *English for Specific Purposes, 7,* 113–122.

Horowitz, D. (1986a). Essay examination prompts and the teaching of academic writing. *English for Specific Purposes, 5,* 107–120.

Horowitz, D. (1986b). What professors actually require: Academic tasks for the ESL classroom. *TESOL Quarterly, 20,* 445–482.

Howatt, A. (1984). *A history of English language teaching.* London: Oxford University Press.

Huckin, T. N., & Olsen, L. A. (1991). *Technical writing and professional communication for nonnative speakers of English* (2nd ed.). New York: McGraw-Hill.

Humphrey, S. (1996). *Exploring literacy in school geography.* Sydney: Metropolitan East Disadvantaged Schools Program.

Hunt, R. (1993). Texts, textoids and utterances: Writing and reading for meaning, in and out of classrooms [On-line]. Available: http://www.stthomasu.ca/~hunt/

Hunt, R. (1994a). Speech genres, writing, genres, school genres, and computer genres. In A. Freedman & P. Medway (Eds.), *Learning and teaching genre* (pp. 243–262). Portsmouth, NH: Boynton/Cook.

Hunt, R. (1994b). Traffic in genres, in classrooms and out. In A. Freedman & P. Medway (Eds.), *Genre and the new rhetoric* (pp. 211–230). London: Taylor & Francis.

Hunt, R. (1998a). Electronic discussions in learning and teaching: Why they don't work, and how they might. *Connexion: Newsletter of the International Society for Exploring Teaching Alternatives, 10,* 1–7 [On-line]. Available: http://www.asu.edu/upfd/www/iseta/connexions/cover102.html.

Hunt, R. (1998b, January). *On the origin of genres by natural selection: Inventing genres online.* Draft paper for the Second Symposium on Genre, Simon Fraser University, BC [On-line]. Available: http://www.stthomasu.ca/hunt/sfu/origin.htm.

Hyland, K. (1996). Talking to the academy: Forms of hedging in science research articles. *Written Communication, 13,* 251–281.

Hyland, K. (2000). *Disciplinary discourses: Social interaction in academic writing*. London: Longman Publishing.

Hyland, K. (in press). Academic attribution: Citation and the construction of disciplinary knowledge. *Applied Linguistics.*

Hymes, D. (1972a). On communicative competence. In J. B. Pride & J. Holmes (Eds.), *Sociolinguistics* (pp. 269–293). Harmondsworth, UK: Penguin.

Hymes, D. (1972b). Towards ethnographies of communication: The analysis of communicative event. In P. P. Giglioli (Ed.), *Language and social context* (pp. 21–44). New York: Penguin Books.

Hyon, S. (1995). *A genre-based approach to ESL reading: Implications for North America and Australia.* Unpublished doctoral dissertation, University of Michigan, Ann Arbor.

Hyon, S. (1996). Genres in three traditions: Implications for ESL. *TESOL Quarterly, 30*, 693–722.

Iancu, M. (1997). Adapting the adjunct model: A case study. In M. A. Snow & D. M. Brinton (Eds.), *The content-based classroom: Perspectives on integrating language and content* (pp. 149–157). White Plains, NY: Longman.

Iedema, R. (1994a). *Literacy in industry research project: Stage 3—The language of administration*. Sydney: New South Wales Department of School Education, Disadvantaged Schools Program, Metropolitan East Region.

Iedema, R. (1994b). Political news reporting: the media as "secondary orality." *Social Semiotics, 5,* 65–99.

Iedema, R. (1995). *Literacy of administration (write it right literacy in industry research project—Stage 3).* Sydney: New South Wales Department of School Education, Disadvantaged Schools Program, Metropolitan East Region.

Iedema, R. (1997a). The history of the accident news story. *Australian Review of Applied Linguistics, 20,* 91–119.

Iedema, R. (1997b). The language of administration: Organizing human activity in formal institutions. In F. Christie & J. R. Martin (Eds.), *Genres and institutions: Social processes in the workplace and school* (pp. 73–100). London: Pinter.

Iedema, R., Feez, S., & White, P. (1994). *Literacy in industry research project: Stage 2—Media literacy.* Sydney: New South Wales Department of School Education, Disadvantaged Schools Program, Metropolitan East Region.

Ingram, D., & Wiley, E. (1984). *Australian second language proficiency ratings.* Canberra: Australian Government Printing Service.

Johns, A. M. (1986). The ESL student and the revision process: Some insights from schema theory. *Journal of Basic Writing, 5,* 70–80.

Johns, A. M. (1990). L1 composition theories: Implications for developing theories of L2 composition. In B. Kroll (Ed.), *Second language writing: Research insights for the classroom* (pp. 24–36). Cambridge: Cambridge University Press.

Johns, A. (1995). Genre and pedagogical purposes. *Journal of Second Language Writing*, 4, 181-90.

Johns, A. M. (1997). *Text, role, and context: Developing academic literacies.* Cambridge: Cambridge University Press.

Johns, A. M. (in press). Genre and ESL/EFL composition instruction. In B. Kroll (Ed.), *Exploring second language writing: Issues for teachers.* Cambridge: Cambridge University Press.

Johns, A. M., & Dudley-Evans, T. (1991). English for Specific Purposes: International in scope, specific in purpose. *TESOL Quarterly*, 25, 297–314.

Johns, A. M., & Paz, D. (1997). Text analysis and pedagogical summaries: Revisiting Johns and Davies. In T. Miller (Ed.), *Functional approaches to written texts: Classroom approaches* (pp. 33–49). Washington, DC: United States Information Agency.

Johns, T., & Davies, F. (1983). Text as a vehicle for information: The classroom use of written texts in teaching reading in a foreign language. *Reading in a Foreign Language, 1,* 1–19, 61–83.

Johns, T., & Dudley-Evans, T. (1980). An experiment in team teaching of overseas graduate students of transportation and plant technology. In *Team teaching in ESP* (pp. 6–23) (ELT Document No. 106). London: British Council.

Jolliffe, D. A. (1995). Discourse, interdiscursivity, and composition instruction, In J. Peraglia (Ed.), *Reconceiving writing, rethinking writing instruction* (pp. 197–216). Mahwah, NJ: Lawrence Erlbaum Associates.

Jones, J., Gollin S., Drury, H., & Economou, D. (1989). Systemic-functional linguistics and its application to the TESOL curriculum. In R. Hasan & J. R. Martin (Eds.), *Language development: Learning language, learning culture. Meaning and choice in language: Studies for Michael Halliday. Vol. 27: Advances in discourse processes* (pp. 226–293). Norwood, NJ: Ablex.

Jordan, R. R. (1997). *English for academic purposes: A guide and resource book for teachers.* Cambridge: Cambridge University Press.

Journet, D. (1991). Ecological theories as cultural narratives: F. E. Clement's and H. A. Gleason's "stories" of community succession. *Written Communication, 8,* 446–472.

Journet, D. (1995). Synthesizing disciplinary narratives: George Gaylord Simpson's *Tempo and mode in evolution. Social Epistemology, 9,* 113–150.

Joyce, H. (1992). *Workplace texts in the language classroom.* Sydney: New South Wales Adult Migrant English Service.

Just, M., & Carpenter, P. (1992). A capacity theory of comprehension: Individual differences in working memory. *Psychological Review, 99,* 122–149.

Kalantzis, M., & Wignell, P. (1988). *Explain, argue, discuss.* Leichhardt, New South Wales, Australia: Common Ground.

Kamberelis, G. (1995). Genre as institutionally informed social practice. *The Journal of Contemporary Legal Issues, 6,* 115–171.

Kasper, L. F. (1995). Theory and practice in content-based ESL reading instruction. *English for Specific Purposes, 14,* 223–230.

Kellogg, R. (1994). *The psychology of writing*. New York: Oxford University Press.

Kent, T. (1993). *Paralogic rhetoric: A theory of communicative interaction.* London: Associated University Press.

Kilborn, P. T. (1991, July 7). From homemaker to wage earner in Appalachia. *The New York Times,* pp. L1, L14.

Kiniry, M., & Rose, M. (1993). *Critical strategies for academic thinking and writing: A text and reader* (2nd ed.). Boston: Bedford Books/St. Martin's Press.

Kintsch, W. (1988). The use of knowledge in discourse processing: A construction-integration model. *Psychological Review, 95,* 163–182.

Kintsch, W. (1998). *Comprehension: A paradigm for cognition.* New York: Cambridge University Press.

Kintsch, W., & Van Dijk, T. (1978). Towards a model of text comprehension and production. *Psychological Review, 85,* 363–394.

Kirsch, I., & Mosenthal, P. (1991a). Understanding definitions, descriptions, and comparison/contrast. *Journal of Reading, 35,* 156–160.

Kirsch, I., & Mosenthal, P. (1991b). Understanding mimetic documents. *Journal of Reading, 34,* 552–558.

Kirsch, I., & Mosenthal, P. (1991c). Understanding process knowledge models. *Journal of Reading, 35,* 490–497.

Knowles, M. (1990). *The adult learner—A neglected species.* Houston: Gulf Publishing.

Krashen, S. (1988). *Second language acquisition and second language learning.* New York: Prentice-Hall.

Kress, G. (1985). *Linguistic processes in sociocultural practice.* Geelong, Victoria: Deakin University Press.

Kress, G. (1987). Genre in a social theory of language: A reply to John Dixon. In I. Reid (Ed.), *The place of genre in learning: Current debates*

(Typereader Publication No. 1, pp. 35–45). Geelong, Victoria: Deakin University Press.

Kress, G. (1991). *Texture and meaning: Working with genre.* Papers from the 1989 Conference, University of Technology, Sydney. Sydney: Common Ground.

Kress, G. (1995). *Writing the future: English and the making of a culture of innovation.* Sheffield, UK: The National Association for the Teaching of English.

Kress, G., & Van Leeuwen, T. (1996). *Reading images: The grammar of visual design.* London: Routledge.

Kronick, D. A. (1985). *The literature of the life sciences.* Philadelphia: ISI Press.

Kucan, L., & Beck, I. (1996). Four fourth graders thinking aloud: An investigation of genre effects. *Journal of Literacy Research, 28,* 259–287.

Kucan, L., & Beck, I. (1997). Thinking aloud and reading comprehension research: Inquiry, instruction, and social interaction. *Review of Educational Research, 67,* 271–299.

Kusel, P. A. (1992). Rhetorical approaches to the study and composition of academic essays. *System, 20,* 457–469.

Labov, W., & Waletzky, J. (1967). Narrative analysis: Oral versions of personal experience. In J. Helm (Ed.), *Essays in the verbal and visual arts* (pp. 12–44). Seattle: University of Washington Press.

Lackstrom, J., Selinker, L., & Trimble, L. (1973). Technical rhetorical principles and grammatical choice. *TESOL Quarterly, 7,* 127–136.

Larson, R. L. (1982). The "research paper" in writing course: A non-form of writing. *College English, 44,* 811–816.

Lave, J., & Wenger, E. (1991). *Situated learning: Legitimate peripheral participation.* Cambridge: Cambridge University Press.

Lee, A. (1997). Questioning the critical: Linguistics, literacy and pedagogy. In P. Freebody, S. Muspratt, & A. Luke (Eds.), *Constructing critical literacies: Teaching and learning textual practice* (pp. 409—432). Cresskill, NJ: Hampton Press.

Leech, G., & Svartvik, J. A. (1994). *A communicative grammar of English* (2nd ed.). London: Longman.

Leki, I. (1992). *Understanding ESL writers*. Portsmouth, NH: Heinemann/ Boynton-Cook.

Lemke, J. (1988). Genres, semantics, and classroom education. *Linguistics and Education, 1,* 81–99.

Lemke, J. L. (1995). *Textual politics. Discourse and social change.* London: Taylor & Francis.

Lemke, J. L. (1998). Multiplying meaning: visual and verbal semiotics in scientific text. In J. R. Martin & R. Veel (Eds.), *Reading science: Critical and functional perspectives on discourses of science* (pp. 87–113). London: Routledge.

Lewin, T. (1990, June 2). Data show rising plight of displaced homemakers. *The New York Times*, p. L13.

Lorch, R., & Van Den Broek, P. (1997). Understanding reading comprehension: Current and future contributions of cognitive science. *Contemporary Educational Psychology, 22,* 213–246.

Love, A. M. (1991). Process and product in geology: An investigation of some discourse features of two introductory textbooks. *English for Specific Purposes, 10,* 89–109.

Luke, A. (1996). Genres of power? Literacy education and the production of capital. In R. Hasan & G. Williams (Eds.), *Literacy in society* (pp. 308–338). London: Longman.

Lyons, E. T., Tolliver, S. C., Drudge, J. H., Grantrom, D. E., Stamper, S., & Collins, S. S. (1991). Transmission of some internal parasites in horses born in 1989 on a farm in central Kentucky. *Journal of the Helminthological Society of Washington, 58,* 213–219.

Macken, M. R., Martin, J. R., Kress, J. R., Kalantzis, M., Rothery, J., & Cope, B. (1989a). *An approach to writing K–12: Introduction. A genre-based approach to teaching writing, years 3–6.* Sydney: Literacy and Education Research Network in conjunction with NSW Department of Education, Directorate of Studies.

Macken, M. R., Martin, J. R., Kress, J. R., Kalantzis, M., Rothery, J., & Cope, B. (1989b). *An approach to writing K–12: The theory and practice of genre-based writing, years 3–6. A genre-based approach to teaching writing, years 3–6.* Sydney: Literacy and Education Research Network in conjunction with NSW Department of Education, Directorate of Studies.

Macken, M., & Rothery, J. (1991). *Developing critical literacy: A model for literacy in subject learning* (Monograph 2: Issues in Education for the Socially and Economically Disadvantaged). Erskinville, Sydney: Metropolitan East Disadvantaged Schools Program.

Macken, M., & Slade, D. (1993). Assessment: A foundation for effective learning in the school context. In B. Cope and M. Kalantzis (Eds.), *The powers of literacy: A genre approach to the teaching of writing* (pp. 203–230). London: Falmer Press.

Macken-Horarik, M. (1996). *Construing the invisible: Specialized literacy practices in junior secondary English.* Unpublished doctoral thesis, University of Sydney.

Madden, C., & Myers, C. (1998, March). *Investigating genre as instruction in an EAP context.* Paper presented at the Annual Meeting of American Association for Applied Linguistics, Seattle, WA.

Malcolm, L. (1987). What rules govern tense usage in scientific articles? *English for Specific Purposes, 6,* 31–42.

Malinowski, B. (1923). The problem of meaning in primitive languages. Supplement 1. In C. K. Ogden & I. A. Richards (Eds.), *The meaning of meaning* (pp. 296–336). London: Kegan Paul.

Mann, W. C., & Thompson, S. A. (1986). Relational propositions in discourse. *Discourse Processes, 9,* 57–90.

Mann, W. C., & Thompson, S. A. (1988). Rhetorical structure theory: Toward a functional theory of text organization. *Text, 8,* 243–281.

Manning, L. M. (1996). Economics on the Internet: Electronic mail in the classroom. *The Journal of Economics Education, 27,* 201–204.

Martin, J. R. (1984). Language, register, and genre. In F. Christie (Ed.), *Language studies: Children writing leader* (pp. 21–30). Geelong, Victoria: Deakins University Press.

Martin, J. R. (1985a). *Factual writing: Exploring and challenging social reality.* Geelong, Victoria: Deakin University Press [republished by Oxford University Press, 1989].

Martin, J. R. (1985b). Language, register and genre. In F. Christie (Ed.), *Children writing study guide* (pp. 21–30). Geelong, Victoria: Deakin University Press.

Martin, J. R. (1985c). Process and text: Two aspects of human semiosis. In J. D. Benson & W. S. Greaves (Eds.), *Systemic perspectives on discourse* (Vol. 1, pp. 248–274). Norwood, NJ: Ablex.

Martin, J. R. (1992). *English text: System and structure*. Philadelphia and Amsterdam: Benjamins.

Martin, J. R. (1993a). Genre and literacy—Modeling context in educational linguistics. In W. Grabe(Ed.), *Annual Review of Applied Linguistics, 13 (Issues in second language teaching and learning)* (pp. 141–172). New York: Cambridge University Press.

Martin, J. R. (1993b). Life as a noun. In M. A. K. Halliday & J. R. Martin (Eds.), *Writing science: Literacy and discursive power* (pp. 221–267). London: Falmer.

Martin, J. R. (1994). Macro-genres: The ecology of the page. *Network*, 21, 29–52.

Martin, J. R. (1995). Text and clause: Fractal resonance. *Text, 15*, 5–42.

Martin, J. R. (1996a). Evaluation disruption: Symbolizing theme in junior secondary narrative. In R. Hasan & G. Williams (Eds.), *Literacy in society* (pp. 124–172). London & New York: Longman.

Martin, J. R. (1996b). Types of structure: Deconstructing notions of constituency in clause and text. In E. Hovy & D. Scott (Eds.), *Burning issues in discourse: A multidisciplinary perspective* (pp. 39–66). Heidelberg: Springer.

Martin, J. R. (1997a). Analyzing genre: Functional parameters. In F. Christie & J. R. Martin (Eds.), *Genre and institutions: Social processes in the workplace and school* (pp. 3–39). London: Cassell.

Martin, J. R. (1997b). Register and genre: Modeling social context in functional linguistics-narrative genres. In E. Pedro (Ed.), *Proceedings of the First Lisbon International Meeting on Discourse Analysis* (pp. 305–344). Lisbon: Colibri/APL.

Martin, J. R. (1998a). Mentoring semogenesis: "Genre-based" literacy pedagogy. In F. Christie (Ed.), *Pedagogy and the shaping of consciousness: Linguistic and social processes*. London: Cassell.

Martin, J. R. (1998b). Practice into theory: Catalyzing change. In S. Hunston (Ed.), *Language at work* (pp. 151–167) (British Studies in Applied Linguistics No. 13). Clevedon, England: Multilingual Matters.

Martin, J. R. (2000). A context for genre: Modeling social processes in functional linguistics. In R. Stainton & J. Devilliers (Eds.), *Communication in linguistics* (pp. 1–41) (Collection Theoria). Toronto: GREF.

Martin, J. R. (in press). From little things big things grow: ecogenesis in school geography. In R. Coe, L. Lingard, & T. Teslenko (Eds.), *The rhetoric ideology of genre: Strategies for stability and change*. Cresskill, NJ: Hampton Press.

Martin, J. R., & Matthiessen, C. M. I. M. (1991). Systematic typology and topology. In F. Christie (Ed.), *Social processes in education: Proceedings of the first Australian systematic network conference, Deakin University, January 1990* (pp. 345–383). Darwin: Center for Studies in Language Education, Northern Territory University.

Martin, J. R., & Peters, P. (1985). On the analysis of exposition. In R. Hasan (Ed.), *Discourse on discourse (Workshop reports from the Macquarie Workshop on Discourse Analysis)* (pp. 61–92) (Occasional Papers No. 7). Melbourne: Applied Linguistics Association of Australia.

Martin, J. R., & Plum, G. (1997). Construing experience: Some story genres. *Journal of Narrative and Life History, 7,* 299–308 [Special Issue: Oral Versions of Personal Experience: Three decades of narrative analysis; M. Bamberg, Guest Editor].

Martin, J. R., & Veel, R. (Eds.). (1998). *Reading science: Critical and functional perspectives on discourse of science*. London: Routledge.

Martin, W. R. (1991). The Fisheries Research Board of Canada. *Bulletin of the Canadian Society of Zoologists, 22*(3), 36–40.

Matthiessen, C. M. I. M. (1995). *Lexicogrammatical cartography: English systems*. Tokyo: International Language Sciences Publishers.

Mauranen, A. (1993). Contrastive ESP rhetoric: Metatext in Finnish-English economics text. *English for Specific Purposes, 12,* 3–22.

McCarthy, L. P. (1987). A stranger in strange lands: A college student's writing across the curriculum. *Research in the Teaching of English, 21,* 233–265.

McCarthy, M., & Carter, R. (1994). *Language as discourse: Perspectives for language teaching*. London: Longman.

McDaniel, M., & Einstein, G. (1989). Material appropriate processing: A contextualistic approach to reading and study strategies. *Educational Psychology Review, 1,* 113–145.

McDaniel, M., Hines, R., Waddill, P., & Einstein, G. (1994). What makes folk tales unique: Content familiarity, casual structure, scripts, or superstructures? *Journal of Experimental Psychology: Learning, Memory, and Cognition, 20,* 169–184.

McKenna, M., & Robinson, R. (1997). *Teaching through text* (2nd ed.). New York: Longman.

McNamara, D., Kintsch, E., Songer, N., & Kintsch, W. (1996). Are good texts always better? Text coherence, background knowledge, and levels of understanding in learning from text. *Cognition and Instruction, 14,* 1–43.

Medway, P. (1993). *Shifting relations: Science, technology and technoscience.* Geelong, Victoria: Deakin University Press.

Melander, B., Swales, J. M., & Fredrickson, K. M. (1997). Journal abstracts from three academic fields in the United States and Sweden: National or disciplinary proclivities? In A. Duszak (Ed.), *Culture and styles of academic discourse* (pp. 251–272). Berlin: Mouton de Gruyter.

Melrose, R. (1991). *The communicative syllabus: A systemic-functional approach to language teaching*. London: Pinter.

Meyer, B. (1987). Following the author's top-level organization: An important skill for reading comprehension. In R. Tierney, P. Anders, & J. Mitchell (Eds.), *Understanding readers' understanding* (pp. 59–76). Hillsdale, NJ: Lawrence Erlbaum Associates.

Meyer, J. E. (1994). *The contribution of genre theory to theme-based EAP: Navigating foreign fjords*. Unpublished master's thesis, Carleton University, Canada.

Michaelson, H. B. (1986). *How to write and publish engineering papers and reports* (2nd ed.). Philadelphia: ISI Press.

Miller, C. (1984). Genre as social action. *Quarterly Journal of Speech, 70,* 151–167.

Miller, C., & Halloran, M. (1993). Reading Darwin, reading nature; or on the ethos of historical science. In J. Selzer (Ed.), *Understanding scientific prose* (pp. 106–126). Madison: University of Wisconsin Press.

Miller, T. (Ed.). (1995). *Functional approaches to written text: Classroom applications*. Washington, DC: United States Information Agency.

Mohan, B. (1986). *Language and content*. New York: Longman.

Mokhtari, K., & Sheorey, R. (1994). Reading habits of university ESL students at different levels of English proficiency and education. *Journal of Research in Reading, 17,* 46–61.

Moll, L. C. (1990). Introduction. In L. C. Moll (Ed.), *Vygotsky and education: Instructional implications and applications of sociohistorical psychology* (pp. 1–16). New York: Cambridge University Press.

Moore, T., & Morton, J. (1998, January). *Contrasting rhetorics: Academic writing and the IELTS test.* Paper presented at the Australian Council of TESOL Associations, Victorian Association for TESOL and Multicultural Education National Conference, Melbourne.

Mosenthal, P. (1985). Defining the expository prose continuum. *Poetics, 14,* 387–414.

Mosenthal, P., & Cavallo, A. (1998). Profiling changing states of conceptual knowledge: With designs towards developing a universal knowledge interface system for the 21st century. *Peabody Journal of Education, 73*(3/4), 145-177.

Mosenthal, P., & Kirsch, I. (1991a). Extending prose comprehension through knowledge modeling. *Journal of Reading, 35,* 58–61.

Mosenthal, P., & Kirsch, I. (1991b). Using knowledge models to understand steady states. *Journal of Reading, 35,* 250–255.

Mosenthal, P., & Kirsch, I. (1992). Understanding knowledge acquisition from a knowledge model perspective. *Journal of Reading, 35,* 588–596.

Muchiri, M. N., Mulamba N. G., Myers, G., & Ndoloi, D. B. (1995). Importing composition: Teaching and researching academic writing beyond North America. *College Composition and Communication, 46,* 175–198.

Myers, G. (1985). The social construction of two biologists' proposals. *Written Communication, 2,* 219–245.

Myers, G. (1989). The pragmatics of politeness in scientific articles. *Applied Linguistics, 10,* 1–35.

Myers, G. (1992). Textbooks and the sociology of scientific knowledge. *English for Specific Purposes, 11,* 3–17.

National Council of Teachers of English. (1979). *Standards for basics skills writing programs.* Urbana, IL: NCTE.

Newkirk, T. (1987). The non-narrative writing of young children. *Research in the Teaching of English, 21,* 121–144.

New South Wales Adult Migrant English Service Writing Team. (1995). *Certificates in spoken and written English I, II, III, and IV.* New South Wales, Australia.

New South Wales Adult Migrant English Service Writing Team. (1997). *Wanyarri: Indigenous Australia in the ESL classroom.* New South Wales, Australia.

Noble, E. R., & Noble G. A. (1971). *Parasitology: The biology of animal parasites* (3rd ed.). Philadelphia: Lea & Febiger.

Noss, R. F. (1993). Wither conservation biology? *Conservation Biology, 7,* 215–217.

Nunan, D. (1987). *The teacher as curriculum developer.* Sydney: National Center for English Language Teaching and Research.

Nunan, D. (1988). *Syllabus design.* Oxford: Oxford University Press.

Nunan, D. (1991). *Language teaching methodology: A textbook for teachers.* Englewood Cliffs, NJ: Prentice-Hall.

Nunan, D. (1993). *Introducing discourse analysis.* London: Penguin.

Nuttall, C. (1982). *Teaching reading skills in a foreign language.* London: Heinemann Educational Books.

Nwogu, K. N. (1991). Structure of science popularizations: A genre-analysis approach to the schema of popularized medical text. *English for Specific Purposes, 10,* 111–123.

Nystrand, M. (1986). *The structure of written communication: Studies in reciprocity between writers and readers.* Orlando, FL: Academic Press.

O'Brien, T. (1995). Rhetorical structure analysis and the case of inaccurate, incoherent source-hopper. *Applied Linguistics, 16,* 442–482.

O'Carroll, P., Drury, H., & Jones, J. (1998). Writing a lab report. Computer-based integration of academic literacy skills. Poster presentation at the 1998 Australian Commuinication Skills Conference, The University of Melbourne.

Ogburn, J., Kress, G., Martins, I., & McGillicuddy, K. (Eds.). (1996). *Explaining science in the classroom.* Buckingham, UK: Open University Press.

Ohmann, R. (1979). Use definite, specific, concrete language. *College English, 41,* 390–397.

Olsen, B., & Lepeintre, S. (1995). Academic argument and e-mail discussion lists: Bringing collaboration and debate into the writing course. In T. Warschauer (Ed.), *Virtual connections: Online activities and projects for networking language and learners* (pp. 43–46). Manoa: University of Hawaii at Manoa, Second Language Teaching and Curriculum Center.

Ongstad, S. (1999). Self-positioning(s) and students' task reflexivity. A semiotic macro concept exemplified. *Journal of Structural Learning and Intelligent Systems, 14,* 125–152.

Ostler, S. E. (1980). A survey of academic needs for advanced ESL. *TESOL Quarterly, 14,* 489–502.

Painter, C. (1985). *Learning the mother tongue.* Geelong, Victoria: Deakin University Press.

Painter, C. (1986). The role of interaction in learning to speak and learning to write. In C. Painter & J. Martin (Eds.), *Writing to mean: Teaching genres across the curriculum* (pp. 62–97) (Applied Linguistics Association of Australia Occasional Paper No. 9). Sydney: University of Sydney, Department of Linguistics.

Painter, C. (1996). The development of language as a resource for thinking: A linguistic view of learning. In R. Hasan & G. Williams (Eds.), *Literacy in society* (pp. 50–85). London: Longman Publishing.

Paltridge, B. (1996). Genre, text type, and the language learning classroom. *ELT Journal, 50,* 237–243.

Paltridge, B. (1999). Reading across the curriculum: A genre-based perspective. In D. Short (Ed.), *New ways in teaching English at the secondary level* (pp. 165–167). Alexandra, VA: TESOL.

Paltridge, B. (2000). *Making sense of discourse analysis*. Gold Coast, Australia: Antipodean Educational Enterprises.

Pappas, C. (1991). Young children's strategies in learning the "book language" of information books. *Discourse Processes, 14,* 203–225.

Pappas, C. (1993). Is narrative primary? Some insights from kindergartners' pretend readings of stories and informational books. *Journal of Reading Behavior, 25,* 97–129.

Paré, A. (1991). Ushering "audience" out: From oration to conversation. *Textual Studies in Canada, 1,* 45–64.

Paré, A., & Smart, G. (1994). Observing genres in action: Towards a research methodology. In A. Freedman & P. Medway (Eds.), *Genre and the new rhetoric* (pp. 146–154). London: Taylor & Francis.

Park, D. B. (1982). The meanings of "audience." *College English, 44,* 247–257.

Partee, M. H. (1996). Using e-mail, web sites & newsgroup to enhance traditional classroom instruction. *Technological Horizons in Education,* 23, 79–82.

Pearson, P. D., & Fielding, L. (1991). Comprehension instruction. In P. D. Pearson, R. Barr, M. L. Kamit, & P. Mosenthal (Eds.), *Handbook of reading research* (Vol. 2, pp. 815–860). New York: Longman.

Peng, J. (1987). Organizational features in chemical engineering research article. *ELR Journal, 1,* 79–116.

Pennycook, A. (1996). TESOL and critical literacies: Modern, post or neo? *TESOL Quarterly, 30,* 163–171.

Petraglia, J. (1995). Introduction: General writing skills instruction and its discontents. In J. Petraglia (Ed.), *Reconceiving writing, rethinking writing instruction* (pp. xi–xvii). Mahwah, NJ: Lawrence Erlbaum Associates.

Pilegaard, M., & Frandsen, F. (1996). Text type. In J. Verschueren (Ed.), *Handbook of pragmatics 1996* (pp. 1–13). Amsterdam: John Benjamins.

Plum, G. (1988). *Text and contextual conditioning in spoken English: A genre-based approach.* Unpublished doctoral dissertation, University of Sydney.

Pressley, M., El-Dinary, P., Gaskins, L., Schuder, T., Bergman, A. B., Almasi, L., & Brown, R. (1992). Beyond direct explanation: Transactional instruction of reading comprehension strategies. *Elementary School Journal, 92,* 511–554.

Pressley, M., & Woloshyn, V. (Eds.). (1995). *Cognitive strategy instruction that really improves children's academic performance*. Cambridge, MA: Brookline Books.

Prior, P. (1991). Contextualizing writing and response in a graduate seminar. *Written Communication, 8,* 267–310.

Prior, P. (1992). *Contextualizing writing and response in graduate seminars: A sociohistorical perspective on academic literacies*. Unpublished doctoral dissertation, University of Minnesota, Minneapolis.

Prior, P. (1994). Girls talk tales, causal models, and the dissertation: Exploring topical contours of context in sociology. *Language and Learning Across the Disciplines, 1,* 5–34.

Prior, P. (1995). Redefining the task: An ethnographic examination of writing and response in graduate seminars. In D. Belcher & G. Braine (Eds.), *Academic writing in a second language: Essays on research and pedagogy* (pp. 47–82). Norwood, NJ: Ablex.

Prior, P. (1998). *Writing/disciplinarity: A sociohistoric account of literate activity in the academy.* Mahwah, NJ: Lawrence Erlbaum Associates.

Purves, A. C. (1991). The textual contract: Literacy as common knowledge and conventional wisdom. In E. M. Jennings & A. C. Purves (Eds.), *Literate systems and individual lives: Perspectives on literacy and schooling* (pp. 51–72). Albany: State University of New York Press.

Quirk, R., Greenbaum, S., Leech, G., & Svartvik, J. (1985). *A comprehensive grammar of the English language*. London: Longman.

Raimes, A. (1991). Out of the woods: Emerging traditions in the teaching of writing. *TESOL Quarterly, 25,* 407–430.

Ramanathan, V., & Kaplan, R. B. (2000). Genres, authors, discourse communities: Theory and application for L2 writers. *Journal of Second Language Writing, 9,* 171–192.

Ratterey, O. M. T. (1985). Expanding roles for summarized information. *Written Communication, 2,* 257–272.

Ravotas, D., & Berkenkotter, C. (1998). Voices in the text: The uses of reported speech in a psychotherapist's notes and initial assessments. *Text, 18,* 211–239.

Reid, I. (1987). A generic frame for debates about genre. In I. Reid (Ed.), *The place of genre in learning: Current debates* (pp. 1–8). Geelong, Victoria: Deakin University, Centers for Studies in Literary Education.

Reid, J. (1993). Historical perspectives on writing and reading in the ESL classroom. In J. G. Carson & I. Leki (Eds.), *Reading in the composition classroom: Second language perspectives* (pp. 33–60). Boston: Heinle & Heinle.

Richards, I. A. (1936). *The philosophy of rhetoric.* London: Oxford University Press.

Richards, J. C., Platt, J., & Platt, H. (1992). *Longman dictionary of teaching an applied linguistics.* London: Longman.

Richards, J. C., & Rodgers, T. S. (1986). *Approaches and methods in language teaching: A description and analysis.* Cambridge: Cambridge University Press.

Rogoff, B. (1990). *Apprenticeship in thinking.* New York: Oxford University Press.

Rogoff, B., & Lave, J. (1984). *Everyday cognition: Its development in social context.* Cambridge, MA: Harvard University Press.

Rose, D. (1997). Science, technology and technical literacies. In F. Christie & J. R. Martin (Eds.), *Genres and institutions: Social processes in the workplace and school* (pp. 40–72). London: Pinter.

Rose, D. (1998). Science discourse and industrial hierarchy. In J. R. Martin & R. Veel (Eds.), *Reading science: Critical and functional perspectives on discourse of science* (pp. 236–265). London: Routledge.

Rose, D., McInnes, D., & Korner, H. (1992). *Literacy in industry research project: Stage 1—Scientific literacy.* Sydney: New South Wales Department of Education, Disadvantaged Schools Program, Metropolitan East Region.

Rose, M. (1983). Remedial writing courses: A critique and a proposal. *College English, 45,* 109–126.

Rothery, J. (1980). Narrative: Vicarious experience. In J. R. Martin & J. Rothery (Eds.), *Writing Project 1, Working papers in linguistics* (pp. 1–44). Sydney: University of Sydney.

Rothery, J. (1989). Learning about language. In R. Hasan & J. R. Martin (Eds.), *Language development: Learning language, learning culture. Meaning and choice in language: Studies for Michael Halliday, Vol. 27: Advances in discourse processes* (pp. 199–256). Norwood, NJ: Ablex Publishing Company.

Rothery, J. (1990). *"Story" writing in primary school: Assessing narrative type genres.* Unpublished doctoral dissertation, University of Sydney.

Rothery, J. (1994). *Exploring literacy in school English (Write it right resources for literacy and learning).* Sydney: Metropolitan East Disadvantaged Schools Program.

Rothery, J. (1996). Making changes: Developing an educational linguistics. In R. Hasan & G. Williams (Eds.), *Literacy in society* (pp. 86–123). London: Longman.

Rudestam, K. E., & Newton, R. R. (1992). *Surviving your dissertation: A comprehensive guide to content and process.* Newbury Park, CA: Sage.

Samraj, B. (1995). *The nature of academic writing in an interdisciplinary field.* Unpublished doctoral dissertation, University of Michigan, Ann Arbor.

Schryer, C. (1995, May). *Advocacy communication: A case study of ideology, power and culture.* Paper presented at the annual conference of the Canadian Association of Teachers of Technical Writing, Montreal, Canada.

Schryer, C. (1998, January). *Genres and power: Or whose time is it?* Paper presented at the Second Symposium on Genre, Simon Fraser University, British Columbia, Canada.

Scollon, R. (1995). Plagiarism and ideology: Identity in intercultural discourse. *Language in Society, 24,* 1–28.

Scollon, R. (1997). Attribution and power in Hong Kong news discourse. *World Englishes, 16,* 383–393.

Scollon, R., & Wong Scollon, S. (1995). *Intercultural communication: A discourse approach.* Oxford, UK & Cambridge, MA: Blackwell.

Selinker, L. (1991). *Rediscovering interlanguage.* London: Longman.

Selzer, J. (1993). Intertextuality and the writing process: An overview. In R. Spilka (Ed.), *Writing in the workplace: New research perspectives* (pp. 171–180). Carbondale: Southern Illinois Press.

Shih, M. (1992). Beyond comprehension exercises in the ESL academic reading class. *TESOL Quarterly, 26,* 289–318.

Shor, I. (1980). *Critical teaching and everyday life.* Boston: South End Publishing.

Silva, T. (1990). Second language composition instruction: Developments, issues and directions in ESL. In B. Kroll (Ed.), *Second language writing: Research insights for the classroom* (pp. 11–23). Cambridge: Cambridge University Press.

Smagorinski, P. (1992). How reading model essays affects writers. In J. Irwin & M. Doyle (Eds.), *Reading/writing connections: Learning from research* (pp. 160–176). Newark, DE: International Rcading Association.

Smart, G. (1993). Genre as community invention: A central bank's response to its executives' expectation as readers. In R. Spilka (Ed.), *Writing in the workplace: New research perspectives* (pp. 124–140). Carbondale: Southern Illinois University Press.

Soule, M. E. (1985). What is conservation biology? *BioScience, 35,* 727–734.

Spack, R. (1988). The author responds to Johns . . . . *TESOL Quarterly, 28,* 707–708.

Spilka, R. (Ed.). (1993). *Writing in the workplace: New research perspectives.* Carbondale: Southern Illinois University Press.

Spiro, R., & Taylor, B. (1987). On investigating children's transition from narrative to expository discourse: The multidimensional nature of psychological text classification. In R. Tierney, P. Anders, & J. Mitchell (Eds.), *Understanding readers' understanding: Theory and practice* (pp. 77–93). Hillsdale, NJ: Lawrence Erlbaum Associates.

Strevens, P. (1987). English as an international language. *English Teaching Forum, 25,* 56–63.

Strunk, W., Jr., & White, E. B. (1959). *The elements of style*. New York: Macmillan.

Swales, J. M. (1981). *Aspects of article introductions*. Birmingham, UK: University of Aston Language Studies Unit.

Swales, J. M. (1988). *Episodes in ESP: A source and reference book for the development of English for science and technology*. New York: Prentice-Hall.

Swales, J. M. (1990). *Genre analysis: English in academic and research settings*. Cambridge: Cambridge University Press.

Swales, J. (1996). Occluded genres in the academy: The case of the submission letter. In E. Ventola & A. Mauranen (Eds.), *Academic writing: Intercultural and textual issues* (pp. 45–58). Amsterdam: Benjamin.

Swales, J. M. (1998). *Other floors, other voices: A textography of a small university building*. Mahwah, NJ: Lawrence Erlbaum Associates.

Swales, J. M., & Feak, C. B. (1994). *Academic writing for graduate students: Essential tasks and skills*. Ann Arbor: University of Michigan Press.

Tadros, A. A. (1985). *Prediction in text*. Birmingham, UK: English Language Research.

Tarone, E., Dwyer, S., Gillette, S., & Icke, V. (1981). On the use of the passive in two astrophysics journal papers. *ESP Journal, 1,* 123–140.

Tarone, E., & Yule, G. (1987). Communication strategies in East-West interactions. In L. Smith (Ed.), *Discourse across culture: Strategies in world English* (pp. 49–65). Hertfordshire, UK: Prentice-Hall.

Taylor, B. (1992). Text structure, comprehension, and recall. In S. Samuels & A. Farstrup (Eds.), *What research has to say about reading instruction* (2nd ed.) (pp. 220–235). Newark, DE: International Reading Association.

Taylor, B., & Samuels, S. (1983). Children's use of text structure in recall of expository material. *American Educational Research Journal, 20,* 517–528.

Tedick, D. J. (1990). ESL writing assessment: Subject-matter knowledge and its impact on performance. *English for Specific Purposes, 9,* 123–143.

Teich, N. (Ed.). (1992). *Rogerian perspectives: Collaborative rhetoric for oral and written communication.* Norwood, NJ: Ablex.

Thompson, D. (1993). Arguing for experimental "facts" in science: A study of academic papers. *Applied Linguistics, 12,* 365–382.

Thompson, G., & Ye, Y. (1991). Evaluation in reporting verbs used in academic papers. *Applied Linguistics, 12,* 365–382.

Thornbury, S. (1997). *About language: Tasks for teachers of English.* Cambridge: Cambridge University Press.

Tribble, C. (1996). *Writing.* Oxford: Oxford University Press.

Trimble, L. (1985). *English for science and technology: A discourse approach.* Cambridge: Cambridge University Press.

Trimmer, J. F. (1985). Faculty development and the teaching of writing. *WPA: Writing Program Administration, 9,* 11–30.

Unsworth, L. (1997). Scaffolding reading of science explanations: Accessing the grammatical and visual forms of specialized knowledge. *Reading, 31,* 30–42.

Unsworth, L. (1998). "Sound" explanations in school science: A functional linguistics perspective on effective apprenticing texts. *Linguistics and Education, 9*, 199–226.

Ur, P. (1996). *A course in language teaching: Practice and theory.* Cambridge: Cambridge University Press.

Vacca, R., & Vacca, J. (1996). *Content area reading.* New York: HarperCollins.

Van Ek, J., & Alexander, L. G. (1980). *Threshold level English.* Oxford: Pergamon Press.

Van Leeuwen, T. (1992). The schoolbook as a multimodel text. *Internationale Schulbuchforschung, 14,* 35–58.

Van Nostrand, A. D. (1994). A genre map of R & D knowledge productions for the U.S. Department of Defense. In A. Freedman & P. Medway (Eds.), *Genre and the new rhetoric* (pp. 133–145). London: Taylor & Francis.

Veel, R. (1997). Learning how to mean—scientifically speaking: Apprenticeship into scientific discourse in the secondary school. In F. Christie & J. R. Martin (Eds.), *Genres and institutions: Social processes in the workplace and school* (pp. 161–195). London: Pinter Publishing Company.

Veel, R. (1998). The greening of school science: Ecogenesis in secondary classrooms. In J. R. Martin & R. Veel (Eds.), *Reading science: Critical and functional perspectives on discourse of science* (pp. 114–151). London: Routledge.

Veel, R., & Coffin, C. (1996). Learning to think like an historian: The language of secondary school history. In R. Hasan & G. Williams (Eds.), *Literacy in society* (pp. 191–231). London: Longman Publishing Company.

Ventola, E. (1987).*The structure of social interaction: A systemic approach to the semiotics of service encounters* (Open Linguistics Series). London: Pinter Publishing Company.

Ventola, E. (1994). Orientation to social semiotics in foreign language teaching. *Applied Linguistics, 5,* 275–286.

Vosniadou, S., & Brewer, W. (1987). Theories of knowledge restructuring in development. *Review of Educational Research, 57,* 51–67.

Voss, J., & Silfes, L. (1996). Learning from history text: The interaction of knowledge and comprehension skill with text structure. *Cognition and Instruction, 14,* 45–68.

Vygotsky, L. (1978). In *Mind in society: The development of higher psychological processes,* M. Cole, V. J. Steiner, S. Scribner, & E. Souberman, (Eds.). Cambridge, MA: Cambridge University Press. (original work published 1934)

Vygotsky, L. (1986). *Thought and language* (A. Kozulin, Trans.). Cambridge, MA: MIT Press.

Walvoord, B., Anderson, V., Breihan, J., McCarthy, L. P., Robinson, S., & Sherman, A. K. (1995). Functions of outlining among college students in four disciplines. *Research in the Teaching of English, 29,* 390–421.

Walvoord, B., & McCarthy, L. (1990). *Thinking and writing in college: A naturalistic study of students in four disciplines.* Urbana, IL: Council of Teachers of English.

Webb, C., & Drury, H. (1995). *Essay writing module*. Sydney: University of Sydney Learning Assistance Centre Publications.

Weissberg, R., & Buker, S. (1990). *Writing up research: Experimental report writing for students of English.* Englewood Cliffs, NJ: Prentice-Hall Regents.

Werlich, E. (1976). *A text grammar of English.* Heidelberg: Quelle and Meyer.

Whitaker, E. (1993). A pedagogy to address plagiarism. *College Composition and Communication, 44,* 509–514.

White, P. (1997). Death, destruction and the moral order: The narrative impulse in mass-media "hard news" reporting. In F. Christie & J. R. Martin (Eds.), *Genre and institutions: Social processes in the work place and school* (pp. 101–133). London: Pinter.

Widdowson, H. G. (1979). *Explorations in applied linguistics.* Oxford: Oxford University Press.

Widdowson, H. G. (1990). *Aspects of language teaching*. Oxford: Oxford University Press.

Widdowson, H. G. (1993). The relevant conditions of language use and learning. In M. Krueger & F. Ryan (Eds.), *Language and content: Discipline and content-based approaches to language study* (pp. 27–36). Lexington, MA: D. C. Heath.

Wilkins, D. (1976). *Notional syllabuses*. Oxford: Oxford University Press.

Williams, J. M., & Colomb, G. G. (1993). The case for explicit teaching: Why what you don't know won't help you. *Research in the Teaching of English, 27,* 252–264.

Williams, R. (1986). "Top ten" principles for teaching reading. *ELT Journal, 40,* 42–45.

Wilson, K. (1997). "Wording" it up: Plagiarism in the interdiscourse of international students. In *Advancing international perspectives* (pp. 763–770), Proceedings of the International Conference of the Higher Education Research and Development Society of Australasia.

Wolfson, L., & Willinsky, J. (1998). What service-learning can learn from situated learning. *Michigan Journal of Service Learning, 5,* 22–31.

Woodford, F. P. (Ed.). (1976). *Scientific writing for graduate students: A manual on the teaching of scientific writing*. Bethesda, MD: Council of Biology Editors.

Yalden, J. (1987a). *Principles of course design for language teaching*. New York: Cambridge University Press.

Yalden, J. (1987b). *The communicative syllabus: Evolution, design and implementation*. Englewood Cliffs, NJ: Prentice-Hall International.

Yates, J., & Orlikowski, W. (1992). Genres of organizational communication: A structurational approach to studying communication and media. *Academy of Management Review, 17,* 299–326.

Young, L. (1994). University lectures: Macro-structure and macro-features. In J. Flowerdew (Ed.), *Academic listening: Research perspectives* (pp. 159–176). Cambridge: Cambridge University Press.

Young, R., Becker, A., & Pike, K. (1970). *Rhetoric: Discovery and change*. New York: Harcourt, Brace & World.

Yunik, S. (1997). Genres, registers and sociolinguistics. *World Englishes, 16,* 321–336.

Zamel, V. (1985). Responding to student writing. *TESOL Quarterly, 19,* 79–102.

Zamel, V. (1995). Strangers in academia: The experiences of faculty and ESL students across the curriculum. *College Composition and Communication, 46,* 506–521.

Zwaan, R. (1996). Towards a model of literary comprehension. In B. Britton & A. Graesser (Eds.), *Models of understanding text* (pp. 241–255). Mahwah, NJ: Lawrence Erlbaum Associates.

Subject Index

J

K

L

M

N

P

Q

R

S

Author Index

A

B

C

L

M

N

O

P